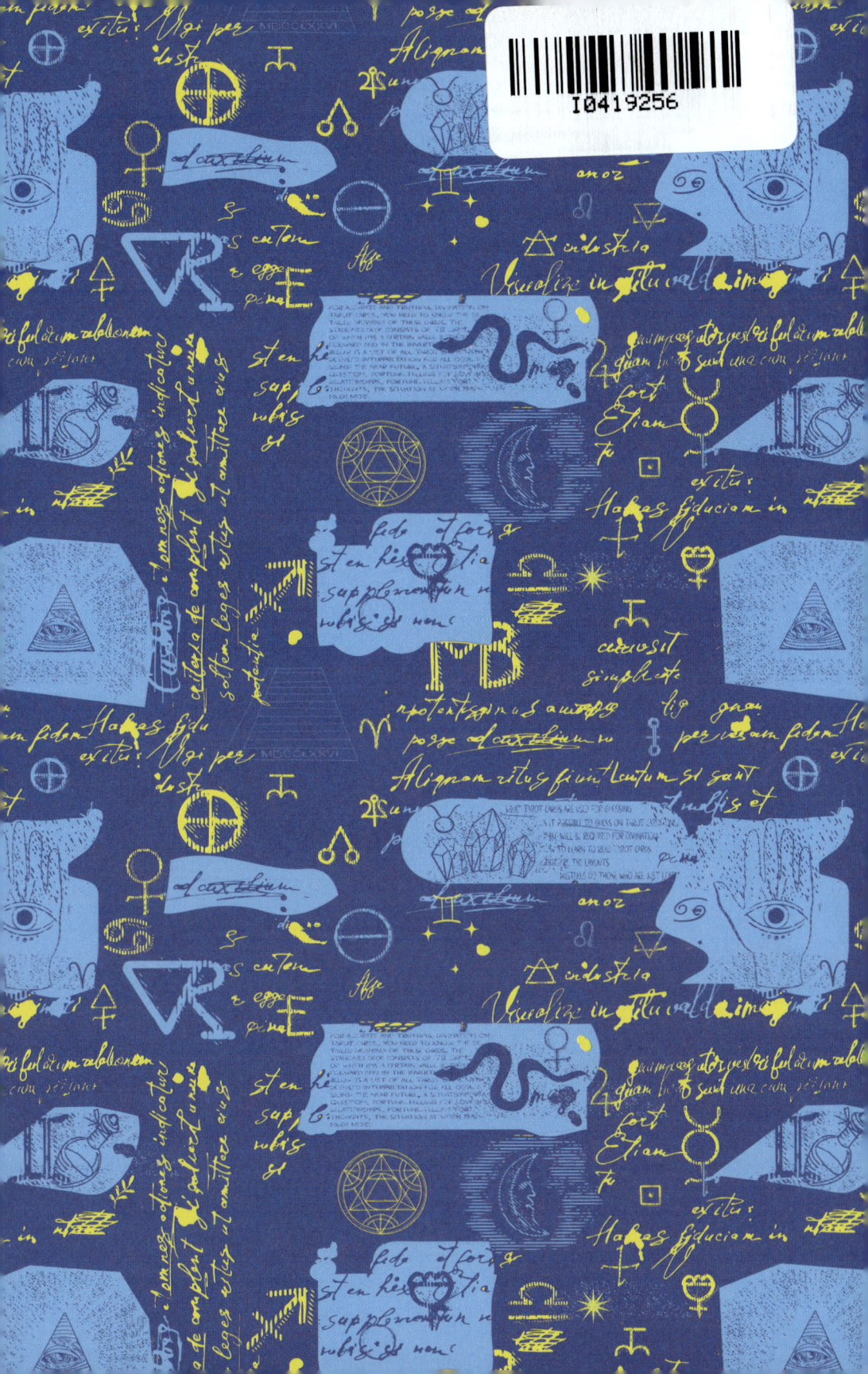

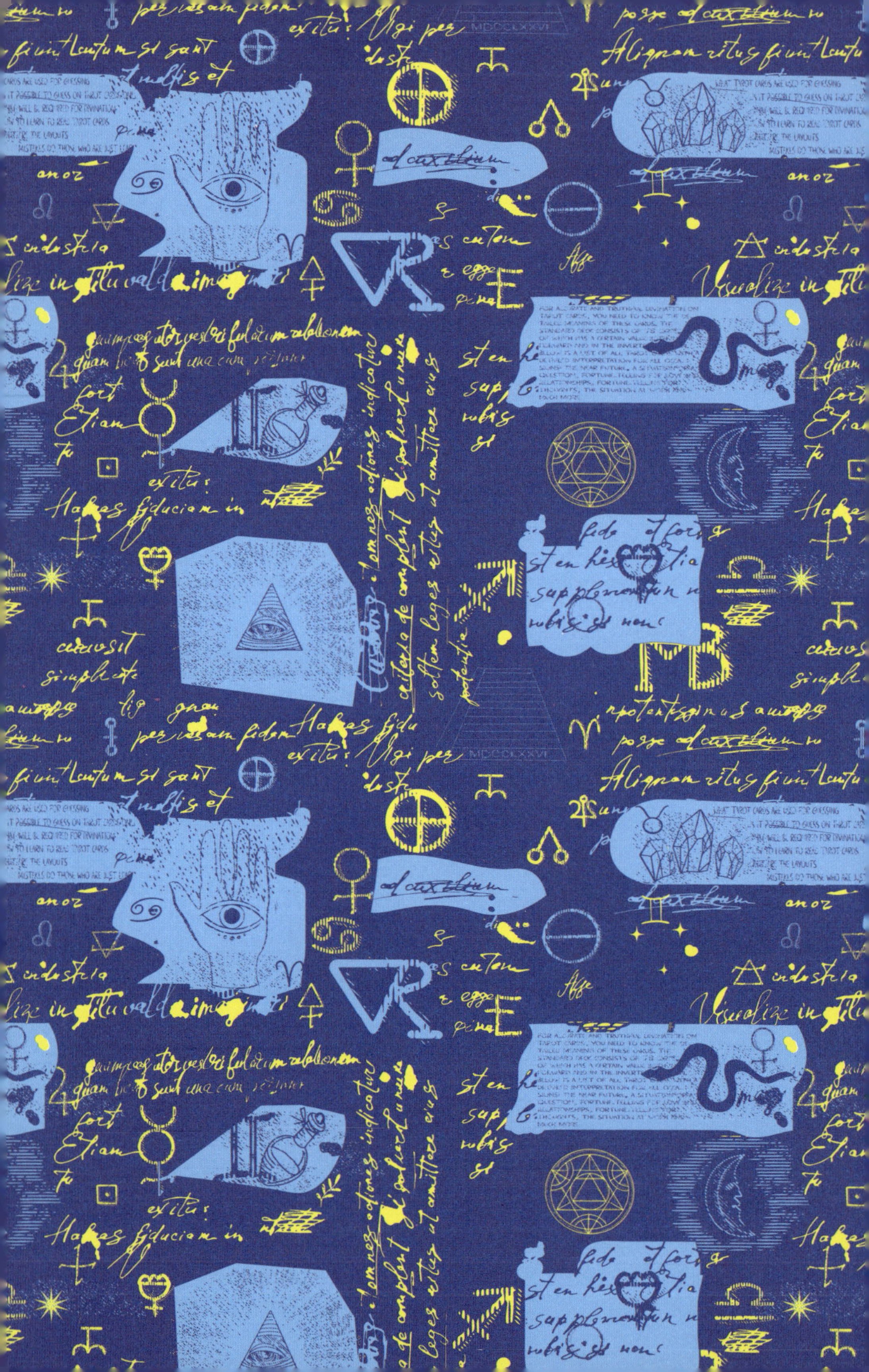

Surrealism and Operative Alchemy

Surrealism and Operative Alchemy

The Secret Language at the Origins of the Surrealist Movement

Patrick Lepetit

Translated by Jon E. Graham

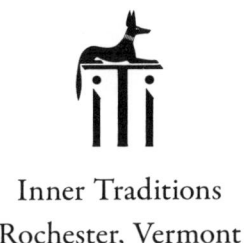

Inner Traditions

Rochester, Vermont

Inner Traditions
One Park Street
Rochester, Vermont 05767
www.InnerTraditions.com

Cataloging-in-Publication Data for this title is available from the Library of Congress

ISBN 979-8-88850-167-2 (print)
ISBN 979-8-88850-168-9 (ebook)

Printed and bound in China by Reliance Printing Co., Ltd.

10 9 8 7 6 5 4 3 2 1

Text design by Kira Kariakin and layout by Kenleigh Manseau
This book was typeset in Garamond Premier Pro with Bookmania, Regulator and Lucida Sans Typewriter Std used as display typefaces

To send correspondence to the author of this book, mail a first-class letter to the author c/o Inner Traditions, One Park Street, Rochester, VT 05767, and we will forward the communication.

Scan the QR code and save 25% at InnerTraditions.com. Browse over 2,000 titles on spirituality, the occult, ancient mysteries, new science, holistic health, and natural medicine.

Igne Natura Renovatur Integra

To Bernard Roger and Serge Pey
and in memory of
Elie-Charles Flamand and Michel Butor

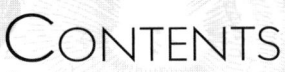

CONTENTS

It is important to restate here the Maranatha* of the Alchemists placed at the threshold of the Work to halt the profane.

ANDRÉ BRETON,
SECOND MANIFESTO OF SURREALISM

It could almost be said that time doesn't pass in the Golden Lane in Hradčany. If you wish to live for five hundred years, drop everything and apply yourself to alchemy.

VÍTĚZSLAV NEZVAL,
ZPÁTEČNÍ LÍSTEK†

For myself, I am fraught with fear before the difficulties of analogy.

MICHAEL PSELLOS,
"DE AUREA CATENA," *PHILOSOPHICA MINORA*

I don't give instruction, I awaken.

VILLIERS DE L'ISLE-ADAM, *AXËL*

---

*As was brought to my attention by Jacques Simonelli, "Maranatha," which is Aramaic in origin and means "Come, Lord!," appears in the First Epistle of Saint Paul to the Corinthians and in the epilogue of Revelations. We also find this word in the first line of Nicholas Flamel's *Hieroglyhical Key* (and often repeated therein), which is "filled with great execrations and curses against every person that should cast his eyes upon it if he were not sacrificer or scribe."

†Vítězslav Nezval, *Zpáteční lístek* [Round Trip Ticket] (Prague: Editions Borovy, 1933). A signed copy of this book was in André Breton's library.

Acknowledgments

Thanks for their help, both conscious and unconscious, and their encouragement:

Jean Artero, Henri Béhar, Gilles Bucherie, Margarita Camacho, Jean-Marie Castex, Camille Coppinger, Didier Deroeux, Laurent Doucet, Marie-Claire Dumas, Béatrice Dunner, Bruno Duval, Obéline and Elie-Charles Flamand, Bruno Geneste and Isabelle Moign, Yoan Armand Gil, Alain Gruger, Daniel Guéguen, Charles B. Jameux, Marc Kober, Jacques Lacomblez, Yann Lauthe, Jacques Lennep, Gérard Lioret, Marie-Dominique Massoni, Pierre Mollier, David Nadeau, Fabrice Pascaud, Michel Passelergue, Serge Pey and Chiara Mulas, Françoise Py, Dominique Rabourdin, Bernard Renaud de la Faverie, Olivier Renaud de la Faverie, Bernard Roger, Etienne Ruhaud, Paul Sanda, Richard Shillitoe, Jacques Simonelli, Aleksandra Sokolov, and Dominic Tétrault.

INTRODUCTION

ALCHEMY OF THE WORD

There is no reading after which we cannot continue seeking for the philosopher's stone.

ANDRÉ BRETON,
LES PAS PERDUS (THE LOST STEPS)

Born at the end of the nineteenth century, a period often considered the golden age of esotericism and "occultism" (a rather catch-all term* coined shortly before by Éliphas Lévi), the intellectual development of the first generation of surrealists was truly immersed in the cerebral ferment that characterized this prewar period. A reaction against the prevailing positivist hegemony, this ferment shook the esoteric world, as evidenced by the emergence of a number of more or less secret societies. These included the various Rosicrucian orders in France, such as Sar Peladan's Aesthetic Rosicrucian Order Emerging from the Shadow of Martinism,[1] and the Golden Dawn in England, as well as the publications of individuals such as Leví himself, Papus, or Helena Blavatsky, to name but a few.

---

*It was René Alleau who, in a 2010 interview in the magazine *3ème Millénaire*, called occultism a "catch-all" and "a kind of junk room in which everything is piled up: esotericism, Kabbalah, theosophy, witchcraft, alchemy, Gnosticism, cartomancy, paranormal phenomena, astrology, tea leaves, ghosts, magic, high initiation, talismans, and so on." (The words *alchemy* and *artist* will appear in either uppercase or lowercase in quotations in accordance with their authors' preference.) This term appears again in Alleau's

1

As noted by Patrick Krémer, André Rolland de Renéville, a prominent member of the Grand Jeu (a group organized by two young seers from Reims, Roger Gilbert-Lecomte and René Daumal, and their Czech friend Joseph Sima), emphasized in *Univers de la parole** that "the fight of the Encyclopedists against religious dogmas had its counterpart in the freedom they gave to certain minds to devote themselves to the study of the philosophies and religious messages of all times and all countries, from which the obstacle of a traditional prohibition had just been removed."[2] He formulated the hypothesis that "the crisis of agnosticism that turned the Western world upside down was overshadowed by a leap toward the marvelous and a passion for the so-called forbidden sciences, something that could be seen in the most educated classes of society."

From this point of view, and considering that this crisis lasted throughout the nineteenth century and only really ended in 1914, how could we not be struck by the blinding evidence that the surrealists were, at least in part, the heirs of these "accursed poets" who were engaged in the elucidation of what Baudelaire calls "the immense universal analogy"? Moreover, are they not cursed "by virtue of the fact that they follow a direction similar to that of the so-called accursed sciences . . . from which they draw the very basis of their thought"?[3] These "accursed sciences" are those, Breton notes in his *Prolegomena to a Third Manifesto*, "with which a tacit contact has always been maintained through the intermediary of 'accursed' poetry." Likewise, in "Before the Curtain," the preface to the catalog of the 1947 exhibition at the Maeght Gallery, he observes that "it cannot be a coincidence that recent research has discovered at the intersection of poetic and social transformative thought (the great figures of the Convention, Hugo, Nerval, Fourier) the continuing vitality of an esoteric understanding of the world (Martinès, Saint-Martin, Fabre

---

(cont.d.) preface to Louis Figuier's *L'alchimie et les alchimistes* (*Bibliotheca Hermetica*), in which he harshly criticizes the "scientism style" of that time. As far as I know, the word *occultism* never appeared before 1853, the time of the *Revue progressive* founded by Alphonse Louis Constant, better known as Éliphas Lévi.

*Renéville is also the author of *L'expérience poétique*.

d'Olivet, the Abbé Constant)." And he adds that their more or less direct influence can be seen, crystalizing around Saint-Yves d'Alveydre, on "the major poets of the second half of the nineteenth century (Lautréamont, Rimbaud, Mallarmé, Jarry)." Rolland de Renéville, author of *The Poetic Experience*, went further, saying: "It is now possible to feel that the assertions of nineteenth- and twentieth-century poets about the meaning of symbols, the power of the word, and the infinite richness of the unconscious will be remote but undeniable consequences of the currents of thought expressed in the Martinist and Swedenborgian doctrines* at the dawn of Romanticism." In support of his claim, he cites "Nerval, Baudelaire, and Poe," but also Hugo,† Mallarmé, Rimbaud, and Jarry, not to mention Balzac and Villiers de L'Isle-Adam,‡ who were influenced by Martinès de Pasqually,** the founder of the Order of the Mason Knights

---

*I think it is important to make a distinction between Martinism and Martinésism, the latter arising directly from the thought and writings of Martinès de Pasqually personally while, according to Rolland de Renéville, "under the impetus of Claude de Saint-Martin [*sic*], the doctrine inaugurated by Martinez [*sic*] de Pasqually tends to blend with that of Swedenborg," and, with the help of Papus, creates Martinism.

†In his introduction to Basil Valentine's *Twelve Keys of Philosophy* (Paris: Editions de Minuit, 1956), Eugène Canseliet writes that the "sketches and drawings" of Hugo, which alone showed his "inclination . . . for transcendental poetry," are "overwhelmingly a precursor to Surrealism."

‡With respect to Villiers de L'Isle-Adam, for example, Jacques d'Ares recalls that Canseliet considered his posthumous book *Axël* to "contain a substantial initiatory doctrine of real value" (*Atlantis*, n° 322). And according to Van Lennep, Mallarmé (about whom, Breton recalls in "Fronton Virage," the "*enchantment*" he felt when he discovered one of his "little sonnets") "also believed in the magic of words" and "stated that occultism [was] the commentary of pure signs, which all literature followed because he was convinced that each letter transmitted a portion of sidereal power." He added moreover that "occultism partially uncovers the mechanisms of universal symbolism," a "fervor" he shared with Villiers de L'Isle-Adam, who was often his confidant on the subject. Robert Amadou devoted the tenth issue of his journal, *La tour Saint-Jacques*, to J. K. Huysmans.

**Breton quoted *Le crocodile* by his disciple, Louis-Claude de Saint-Martin, the "Unknown Philosopher" in his text "Languages of Stones." Breton was familiar with the work of his friend Robert Amadou whose "silhouette" crosses through the pages of "Surrealism in its Living Works" in 1955, according to Etienne-Alain Hubert. Breton's library also contained a copy of *Gnostiques de la révolution* by Claude [*sic*] de Saint-Martin, a collection of texts presented by André Tanner and published in 1946 by Éditions Egloff (Paris and Fribourg).

Elect Cohen of the Universe. There were also Blake, Swedenborg, and several other "accursed philosophers [who] created their personal works in the secret radiance of the Kabbalah,* and thereby, without seeking it, earned credit as initiators of Romanticism."

In the same spirit, Breton (in the third part of *Ajours*, the section that concludes *Arcane 17*), hails in a footnote "the publication of a major work entitled *La symbolique de Rimbaud*," which definitively establishes that "the influence of Éliphas Lévi, about which A. Viatte had shown the predominant role it played in the development of Victor Hugo, was experienced by Rimbaud with equal importance." Breton did this despite the fact that the author was "a young Jesuit" named Jacques Gengoux.† As a sign of his possible approval, he quoted the following sentences: "Fourier and Lévi formed part of a massive trend of thought that we can follow from the Zohar to its diversification in the visionary schools of the eighteenth and nineteenth centuries. We then find it at the base of the idealistic systems, including that of Goethe, and in general in all those who refuse to believe that a mathematical identity is the ideal unifying principle of the world." Breton emphasized Éliphas Lévi's ties to the Phalansterian bookshop on Quai Voltaire, while pointing out that Fourier had insisted on "the symbolism of colors" before Rimbaud.

In words close to Breton's, but which will not surprise anyone who is aware of the closeness of the two men, Pierre Mabille mentions in his preface to the new French edition of *Alice in Wonderland and Through the Looking Glass* (published by Stock in

---

*There is a clear distinction between the Hebrew Kabbalah, which is an esoteric tradition of Judaism, Christian Kabbalah, the philosophical trend, due to the Neoplatonic philosophers of the Renaissance who made it possible to use kabbalistic techniques to interpret the New Testament in particular, and the phonetic cabala—which is nothing other than the Language of the Birds.

†The exact title of the book, published by the Parisian publisher Éditions du Vieux Colombier in 1947, is *La symbolique de Rimbaud: Le système, ses sources*. But the book in Breton's library was this author's *La pensée poétique de Rimbaud*, which he had inscribed to him. Jacques Gengoux abandoned his plans to join the Jesuit order.

1947),* two works which he said "were almost as widespread in English speaking countries as the Bible," "the initiatory nature of Art" that "can never be stressed too highly" (art in the sense he gives it), even if "membership in secret societies is not enough in itself to awaken poetic genius."† Referring to the works of Auguste Viatte,‡ he writes: "To explain the extraordinary success of certain books, signed or not, the occultists of the end of the last century, Éliphas Lévi, Saint-Yves d'Alveydre, [and] Schuré stated that these works were initiatory and that their authors belonged to a kind of occult chain or, more exactly, a fraternity that has passed down a secret teaching since the dawn of time." Then, recalling in passing Etiemble's study of "the singular readings of Rimbaud at the Charleville Municipal Library when he was a child," he concludes that while "definitive proof" has "not been produced"—how could it be?— "disturbing facts have been discovered." This should come as no surprise, since "the poet expresses the resolution of that ancient conflict to which the initiate claims to hold the key through knowledge of the Arcana," and since "poetry seeks through the word (words and images) to express the ceaseless communication between the world of external phenomena and that of the internal representation animated by the violence of our passions."

This happens in the secret radiance of the Hebrew Kaballah, as Breton puts it, and of the *Zohar*, but certainly also of Hermeticism, whose foundational text, the *Emerald Tablet*, establishes precisely this analogy, that "targets the intelligence of the heart and its creativity," as the manifestation of a universal law. In addition, as René Alleau points

---

*In this text, republished in *Traversées de nuit* (Paris: Éditions Plasma, 1981), Mabille points out that the work of Lewis Carroll "constitutes . . . a text of the highest occult scope by directly questioning the foundations of logic and reason and by demonstrating the weakness of our certainty."

†It seems helpful to me to recall that Mabille knows what he's talking about here as he was a Freemason of high degree in Le Droit Humain.

‡"Who isn't," Mabille thought it worthwhile to spell out, probably intended to silence malicious critics, "an occultist but a lucid and well-informed professor."

out, this analogy "arises from the poetic and forms the basis of traditional alchemy."[4] "It is one of the paths of the Living," says Jean Biès, whose "definitions mutually converge, intersect, and fertilize each other and whose inexhaustibility leaves the seeker forever dissatisfied."[5] Alleau, in his *Aspects de l'alchimie traditionnelle* (Aspects of traditional alchemy), also pointed out that Hermeticism was based on the myth of Hermes Trismegistus, whom Neoplatonists and Christians, under the influence of Euhemerist ideas, considered to be an ancient Egyptian king and the inventor of all sciences, whose secrets he had enclosed in mysterious books. Their solemn procession was described by Clement of Alexandria.* This *"thrice great figure"*† whom "the ancient Egyptians," Camacho tells us, "worshipped under the name of Thoth," is the one "who knows the *Word* with which the gods gave birth to the universe, which they considered to be the *heart* of the god RA, and who possessed the knowledge of the secret language. This is the figure whom the Greeks . . . called HERMES, who by his nature corresponds to the *Artist* of our Hermetic Science" (italics and capitalization in the original).[6] Meanwhile Henri Hunwald shares the view of Rolland de Renéville and writes simply and clearly: "It has thus been decided to designate in this way a set of doctrines, which according to tradition go back to Ancient Egypt in the figure of the legendary Hermes Trismegistus. All of those doctrines and the practical applications they promoted find a common denominator in the *theory of correspondences* according to which the entire universe is composed of a number of analogous realms, whose elements correspond to one another, and can thus be used mutually as symbols, to reveal their respective properties, or even to act upon one another."[7]

---

*René Alleau, *Aspects de l'alchimie traditionnelle* (Paris: Edition de Minuit, 1953). However, in the book he wrote on Alleau (*René Alleau et l'écriture philosophale*, Saint-Gervais: SELENA Editions, 2022), Gilles Bucherie points out that as "in Fulcanelli's two books, *The Mystery of the Cathedrals* and *The Dwellings of the Philosophers*," few developments are carried out in Alleau's work "around the study of Egyptian myth and its connection with the Great Work."

†"Thrice great," writes André Coia-Gatié in his book *Chevalerie errante* (Paris: La Table d'Emeraude, 1992), "because he acts simultaneously in the heavens, earth, and hell."

Continuing his demonstration, Rolland de Renéville, alluding directly to Swedenborg, says: "By a bold and grandiose effort that surpasses all in the Romantic style of composition . . . Baudelaire, at the same time as Nerval,* and under the influence of a shared mystical theory, introduces the method of *Correspondences* into French poetry. This innovation had such a great impact on our aesthetics that neither the Symbolist movement nor the later Surrealist movement could exhaust its possibilities!" Speaking of the same correspondences Pierre Mabille notes,† "There is no question that Baudelaire borrowed this idea from the Swedish mystic Swedenborg," to whom Baudelaire expressly refers in another passage in *L'art romantique*. "Swedenborg," the poet says, "has already taught us that everything: form, movement, number, colors, and aromas in the spiritual as well as in the natural world, is meaningful, reciprocal, contrary, and corresponding." "From there," Mabille continues, "the poet's task will be to follow his inner sense of divination in order to perceive the analogies and correspondences concealed by the literary aspect of the metaphor." He continues, "The equivalence between the sensory elements, the reflection of the spiritual world in the material world, is where we see the first two levels on which correspondences develop." The third, which is concerned with the ability to discern—not given to everyone—"through appearances reduced to the rank of signs and symbols, the reflections of a supersensory universe," allows the poet to perceive "the Saturnine and profound unity" of the world, of which these correspondences serve as proof. Van Lennep confirms the existence of these correspondences, although he traces their origin only to Cornelius Agrippa,‡ the famous Kabbalist from the early Renaissance who "specifically revealed the magic liaison between the

---

*Nerval was highly esteemed by the members of the *Grand Jeu*. Van Lennep writes that "his poem 'El Desdichado' was conceived as a typical hermetic riddle, revealing in a remarkable way the influence of alchemy" ("L'art alchimique et le surréel").

†In his first press conference on poetry, included in *Traversées de la nuit* (Paris: Editions Plasma, 1981).

‡Heinrich Cornelius Agrippa von Nettesheim (1486–1535), a highly influential German esotericist best known for his work *De occulta philosophia*. Breton compared Max Ernst to the "great Corneille Agrippa."

conceptual world, that of images, and the universe. These liaisons, which Bruno calls 'chains,' survived in Swedenborg's 'Correspondences' and in Baudelairean analogies, to which the Surrealists were not deaf." Before them they survive in Rimbaud's work, whose "alchemy of the word," according to Michel Carrouges, "was sufficient from the time of its inception to magnetize the entire line of great modern poets."* In his *Second Manifesto*, Breton, while emphasizing its limitations, wanted to see this phrase "taken literally." There is certainly a connection with those quoted above! Bernard Roger[8] extends these correspondences "to the destiny of all humanity and the life of civilizations inasmuch as . . . the birth and death of religious systems is connected to astronomical events." He points out in a footnote that this point of view is shared by René Guénon (in *The Reign of Quantity*), Pierre Mabille (in *Egregores*), and Isha Schwaller de Lubicz (in *Herbak*).

This is all the more significant because, as the author of *Art and Alchemy* reminds us, "nourished by the occult sciences [Rimbaud] composed a poetic science that he expressed in his 'Sonnet of the Vowels,' which reflects a profound initiation into the symbology of letters and colors." "The Surrealist poet," Van Lennep says, "who was enchanted by the relations between alchemical transmutation and poetic transformation, which Surrealism had to maintain with a particular fervor, found beyond Rimbaud and Nerval, the verses of Clovis Hesteau de Nuysement† or the prose of Hermes Trismegistus!"[9] Not to mention that "alchemical emblems probably respond most perfectly to the imperatives of a magical art based on universal sympathy, as advocated by the humanists interested in the occult sciences or as later envisioned by André Breton." Convinced

---

*Michel Carrouges, "Poésie moderne et alchimie," in *L'alchimie*, by E. J. Holmyard. Incidentally, Michel Carrouges was a good friend of many of the figures appearing in this book, with whom he maintained correspondence. This included René Alleau, Eugène Canseliet, Henri Hunwald, Maurice Fourré, and Breton, of course.

†Clovis Hesteau de Nuysement (1555–1623), poet and alchemist and author of *Traittez de l'harmonie, et constitution generalle du vray sel, secret des philosophes, & de l'esprit universel du monde*.

that surrealism and alchemy could both be defined as "a kind of occulto-materialism" Carrouges, who had already noted "the deep bond between alchemy and surrealism, between alchemical transmutation and poetic transformation" in his *André Breton and the Basic Concepts of Surrealism*, plows the same furrow when stating, "And just as alchemical literature is an initiation to transmutation, surrealist poetic manifestations are an initiation into the transformation of the relationship between man and the universe." "Because," he goes on to say, "the practice of poetry, not as an object of verbal art but as an irreplaceable mental process, has immediate value as a first apprenticeship in the world of transmutation and transformation." "*In this way,*" he states explicitly with the ability to state things succinctly and clearly, for which he is known, "*alchemy is poetry in the strongest sense of the word and surrealism is really an alchemical transmutation.*" (My italics.) To ensure that this is fully understood, he then notes, "Through the transmutation of matter, mineral or verbal, the goal of both is the metamorphosis of man and the cosmos."* He then goes on to say that it is "this myth of the transformation of man, stripping himself of his wretched appearance in order to put on a glorious body by means of a transmutation analogous to that of the mystical lead of the alchemists transformed into mystical gold, that inspires the bulk of the essential themes of surrealist symbology, including that of Breton."

Then we have Elie-Charles Flamand, who says in "La quete du verbe," (his preface for his anthology *Attiser la rose cruciale*) "that some of the phases of poetic alchemy consist in recovering, as best as possible, the inflections and the rhythm of the mystical voice, in embodying the idea it expresses in living images that tend to make it possible to grasp what is most elusive, to precipitate, clarify and intensify this vibration, which is sometimes so tenuous and so difficult to capture and translate." He goes on to say that although "throughout the ages, some poets have

---

*Jörg Völlnagel, in his book *Alchimie, l'art royal* (Paris: Imprimerie Nationale editions, 2012), explains that alchemists believe their art "like a hermetic promise of salvation . . . would be able to complete and perfect the divine creation of nature and lead humanity into a new era of paradise."

suspected or known that, as in the handling of the Great Work, the operations whose goal is the transmutation of verbal matter are inseparable from the work on the self that can give birth to enlightenment," it was the Romantics, he adds—"and especially the French Romantics"—who "began to favor metaphor and to consider the system of correspondences that underlies it as one of the fundamental principles of poetry," an "idea that has been further developed by Symbolism and more recent poetic movements such as Surrealism." It's this "concept of the image, so close to that of the hermeticists," which, "accompanied by a clearer realization of the true essence of the [imagined] poetic act," when it is "carried to its highest degree," as a rebirth of the "whole psychological and spiritual individual" through writing, has made "the kinship between poetry and alchemy"* more immediately visible. As Bernard Roger puts it, in describing this kinship: "Like all activity that comes from poetry, alchemy is very receptive in its own depths to infinite possibilities and heavens. Access to it is all the more forbidden to those who have closed their ears to nature, just as poetry will always be to those who have lost contact with the spirit."[10] For this reason, Flamand resumes, "elements of the high wisdom of the *Ars Magna* can be detected" in the works of "Gérard de Nerval, Stéphane Mallarmé, Arthur Rimbaud, Oscar Vladislas de Lubicz-Milosz, and André Breton, for example," while others such as Saint-John Perse, Pierre Jean Jouve, Paul Éluard, René Char, (and) Edmond Humeau,† "without having frequented the sanctuary of the Adepts, intuitively rediscovered the very spirit of the science of the Great Work and often practiced true verbal alchemy."[11]

---

*A reversible proposition, as can be seen in the highly poetic nature of numerous titles for alchemical works, such as those cited by Caron and Hutin: *An Open Entrance to the Shut-palace of the King, The Great Work Unveiled in Favor of the Children of the Light, The Light Coming Out of the Darkness, The Desired Desire, The Book of Twelve Gates, The Tomb of Semiramis Open to the Wise,* and *The Great Mirror of the World.*

†Edmond Humeau (1907–1998), a friend of E. C. Flamand and author of, most notably, *Le tambourinaire des sources.* He was one of the "comrade-kings" who channeled all his brilliance into *La tour de feu* (1946–1981), the magazine of Pierre Boujut (1913–1992).

A little later in Great Britain, Toni del Renzio (1915–2007), a dissident surrealist who like Ithell Colquhoun* was expelled by E. L. T. Mesens and Jacques Brunius for the importance he attached to the same esoteric thought toward which Breton had turned, stated in his short manifesto, "Incendiary Innocence":

Alchemy of the word—released from the limitations Rimbaud had placed upon it—plays a miraculous role in the surrealist drama, and as psychology becomes more precise upon the nature seen by Philosophers, so the accuracy with which Breton identified Alchemical and Surrealist researches continues to astound and to confound. Flamel and Lulle† have both been listed as Surrealists, while from the former's transcription of the *Book of Abraham the Jew*‡ has been drawn a description typifying *the* surrealist picture. The parallelism of these two *revolté* movements, separated by several centuries, yet intertwined, is most marked in a recent important text, *Genesis and Perspective of Surrealism*, written by André Breton for the catalog of *Art of this Century*, where deliberate and conscious references are made to occultists and mystics such as Giordano Bruno, Joachim of Flora, Meister Eckhart, an intimate acquaintance with the *Chemical Wedding of Christian Rosenkreutz*, and to the very fount of alchemy, *The Smaragdine Tables of Hermes Trismegistus*,** cited in the work. [Del Renzio's italics, above.]

---

*To whom he was briefly married.

†Raymond Lulle, or Ramon Lull (1232–1315), was a poet and mystic philosopher of the thirteenth century. Numerous alchemical treatises have been attributed to him, such as *Testament in Two Books of the Complete Universal Chemical Art—Of which one volume concerns how to transmute the soul of metals*, and *On the Secrets of Nature and Its Quintessence*, but recent scholarship has called this into question.

‡This would be no less than "the lost work of Rabbi Abraham, the *Ash Mesareph*, that was believed to have been totally destroyed," according to Jacques Sadoul in *Le trésor des alchimistes* (Paris: Editions Publications Premières, 1970).

**The "Smaragdine Table" is also known as the "Tabula Smaragdina" or more prosaically as the "Emerald Tablet."

He then goes on to say: "Vision must return to its pristine clarity, which the occultists accord to innocence—an innocence more precisely situated than that mask beneath which ignorance and ill will have hid themselves—incendiary innocence bursting into the flames of the primitive temptations of Bosch."[12]

Alleau, in his analysis, thought that "being only means actively being in every moment" and that "any ontology that overlooks this makes us slaves to an abstract idea of the being and leads us astray." He counters this with "the ceaselessly reanimated life of 'active being,'" in other words the ceaselessly recreating Word, for the preeminent poetic Word, essentially operative and concrete, which the ideological abstractions of contemporary "false consciousness" never ceases to take us away from. He then emphasizes "the primitive liaison between poetry and metallurgy," "later vouched for by the double meaning of the Greek poiein," and reminds us that fiction is "literally a transformation of 'fact' into 'fiat,' a *recreation of the created*. Hence the demiurgic nature of poetry and alchemy."* "This is why," Elie-Charles Flamand concludes in a similar vein, "Photius and the anonymous author of a papyrus text in the Leyden library, among many others, use the word ποιηεις (poiesis) instead of χρυσοποια (chrysopoeia),† which means the transmutation of metals into gold. Moreover, in some manuscripts, like one in Saint Mark's Library in Venice, alchemists are called ποιητής (poietes)." "What's at work here," he adds, "is a play on words. These two words,

---

*René Alleau, "Hypnos et thanatos ou le philosophe dans le paysage" in *Jorge Camacho, la danse de la mort*, exhibition catalog, Galerie de Seine, Paris, for the first part of the citation, and *Aspects de l'alchimie traditionnelle* for the second. It will easily be seen that this expression, "recreation of the created," was reused by Bernard Roger in the introductory "text" dedicated to Alleau in the republication of Basil Valentine's *De la nature des métaux*.

†Speaking of chrysopoeia, we may recall that a painting by Leonora Carrington from 1964 is entitled *Chrysopoeia of Marie the Jewess*. This woman is considered to be one of the founders of alchemy. She invented a number of tools and procedures and for this reason was cited in the treatises by Zosimus of Panopolis. Marie the Jewess is believed to have lived in Alexandria between the second and third century CE.

which are connected to the root of the verb ποιειν, poiein, can be either taken in their etymological sense of creator and maker, or in the more common definition of poet and poetry."[13]

This is why the sacred art, "according to the traditional expression of the Adepts," should be seen as a means of considering the connections between the different levels of reality, to the extent that, as Mircea Eliade says, "the experiments of the alchemists on mineral or plant substances have a more audacious goal than simple experimentation; it is to alter their very way of being."* This happens, according to Alleau and then Canseliet, "in the disruption of the balance of the logical mechanics of profane consciousness, the prime material and, consequently, the *chaos* of the Great Work on the mental and spiritual planes,"[14] and "therein resides the esoteric explanation of some poetic works, the justification of the *inspired poets*, labeled as *accursed*." This cannot help but cast a new light on the well-known formula concerning the "long, immense, reasoned derangement of all the senses" that Rimbaud wrote in a letter to Paul Demeny and which Breton repeated in the *Manifesto*. In a bit of a breathtaking abridgement, he even went on to say (in *Surrealism*), "we should recall, on that respect, with Yves Duplessis, 'the gnostic meaning of the whirlwind of life that devours the darkness' (Surrealism), and which could explain, for example, Rimbaud's sonnets on the vowels, and also holds a certain kabbalistic connection with Raymond Roussel's *Poussière de soleils* [The dust of the suns]." A sonnet in which the *man with the soles of the wind* mentions, as someone accustomed to the inn of the Great Bear,† alchemy and its "broad, studious brows," and whose famous image, "O the Omega!

---

*Mircea Eliade, *Le mythe de l'alchimie suivi de l'alchimie asiatique*. Eliade's statements are confirmed by Stanislas Klossowski de Rola in *Alchimie: Florilège de l'art secret*, when he asserts that "while the transmutation of metals is not the final goal of the Great Work, it is nonetheless certain that it plays a major and absolutely indispensable role, so that the Great Work is both a spiritual and material realization."

†Arthur Rimbaud, "Ma bohème" (*Cahier de Douai*, 1870): "My Inn was at the *Grande Ourse* [the Great Bear, the Big Dipper—*trans.*]," which in an alchemical context assumes a very specific meaning.

Violet beam from his Eyes!," inspired Fulcanelli's disciple to write the following commentary (which will be helpful to remember later): "The last verse of the famous sonnet sings of Hermes's small fish, the *Ichthys* of the Christian catacombs, the *remora* of the old alchemists, that tablet, which is miniscule in comparison to the mineral mass involved, and of which it is the pure and spiritual sulfurous part, laboriously gleaned during the course of the second work, and whose fracture reveals to be superbly shiny and purplish-blue."[15]

In a very complementary way, Bernard Roger rightly shows, while leaving everyone to draw their own conclusions, that the birth of the two "liberating movements of the mind" that promoted an awakening of consciousness—Romanticism in the nineteenth century and surrealism in the twentieth century—coincides with the appearance "after centuries of silence" of books by two *Sons of science*, Cyliani's *L'Hermès dévoilé* (Hermes unveiled) and the two books by Fulcanelli, *The Mystery of the Cathedrals* and *The Dwellings of the Philosophers*, in 1926* and 1930. Let's say straight off that we know very little about Cyliani, whose book may have inspired Balzac to write *La recherche de l'absolu* (The search for the absolute). In any case it was obviously one of Canseliet's first links to alchemy—at least with certain aspects of this "nebula with multiple configurations," to use Jean Biès's words. However, Papus wrote about this figure in his book *La pierre philosophale* (1889) saying, "the

---

*As Richard Khaitzine points out in his *Secrets d'alcôves—Fulcanelli et la cosmosphère* (Bosguérard-de-Marcouville, Eure: Editions Philomène Alchimie, 2020), 1926 was the year in which Werner Heisenberg formulated—he only released it in 1927—his famous Uncertainty Principle, which in a nutshell expresses that the results of an experiment can vary according to the quality of the observer, or even because of the observer's presence or absence. We should not fail to emphasize that, according to Canseliet's remarks in the preface to the second edition, "when the *Mystery of the Cathedrals* was released in 1922, Fulcanelli had not received the Gift of God yet but he was so close to supreme illumination that he deemed it necessary to wait in personal anonymity, which he consistently observed." Other documents published by Canseliet give reason to believe that this event took place before 1920—perhaps occurring between 1917 and 1919.

alchemist Cylani (1832) who, as he said, discovered the philosopher's stone after forty years of labor, lived as a man of modest independent means after his wife persuaded him not to offer the precious secret to King Louis XVIII."

"While alchemy in its operative aspect," writes Jean-Louis Bédouin in *Vingt ans de surrealism*, "has as its goal the capture of the germinating energies of the 'metal spirits' in order to regenerate their bodies and bring them to perfection by means of the Art, we now see that the surrealist experience proposes nothing less than the discovery of the *signifying* principle of language in order to restore it to true life."[16] Indeed he later goes on to say, "On the basis of the testimony of those who have gone a long way along the narrow and *steep* path, sown with *snares*, that leads to the discovery of the 'Golden Bough,' there would be no impassable border, nor even a sharp demarcation, between certain revelations that can be produced in a state of poetic enlightenment and those that, as Artephius* says, come from the mouth of the *student* when he or she reaches the threshold of enlightening knowledge." However, a word of warning is in order: "It is not a question of establishing a strict parallel between a 'sacred science' and poetic experience,† but of establishing, as the alchemists themselves seem to suggest, not only the analogy of the end but, to

---

*Artephius is a twelfth-century Jewish or Arab alchemist "whose works," according to Bernard Roger," "were circulated in Latin through the scholarly world of the cloisters at that time." Michel Caron and Serge Hutin have suggested that "the poet Al-Tughräi (executed for apostasy around 1120)," who "founded the alchemical art on revelation and initiation," "was none other than the mysterious alchemist known as Artephius."

†It seems appropriate to recall that René Alleau, in his foreword to the republication of Nicolas Flamel's *Book of Hieroglyphic Figures*, said that "the poetic experience in the most general sense of the term . . . was not limited to art, to works, or even less, to their forms, because it extends to *any magical experience of the Sacred*." He added, "It involves, even in the most trivial activities, a pure ability to recreate the data of the outside world, our lifestyle, and the logical modes of our understanding, within." (The uppercase and italics are Alleau's.)

a certain extent, the analogy of the means between hermetic science and poetry, in the highest acceptance of the term." For while "the alchemist is both the demiurge of the philosophical microcosm and the operator who leads the material to a regeneration whose nature is analogous to the transformation that poetry imposes on language,"[17] poetry alone "is the guardian of that lost word, the true subject of the art according to Bernard le Trévisan. But it's an art of connivance, capable of the ultimate reformation, of the final revolution, the one that carries away all the others after having prepared and fulfilled them," Vincent Bounoure sums up in his "Preface to a Treatise on Matrixes." He takes great pains at the beginning of this text to make it clear that the "purely profane" perspective he is expressing "is far from the intelligence of a science that has always presented itself as sacred," but he nevertheless suggests that alchemy "fits into the great current that takes as its primary objective the regeneration of man," a "project based on the primordial powers of thought, on the expectation of their restoration."* He offers a "layman's" way of saying what Stanislas Klossowki de Rola said in words more directly inspired by traditional esotericism, difficult to handle for a scientifically trained surrealist. Namely that "the Great Work, when all is said and done, is nothing other than the restoration of the primordial divine state and the universal salvation of all beings and all things." Or, as Jean Biès puts it, alchemy is "entirely concerned with recreating the process that would allow this life to recover the fullness and purity of the time before the fall of Adam."

We should not lose sight, however, of the fact that, as Bounoure goes on to say, "the Adepts may have devoted themselves to literary

---

*Vincent Bounoure, "Préface à un traité des matrices." The Trévisan who Bounoure discusses is Bernard "Earl of the Trévisan Marches," and notably author of the *Songe verd* who is supposed to have attained the Adeptat at the age of eighty-two, and whose book *La parole délaissée* is cited in *La nouvelle assemblée des philosophes chimiques* by Claude d'Ygé. Vincent Bounoure, a member of the surrealist group during Breton's time, attempted to prevent the rupture of the group after Breton's death.

exercises" in writing their treatises, which is far less "evidence of their indulgence or commiseration for lost seekers than for the necessity of a writing, which is what we call poetry, in whose operations the same procedures are at work as in alchemical work." While concluding that the "hermetic work . . . appeared as a particular case of a general poetics," he added, "this is why for the Adept, the cabala and its practice are both a key to reading the texts, and the means of an invention that implements the same intellectual resources, whether its results are of an operational or poetic order." However, it is a good idea to keep in mind what René Alleau said: "Although the symbology of the Great Work can receive a boundless expansion, its inner consistency is nonetheless so precise and rigorous that it cannot cater to the arbitrary or fantastic interpretations of its users, because its experimental basis makes it possible for mistakes to be found immediately."[18]

In her short and little-known book, *A razão ardente—do romantismo ao surrealismo*, Nora Mitrani, who according to Fernando Sabido Sanchez "was one of those poet-philosophers for whom surrealism was inseparable from life," anticipated in 1950 J. L. Bedouin's later claim: "The art of the surrealists is only the constant tension toward the way of the Great Art, the ARS MAGNA according to Ramon Lull, the golden chain that connects all the events and things of this world—the desire to realize on the plane of language the effort of the Alchemists."* She goes on to write, "From this perspective, we understand Rimbaud's failure. Breton himself foresees his own—certain of not achieving it, but too little concerned about his own death to not reckon with the joys of such a possession." Breton says, perhaps a bit hastily in 1955: "The whole point for Surrealism was to convince ourselves that we had got our hands on the 'prime matter' (in the alchemical sense) of language," "something like language in

---

*Nora Mitrani, *A razão ardente—do romantismo ao surrealismo* (Cuadernos Surrealistas, 1950). The capitalized letters are in the original. Breton had a copy of the typewritten manuscript in French in his library.

the raw state, one on which the operation separating speaking from saying has not yet been performed."* Words that could not help but complement this extract from one of René Alleau's still-unpublished *Notebooks*, which is obviously on the same wavelength:

> *The whole point for Surrealism*
> *was to convince ourselves*
> *that we had got our hands*
> *on the PRIME MATTER*
> *(in the alchemical sense) of language;*
> *AFTER THAT, WE KNEW WHERE*
> *TO GET IT, and it goes without saying*
> *that we had no interest in*
> *reproducing it to the point of satiety; THAT'S for those*
> *who are so surprised that the practice*
> *of automatic writing among us*
> *had been abandoned.†*

Jean-Claude Silbermann, in a rare text entitled *Le saumon, la cerise et le gardien du trait, texte sur l'art* (The salmon, the cherry, and the guardian of the line), brought his own evidence to bear on this question of the relationship between surrealism and alchemy, stating:

I don't have the expertise to identify the reasons and place the circumstances (Christianity? The Renaissance? The Enlightenment?) that led us to cut ties with our own primordial myths, but there

---

*André Breton, "Du surréalisme dans ses oeuvres vives," in *Oeuvres complètes,* vol. 4. As Etienne-Alain Hubert points out, the phrase quoted was first published in the fourth issue of *Médium,* and the second part of the citation corresponds to an "author's note connected with language."

†The capitalization is René Alleau's. This dates probably from the beginning of the aughts.

is at least one traditional discipline in the West: alchemy. The "Sons of Science" have brought the "Art of Hermes into our day." Poets—Jean-Pierre Brisset, Raymond Roussel, Ghérasim Luca, Guy Cabanel—have, in this century, known how to loosen the bridle on the "horse of the word." Artists who, for the most part, emerged from surrealism in a specific and decisive fashion, among them Jorge Camacho, may well have succeeded in momentarily "fixing the volatile" and "volatilizing the fixed." But this traditional art, like all others, is transmitted by *initiation*, and in the study, reading, and rereading of *inspired* texts. The secret it holds is the key and the lock that this key fits is it own imprint.[19]

It is Gherasim Luca who writes, for example, "For us, the dream of the alchemists, like all dreams, belongs to a reality," and it was again Jean-Claude Silbermann who in 2019 created a series of original drawings for the deluxe edition of Philippe Audoin's previously unpublished *Les capucines aux lèvres d'émail* by Editions du Grand Tamanoir. Some of these drawings, such as the court jester spurting out of a flask, undeniably bear the stamp of the Art of Music! With respect to this Art of Music, "we know," Bernard Roger writes in his introduction to *The Light Coming Out of Darkness by Itself,* a book attributed to Marc-Antonio Crasselame[20] (which was also cited at length by the author of *L'alchimie expliquée sur ses textes classiques,* Eugene Canseliet), that many authors "use this periphrasis to refer to alchemy" in order to thus convey that on the practical level of the work the concern was to achieve harmony between the elements by means of the "salt" while on the level of theoretical instruction, the texts are considered to be a unique musical theme—engendered by the word of Hermes, regarded as the "Father of all alchemists."

But in any event, it is clearly an expert in this field, Eugene Canseliet, to whom I should give the last word. In a later text from 1978 happily dismissing one of the inescapable assumptions of the current of thought represented by Breton and his friends, he deemed "that it was not disputable that surrealism had played a large role in the revival of alchemy, just as *Atlantis* had played no less important a role." "Between the two great movements," he added, "the dissimilarity is only in appearance because the first recovers from dream what atheism had caused it to lose on the level of reality."[21]

1

SURREALISM AND ESOTERICISM

The surrealists are the investigators of a new kind of science—and they must follow the same path as the candidates for the status of Adept [Sons of Science], the path of illuminated knowledge.

JEAN-LOUIS BÉDOUIN,
TWENTY YEARS OF SURREALISM

It might be a good idea here to say a few words about surrealism, which cannot be reduced to a simple "avant-garde" philosophy while overlooking the fact that it took root in symbolism, "the flowering of all the secret and mystical philosophy that French Romanticism possessed," as Rolland de Renéville noted. In fact surrealism, like symbolism before it, grew out of Romanticism, a movement of *reaction* against the Enlightenment. Chateaubriand, the "surrealist in exoticism" so often quoted by Breton's friends, was a figurehead of this movement in France. Mainly through the intervention of the "Knight Errant of Theosophy," his friend Louis-Marie de la Forest-Divonne, a disciple of Louis-Claude de Saint Martin,* Madame de Staël, herself quite close

---

*Who Canseliet assumes to be, like Joseph de Maistre, "an alchemist though uncertain if he was an operative one . . . like Willermoz and many other Illuminated brothers" who "all studied the text of *Nature Uncovered: For the children of Science only and not for*

to the author of *Memoirs from Beyond the Grave*, grew familiar with the philosophy of the man known as the Unknown Philosopher, Saint-Martin, and those Canseliet called the "Illuminated theosophists." Not to mention that other link between Chateaubriand and Illuminism in Lyons,* Pierre Simon Ballanche (1776–1847) who Paul Bénichou ironically called "a progressive counter-revolutionary!" Therefore, as one thing leads to another, we can't help but observe when following the course of ideas that the movement founded by Breton† was also influenced to some extent by the Illuminism of the second half of the seventeenth century, the "illuminated Masonry singularly illustrated by Martinez [*sic*] de Pasqually."‡ It also drew on even earlier systems of thought such as those of "that strange Swiss-German Faustian figure of the sixteenth century,"[1] Paracelsus, "the spirited innovator, [the] fierce tribune of Nuremberg, Saint Gall, and other places, [the] brilliant wild man to whom modern medicine seems to owe the very basis of its therapy."[2] There is also Jakob Böhme, who "according to some critics . . . was the last to seriously pursue the quest of the Adepts, but by altering its symbols so that under [his] pen . . . alchemy became . . . a

(cont.d) *ignorant Sophists* by the Unknown Knight," which the Master, that is to say Canseliet, was to republish in *Trois anciens traités d'alchimie* ("Short observations inspired by a great mystic," Eugene Canseliet, *Alchimie, nouvelle etudes diverse sur*).

*In a 1968 interview with Roger Otahi in the Lyonnais magazine *Objectif*, E. C. Flamand, describing Lyon as a "secret city" said, "I spent my whole youth in Lyon and I really believe that the very special mystical climate in which this city is immersed has definitely left its mark on me."

†Who cites Martinès de Pasqually and Louis-Claude de Saint Martin by name in several texts.

‡The two quotes from Rolland de Renéville are from *Sciences maudites & poètes maudits*. Moreover, Breton owned the two 1947 issues of the magazine de Renéville published, *Les cahiers d'Hermès*. An article by Eugene Canseliet appears in the first, "Cyrano de Bergerac, philosophe hermétique" and another by Émile Dermenghem on "Joseph de Maistre et la tradition." Also there is an article by Léo Margot, "Rabelais et l'alchimie," and the article I mentioned earlier by Jacques Gengoux, "Le grand oeuvre de Rimbaud." In the second appears an article by Robert Kanters on "La réalisation théomorphique chez Martinez [*sic*] de Pasqually," as well as extracts from his *Traité de la réintégration des êtres,* and a text by Michel Carrouges, "Surréalisme et occultisme."

Christian mysticism."* This can only irresistibly bring to mind Mircea Eliade's observation in *The Myth of Alchemy*, "In short, all alchemists say that their art is an esoteric and mystical technique."[3]

It is not so easy, however, to define surrealism, a movement of thought that is still alive today and that, without being, with all due respect to the university, just another simple literary or artistic school, has produced a good number of the masterpieces of the last century. If Breton initially presented it as "pure psychic automatism by which one proposes to express . . . the actual functioning of thought . . . in the absence of any control exercised by reason, exempt from any aesthetic or moral concern," this definition was soon revealed to be too narrow. Although he also said in *La révolution surréaliste* he wanted "to come to a new declaration of the rights of man," and made his watchwords those of Marx, "to transform the world" (which evolved into re-enchanting the world), and Rimbaud, "to change life," and later Fourier,† "to remodel human understanding," it soon proved to be clear that the primary goal of surrealism was to restore full power to the imagination by opening oneself to the marvelous—the marvelous that, in the words of the author of *Nadja*, is located "at the extreme point of the vital movement." Although by only seeking, out of disdain for the beyond, to explore reality as it is by all means even if it means, as Fabrice Flahutez notes, drawing from "the timeless storehouse of traditional images and symbols in order to create something new." All this was to restore to Man his freedom—hence the political commitment of surrealism and its revolt against the rich and the system they built,

---

*Jennifer Waelti-Walters, *Alchimie et littérature*. Concerning Böhme, though, Fabrice Bardeau in his article "Alchimie vraie et alchimie métaphysique" (*Atlantis*, no. 401) maintains he "was not an alchemist. He used alchemical vocabulary, phraseology, and imagery to illustrate his religious notions. He was a prophetic dreamer, but certainly no seeker and practitioner. His writings are those of kabbalists and theosophists formulated with an alchemical vocabulary . . ."

†We should recall in passing that Simone Debout's studies of Fourier clearly established the influence on his thought of the work of Martinès de Pasqually's disciple, Louis-Claude de Saint-Martin, by way of Chateaubriand's friend, Pierre-Simon Ballanche.

a revolt that is undeniably echoed in this extract from the third paragraph of Fulcanelli's *Mystery of the Cathedrals*, cited by Bernard Roger, in the tone that is still so appropriate today:

> In our day, cant is spoken by the humble people, the poor, the despised, the rebels, calling for liberty and independence, the outlaws, the tramps and the wanderers. Cant is the cursed dialect, banned by high society, by the nobility (who are really so little noble), the well-fed and self-satisfied middle class, luxuriating in the ermine of their ignorance and fatuity. It remains the language of a minority of individuals living outside accepted laws, conventions, customs and etiquette. The term *voyous* [street-Arabs], that is to say *voyants* [seers] is applied to them and the even more expressive term *Sons* or *Children of the Sun*.[4]

A friend of Bataille, but also of Roger Gilbert-Lecomte, André Rolland de Renéville, and Antonin Artaud, the last of whom he invited to give lectures at the Sorbonne to the members of his association of philosophical and scientific studies for examination of new trends, Doctor René Allendy, author of a thesis on "medicine and alchemy," was thus in good company when he asserted in his *Paracelse, le médecin maudit* (published by Gallimard in 1937): "The very idea of alchemical transformism and the ideal of transmutation automatically leads, on the social level, to a reformist attitude that takes on a revolutionary spirit when it confronts the institution with immutable and definitive claims."

At any rate, while Fourier's maxim, "Remodel human understanding," forms one of its pillars, the convergence of surrealism and alchemy's goals becomes quite clear when compared to this sentence from Alleau's *Aspects de l'alchimie traditionnelle*: "*The ancient dream of the alchemists*," "*the most illustrious dreamers humanity has ever known*," he adds elsewhere, "*was to transform the human ape into a true man*." (Italics are mine.)

This point of view, expressed by Flahutez, is shared by Alain Joubert, who brings it back to the subject by writing: "What interests us in Alchemy is first and foremost the inexhaustible reservoir of images that it consists of, as well as a certain poetic practice of language, of which the image is an intrinsic part."[5] This is explained, according to Carrouges, by the fact that "the writings of the alchemists have a distinctly pre-surrealist look" and that surrealist poetry "takes place precisely as an extension of that of the alchemists.[6] The example he cites, a phrase attributed to "Hermes" that Breton borrowed from Éliphas Lévi for a text on Matta in his book *Surrealism and Painting*—"The raven's head disappears with the night; by day, the bird flies without wings, he vomits the rainbow, his body becomes red, and on his back floats pure water"—is in this regard quite meaningful.

And this is, in a sense, what is implied by the question with which Bernard Roger opens his preface to the new edition of Basil Valentine's *De la nature des métaux* (On the nature of metals):[7] "How could alchemy not have made the most extensive use of the image since it recognizes in its founding principles that no knowledge is possible without images?" René Alleau, however, deemed it wise to qualify this by reminding us that images especially "of sexuality, however veiled, are given free rein behind the décor of a religious lyricism intended to pull the wool over the eyes of the inquisitors," and that "by all evidence, the claims of religious orthodoxy that abound in medieval alchemical literature are repeated too often to not appear somewhat suspect." Now, while this cautious attitude is obviously caused by the "prohibition of the traditional magical arts" orchestrated "by the dominant religion" and the consequent risks incurred by their practitioners, everything here suggests that it arises from a desire, more or less assumed, but objectively consistent with that of surrealism, to subvert the system—or at least skirt the attempts, "in all eras, to censure by any means the manifestations of the collective unconscious, source of the permanent claims of human desire, always considered as dangerous for the established order."[8] But we should also bear in mind the warning of Jacques

Van Lennep who saw alchemical art "in no way as an illustrative art but forming a complete and autonomous language." He topped off this observation by pointing out that "it is primarily in accordance with the desire to evoke objects that could not be perceived by any rational operation that alchemy has one of the most fertile symbolic imaginations."[9]

René Alleau (in his book *Aspects de l'alchimie traditionnelle*) takes great pains to recall "that profound and grandiose idea that we have despised and lost," namely "that traditional thought does not separate the physical world from the social world," and that it is "linked to the metaphysical world of which it is simply an adaptation." Alleau doesn't fail to emphasize that it still involves "*initiation into mysteries* that cannot be attained through reason alone," and goes even further when he asserts, "It seems that alchemy corresponds less to a physical science than an *aesthetic* knowledge of matter and that it should be situated halfway between poetry and mathematics, between the world of symbols and the world of numbers."

Meanwhile, Elie-Charles Flamand (who, however, did not thumb his nose at transcendence), in his book *Les méandres du sens* (The meanders of meaning),[10] writes a few lines on the philosophy of the movement, which, with their multiple implications, seem to ring quite true:

> I have always been deeply sensitive to the marvelous that lies hidden beneath the everyday appearance of things. Breton initiated me into the quest for the disturbing glimmers of pure Reality that come thick and fast—but only if one keeps their attention on full alert—in the sudden cracks of appearances, the overlaps of events, the margins of life, and the auras of objects. These signs, intuitions, and premonitions bring us a piece of true knowledge and make us aware that quite often, reason is far from being right. Here life rises to a sublime intensity. Just like knowledge, begins with awe and wonder.

Surrealism, which Michel Leiris (in the first issue of *Archibras*) considered to be "a new poetic humanism," is for Stanislas Rodanski nothing less than "a free cause at the heart of men who walk," and for Jacques Abeille, "the incandescent demand of reality, in other words, since always, since before history, the quest born of passion." Meanwhile the cofounder of the Chicago surrealist group, Penelope Rosemont, calls it "the search for that moment in history when the awakening of the mind and the romantic magic of the imagination cease to be seen as contradictory."[11]

As I've had occasion to show elsewhere,[12] André Breton and his friends, including Rolland de Renéville, who in this instance shared these ideas, "sought to expand the perception of reality by all possible means, including traditional ones," as Marc Kober points out. "Hence," he adds, "this great moment of surrealism, which lasted some several decades, when an esoteric reading of the world was honored."[13] In fact they exhibited a systematic and great interest in all the forms esotericism took,* an esotericism whose message is even more scrambled today that only a few are capable of grasping it. This is even more true of alchemy, which Bernard Roger tells us "is primarily situated in the subtle world of transitions, mutations, and births."[14] "It is one of the most vertiginous interrogations experienced by surrealism,"[15] which appears as "one of the major secular expressions of the universal unconscious,"† and at the same time is that "traditional magic art."‡ Van Lennep

---

*And they continue to do so! I will cite just two recent occurrences as proof: the June 2022 publication in New York by surrealists Allan Graubard, Paul McRandle, and Valery Oisteanu of the magazine *Nigredo*, whose name says it all; and the 2021 republication—the second issue of the new series, in July 2022—of the mythical journal *The Philosophical Egg* created by Ludwig Zeller and Suzanna Wald at the beginning of the 1980s thanks to the efforts of their daughter Beatriz Hausner and Peter Dubé.

†Jacques Van Lennep, "Jacques Lacomblez." This catalog was published following the exhibition held at the Granell Foundation in Santiago de Compostela during the summer of 2019. Jacques Van Lennep opportunely noted that "its initiatory pilgrimage was recommended to alchemists to follow in the example of Ramon Lull, Nicolas Flamel, and Basil Valentine."

‡Term used by Alleau in his book *Aspects de l'alchimie traditionnelle* in preference to that of "occult science." "Traditional," he says elsewhere, "in other words linked . . . to a veritable esoteric and initiatory tradition." He believed, however, unlike Guénon, for example, "that the tradition has meaning only if it is constantly reinvented according to the ever new needs of the human spirit" ("Hypnos et thanatos").

demonstrated* how it allows the "sounding of the collective unconscious, going back to the very origin of myths." These are characteristics
that, in his opinion, "explain the favor that Alchemy continues to enjoy
in our age of demythification, especially among the surrealists, who systematically focus on tuning in to the unconscious."[16]

So it is no cause for surprise to see that so many surrealists (as well
as Canseliet and Amadou, for example), curtly rejected the author of
the magisterial *Psychology and Alchemy*,† Carl Gustav Jung, first published in German in 1944. This is probably due to the greater influence
of Freudian ideas in France, in contrast to what was already beginning
to happen in the English-speaking world,‡ so it is not surprising to see
his influence was stronger among surrealist women, of mainly English
origin like Ithell Colquhoun, who was close friends with Jungian psy-
choanalyst Alice Buck** of London, Dorothea Tanning,†† Leonora
Carrington, and her friend Remedios Varo as well. But there were also a
few men like Kurt Seligmann, Tristan Tzara, and Elie-Charles Flamand

---

*As Jung clearly saw!

†Carl Gustav Jung, *Psychologie et alchimie*, Paris: Buchet-Chasterl, 2004. Of Jung, who
saw alchemy as a search for spiritual equilibrium based on the creation of archetypes
and taking eventually the metaphorical form of the philosopher's stone, Mircea Eliade
wrote, "His discovery essentially proves this: processes take place in the depths of the
unconscious that have a surprising resemblance to the stages of a spiritual work—gnosis,
mysticism, alchemy—which is not provided in the world of profane experience"
("C.G. Jung et l'alchimie," in Holmyard, *L'Alchimie*).

‡The first edition of this book in English appeared in 1953 but it was necessary to wait
until 1970 for the French translation!

**Richard Shillitoe describes Alice Buck as a medical doctor and Jungian psychothera-
pist interested in theological issues. In addition to being Ithell Colquhoun's analyst,
she ran the London-based Buck Research Unit in Psychodynamics, specializing in the
interpretation of dreams and premonitions, which hold a prominent place in the concept of objective chance developed by Breton.

††Danielle Dumas-Pux mentions a series of lithographs by Dorothea Tanning "close
to Jung," "that were created in tandem with a series of poems by André Pieyre de
Mandiargues . . . in 1948 and 1950," that "featured mythical female figures in quest of
a secret, oneiric, magic, and surrealist knowledge" and "evoke Jung's mandalas in their
search as an expression of profound emotions and personal, intuitive explorations of
inner life."

who studied the—yet consistent—work of the man from Zurich. Flamand even went so far as to write in *Les méandres du sens*, "It is certain that everything is within us. Cosmogonic and mythic knowledge, all the knowledge of the human condition has been transported thanks to the genetic heritage and the memory of the species. . . . And beyond, throughout the fabled almost inconceivable geological past, this chain continues through our animal nature, connecting us to the very source of life." He adds, "To attune again with our roots like this is to open ourselves to the sovereign freedom of the creative spirit; to regain harmony with our ancestors, which is to reconcile with ourselves." He concludes by noting: "As Carl Gustav Jung observed, 'I am an answer to one of my ancestors' questions'."

It was probably Flamand who established the most direct parallel between the two systems of thought by pointing out (in the same book) the unsettling similarity between the *objective chance* dear to Breton and the *synchronicity* discovered by Jung, even if he scolded both, despite the rigor of their "effort of interpretation," of having stayed "within the narrow confines of logic" and therefore "not grasping the symbolic resonance and the metaphysical dimension of these manifestations," which he had the opportunity to experience and saw as "true hierophanies . . . an unveiling of the sacred." "Close to this same time," he writes, "when Breton was passionately interested in these same phenomena," "these coincidences that carry a value, a decisive meaning and that occur at certain essential times of life," "and was trying to craft a theory to encompass them, Carl Gustav Jung's mind was also occupied by these kinds of major encounters. And I would note that this too forms a case of objective chance or synchronicity—the name the Swiss psychologist gives to these manifestations."

While "Jung never made any reference to surrealism," Breton, whose references are essentially Freudian, was hardly any more loquacious about the writings of Freud's rival, as Danielle Dumas-Pux points out, even if "their procedures for approaching the unconscious" are similar. "However," she explains, "Jung and Breton have much in common. They were contemporaries who granted an important place to intuition, to the association of ideas, and to dreams. To their shared interest in alchemy, parapsychology, and travel to remote places we can add their taste for Oceanic and Native American art."[17] There is also "the attention to inner images, raw matter for the work to come," "the constant exploration of levels of the mind located above or below the threshold of everyday logic formed by means of explorations within the confines of waking life," the "desire to go beyond the ordinary mental and emotional conditions," the "series of creative acts aimed at freeing the imagination," and the "desire to shed light on the irrational forces that influence the conscious mind of each and every one of us." Not to mention the "desire for individuation" and the "search for a new myth!" In fact, as Mircea Eliade points out in his brief study of Jung and alchemy, published this time in the French edition of E. J. Holmyard's book cited above, for the psychologist, alchemy, "with all its symbolism and its operations, is a projection into the concrete of the archetypes and processes of the collective unconscious." "In the depths of the unconscious, processes take place which bear a surprising resemblance to the stages of a spiritual work—gnosis, mysticism, alchemy—which . . . contrast sharply with the profane world" and lead to "the discovery and possession of one's own self." He therefore saw in "the process of individuation through which one becomes the Self," "a foreshadowing of the *opus alchymicum*, or more precisely . . . an 'unconscious imitation' . . . of an extremely difficult initiatory process and thus reserved for an elite few," who, "on the level of dreams and other unconscious processes" bring about a "spiritual reintegration." The convergence with the surrealist desire to *"remodel human understanding,"* to *"recuperate lost powers,"* leaps out at even the less sophisticated—although the elitist nature suggested here could only anger the members of the groups!

At the same time we cannot pass over in silence the proximity of Bachelard's* thought to that of the surrealist spirit, inasmuch as

---

*Whose shadow, because of his proximity to René Alleau, will hover over this book!

Breton, who believed that his "surrationalism" accompanied and both heightened and restrained surrealism, wrote in 1936, in "Crisis of the Object," "The recent introduction by Gaston Bachelard into the vocabulary of science of the word *surrationalism*, with the aim of defining a whole mode of thought, lends additional immediacy and force to the word 'surrealism,' whose acceptation had hitherto remained confined to the world of art. Once again, each of these two terms confirms the other, a fact which provides ample proof of the unity and depth of feeling animating all human speculation in our times, just as much in the fields of poetry and painting as in that of scholarship." And Bachelard, while remaining a philosopher of science, took an interest in alchemy, seeing it as a path of moral initiation in which "the symbols of objective experience are immediately translated into symbols of the subjective culture."[18] This permitted Catherine Backès-Clément and Bernard Pingaud to feel authorized to advance the idea, especially with regard to the later Bachelard, that the man who "had planned to write a *Poétique du Phoenix*," he who "defined himself as a dreamer of words," was a man in whom "it might be more appropriate to see . . . the last alchemist": "The solitude that provides the keys to the dreamer's language, that of alchemy, offers us a last mythical figure of philosophy: Bachelard the alchemist alone in his room, lit only by a flame like the lonely people of La Tour, an unstill life of Bachelard that serves as a counterweight to the intimate still life."[19] Now even Bachelard, still an epistemologist of his situation and "at the crossroads . . . of realism and rationalism,"[20] a man whose testimony is all the more valuable because it combines an extensive philosophical culture with real scientific training,[21] said of this "Art of Music," albeit from a different point of view, that it is "pervaded by an immense sexual reverie,* by a reverie of wealth and

---

*In his book *Érotique de l'alchimie*, Elie-Charles Flamand speaks of "alchemical pansexuality"! Didn't Canseliet quote Bachelard as saying that "from some angles, alchemy could be said to be the secret vice"?

rejuvenation, by a reverie of potency!" From this point of view, didn't Elie-Charles Flamand take the trouble to remind us that this "Celestial Agriculture"—another name for the art whose Adepts could therefore also be called, as Fulcanelli did, plowmen—was also that "long poem that magnifies the union of the individual and the universe" and that in some esoteric texts the word *alchemist* is replaced by the word *poet*?

2

SURREALISM AND ALCHEMY

The dream of the transmutation of metals, chrysopeia,
spun the most able minds of this time.

PHILIPPE AUDOIN, *BOURGES CITÉ PREMIÈRE*

In a short book intended for the general public published in France in 2013, Stanislas Klossowski de Rola, son of the painter Balthus, who cites Grillot de Givry, Claude d'Ygé, René Alleau, and Eugene Canseliet among his sources, clearly puts his finger on the reasons why it's so difficult to address the question of the exact nature of the traditional science we're examining here. He writes: "If the ephemeral alchemy refuses to be easily encircled and defined, it's because it's a sacred Science, a hermetic Philosophy, and a secret Art; and still holds the key to the mysteries of the universe. For hidden beneath the obscure detours of its esoteric texts, veiled by the subtle nature of its hieroglyphic figures, are the means to penetrate to the heart of the mysteries of Nature, Life, and Death, and to conquer the arcana of the Absolute."* René Schwaller

---

*Stanislas Klossowski de Rola, *Alchimie, florilège de l'art secret*. The capitalization is the author's. A footnote at the end of the book reveals that Eugene Canseliet had read the manuscript before its initial publication in English. Although using the book *Alchemy* (London: Thames and Hudson, 1973), Klossowsi de Rola's text is substantively longer and more detailed. Although the imagery is the same, the other content is quite different—*trans.*

de Lubicz, in his "notes and observations on Hermeticism" collected in his book, *Notes et propos inédits*, explains that "this word *Alchemy* . . . means, in the sense adopted by the common man, the means of transmuting base metals into gold or silver." He goes on to point out that "this power is linked to another, even more important one, that of the 'Universal Panacea,' the means of curing all ills in one fell swoop and rejuvenating the individual, or at least preserving his health. We can add to these marvels, as the mystic alchemists did, the means of acquiring illumination or wisdom as well as health, the key to all knowledge and all consciousness."[1] This is indicative of the real stakes in the game.

In his *Mirror of Magic*,[2] Kurt Seligmann puts forth the notion that "as in the age of Gnosticism and Neoplatonism, fable and philosophy of East and West were syncretized into an astounding world image. The heavens of theology and that of Greek philosophy, the monsters of the Orient, and the mythical figures of Hellas were joined under the sign of Hermes." Like Breton's friend, Robert Amadou, who in his book *West, East, the Journey of a Tradition*,[3] states that alchemy was based on "the permanent correlation between the material phenomenon and what takes place on the spiritual level," like René Alleau who said that "the alchemists required their disciples to complement their laboratory work with oratorical work, and feel the reality of their faith and theories alike through the observation of things that do not know how to lie,"[4] Claude d'Ygé believed "there was no true alchemy without perfect knowledge of the metaphysical principles and without oratory," but also that "there was no true alchemy possible without the daily communion of the alchemist with nature, with his material (his Beatrice, the lady of his thoughts) and without laboratory experience." *Ora et labora*.*

For his part, Jacques Van Lennep, in the third book he dedicated to the *Ars Magna*, explains that "Alchemy is a wisdom inseparable from experiments on matter," that "the search for the elixir of long life and a philosopher's stone expresses nothing other than the desire for

---

*Pray and work, the motto of the Benedictines—*trans.*

the perfection of man that cannot be successfully achieved without knowledge of nature, with which man forms a whole," and that "for the alchemist, nature is a mirror in which he tries to discover the secrets of the human condition." He goes on to add that "the archetypal secret of the Great Work"* is nothing other than "the passage from darkness to light."† Jacques Sadoul confirms these observations in his *Treasure of the Alchemists* when he asserts that "it is absurd to say that the Stone is used to transmute metals *and* to prepare the universal medicine *and* to create the elixir of long life," "since the *chrysopeia* was merely a practical *test* to ensure that the substance obtained was really the Philosopher's Stone." In fact, according to Sadoul, who presents this fact as "an essential point of the hermetic art," "the alchemists . . . only had to perform one transmutation to guarantee the quality of their stone." This would sufficiently explain "why it was rare for the Adepts to become rich." Moreover, "the possession of worldly goods, particularly gold" was meaningless to Adepts. The two or three projections they made over the years were really only "to renew their supply of elixir."[5]

But René Alleau has something more to add about the "closed space of the alchemical universe, its opaque language, its logical labyrinths, its singular gleams, and sudden shadows. It is a house of mirrors in which dragons and naked goddesses circulate silently," as well as "slaughtered crowned children and burning kings, lovers and musicians, executioners and eagles, lions and queens. This fascinating and luxurious imagery, this enigmatic host of actors and performers who stubbornly conceal their true faces, evoke, in their abandoned palaces near rivers, in ruins, or in secret gardens, a complete cosmological drama whose theatrical depth can be instinctively sensed."[6] This fascinating imagery is also beautifully described by Artaud in *The Theater and its Double* (we will revisit this), but also reminds us of the tireless alchemical activity

---

*Jacques Van Lennep, *Une pierre en tête*. It is worth noting that Van Lennep also created artwork under the name of Jacques Lennep—art bearing the stamp of alchemy!
†Didn't Fulcanelli define alchemy as "a permutation of forms by light?"

engaged by Newton, to mention only him, as well as of the small number of the Elect. Alleau goes on to talk about "the nascent experimental method whose deviations, mistakes, and shortcomings were no less fruitful than the logical quartering and emotional upheavals they provoked, opening to rare minds access to an awakened state." This is an awakening that proves to be the result of an "illumination," for which Alleau later gives the following definition: "Illumination indeed opened to the Adept the gates to a kingdom compared to which gold, health, power, and worldly celebrity were but trifles unworthy of a philosopher. This kingdom was—and still is—that of the transcendence or awakening that should be more simply viewed as the TRUE, MATURE, and ADULT state of consciousness, if not our present consciousness." "We can't even imagine," he continues, "what a consciousness would be that could ceaselessly maintain itself at the highest point of extreme lucidity."[7]

Vincent Bounoure has shown that "holding from its own technique a very particular view of this stake [the recuperation of lost powers—*author*], alchemy is developing out of an exact correlation of the various levels of work, through which operate simultaneously the regeneration of the microcosm and the macrocosm, of man in his metallic simulacrum, and quite likely that of the universe in human matter," "the exact center and . . . node of the doctrine," "whose revelation appears to be reserved for the Adept and which distinguishes him from the puffer, had he accomplished many transmutations."[8]

In an interview with Jacques Carletto posted online shortly after Dervy's republication of *Paris and Alchemy* in 2017, Bernard Roger began by clearly laying out just what High Science is *not*. "It is not the simple desire to transform lead into gold," he said, before explaining that "it is first and foremost an initiatory path," "that it's an art, a work in which the consciousness of the operator evolves in parallel with the state of the material." Elsewhere, he happily clarified that "the path offered by alchemy obliges the disciple of Hermes to pass through the intermediary of a material that constitutes the magnet capable of attracting the celestial spirit," or "that light that is essential for the awakening of our consciousness," before emphasizing that "it is through the judicious use of his sharp sensory apparatus that the *artist* can realize with his hands this diaphanous earthly body, and recognize with *sight, hearing, smell, taste,* and *touch* that the light of the stars has finally chosen to take up residence in it."[9] In the end, for Roger, "the success of the Great Work makes the human being a true individual, in other words an Adept,* who has made his or her way to the heart of the human condition." We can see what's at play here!

All this is luminously confirmed by Philippe Audoin in the second appendix, entitled "Summary of the Art of Hermes," in his remarkable *Bourges cité première* (Bourges first city)—a book that gives reason to believe, although the author describes himself as a simple *amateur* and moreover *uninitiated,* that he had solid knowledge of the subject at hand. He writes, "The theory on which [alchemy] is founded posits the unity of animate and inanimate matter,† and by all likelihood, the identical nature of matter and spirit,‡ conceived as modalities of a single "being." On that respect, the basic text is the famous *Emerald Tablet* . . . which proclaims: 'That which is above is as that which is below, and that which is below is as that which is above, to accomplish the miracles of the One Thing. From this point of view, analogy is not only an illustrative means of expressing thought; it recognizes a profound truth and reveals a universal law," this "principle of analogy on which,"

---

*As Khaitzine points out, echoing Canseliet who specifies that it means *one who has received the gift,* the word *adept* comes from the Latin *adeptus,* a past participle used as an adjective and a noun meaning "he who has attained, who has acquired."

†This also seems to be the theory of Carrouges, who writes in his book on Breton and surrealism: "In this way the unity of all things would be already set at the origin of everything, inscribed in matter, and the Great Work's only mission would be to actualize it, to reveal it to man so that he might possess it."

‡Depicted, according to Canseliet, by the oldest of alchemy's allegorical symbols, the ouroboros, often accompanied by "the apothegm Εν το παν—One is All—which was borrowed from the Chrysopoeia of Cleopatra," which symbolizes "the identical nature of matter and spirit" (*L'alchimie expliquée sur ses textes classiques*).

says Bernard Roger, "all the traditional sciences are based!" "The sole value of the Golden Fleece," Audoin also notes, "is to the extent that its possession guarantees a spiritual victory." He adds: "As I've said before, true alchemists are neither magicians nor sorcerers. They do not seek miracles, or rather, only nature is miraculous. They claim themselves of her, she is what they invoke, and all their art, or so they say, is only to help nature realize her intentions. For them the *secretum secretorum** is a natural secret, and while its possession gives full access to spirit, it's because matter and spirit are one just as the various substances of the observable world are made one." At the end of his "Summary," in conclusion of his book, he deems it wise to remind us once again that "in the logic of Alchemy—which is that of every sacredness that has been mastered and experienced by human beings—a material operation can only succeed if the sacrificer has made himself worthy of achieving it and, conversely, the degree of dignity that he achieves depends on the success of the operation."[10]

We should not fail to keep in mind that such assertions by Audoin, even though he clearly does not seem to have engaged in operative activity, cannot be taken lightly, since the impressive science he deploys in his alchemical reading of the ceiling of the "study" in the Hôtel Lallemant in Bourges, for example, *very simply* completes that of Fulcanelli himself, who was the first to see it as a "philosophical dwelling"—in other words, to use his definition, "a symbolic support of the hermetic truth, whatever its nature and importance may be."† If we can wonder why Audoin deemed it necessary to write a book on Bourges (see plate 10), the city of Jacques Coeur, in any case the man whom Fulcanelli called

---

*The "secret of secrets," an allusion to a highly influential medieval, pseudo-Aristotle treatise of Arab origin that deals mainly with occultism, astrology, alchemy, and the magical properties of plants, stones, and numbers, and of which a later version includes the *Emerald Tablet*.

†"Namely, for example," he adds," the miniscule knick knack housed under glass, the piece of iconography as a simple sheet or painting, the architectural monument, whether it's a detail, a remnant, or a lodging, castle or even a church, in their entirety."

a "proven" Adept, "possessing the precious gift of the white stone," an ennobled bourgeois whose arms are singing, to say the least, it seems that his interest was longstanding and he left us a few clues in one of his books that was not published until almost forty years after his death: a small collection with the title *Les Capucines aux lèvres d'émail* (The capuchins with enamel lips).[11] Some of these clues put us on the trail of René Alleau, whom Breton made it possible for Audoin to meet! In the first of these texts, "Au gué d'orge" (At the barley ford), the author recounts how, after having written a poem in September 1958*—which was necessarily unsatisfactory because of "the influences it brought to light"—he had been audacious enough to add, "rather childishly," "a dedication to Nicolas Flamel, Jean Lallemant, Gérard de Nerval, Lautréamont, and André Breton—to whom I was . . ." These names clearly show that he had at least a rudimentary knowledge of alchemy, especially since, immediately afterward, he explicitly says: "The figure of Jean Lallemant, while referring in general to Hermeticism, more specifically evokes the mansion he had built at the beginning of the sixteenth century, and which can still be admired in Bourges." Audoin went on to say, "For several years, this elegant dwelling really fascinated me, and some of the emblems there could in a pinch be recognized in the poem dedicated to him" (which unfortunately we do not have). A few lines later, Audoin continues: "The following summer, that would be 1959, I decided to study the Hôtel Lallemant more seriously," noting in passing that "with this in mind, I expanded my very vague notions of hermeticism and undertook to pick out the most striking emblems on the premises." But what seems most striking is that Audoin, next mentioning his budding friendship with Breton and subsequent entry into the group, concluded, "It is too soon to speak of what happened next. I will only say that two months later, his friend René Alleau agreed to meet me and entrusted me with documents of rare value about the

---

*He was then thirty-four years old. He would not publish *Bourges, cité première* for another fourteen years.

Hôtel Lallemant." In the same vein, we should recall that "during a brief stay," probably later in Nantes "in fealty to Evangeline, the black ancestor of Monsieur Governor,"* what Breton's companion "kept in his memory" was "the hermetic sun that adorns the pommel of the sword held by Justice on the southwest corner of the tomb of François II, the last Duke of Brittany" and also "the double face of Prudence that flanks [it] and shows the face of a youth in front and the face of an old man in the back."† There are again his wanderings, probably comparable to those of the members of the Hermes Circle in Paris, in the old city, where, "we can see embedded in a façade on the rue de la Juiverie an alchemical bas-relief depicting a sleeping young man. His left foot, winged like Mercury's, is posed flat on the ground. His other foot is raised. With his right hand, the sleeper holds a turtle at arm's length. Behind him there is a small temple, the triangular pediment of which bears a realistic representation of a *fire*," "an allegory," he adds, "of the necessary balance between the Fixed and the Volatile." Quite an astute observation for a simple amateur.

A simple amateur who, in 1968, in the text "La fontaine du bonheur," (The fountain of happiness), which Audoin had contributed to the *Princip slasti* (The principle of pleasure—the catalog of the exhibition, which was shown in various places in Czechoslovakia at that time), established, by means of Nicolas Flamel, a connection—quite natural—between Paris and the city that Breton considered to be the magical capital of Europe, Prague, writing: "Given the effect of a certain hindsight, the staircase on which Duchamp's *Nude* descends is transformed into that of the Tour Saint Jacques; an endlessly spiraling, winged and armor-piercing vehicle of what the modern spirit

---

*An allusion to *La nuit du rose-hôtel,* a novel by Maurice Fourré. The quote comes from Audoin's article "Baron Zéro" published in the seventh issue of *Archibras* in March 1969. The capitalization is his.

†This tomb was masterfully analyzed by Fulcanelli in the second volume of *The Dwellings of the Philosophers*. It is worth noting that it was designed by Jean Perréal, the author of the *Complainte de nature à l'alchimiste errant*.

can most aggressively offer when it comes to drilling into the depths of time—and casting toward an inverse coronation of the one that signals, in the clouds, the tetramorphic chiasmus, the increased form of Nicolas Flamel's *Awaited Bride.*" "We know," he adds, "that when Flamel was said to have died, the Adepts of the Sublime Science had already found a haven beneath the great heretical porch of Notre Dame. Later, all those who were subject to the whims of Emperor Rudolph knew the figures that the Parisian writer had had drawn on the Charnel House of the Innocents. Alchemical gold* was struck secretly in Prague and Paris, as if at the two stable poles of an intransitive universe, which underlays the official world of tottering courts and religious massacres."[12]

A simple amateur recidivist, Audoin, in *Bourges cité première*, approached the myth of Tristan and Yseult (see plate 12), this time from the perspective of alchemy, particularly the texts of Fulcanelli. He noted that the scene depicted on "one of the corbel rib supports" in the treasury room in the keep of Jacques Coeur's palace is none other than the "episode of the famous romance of *Tristan and Yseult* [that] P. Gauchery† . . . describes this way: *Queen Yseult is lying down near a fountain; Tristan, represented as a richly clad figure, approaches her followed by a fool with his jester's head on a stick. In the background, the head of King Mark can be seen in the foliage of a tree.* An owl indicates that the scene takes place at night."

---

*Alchemical gold that Canseliet, citing Marc-Antonio Crassellame in his *Alchimie expliquée par ses textes classiques*, describes as follows: "A gold of complete sulfur and true gold sulfur. A gold of all fire and true gold fire. A gold, I say, that is engendered in the caves of the Philosophers and their mines. A gold that is not altered or overcome by any element when it itself is the master of elements. A fixed gold when the sole fixity is to be found in it. A very pure gold when it is itself the sole purity. A very potent gold, when outside of it all strength languishes. A balsamic gold that preserves all bodies from putrefaction."

†Paul Gauchery (1846–1925) wrote with Albert de Grossouvre a book entitled *Le palais Jacques Coeur*, published in 1919 in *Les mémoires de la société des antiquaires du centre*, and republished in 1949 and again in 1954 by Desquand.

After citing the episode as it appears in the adaptations of Joseph Bédier that were current at this time, Audoin begins to wonder about the reason that had led Jacques Coeur, "who it's hard to imagine as sentimental [to have had] this disturbing scene sculpted in his most personal retreat" before firmly suggesting an alchemical reading of it on the grounds that "we find there a tree and a fountain!" Now Audoin, who considers this *image* as a "snapshot of alchemical symbolism," sees there "an allegory of the first raw matter: the oak, and of the Mercury to which it gives birth, the water of the Sages." And actually, how could we not think of that medallion—extremely damaged—of the Door of Judgment at Notre Dame de Paris, "The Mysterious Fountain at the foot of the Old Oak" that appears in Fulcanelli's *Mystery of the Cathedrals* (Plate IV)? How could we avoid thinking of the innumerable fountains found throughout alchemical texts? Breton's friend also sees this as "an acceptable image of the Philosophical Marriage of the two natures: the female mercury and the male sulfur, which cannot be achieved without the agreement of the third principle: the salt—or *scel*—represented by the king." Moreover, with respect to the bird of Minerva, so often present in alchemical documents, he reminds us that "the owl indicates that the night is favorable for the operation." Again referring to the writings of the Unknown Master for support, he points out that "the fool in itself constitutes a hermetic signature," insofar as it is "the hieroglyph of the manufacture of the Green Lion—hence the name of *Leonois* or *Leonnais* borne by Tristan." Still quoting the author of *The Dwellings of the Philosophers*, Audoin continues: "Fulcanelli next observes that the dissolvent, the stakes of the battle (between the eagle and the dragon*), alone can restore to gold (to the old king) his first youth (assumed here by Tristan)." "Mark and his nephew," he continues, "are thus one individual,† which is why they have the same single

---

*In other words, between the volatile part of matter, the mercury of the philosophers, and the fixed part, the sulfur of the philosophers—*author*.

†"Are only," Fulcanelli writes, "chemically speaking, one and the same thing, of the same type and of similar origin."

spouse in order to maintain the hermetic tradition that makes the king, the queen, and the lover the mineral triad of the Great Work." Finally, by pointing out in a footnote that "the Forest of *Morois* [my italics] is one of the places where Tristan and Yseult met," our author finds arch humor in highlighting a short phrase of Fulcanelli's: "strange forest in fact, truthfully speaking, that of the Mort-Roi,"—especially if we invoke the Language of the Birds (see plate 9).

It is also the same Audoin who published an article with the supremely suggestive title, "Inaugural Lesson in the Schools of Saturn," in the third issue of *L'archibras.* It is full of allusions, each more subtle than the one before, to the art of music, "the ringing of the jingle bells," "the simultaneous trial of the SOLVE and the COAGULA," "at least the withered tree will cease to oppose the living tree," "the hermetic thicket," and "the philosophical hare." In a kind of postscript to this text, entitled "Side Road," Audoin explains that, in his search for illustrations, he had finally chosen the statue of Velleda by Hippolyte Maindron in the Luxembourg Gardens, the figure of the prophetess serving as a guiding line for his remarks. And the anecdote he tells, which brings another protagonist of this story on the stage, as well as the amazement he felt at the "consonance between the hermetic vocabulary that [he] had spontaneously borrowed from the dry tree* and the multiplied signatures on the statue and around it," are extremely significant in that they are proof of a deeper knowledge of the subject of alchemy. He writes:

Bernard Roger had offered to photograph it for me. On Saturday, October 28 . . . we found ourselves at the foot of the statue—not without noticing that she was leaning against a hollow tree trunk

---

*"The dry tree depicts," according to Fulcanelli, "metallic inertia, in other words the special state that human industry makes reduced and melted metals assume" (Jorge Camacho and Bernard Roger, *La Cathédrale de Séville et le bestiaire hermétique du portail de Saint Christophe et de l'Immaculée Conception* (Brussels: Fondation Pol François Lambert, 2001).

with her hair flowing freely, that her crown was woven from oak leaves, and that she was wearing, on her left hip, a scallop shell called a Saint Jacques or a Saint Michel. It is impossible not to think of the *chesne creux* of the alchemists, an emblem of ore, the leprous mineral from which the artist makes the *hidden fountain* spring forth: the first mercury for which the scallop shell is one of the most widespread symbols."

"The shadow of the neighboring school," he adds, "seemed propitious since Velleda's crossed legs, curved and sensual as they were, no longer brought anything to mind but the spagyric X of the crucible"*— this X, the Greek X (Khi) that, "just like the cross, offers the graphic formula of radiance, which it is impossible to simplify any further."† This is precisely what Bernard Roger wrote in *Paris and Alchemy*: "The Greek X and the French X represent the writing of light by light itself, the trace of its passage, the manifestation of its movement, the affirmation of its reality. It is its true signature."[13] In his most recent work, *Les Demeures de l'invisible*,[14] Roger adds, "A similar sign should be visible, based on the testimony of those who have performed the experiment, on the surface of the matter when it has been 'canonically' prepared with an eye to the happy continuation of the work."

In the last months of his life Artaud felt compelled to express a much more modest enthusiasm for occultism in general and for the "Art of Music" in particular, explaining for example that "in history, alchemy

---

*"The cross," Fulcanelli writes in *The Mystery of the Cathedrals*, "is the alchemical hieroglyph for the crucible."

†Eugene Canseliet, introduction to the 1996 reprint of *Mutus Liber* by Isaac Baulot. The *Mutus Liber* is this "mute book" published in La Rochelle in 1677. In his preface to Basil Valentine's *Twelve Keys*, Canseliet adds that it's "the ray in the ashes at whose heart remains the precious glass . . . when all exterior ornaments, despite their wealth and beauty, have vanished." In *Dwellings of the Philosophers*, Fulcanelli, who speaks of this at length, shows that "all the meanings revealed by the sign X have a transcendent or mysterious value, making it quite singular." René Alleau devoted the entire second part of his book *De la nature des symboles*—in other words, sixty pages—to this sign.

like the rest is nothing more than the alphabet primer of a number of quantified scientific abortions. It's a textbook that has not been entirely catalogued, nor can it be except when speaking of it makes it real, consisting of operations that only crime allows man to target, and for which only a few rare great poets like Baudelaire, Edgar Allen Poe, Rimbaud, Lautréamont, and especially Gérard de Nerval have restored for us an equivalent." He voiced similar doubts in a reply to two articles by George Le Breton, "La clé des chimères: l'alchimie" and "Aurélia: les mémorables," which appeared in 1945 in issues 44 and 45 of the journal *Fontaine*. Antonin Artaud, an essential figure of the movement, unquestionably discusses it in a 1932 text with the title "Le théâtre alchimique"* that looks at "all that is *representative*, i.e., theatrical, in the whole series of *symbols* by which the Great Work is to be realized spiritually while awaiting its actual and material realization, as well as in the digressions and errors of the ill-informed mind among these operations, in the almost '*dialectical*' sequence of all the aberrations, phantasms, mirages, and hallucinations that those who attempt to carry out these operations by *purely human means* cannot help but encounter." This text was initially published in the journal *Sur* in Buenos Aires, and republished in 1938 in his manifesto-book *The Theater and its Double*. We can indeed see surfacing there what René Alleau called "an entire cosmological drama":

> We must believe that the essential drama, the one at the root of all the Great Mysteries, is associated with the second phase of Creation, that of difficulty and of the double, that of matter and the materialization of the idea. . . . Now these conflicts which the Cosmos in turmoil offers us in a philosophically distorted and impure manner, alchemy offers them to us in all its rigorous intellectuality, since it permits us to attain once more to the sublime, *but with drama*, after

---

*This title is also that of one of the chapters of the foreword that René Alleau wrote for the *Book of Hieroglyphic Figures* that he published in his *Bibliotheca Hermetica*, which fairly clearly shows the influence that the figure of the *Momo* (i.e. Artaud) had on him!

a meticulous and unremitting pulverization of every insufficiently fine, insufficiently matured form, since it follows from the very principle of alchemy not to let the spirit gain momentum until it has passed through all the filters and foundations of existing matter, and to redouble this labor at the incandescent limbo of the future. For it might be said that in order to merit material gold, the mind must first prove that it was capable of the other kind, that it would have earned it, would have attained to it, only by assenting to it, by seeing it as a secondary symbol of the fall it must experience in order to rediscover in solid and opaque form the expression of light itself, of rarity, and of irreducibility.[15]

It was also Artaud who said (in 1934, in *Héliogabale ou l'anarchiste couronné* [Héliogabale or the anarchist crowned]), that "for alchemists these moments of eternity when they get fixed correspond to the appearance of the star* in the crucible," which explains why Ilios Chailly entitled his study of this book *Héliogabale ou l'anarchiste couronné*![16]

Like several of his surrealist friends, Sarane Alexandrian often showed evidence of a vast alchemical erudition, even if he didn't use the furnace. In his *Histoire de la philosophie occulte*, for example, he devoted thirty pages to the Art of Music. In his book *L'Érotisme en alchimie*, with its sweeping view of the history of this traditional science, he briefly touches upon Zosimus's *On Virtue*, the *Rosarium Philosophorum* and *Flos Florum* attributed to Arnaud de Villeneuve, the *Philosophia Reformata* by Johann Daniel Mylius, Michael Maier's *Atalanta Fugiens*,

---

*In chapter XI, "L'étoile polaire des Mages," in *Alchimie expliquée sur ses textes classique*, Eugène Canseliet thought it worth pointing out: "In operative alchemy, it's necessary to know fully, and for the disciple of the science in particular, that the star is not a fiction nor only a symbol. The hermetic and religious star, we'd like to add, appears to the five senses of the artist who can hear it audibly, see it, touch it, taste it, and even smell it." Fulcanelli's disciple then continues: "In reality, it is his good star that will guide him to the cavern, from the moment he made his choice with great determination. The alchemist is also the magician for whom the awakening bestowed by the herald star of the eternal miracle is intended."

Louis Cambriel's *A Course in Hermetic Philosophy*, as well as Geber and Morien.* They as well as Fulcanelli and Canseliet are also mentioned in his *History of Occult Philosophy*, not to mention "the surrealist poet, Elie-Charles Flamand." But he dwells at length on the little-known work of Béroalde de Verville,† *The Voyage of the Wealthy Princes*. This is a "steganographic" book that, in the author's own words, "contains under the pleasant guise of amorous discourse all the most exquisite secrets sought by the curious of the good sciences."‡ All in all, it is "one of the most stimulating and rich [books] of its time,"[17] whose alchemical symbology is summarized and eruditely analyzed by Alexandrian.

---

*Zosimos of Panopolis: Born in Egypt between the third and fourth centuries CE, this "Gnostic" was one of the principal exponents of alchemy of Greek language and culture, including in its operative dimension. "The first alchemist worthy of the name," Alexandrian writes in his *Histoire de la philosophie occulte*, adding that *The Book on Virtue* is the "model for the allegories dear to later alchemists." Arnaud de Villeneuve (1240–1311): Physician, theologian, and alchemist possibly born in Catalonia, he was one of the most learned men of the thirteenth century. Johann Daniel Mylius (1583–1642): German composer, physician, and alchemist. Michael Maier (1568–1622): German Hermeticist born in the Holstein region, he was raised to the rank of Imperial Count Palatine by Rudolph II of the Habsburgs, "Emperor of the alchemists," for whom he was the counselor and personal physician. Louis Cambriel (1774–c.1850): Author of only this book, this Hermetic and alchemical philosopher was cited by both Fulcanelli and Canseliet. Geber (Jabir ibn Hayyan): "King of the Arabs and prince of the philosophers" is Alleau's description of him in his entry in the *Encyclopedia Universalis*, before adding, "The considerable work of Jabir ibn Hayyan, Geber in Latin, numbers some three thousand treatises, if we can believe tradition and even some Orientalists. It has been assumed that Jabir, whose birth and death would be approximately between 730 and 804, would have been the name chosen by the *Ikhwan al Safa*, the Brotherhood of Purity and Loyalty who were headquartered in Basra where they composed an encyclopedia in the tenth century." Morien: "It is said," Alexandrian writes in his *Histoire de la philosophie occulte*, "that Morien was an eleventh-century Roman alchemist, who had lived as a hermit in the Syrian mountains, before being summoned to Egypt by the Khalid sultan who wanted to learn his secret." According to Caron and Hutin, he wrote the *Liber secretorum alchemiae* and the *Liber trium verborum*.
†François Béroalde de Verville (1556–1626): A close associate of the Paracelsian physicians in the entourage of Henri IV and translator of Franceso Colonna's *Hypnerotomachia poliphili*, with his *Voyage des princes fortunés* he offers a text with strong alchemical content in the guise of an orientalized narrative.
‡In the title of the "Avis aux beaux esprits" that precedes the novel.

With regard to alchemy again, one of "the rare esoteric disciplines still alive in the West,"[18] René Alleau, as opposed to his friend Jean Palou,* who here follows René Guénon's lead, and asserts that it is "essentially spiritual" and therefore that "the material operations described or alluded to in alchemical treatises would actually be symbolic in nature,"[19] decisively explains in his *Aspects de l'alchimie traditionnelle* that "positive, experimental and concrete," alchemy "borrows its principles from traditional metaphysics, of which it represents one implementation to in the formal domain as well as the relationship between form and light," but "corresponds less to a physical science than to an *aesthetic* knowledge of matter." It is therefore necessary "to place it halfway between poetry and mathematics, between the world of symbols and that of numbers."

Bernard Roger, in his *À la découverte de l'alchimie*, states that "its material goal is the manufacture of the *universal medicine* whose virtue is to free the individual from the three kingdoms of *accidents* which prevent them from attaining the *perfection* toward which tend their desires and to which nature, with its means alone, is incapable of leading them without the help of the *artist* whose role is only to help them along their paths." He also thinks that "its origins are commingled with those of the man to whom it offers the fulfillment of his destiny as a poet, in other words the creator that tradition calls the *true man.*" Elsewhere, he takes the trouble to point out that "if it is not an *exact science* in the present sense of the term," it "is no less a *real science*." He speaks of it as the true "Art of Love"† in which "*matter* and *spirit*, in the richness of

---

*Jean Palou (1917–1967), surrealist and a member of the Thebah Lodge of the Grand Lodge of France (among others), is the author of a continuously republished reference work, *La Franc-maçonnerie* (Paris: Payot, 1964). Philippe Audoin cites his article on Jean de Berry's tomb in his *Bourges cité première.*

†In his *À la découverte de l'alchimie*, Roger writes, "The function of an *Art of Love* could not be better evoked: this is how traditional alchemy was described, the purpose of which seems to merge with man's true raison d'être on earth according to the traditions, and the true meaning of his legitimate progress: to ascend to the light by giving light to nature or, to use René Alleau's expression defining the principal function of alchemy, 'to liberate spirit through matter by liberating matter itself through spirit.'" These words come from his entry on alchemy in the *Encyclopedia Universalis*.

their complementarity, rejoice and liberate each other to form the vessel over which the spiritual adventure of each individual plays out." At the same time, he adds: "All those who have practiced it affirm that the purpose of its operative technique is to contribute, by means of the concrete support of mineral and metallic materials, to the conception and birth of a new body, which, without the intervention of *art* to help it, nature is incapable of producing by itself. A body that can be weighed, but is swollen with energy, known as the *philosopher's stone* and sometimes called the *miracle of the world* because of the virtues that have been the subject of too many testimonies (throughout history) to give anyone the authority to consign it without examination to the drawer of chimera." He concludes by saying: "This philosopher's stone, which all the ancient treatises explicitly say is of two kinds: the *white*, capable, according to the purpose it is given, of transforming metals into silver or *moon*, or curing *lunar diseases*; and the *red*, which transforms itself into gold or sun and cures *solar diseases*."[20] The pilgrims of Hermes also call it the *Rosa Hermetica*, Elie-Charles Flamand reminds us, because "the rose is the symbol of esoteric Knowledge and mystical love."*

Although Michel Leiris, having seen "shining in alchemy the imaginary glimmer of the Absolute," drew, in 1927, his friends' attention "to the golden sign in an article on John Dee's Hieroglyphic Monad,"[21] it was Breton who first brought up this "traditional science." "Of course, since

---

**Elie-Charles Flamand, *La Tour Saint-Jacques*. It is hard to overlook the dedication in this book: "In memory of my friends Henri Hunwald, Claude d'Ygé, Gerard Heym who live in the Light of which this tower reflects a ray." Sir Gerard Heym was the founder of the Society for the Study of Alchemy and Chemistry and head editor of the university journal *Ambix*. He collaborated on issue 11–12 of Robert Amadou's *La tour Saint-Jacques* with a text on John Dee. With respect to this researcher, the British surrealist Ithell Colquhoun (who was herself an accomplished esotericist) writes (in the twentieth chapter—on alchemy—in her book on MacGregor Mathers and the Golden Dawn, *Sword of Wisdom*, published in 1975): "His introduction to the French translation of Gustav Meyrink's novel *Le dominicain blanc* (1963) shows his insight into the theory of Taoist alchemy, traceable to China in the sixth century B.C., and refers to the tradition that a Sword is found materialized in the coffin of an adept whose corpse has been transmuted by the Elixir into a Body of Light."

the Manifesto of Surrealism in 1924," writes Annie Le Brun, "Breton never ceased to refer to the alchemist current in order to emphasize the points where it met the poetic approach as he saw it."* In fact, we suspect his interest in the subject from the time of *Littérature*, but it is in his "Lettre aux voyantes" that he makes this observation (in 1925):

> He [Flamel's detractor] scarcely believes in the invention of the Philosopher's Stone by Nicolas Flamel, for the simple reason that the great alchemist does not seem to have gotten rich from it. Outside of the religious scruples he might have had about taking such a vulgar advantage, however, one may wonder how the obtaining of more than a few bits of gold could have interested him, when it had been above all building up a spiritual fortune. This need for industrialization, which is uppermost in people's objection to Flamel, is to be found almost everywhere: it is one of the principal factors in the defeat of the spirit."

It is precisely here that he clearly identifies alchemy with "moral truth,"† a truth that undergirds the "quest for the gold of time, the eternal motor of surrealism," in which he and those close to him were engaged, according to Eugène Canseliet.

The truth that the Adept,‡ the "ruril [native] of Pontoise," and his wife Pernelle would look for, like the other "disciples of the Science of Love, based on the natural law of analogy through which all the kingdoms and levels of life communicate," as Bernard Roger writes in his introduction to Basil Valentine's *On the Art of Metals*. Did Philalethes not state: "I rightly despise and detest this idolatry of gold and silver

---

*On her November 2, 2013, guest post on Paul Jorion's blog.
†Artaud, in his text "Le théâtre alchimique," in *Le théâtre et son double*, also refers to a "moral truth."
‡"An adept, in other words . . . a hermetic philosopher who has carried out the labors of the Great Work to their conclusion" (Bernard Roger, "Introduction" to *La lumière sortant par soi-même*).

by which everything is gaged and which serves only worldly pomp and vanity"? It is in a similar spirit that Bernard Roger and Jorge Camacho note in *Typus Mundi*:

> *Our gold is not the gold of the vulgar.*
> *Choose well among the*
> *common currencies.*
> *Take the green gold, in other words, the*
> *central salt.*
> *And hasten slowly.**

On that respect, the anecdote reported with malicious humor by Van Lennep talking about a dream recorded by Breton in 1925 is quite symptomatic. "He found himself in the Saint Malo marketplace where he discovered a kabbalistic book that looked as strange as the *Book of Abraham* that an angel had revealed to the Parisian alchemist. Aside from the angel, this coincidence might lead us to believe that Flamel, who reappears throughout the centuries, personally gave it to the 'Pope of Surrealism!'† Van Lennep, in this case, seems to be cheerfully

---

*Here we recognize the *Festina lente* attributed to Horace, which is also associated with the dolphin and the anchor in the *Hypnerotomachia poliphili* by Franceso Colonna, which Fulcanelli presents in *The Dwellings of the Philosophers* as a hermetic text including knowledge useful for the realization of the Great Work. Bernard Roger writes in *Les demeures de l'invisible* that this is "a strange book not easily accessible; on every page we find allegories, symbols, punning references, and the language of the birds," a work that "belongs in the category of closed books like the works of Rabelais, Dante, Cyrano Bergerac, and many others that are less well known but which nevertheless marked their time in secret. They are called closed because only those who possess the keys know how to open them." Green gold, moreover, which is also, as Canseliet tells us, the "*philosophical vitryol* [sic] that in its former spelling was, according to Fulcanelli, a perturbing anagram of a brief exclamation: L'OR Y VIT! [the gold lives there—*trans.*]"

†Jacques Van Lennep, "L'art alchimique et le surréel . . .". Philippe Audoin also mentions Flamel in his book on Bourges and describes his despair "about finding the meaning of the figures in the *Book of Abraham* that led him to make the pilgrimage to Compostela where he received initiation," but doesn't fail to mention that "Fulcanelli showed that this traveler's tale of the famous Parisian alchemist was in fact an allegory for the Great Work."

embroidering a little more around a sentence from the *Second Manifesto*, in which its author states, "I am not yet of a mind to admit that a certain Paul Lucas encountered Flamel in Brusa at the beginning of the seventeenth century, that this same Flamel, accompanied by his wife and one son, was seen at the Paris Opera in 1761, and that he made a brief appearance in Paris during the month of May 1819, at which time he was purported to have rented a store at 22 rue de Cléry in Paris."

But it is true that Flamel has always inspired many texts in surrealist circles, and that many of the traces around him have been followed more or less persistently. Thus, Alleau quotes (in the Breton spirit) a certain "Alexis Monteil [who] swears in his *Histoire des Français des divers états* that an old clergyman named Marcel claimed, more than four hundred years after the death of the adept, to have met Flamel near his home, an underground laboratory protected by seven gates, built in the heart of Paris." The same Alleau, in his book *Énigmes et symboles du Mont Saint-Michel* mentions the relationship that the parishioner of Saint Jacques de-la-Boucherie (which he considers more Miquelot than Jacquet*) would have had with the Marvelous in these terms: "Is it not significant to note, for example, that the famous alchemist Nicolas Flamel, whose renowned pilgrimage to Santiago de Compostela has been taken as a learned allegory, in fact belonged to a brotherhood of *Pilgrims of Saint Michael of the Mountain of the Sea*, founded in Paris during the thirteenth century." And he continues: "The historian Corrozet† also points out that the chapel of Saint Michael in the Paris Palace Compound was formerly called the *chapel of Saint Nicolas*. Nicolas Flamel's membership in the Brotherhood of Saint Michael was noted by the historian S. J. Morand in his *Histoire de la Sainte-Chapelle*

---

*Miquelot refers to pilgrims of Saint Michael while Jacquet refers to those of Saint James—*trans.*

†This would probably be Gilles Corrozet (1510–1568), a Parisian bookseller and printer who was one of the first historians of the City of Light. More than thirty works of history and literature are attributed to him, including *Les blasons domestiques* and the *Hecatomgraphie*.

royale du Palais, published in Paris in the eighteenth century." (Italics are Alleau's.)

Contrary to what Alleau seems to think and what Gérard Legrand asserts in the entry on him he wrote for the *Dictionnaire général du surréalisme et ses environs*, the most recent studies on Flamel tend to give the impression that he was a simple mythical figure and never the Adept of tradition, nor even the author of the *Book of Hieroglyphic Figures* generally attributed to him! Moreover, Canseliet, saw the *Roman de la Rose* as "the unsuspected and extremely distant ancestor of surrealism of our time," who, "after the excesses of a tumultuous youth," had "seized the great problem of plucking the *Rose* and, through *It,* of the return to primordial androgyny."[22] At the same time he saw "the physical and scientific expression of surrealism" in alchemy and even explained, sometimes a little boldly (as Jacques Van Lennep reports in his recently cited book), Breton's interest in it by the fact that "it is linked to the unanimous Tradition, that it remains the keeper of the ancient arcana, as well as the inexhaustible source of the Marvelous, without which natural Truth would be incapable of manifesting itself!"

And from the standpoint of these words by Jakob Böhme, "Paradise is still of this world, but man is far from it, for he must regenerate himself. . . . And here is the gold hidden in Saturn," while keeping in mind that "Saturn has appeared since Antiquity as the personification of time,"[23] we should take great pains not to underestimate the symbolic as well as esoteric content of this saying from Breton's "Introduction to the Discourse on the Paucity of Reality," the maxim, which was specifically chosen by his friends after his death as an epitaph, "I seek the gold of time." René Alleau, in an interview with Robert Benayoun, thought it worthy of a luminous explanation:*

---

*On April 19, 1970, in a program of the *Bibliothèque de Poche*, a literary television show with Michel Polac for the national office of French radio and television broadcasts. The interview, entitled *René Alleau, l'ésotérisme et Breton* was produced by Robert Benayoun.

But I would just like to remind you that the god of time was Saturn for the Romans and Chronos for the Greeks, in whom some have seen the Satan of Scripture. This god was associated with lead, a gray and opaque metal, heavy like the Lord of History, while the metal associated with the Sun was gold, which is the supreme metal of light. To seek the gold of time is to seek the meaning of eternity through time and almost against historical consciousness. I think that poetic experience, in the sense that Breton was able to extend it through surrealism, was essentially in opposition to reductive historical consciousness. The amplifying poetic experience, which is the search for light, the search for inner regeneration, corresponds here to a certain extent to the experience of the alchemists, although it is clearly different because it is an essentially poetic experience. . . ."

Eugene Canseliet, who was also convinced that the choice of this phrase owed nothing to chance and who was also appealing to youth,* says nothing else when he writes in *L'alchimie expliquée sur ses textes classiques* (Alchemy explained by its classic texts): "It is not without great interest that young students learn that the star exerted an intense fascination on André Breton.† It was destiny, therefore inevitable, that the leader of the Surrealists should discover this polyhedron with eight points and twenty-four faces during an excursion, unfortunately his last, to the village of Domme in the Dordogne."

The gigantic crystal‡ that replicates the system incorporating the

---

*As Bernard Roger did in his text "Melius spe licebat." See chapter 10.

†And for good reason; he had probably read in *The Dwellings of the Philosophers* the sentence in which Fulcanelli makes the star "the outer manifestation of the inner sun!"

‡In *Soleil noir et main de feu*, a small book subtitled *Alchimie et surréalisme* (Venus d'Ailleurs, no date), Patrick Rivière puts it in these terms: "The volumetric projection in the space of the hexagram also symbolically defined the philosopher's stone, the transformation of elements represented graphically by intersecting triangles, thus realizing the most perfect harmony."

Universal Medicine or the Philosopher's Stone now decorates Breton's very humble grave in the Batignolles Cemetery of Paris, where he was probably destined from all eternity. On its edge, how luminous in its inscrutability, appears the alchemical confession of the poet's faith: *I seek the gold of time.*

3

EUGÈNE CANSELIET, F.C.H.

Alchemy arises precisely from that state of consciousness,
or true grace, which finds in the Sage the harmony of the
fruitful duality of love and knowledge, the generatrix of
the permanent desire for improvement.

EUGÈNE CANSELIET, INTRODUCTION TO
THE REPRINT OF THE *MUTUS LIBER*

I feel I should say a word here about Eugène Canseliet, even if his name
is familiar to fans of alchemy. He is the key person in this whole affair,
one with whom a certain number of surrealists were closely or remotely
connected. He is most likely the person to whom Jorge Camacho and
Bernard Roger referred when they wrote in *La cathédrale de Seville*
(published in 2001): "More than five lustrums have passed since the
day our old Teacher, now deceased, let us know that a few sincere
words whispered in the ear of the student of the Science were often of
greater value to him than many years of study." In particular, Breton,
whom he called a "hermetic poet" in the best sense of the word, seems
to have met him in 1948,* and they corresponded until 1966. Other

---

*We know that Breton spoke of his reading Fulcanelli's *Demeures philosophales* in a letter
to Victor Brauner in 1948. All in all, Canseliet says that the author of *Nadja* sent him,

56

sources even suggest that their paths may have crossed much earlier, when the young Symbolist poet met him, in the company of his Master Fulcanelli, at 11 avenue Montaigne* or at 22 in the famous Egyptian pavilion built by Jules de Lesseps to house his friend Abd el-Kader and "which partly (served) as a setting for Irene Hillel-Erlanger's beautiful novel, *Voyages en Kaléidoscope*,"† about which I will speak more later. "Like Hillel, Milosz, Roussel, and many others, André did frequent the Lesseps' salon of which Fulcanelli was probably a familiar visitor, and perhaps a member," says the hermeticist Archer on his blog‡ an opinion he claims is shared by Patrick Rivière and Geneviève Dubois. And if Breton didn't necessarily know Fulcanelli, some sources—most notably Canseliet—have let it be known that it's not impossible for Fulcanelli to have known Breton. The fact remains that "around 1950," according to Jacques Van Lennep, the author of the *Surrealist Manifestos* and the Master of Savignies (Canseliet) shared "several philosophical agapes," which René Alleau and Claude d'Ygé also attended.[1]

They knew each other quite well, as shown by the anecdote told by Bernard Roger about the encounter of the two men at the Promenade de Venus on an unspecified date (one that should have taken place somewhere between the end of the fifties and the beginning of the sixties):

(cont.d) "during the summer of 1948," the one-hundred-percent linen copy of the *Cahiers de la Pléiade* containing "Fronton Virage," which "provided a persuasive glimpse of an unexpected exegesis." Gilles Boucherie, meanwhile, pushes the date up to 1953.

*According to Moreh, who wrote the preface to the 2015 Utrecht edition of Irene Hillel-Erlanger's book: "The Lesseps had turned their home into a place where the elite of the occult community and some select members of the Parisian bohemian community could meet. This group included musicians, painters who would later become Cubists, some Dadaist and Surrealist bigwigs, alchemists, and occultists."

†Richard Khaitzine, *La langue des oiseaux*, vol. 3. "The magnificent mansion on Montaigne Avenue," as Irene Hillel-Erlanger described it, in fact.

‡In the article "Julien Champagne et le pape du surréalisme" on his blog (archerjulienchampagne.com). This is what was said in the *Bulletin de liaison d'Atlantis* n° 2 of November 2015, about Archer in a "footnote by the editorial board" after Archer's article "De bonnes nouvelles de Julien Champagne" about Jean Artero's March 14, 2015, conference: "Archer is a close friend of Jean Artero. Together they have managed a blog dedicated to Julien Champagne since 2006." At the very least, Archer is a Janus!

Breton was often the first one there, arriving every day around six o'clock. He would take a seat in the middle of a banquette in the room whose windows looked out on the rue du Louvre. One evening, although the place was almost empty, he found someone sitting in the "perilous seat," as Philippe Audoin called it. This individual was none other than Eugène Canseliet, who had casually dropped in to relax over a drink, entirely unaware of the daily meetings that took place there. Both men were equally surprised and delighted. That evening, Fulcanelli's disciple took part in the group discussion, surrounded by the congenial interest, in spite of the slight reticence of some members.[2]

Khaitzine reminds us that Canseliet himself said (in the opening remarks written for the republication of his *Deux logis alchimiques* in 1979), "that on one of his very rare meetings with Breton" he told him, "that of the various people, always of high quality [that he used to see] around his Master on Montaigne Avenue, it was Raymond Roussel [and we will revisit him] who impressed him the most."* It seems that he knew Roussel quite well! And in 1956, when his translation of Basil Valentine's *Twelve Keys of Philosophy* published by Editions Minuit was released, he didn't fail to have a numbered, deluxe copy sent "to André Breton, the poet, the philosopher, this work by the great German Adept, in whom he shall recognize, better than anyone, the *physical and scientific expression of surrealism*; in affectionate and *fraternal* homage."

---

*As for the relationship of Breton and Roussel, it would clearly seem to date from the very beginning of the twenties. After attending a performance of *Locus Solus*, the future author of the *Surrealist Manifesto* sent his elder colleague a copy of *Clair de terre* (Earthlight) with the following note: "To Raymond Roussel for *Locus Solus*, the only performance I was given the opportunity to attend." In return Roussel sent him a copy of *L'étoile au front* (The star on the brow) in 1926 as a token of gratitude for the beautiful dedication of *Clair de terre*—"proudly cited by me on the program of *La Poussière de Soleils* [The Dust of Suns]." Moreover, in January 1927 he sent a copy with a dedication saying, "To André Breton, whose support is infinitely precious to me," a copy that appears in the recipient's library with six pages of handwritten notes on its presumed alchemical content.

It will be noted, and I have allowed myself to insist by using italics, that the Master of Savignies establishes a direct relationship between alchemy and surrealism, which appears to some extent as its literary counterpart, and that he assumes, on the other hand, a bond of fraternity—but what kind of bond of fraternity?—with his friend.

Of modest origin, as his father was a construction worker, Eugène Canseliet was born on December 18, 1899, in Sarcelles and died on April 23, 1982, in Savignies, the "small locale in the Oise region not far from Beauvais, where he had chosen to live . . . in fraternal communion with nature, which is," as Elie-Charles Flamand explains, "necessary for the practice of the Magisterium." Canseliet didn't follow any specific course of studies, Jacques d'Arès notes in issue 322 of the magazine *Atlantis*, of September-October 1982. In this *Hommage au maître alchimiste Eugène Canseliet, F.C.H., 1899–1982*, he says that Canseliet "was truly exceptional, juggling Greek and Latin—classical or that of the sixteenth century—as he did with other languages from which he could extract the substantive marrow." He adds, "Whether you talked to him about history, economics, chemistry, or technical physics, he knew it all and had a truly astonishing memory. Add to this his remarkable deductive powers and his ability to see the big picture, and you have a portrait of someone who had to be an authentic humanist of the twentieth century. Unfortunately, there are practically no more of them, but he was one of their number because he was an alchemist."

These remarks are corroborated by Flamand in his book *Les méandres du sens* where with respectful affection he shares his memories, which admirably complete the portrait of a man whose "plain appearance and old-fashioned charm" he admired while sensing within him "an individual who possessed the strength of spiritual convictions and who was the keeper of solemn secrets." He goes on to say, "Respecting the timeless discipline of the Arcane, Canseliet during his simple and almost ascetic life conformed with the magnificent and austere precept decreed by Nicolas Valois in the fifteenth century: 'Patience is the ladder of philosophers and humility their garden gate.'"

Even if he claims to have also been "initiated" into alchemy by Cylani, who would have thrown the door to the labyrinth wide open during the course of the week in which his booklet reappeared in 1915,* Canseliet is also the spiritual heir and "editor, then . . . disseminator"† of the books *The Mystery of the Cathedrals* and the *Dwellings of the Philosophers* by the man who was perhaps the sole Adept of the twentieth century, that mysterious Fulcanelli whom he had accompanied from 1916 to 1930 and whose true initiator he claimed was . . . Basil Valentine! Man "outside time" as well as a "craftsman of the royal art" convinced that alchemy is "the fruit of a lengthy ascetic and non-stop labor,"‡ he worked mightily and humbly to transmit and explain it as he explained in an interview with Robert Amadou. "I have published Fulcanelli's works and my own in order to fulfill the responsibility entrusted to me, in other words, to respond in the best possible way to the needs of all those who have participated in the renewal of alchemy and who have become disciples of his great school."[3] As far as this renewal is concerned, he was unquestionably the implementator! Indeed, thanks to his efforts, as Bernard Renaud de la Faverie points out,** "several hundred copies of

---

*In the "Préface à la deuxième edition" of *Le Mystère des cathédrales.* The "reprint" used by Canseliet alludes to the 1915 republication by Chacornac of Cyliani's booklet *Hermès dévoilé—Dédié à la postérité,* initially published in Paris by Félix Locquin in 1832, which was probably, according to Archer, one of the very first books read by this student researcher of Hermeticism.

†In Archer's terms, again, in the article "Cuba Libre" on his blog.

‡There should have been a third book "that would have raised the didactic work into a most extraordinary alchemical trilogy," *Finis Gloriae Mundi,* a title borrowed from a painting made by Juan de Valdès Léal in 1672 and kept in . . . Seville, but Fulcanelli took the manuscript back from Canseliet without any explanation. Canseliet even suggested in his preface to *Héraldique alchimique nouvelle* that the Adept may well have destroyed it. Some also claim that it was Fulcanelli who dictated the text of his book *La rôtisserie de la reine pédauque* to Anatole France! (The book was translated into English as *At the Sign of the Reine Pédauque.* The name refers to a queen with a webbed foot like a goose, which has ties to certain Hermetic symbolism—*trans.*)

**Robert Amadou, *Le Feu du Soleil.* This citation seems to be appropriate even though we know that because of some rude actions committed by Amadou, the publication of this book created a definitive rupture between the two men. It is also

The Mystery of the Cathedrals were published in 1927, then three years later *The Dwellings of the Philosophers.* "For thirty years they only sold in dribs and drabs" and only enjoyed real success when "between 1960 and 1982, five editions of the first and four of the second were printed in runs of several thousand copies each"! Moreover, it cannot be overlooked that, by the curious effect of a more than ever objective chance it was only two years after the publication of *The Manifesto of Surrealism* that the famous work only cited by its truncated title—*The Mystery of the Cathedrals and the Esoteric Interpretation of the Hermetic Symbols of the Great Work*—appeared. It was written out by Canseliet using the notes left by a Fulcanelli* who was apparently no longer in this world and who "like the majority of ancient Adepts, when he threw the *old man*'s corpse in the nettles in the ditch," had only left "on the path, the onomastic trace of his ghost, whose haughty calling card proclaimed the supreme aristocracy."[4]

In this way he himself became the author of several books—in particular *Two Alchemical Abodes* and *Alchemy Explained by Its Classic*

<hr>

(cont.d) indicated by Marie-Claire Dumas in her presentation of "Fronton virage" (in André Breton, *Œuvres completes*, vol. 3), that Breton wrote in his letter to Jean Ferry of March 31, 1948: "It's the pseudonym concealing Monsieur Canseliet, author of *Deux logis alchimiques*, although the author denies it in this book."

*Much has been said—and continues to be said—about the identity of the individual known only by the name of Fulcanelli. "Every adept," Caron and Hutin tell us, "having to take a new name once he had made his way to the end of the Great Work." Opinions are varied and divergent. Some (Walter Grosse) think this was the pseudonym of Paul Decoeur, a French engineer born in 1839 and who died in 1923, but this claim has not been accepted by all. Among the names most often mentioned, it is worth citing those of Alphonse Jobert (Richard Khaitzine); Jules Violle, a French physician born in 1841 and deceased in 1923 (Johann Dreue and Patrick Rivière); and especially Pierre Dujols, concerning whom recent documents have introduced new elements! However, Bernard de la Faverie, who sometimes loses his temper with those who would like to "violate" the secret identity of the adept, rightly points out in his preface to Bernard Chauvière's book, *Mémoires d'un alchimiste contemporain*, that "if Fulcanelli hid his name this way, it's because he wishes to remain unknown while respecting the ancient tradition of the true Adepts."

*Texts**—as well as prefaces whose importance has been demonstrated countless times. All this, as Patrick Rivière, himself a student of Canseliet,[5] points out, helped establish his reputation as a philosopher, in the sense Dom Pernety gives to the word in his *Mythic-Hermetic Dictionary*. Pernety, "a Benedictine of the Congregation of Saint Maur,"† is quoted by Rivière as saying that a philosopher is "a lover of Wisdom, who is instructed in the secret operations of Nature and imitates its procedures to produce things that are more perfect than those of Nature herself. The name of philosopher has been given throughout the ages to those who are truly instructed in the procedures of the Great Work, which we also call Science and hermetic philosophy because we consider Hermes Trismegistus the first to have been made famous by it." But we should keep in mind that the Master of Savignies was never at a loss for words when it came to criticizing "the passive resignation of the peoples enslaved by scientism." "Alchemy," as he told Robert Amadou, "is the preeminent vocation for the one called to it—*vocatus*—and who thereby receives from God the most effective grace."[6] For Canseliet, as he wrote in the introduction to Jean-Jacques Pauvert's 1966 new edition of *Mutus Liber*: "Alchemy presupposes ecumenism, since it is universal and reaches the agreement of science and religions."

I cannot fail to point out that Bernard Renaud de la Faverie, in his preface to Bernard Chauvière's *Mémoires d'un alchimiste contemporain*, asserts that Eugène Canseliet himself, although it is he "to whom we owe the renewed interest in traditional Alchemy," "never claimed to be a master," that "he never had any apprentice working with him in the laboratory and [that] those who claim so are not telling the truth." However, he added that "he nevertheless kindly answered

---

*A work in which he says in a preface that "he could have called it *The Charitable Guide*, as the manuscript which was born in the Great Century, and whose entire incipit was transmitted by Fulcanelli, who holds out a hand to the Curious of Alchemy, in order to free them from this vexing labyrinth in which they are wandering and lost."

†As explicitly stated by Canseliet in his "Étude historique" on Nicolas Flamel in *Le livre des figures hiéroglyphiques*.

the questions he was asked and always at the level of the questioner's knowledge."

With regard to this man, whom this same Bernard Renaud de la Faverie rightly described as being "one of those great figures who pass by on the margins of their century and whose importance and influence are discovered only later,"[7] we can appreciate the full meaning of this confidence shared by Elie-Charles Flamand: "As several of us can testify, he was very close to succeeding in the final phase of the work." This is confirmed by Jean Glasser, who writes, "He enjoyed the unusual gifts that the stone gave him and was already much closer to the state of an adept than to ordinary life."[8] Bernard Roger and Jorge Camacho even went so far as to suggest, "If the Master of Savignies did not receive the 'Present' in his earthly life, at least to the knowledge of his contemporaries, in the double sense of the term he himself defined, who can say that he did not perceive its extreme proximity in the intensity of certain moments during his work at the furnace?"[9]

All in all, as Flamand reveals in *Les méandres du sens*, "even those who haven't benefited from God's Gift that allows them to successfully reach the final phase of the Great Coction are generously rewarded for their zeal. The intimate union and the canonical exchange they have with matter and with the Spirit grant them immense initiatory benefits!"

In this regard, it seems wise to me to recall the description given by Canseliet himself (October 1925) of this "upheaval caused by the spark of the Revelation in the solitary and studious life of the philosopher." "Under the effect of this divine flame, the old man is completely consumed. Name, family, country, all illusions, all errors, all vanities crumble to dust. And out of these ashes, like the phoenix of the poets, a new personality was born." Prudently he went on to say, "At least that is how the philosophical tradition sees it." This description was rounded off by Flamand in the above-mentioned book as follows: "Regeneration of the physical body, extension of life, and illuminating knowledge are acquired to him. The personality of the individual is erased and gives way to a liberated and fully spiritualized being." We could also stick to the definition of the adept proposed by Canseliet in 1960 in these terms: "the alchemist who has successfully completed the Great Work, who has *realized* the Philosopher's Stone in the strict sense of the verb, that is to say, has made it *real, positive*, and *effective*. Having reached this glorious point of his career, the adept simultaneously dies to the fleeting present of illusory contingencies and is born into a single existence without antagonisms, into omnipresence and perpetuity."[10] The *epopteia*, in other words, the highest initiation of the theurgists, the contemplation of the Divine and nature—direct knowledge of the principle of things!

Canseliet, "probably the only one of our contemporaries who knew the true identity of the Adept,* in other words Fulcanelli, was in the habit of adding the mysterious letters of F.C.H., which means *Frère Chevalier d'Heliopolis* (Brother Knight of Heliopolis) to his name. This refers to a discreet, not a secret society. This society maintained ties with the Egyptian Rite, which clearly seems to have a connection again with the De Lesseps family, a society that the data bank of the National Library of France presents as "an alchemical and esoteric brotherhood founded in 1798 by Jean-Baptiste Barthélémy de Lesseps," the uncle of Ferdinand de Lesseps. Going further back, Caron and Hutin explain (in their book *Les Alchimistes*) that "Fulcanelli's own secret society— that of the Brothers of Heliopolis—itself the keeper of much older traditions, is said to have been founded in Alexandria in the second century AD" and that it was "an organization whose purpose was to spread Egyptian initiation, as was the Prague para-Masonic group to which writer Gustave Meyrink belonged. He revealed some of its rites in various chapters of his famous esoteric novel, *The Golem*." In his book, *Tradition alchimique et tradition maçonnique*, Guy Piau clarifies that "the Fraternity of Heliopolis is a community whose existence has

---

*Philippe Audoin, *Bourges cité première*. Unless, but it's most unlikely, it was Fulcanelli himself, as we saw earlier! It should also be noted that the same Canseliet published a text entitled "Notre-Dame de l'alchimie" in issue 209 (November–December 1961) of the magazine *Atlantis*.

been proven. Its members, recognized if not famous alchemists, philosophers and spagyrists, met in the time of Fulcanelli and Canseliet in the back room of a bookshop specialized in hermetic works." In his first preface to *Mystery of the Cathedrals* in 1925, Canseliet went so far as to speak on their behalf! And in his introduction to his Master's second book, whose full name is *The Dwellings of the Philosophers and Hermetic Symbolism in its Connection with the Sacred Art and the Esotericism of the Great Work*, he raises the question of Fulcanelli's true identity and the discretion observed in this regard by "free, powerful, and high ranking figures, who had been able to reveal his true name, even in confidence," but who "kept their silence, as if bound by a tacit agreement." He thought this worth clarifying, while giving us some valuable information on the people with whom the Adept, his Master, associated. "As a youth he was welcomed by Chevreul,* de Lesseps, and Grasset d'Orcet.† He was a friend of Berthelot, Curie, his younger by twenty years, as well as Jules Grevy and Paul Painlevé.‡ But Canseliet recalls that "in Heliopolis, he, found himself always and strictly subject by oath to the ancestral discipline of secrecy." This suggests that the Order was truly ancient and had a strict set of rules. Still, according to Canseliet, the F.C.H. would be identical with the Brothers of the (true) Rosy Cross, as he says about the adepts in his introduction to Basil Valentine's *Twelve Keys* that "having shed [their] human carcass"

---

*Michel-Eugène Chevreul (1786–1889) was a major figure of his time, a chemist of international renown, a member of the Academy of Sciences and of the Royal Society of London. His work on color perception influenced many painters. Canseliet, in the "preliminary considerations" of his book *Alchemy Explained*, said of him that he "was the perfect model of scientific impartiality," and that it was from him that "the valuable alchemical works in the library of the Natural History Museum of Paris came."

†Concerning de Lesseps, see chapter 4, and for Grasset d'Orcet, chapter 5.

‡Marcellin Berthelot (1827–1907) was a scientist whose political activities led him into the Ministry of Foreign Affairs rather than to the field of public education. Pierre Curie (1859–1906) is the famous French physicist who with his wife Marie received the Nobel Prize for their work on radioactivity. Jules Grevy (1807–1891) was a politician and President of the Republic from 1879–1887. Paul Painlevé (1863–1933) was a mathematician and politician who served as council president and war secretary.

they enjoy the "invisibility and omnipresence that belong exclusively to the members of the Rosy Cross, as well as to those of the universal *Heliopolis*" (emphasis is Canseliet's). This brings to mind the work entitled *Le texte d'alchimie et le songe-verd* whose author quoted by Canseliet mentions the "Brothers of the true Rosy Cross!" Perhaps he is also thinking of this mysterious brotherhood when he writes in "Hermétiques rudiments d'héraldique":[11] "In fact, during the embryonic period of the new beginning of the world, only those who have acquired a more or less significant fraction of alchemical teachings and received, each according to their merits, the corresponding position on the hierarchical scale opening at the grade of knight, have the rights of nobility!"

Nor can I pass over in silence the fact that the Master of Savignies was so close to Breton and his friends that they had made him one of the recipients of the questionnaires on "Magic Art" they had addressed to their friends and traveling companions (in the time after the Second World War), for example, or that on "The World Upside Down?" His response to the latter was published in the third issue of *La Brèche* in September 1962. And evidence of this proximity is found again later in 1974 when he mentions (in the Prolegomena to *Three Ancient Alchemical Texts*) his friendship with Robert Lebel, who had shared Breton's American exile and while remaining "a spirit free of all allegiance," as Etienne-Alain Hubert says, participated closely enough with the group for the author of *Nadja* to write a short preface in 1955 for his pamphlet *Chantage à la beauté* (Beauty's extortion). Canseliet analyzed a painting owned by Lebel, *The Hunting of the Owl*, in which he saw evidence that "religion and hermeticism are as one in all expression of elevated symbolism in the Sacred Art," while pointing out that the collector—and "national expert"—had the "double kindness to offer [him] a photograph of it and permission to reproduce it."[12]

One anecdotal detail I found in the long text that the Master of Savignies wrote about Flamel seems so revealing that I have chosen to share it as a conclusion to this look at his profound personality.

Mentioning the alchemist's wife, Perennelle, and spelling her name as it appears in the first pages of *The Book of Hieroglyphic Figures*, he addresses her as follows: "Are you in the catacombs, Perennelle, or do you continue to live with your spouse in some secret and blessed place in this world, where man is fixed in the grace and charm of a past that is irretrievably dead and nostalgic?" And he goes on to say: "Let's leave this language to the poets, though we could ourself be something of a poet."*

---

*Eugène Canseliet, *Alchimie: Nouvelles études diverses sur les portraits alchimiques*. This text was first published in issues 2 and 3 of Robert Amadou's magazine, *La tour Saint-Jacques*, in 1956.

4

KALEIDOSCOPIC JOURNEYS

The star found here again is the early morning star.
ANDRÉ BRETON, *ARCANUM 17*

The surrealist attraction to the "Art of the Scales"* goes back practically to the origins of the movement. Traces can be found from the time of *Littérature*—particularly in Louis Aragon's text (in the ninth issue of November 1919) about the singular book by Irene Hillel-Erlanger, *Voyages en kaléidoscope* (see plate 5),† published in 1919, in which, "under the guise of a surrealist fiction, the author reveals the highest secrets of transcendental Hermeticism." On the threshold of all this history, this small book of a one hundred pages dedicated "to the great soul of L. B."—who, depending on the source, is either the novelist and Christian polemicist, Léon Bloy,‡ or a friend of the author, Louise Barbe, chemist for the Poulenc Brothers and an alchemist—has inspired a great deal of discussion.

---

*"For it requires a great deal of discernment and precision, as does the practice of judgment," notes Antoine Plussihem on his article on "Le tombeau de François II à Saint-Pierre de Nantes," *Atlantis* n° 401, "Mysterious Brittany," May 2000, Vincennes.
†Irene Hillel-Erlanger, *Voyages en kaléidoscope*. The book contains an important preface by Jacques Simonelli to which this chapter owes a great deal. This is the fourth edition. It should be noted that this book, the 1919 edition of course, was in Breton's library.
‡This is notably the opinion of Khaitzine.

It seems amazingly precursory to Khaitzine, who points out that "this strange novel, written in a Dadaist style, contains about thirty (mysteries) that would not seem out of place in an alchemical treatise"[1]—and it is true, as Bernard Roger shows, that "we have every reason to believe that the names of Parisian places [in the book] have been carefully chosen for the resonance they give through the play of the phonetic cabala,"[2] which Simonelli confirms in detail. Although Fulcanelli mentions it in *The Dwellings of the Philosophers*, it seems, according to Khaitzine, "to have caused some consternation among [the adept's] retinue, and was quickly withdrawn from bookstores," and legend even has it that a mysterious person attempted to burn all published copies.* Michel Carrouges discusses it, among many other masterpieces in his mythic book, *Les machines célibataires* (*The Bachelor Machines*).†

In any case, Bernard Roger insists (in *Paris and Alchemy*) that *Kaleidoscopic Journeys* has nothing to do with literature," especially since "the author gave warning of her intentions":

> *This is not a novel*
> *even less a character study,*
> *we have simply tried, fervently,*
> *to grasp and fix some signs . . .*

Despite the initial denials, it is clear that the title of the book assumes a particular meaning after reading what René Alleau explained in a later article entitled "Alchimie et cryptographie"[3] that was the last in the French edition of the book on alchemy by E. J. Holmyard. With this text, which we have good reason to doubt is as innocent as it seems. Alleau first shows that "alchemical symbolism can be compared to the play of

*According to Canseliet, Fulcanelli was quite surprised to find "such symbolism in such a disjointed text, which often lapses into shorthand and pidgin French."

†Michel Carrouges, *The Bachelor Machines*. Carrouges (1910–1988) whose real name was Louis Couturier, was a member of the group from 1949 to 1951 and is also, incidentally, author of the major work, *André Breton and the Basic Concepts of Surrealism*.

a kaleidoscope, which, with the help of a very small constant number of colored elements, shows, with the slightest movement of these elements, infinitely varied figures which people find it hard to believe are composed of exactly the same material parts." A little later he clarifies that "the basis of alchemical symbolism is not abstract but *concrete* and *positive*, material and tangible, so much so that it is completely impossible to understand the hermetic *kaleidoscope* if one has never seen the fundamental elements that it describes and assembles in a multitude of forms and structures that seem to have no relation to each other."

Finally, Canseliet, as a good disciple of his Master, mentions it on several occasions. In a footnote to his 1956 text on "Jacques Coeur,"* Canseliet recalls, "I also mentioned the book by Irene Hillel-Erlanger, in *Two Alchemical Abodes*. This book was born during the heyday of Cubism and Dada style. Michel Carrouges,† gave it a lengthy review, not without verve and perspicacity, in *The Bachelor Machines*." A little later, in *L'hermétisme dans la vie de Swift et dans ses voyage* (a text published in 1957 in number 344 of the *Cahiers du Sud* and later published in 1983, with nine superb illustrations by Camacho, as the first volume of the *Little Library of Traditional Alchemy* by Fata Morgana), Canseliet mentioned Hillel-Erlanger's short novel and again referred always in footnotes yet to the author of *André Breton and the Basic Concepts of Surrealism*: "See also. *The Bachelor Machines,* Arcanes, 1954 in which Michel Carrouges projects dazzling flashes on the magical mystery of certain contemporary works, pages 165 to 177."

In the preface to the new edition of his book *Two Alchemical Abodes*, he also reveals that he "examined" "the question of Joel Joze and his kaleidoscopic journeys, on the occasion of one of their far too rare meetings" with Breton, who owned the book by Irene Hillel-Erlanger. Unfortunately he doesn't give a date!

---

*Eugène Canseliet, *Alchimie*. As noted before, this was first published in *La tour Saint-Jacques*, no. 8 (January–February, 1957).

†In his introduction to *Mutus Liber*, Canseliet speaks of Michel Carrouges as his "dear friend" and mentions his article "'Le sismographe surréaliste,' in *Polarité du symbole*, in *Etudes carmélitaines*, thirty-ninth year (1960)."

Then, in passing, in one of his *Alchimiques mémoires*, published in issues 15 and 16 of the magazine *La tourbe des philosophes** in 1981, he writes: "Many memories link me to Julien Champagne, especially those of the ancient days of my happy youth, also those of the avenue Montaigne and the famous *Voyages en Kaléidoscope*." And on the blog devoted to Julien Champagne that I mentioned earlier the mysterious Hermeticist(s) who goes by the name of Archer says this about the Master of Savignies: "He was also sensitive to the hermeticism of these *Voyages*. In another issue of *La Tourbe* (N° 6, 1979), he compares this work to the medieval alchemical poem by Jean de Lafontaine, *La fontaine des amoureux de science*.†

La tourbe des philosophes is a magazine of alchemical studies that takes its name from the *Turba philosophorum*, a "translation" according to Alleau "from Arabic works" and one of the "first monuments of Western Alchemy." The magazine appeared from 1977 to 1995 under the direction of Jean Laplace (1951–1996) followed by Bernard Renaud de la Faverie. It consists of thirty-nine issues including six double issues and a special issue on spagyrics. With respect to Jean Laplace, it is interesting to note that after having discovered alchemy in Africa (like René Alleau) when he was twenty, he made contact with Canseliet in 1973 concerning philosophical problems raised by mummification by the Ancient Egyptians. On the back cover of the book he published in 1986 with Editions Suger, *Index général des termes spéciaux, des expressions et des sentences propres à l'alchimie se rencontrant dans l'œuvre complète d'Eugène Canseliet* (impressively close to 10,000 entries), one can read: "Disavowed by the Master in 1976 for behavior contrary to the discipline, he undertook through nonstop laboratory work to start his path anew on more solid foundations. This new approach earned him reconciliation with Canseliet in 1980 and, until the Master's death in 1982, the acquisition of advice thanks to which he succeeded to gain knowledge of the *Virbum demissum* [sic] in 1985."

†In fact, the author of this Hermetic poem written in 1413, the text of which can be read in its entirety in Klossowski de Rola's *Alchimie: Florilège de l'art secret*, is Jehan de La Fontaine, "the poet from Valenciennes," "not to be confused with the gloomy fabulist of the *great* century," "an exquisite fabulist of outspokenness," or Canseliet. He is also cited by Bernard Roger in his text "Le jour de l'étoile" (*Archibras* n° 7) and in his preface to the republication of Basil Valentine's *On the Nature of Metals*. In *La Cathédrale de Séville et le bestiaire alchimique du portail de Saint Christophe et de l'Immaculée Conception*, Bernard Roger and Jorge Camacho provide the following precise historical references: "La Fontaine des Amoureux de Science. Composée par Jean de la Fontaine [sic] de Valenciennes, en le Comté de Henault in *Le Roman de la Rose* 'accompagné de plusieurs autres ouvrages,' Amsterdam: 1735, Tome III." Flamand alludes to this work in his book *Les méandres du sens*, stressing that the poem is, like "Jean Perréal's *Complainte de nature à l'alchimiste errant*, . . . composed in octosyllables."

The author tells of discovering a fountain that reminds me of the gushing, salutary spring on Montaigne Avenue that is so similar to that of the Hermetic poet.

> *Water so clear, pure, and fine*
> *that was beneath a hawthorn.*

There two beautiful women, whom I also see in the gentle Grace and the proud Vera of *Kaleidoscopic Journeys*, the same person under two appearances, approach the wandering artist:

> *Friend, my name is knowledge*
> *Here is Reason who accompanies me*
> *through hills, and dales, and countryside.*
> *She can make you very wise.*

The same female couple ruled in the mansion of Countess Vera whose salons experienced their glory days during the roaring twenties and the living Surrealism of Arts and Letters.

Surely, it is far better for a good lineage to lift up the Curtain of Homespun rather than the Curtain of Fine Gold, for only the Simple have entered the Hall of the Treasure.

What can I add to this?

Few friends visit the whole house, which is high and vast behind its ancient facade. It requires special permission, which is rarely granted.

What can I add? Simply that, as Jacques Simonelli clearly saw (in the first republication of this book through his efforts in 1977), Jean Laplace, speaking of the places and curtains seen there, explains that their presence "reveals an aspect of science with generous evidence." He explains it as follows, "Homespun is a reddish-brown cloth that here symbolizes the red silt released by the calcination of the crow's head. This silt will be covered by quicksilver, which sinks in and soaks it. It is the second curtain. Finally, a third curtain is placed over the mercury.

The latter, like the small casting net still used on our Mediterranean coast, catches the fish that come from the deep waters and fixes them in its tight, interwoven mesh!" But to turn the Mediterranean into the philosopher's sea . . .

And after this exceptional experience, the hero of the novel, Joël Joze, who has drunk the water of this "musical living Spring"— Alchemy is the Art of Music—is literally transfigured, as André Coia-Gatié points out, citing the author: "When the Simples emerge from this miraculous Meeting, they are truly so radiant that it is difficult to recognize them. Their oldest relations remain stupid. Now intelligent, they now feel that nothing is impossible, because things are no longer hidden from them because of the great LIGHT on their faces." (Capitalization is Hillel-Erlanger's.)

In an interview with Robert Amadou, another friend of Canseliet, André Savoret* described this little book as "authentically alchemical." Then Philéas Lebesgue† defined it (in his 1979 article "Hermétisme et poésie," published in *La tourbe des philosophes*, no. 7) as "a unique book whose baroque cover hides or protects a dozen precious pages consisting of the testimony that each adept traditionally leaves at the time of his metamorphosis, either according to the fate common to mortals—and that's probably the case here—or as an avatar of a completely different order." Thus Irene Hillel Erlanger was able to attain the status of Adeptat!‡

---

*André Savoret, (1898–1977): druid, alchemist, writer, and Christian mystic. Author in 1947 of a small *Qu'est-ce que l'alchimie?* (What is alchemy?) published by Editions de Psyché—republished by Editions Arqa—in which he writes: "True alchemy, traditional alchemy, is the knowledge of the laws of life in man and nature, and the reconstruction of the process through which this life, adulterated by the fall of Adam, has lost and can recover its primordial purity, splendor, fullness, and prerogatives; what in the ethical man is called redemption or regeneration; the reincrudation in the physical man; purification and perfection of a nature, finally, in the actual mineral kingdom, reduction to the quintessential and transmutation."

†Philéas Lebesque (1859–1958): poet, novelist, essayist, translator, literary critic, druid, and close friend of Canseliet.

‡Adeptat refers to the quality of the Adept who has reached the final stage of alchemical immortality.

Irene Hillel-Erlanger was born in 1878 into the great Sephardic family of the Camondo, "an ancient family of kings and rabbis,"* patrons and philanthropic financiers, the "Rothchilds of the Orient," who came from Constantinople and received titles of nobility during the Second Empire. She was wife of the musician Camille Erlanger, and mother of the high civil servant and historian Philippe Erlanger, and she was also a poet under the name of Claude Lorrey (to be heard as *l'or est* [the gold is] according to Khaitzine or *or y est* [the gold is] according to Patrick Rivière). She became close to Paul Eluard as well as to Tristan Tzara after his arrival to Paris, but above all to Louis Aragon, whose lover she was in 1919, according to Lionel Follet. In his book, *Les demeures de l'invisible*, Bernard Roger confirms that "Benjamin Peret recalls having met Irene Hillel-Erlanger in the company of Louis Aragon at the café where the surrealists then met, at the beginning of the twenties." Follet however, denies Raymond Queneau's claim (citing Michel Leiris in *Journaux 1914–1965*) "that she was the *heroine* of *Le Con d'Irène*," but confirms that she "is the very real pillar of the character of Mary de Perseval in *Aurélien*."4 Described rather mean spiritedly as a "faded blonde" by Philippe Soupault in his *Mémoires de l'oubli 1923–1926*, she worked with Germaine Dulac who much later directed the film *La coquille et le clergyman,* based on a screenplay by Antonin Artaud, "the first surrealist film that owed nothing to the search for pure cinema."† Khaitzine even suggests that she may have met Raymond Roussel! "It's been said, without sufficient proof," Bernard Roger notes, "that Irene Hillel-Erlanger died in mysterious circumstances. Mystery fans would be pursuing a more interesting task if they wanted to know where this young woman of high society (and friend of Louis Aragon

---

*In the newspaper *L'intransigeant* of March 2, 1920, cited by Jacques Simonelli in his afterword to *Voyages en kaléidoscope* by Hillel-Erlanger. See also Pierre Assouline, *Le dernier des Camondo* and Edmund De Waal, *Lettres à Camondo*. It's Assouline who compares them to the Rothchilds.

†Ado Kyrou, *Le surréalisme au cinéma*. It was condemned though by Artaud, in disagreement with Germaine Dulac, as "nutty."

who sometimes took her to the Café in Place Blanche for an evening aperitif, where the future surrealists were already meeting) had received the precise traditional teaching she bestowed throughout her last book, which despite its very *modern* appearance finds a place on the level of the best classics of alchemical literatures"—and that's the real question worth asking!

A great expert in occultism, as Simonelli has clearly shown, she is believed to have received her knowledge of alchemy from Pierre Dujols, "who was no stranger to the genesis of the works signed Fulcanelli"[*] and is considered the "alchemy teacher of Julien Champagne and Coton-Alvart."[†] A friend of Papus, Pierre Dujols de Valois, who notably spent time in the company of Oswald Wirth, Paul Vuillaud, and René Guénon, is also the author of "the hypotyposis[‡] of the *Mutus Liber* in the 1914 Nourry edition, under the pseudonym of Magophon. In it "he emphasizes the existence of a diplomatic language with double meanings" and also cites the little book of the Company of Jesus, *Typus mundi*,[**] which we must revisit.

The main character of *Kaleidoscopic Journeys*, Joël Joze, is "a kind of patient hermit, full of faith," who, as Simonelli explains, "represents the alchemist and would-be initiate," and whose name, "symbolic like those

---

[*]Richard Khaitzine, *Le cabaret du chat noir*. In his introduction to *Mutus Liber*, Canseliet writes, "Pierre Dujols, the bookseller and scholar who many believe was Fulcanelli." But he immediately goes on to say, speaking of himself in the third person as was his wont, "About this great secret, what has not been imagined, what will not be imagined in the future, perhaps even where, less than elsewhere, no one can be a prophet; especially after our earthly disappearance, whether the old man we already are has died in the flesh, or whether we have killed him so that he may live in the spirit . . ."

[†]Henri Coton-Alvart (1894–1988), chemist and astrologer who is said to have reached the Adeptat in the seventies.

[‡]The hypotyposis paints things so vividly and energetically that, especially after we're dead, it brings them before people's eyes to a certain extent, turning a story or a description into an image, a picture, or even a living scene.

[**]See the *Fulcanelli: La rue de l'alchimie* blog of a certain ljnuhbes! Dujol's *The Hypnotyposis of the Mutus Liber* is often cited by Bernard Roger in his books. Roger, incidentally, provided commentary, with Jorge Camacho, in one edition of the *Typus mundi*.

of the other characters, alludes to the famous hermetic maxim *Savoir, Pouvoir, Oser, Se Taire* [to Know, to Be Able, to Dare, and to Keep Quiet]." He also devoted himself for a long time to the study of the occult sciences, mainly by reading the works of Stanislas de Guaïta* and by stroking the concepts of "ANALOGIES, CORRESPONDENCES, and REVERSIBILITY." (Capitalization is Hillel-Erlanger's.) Although he seems to recently have "abandoned the disappointing quest for the Beyond" for the love of a Vera who thinks solely of exploiting him, he has still not abandoned his belief that "the *nothings* . . . are the material of *everything*," and he still cherishes the idea that "*the universe, as our eyes think they perceive it, is completely different from its true form. We see and can only see what is within us.*" This is an original variant of the famous "As above, so below," in a potential "subversive Utopia" where "the simply curious will find the key to striking and piquant analogies everywhere." "A man of about thirty," he is "the very modern inventor of an optical instrument, which he has given the name of KALEIDOSCOPE" that "works according to the natural law of *analogy*," captures "fluids," and "makes it possible to see *beautiful images*." But it "has no comparison with the old one," "that venerable varnished cardboard tube [that] you remember reveals a moving, tiny rosette of multicolored glass shards that has brought joy to several generations of children." It is not like television, says Simonelli, taking a contrary position to Michel Carrouges. "Madame Hillel-Erlanger," who seems to have been quite up to date with contemporary studies of radiation and other forms of radiance, André Coia-Gatié (who devoted numerous pages of his book *La chevalerie errante* to *Kaleidoscopic Journeys*), tells us, "is also kind enough to clarify the exact nature of these mysterious fluids. 'Soon he (Joze) had mastered the fluidic Forces that rule the world—and whose secret has not been entirely buried

---

*Cited by Hillel-Erlanger. Stanislas de Guaïta (1861–1897) is a French poet and occultist of primary importance. He is the author, notably of *Au seuil du mystère* (Paris: G. Carré, 1886).

since the time of the Most Sublime Antiquity. Docile to his commands, these forces merged with their captive brethren: Rays. Radiant Bodies. Effluviums. Electricity. Of which we know nothing. And which serve us. Great Prisoner-Princes, beneath their metal armature and their glass masks.'" In fact, the device, which captures "in the pupils of all living beings the images of all visible things," "condenses, fixes, and compresses them" through "chemical synthesis" into "magnetic waves, skillfully held in the kaleidoscope's propellant." Transformed into the device itself, by means of very mysterious fluids, salts, and precious metals, the visions are immediately concentrated into flattened pellets that can then be used for an unlimited number of experiences, allowing everyone, in the end, "to discover the HIDDEN MEANING of all things," "a relative hidden meaning [that] is restored to us in an absolute sense, by comparison with *another way of seeing*," "The EMBRYONIC HARMONY OF AN EXCHANGE OF VIEWS!" (Capitalization throughout this section is Hillel-Erlanger's.) "The Kaleidoscope," Simonelli continues, "thus transforms, in accordance with its etymology, the images of the Dark Age or Kali Yuga into *beautiful images* appropriate to their archetypes, restoring to everyone a NEW VISION OF THE UNIVERSE."

Abandoned by the cruel and superficial Countess Vera* after the failure, "because nothingness can only contemplate emptiness," of the high society demonstration of the Kaleidoscope that she had organized in the parlour of her "luxurious mansion," Joze, lost in his hermetic solitude, wanders the streets of Paris vociferating when he is rescued by MADAME GRACE, a sublime original with an "IMMEMORIAL NAME." She invites him to her home in the middle of a "palm grove in the middle of Paris," which, according to Bernard Roger, "seems to contain all the mysterious freshness of the Orient," a house whose upper stories are only accessible to the simple and where he will then "spend most of his time." According to Richard Khaitzine,[5] this house

---

*Vera, "Sensual pleasure, Perfect form of ferocious pleasure," "Quite close," Simonelli says, "to the other femme fatale heroines of 1920s cinema."

was inspired by the "Egyptian style pavilion" that I discussed in chapter 3, the "Moorish villa" built by Ferdinand de Lesseps at 22 avenue de Montaigne in the eighth arrondissement of Paris. The palm grove inescapably brings to mind the short poem signed Claude Lorrey (in other words, Irene Hillel-Erlanger herself) as an overture to *Allégorie luminaire*, in her last collection, *La Chasse au bonheur* (The Hunt for Happiness):[6]

> *Under the sun's fire, in the gleam of the Big Dipper*
> *   [Bear, in French]*
> *The pilgrim scales fastidious paths*
> *But finally reaching the end of his journey*
> *In a secret garden, he will find the spring*
> *The pomegranate and the rose and the temple of a god.* *

This "palm grove" . . . strongly resembles this *Roseraie des Philosophes* [Philosophers' Rose Garden] dear to Arnaud de Villeneuve among others, the "enclosed garden of the philosophers," "a sacred and privileged place, kept apart from the profane world," which Bernard Roger has written "is obviously a place where the famous white or red flower, emblem of the philosopher's stone, is cultivated."† A palm grove of any kind is a place where palm trees grow. Here it is helpful to recall that, according to Bernard Roger and Jorge Camacho, this "tree is the one to which the Greeks gave the same name as that of the fabled bird that is reborn from its own ashes, the Phoenix." In their book *The Cathedral of Seville* they also describe this tree as one that alone "symbolizes all the processes of the Great Work" with "the roots at the bottom nour-

---

*A temple that brings to mind the one dedicated to friendship found in the gardens of Natalie Cliff Barney's pavilion at 20 rue Jacob. And the following verse of this short poem is: "Blessed are those who know how to keep a beautiful, intense treasure."

†Bernard Roger, *Paris et l'alchimie*. In his introduction to *On the Nature of Metals* by Basil Valentine, he again mentions "the design of medieval gardens in the very middle of which often stands a clear and joyful fountain."

ished by dark chaotic waters from which, in our world, emerges the scaly trunk that resembles primordial matter," with "a crown of plants whose fruits ensure its continued existence," that "should give birth to the work of art, combined with that of nature."[7]

As for Grace, she turns out to be a being of light* who with a single glance (for the enthralled Joël Joze) "transmutes the most base metal into gold coins: *Rose Nobles*† struck with the royal image of [her] soul." So that her argument is fully understood, the author alerted us in the "frontispiece" that:

> *So contrasting in appearance,*
> *Grace and Vera—essentially—*
> *are intimately related,*
> *or rather, two aspects of the same person.*
> *Vera has mastery over reality*
> *and Grace over Truth.*
> *If one or the other becomes greater*
> *it is to the detriment of the other*
> *and to the danger of the human race.*
> *A twofold emanation of the Unknown*
> *as*
> *Time and Eternity*
> *divine necessity and human freedom*
> *which we will probably understand in*
> *another level. [Capitalization is Hillel-Erlanger's.]*

---

*"I thought I'd seen some weakening in our projections. There was less good light since Madame Grace left," Gilly says.

†A gold coin minted in England in the fourteenth and fifteenth centuries decorated with a rose as an emblem of the House of York or of Lancaster, but also an alchemical symbol of the philosopher's stone. According to Simonelli, "legend has it that it was smelted from the gold of the transmutations that Ramon Llull is said to have performed in London during the reign of Edward II." That's why these coins are also called *Raymondines*! After his coronation, King Ubu distributed some of them to the Polish people in *Ubu roi*.

Two female heroines who "are really" the same person in two aspects opposed in everything so that this opposition is "transposed to the transcendental level of metaphysics," as Simonelli observes. Canseliet emphasizes their opposition in his *Hermeticism in the Life of Swift and His Travels*, comparing them to *Congnoissance* (Knowledge) and *Raison* (Reason) in Christofle de Gamon's 1610 poem, "The Treasure of Treasures," writing that they are "an exciting transposition to the human plane of the feminine duality that triggers the whole drama of philosophical love." In *Two Alchemical Abodes*, however, he clarifies his remarks, pointing out about Grace that "Irene Hillel-Erlanger could not have better named the ideal being of alchemical purity that embodies in woman the inner qualities without which the artist could do nothing in the order of his physical creation. With this creature, he will find peace of mind, spiritual tenacity and physical strength."

"What a shame," notes André Coïa-Gatié, "that Joël Joze couldn't see the big picture and overcome his pride and sensual cravings! He would have found the right balance and deserved to be called a lover of science in the sense that E. Canseliet gives it in a definition whose clarity should not give the impression that its attribution is easy!" He then cites this definition:* "First and foremost, Alchemy is the preeminent esoteric discipline which fundamentally requires a state of mind and consciousness in which disinterestedness is only equaled by the constant desire to love and to know. Hence our familiar expression Lovers of Science, already used by old authors." To which the Master of Savignies brings the following conclusion, "Nothing can be achieved without love. Love and Knowledge form an inseparable duality."

Canseliet in his text on Jacques Coeur again states,[8] "Please don't consider as sacrilege our inability to defend ourselves against the philosophical comparison with the strange female duality in *Kaleidoscopic Journeys*, Grace and Vera, even though these two personifications refer

---

*In a 1975 interview that appeared in the ninth issue of *Revue Hansa* entitled "Qu'est` ce que l'alchimie?"

solely to the two paths of progression open to man on earth. Were they not announced, at the beginning of the World by the Tree of Science and the Tree of Life of the biblical paradise?" And he compares them, this time with Joan of Arc and Agnes Sorel, both contemporaries of the financier.* And again Jacques Simonelli emphasizes the influence of Stanislas de Guaïta† on Hillel-Erlanger: "*Grace has command over truth,* that is to say over the archetypal and provocative form/shape (*eidos*), whereas Véra has command over reality, that is to say over the passive and receptive substance (*kylê*) that develops the appearances of manifestation, to which this externalization gives their power of illusion." From this perspective, the kaleidoscope, Bernard Roger concludes, "is for Joël Joze the instrument of a quest for the *truth* behind the shapes of *reality*."[9] Moreover, this author contends that from the cover (of the book) we are invited to make the difficult transition from the domain of Vera to the domain of Grace, from "reality" to "truth," with the help of Gilly's right eye. Gilly is the "faithful servant"—the "faithful and loyal servant" who according to André Coia-Gatié, in *The Knighthood Errant*, is the "first mercury, of cold and passive quality."

Having probably grasped, in one way or another, the potential revealed by the machine, Grace advises her loving friend to "entrust [his] Kaleidoscope to a child"—*Ludus puerorum*—thus in passing becomes Gilly's Godmother, a "thirteen-and-a-half-year-old" newspaper hawker, whom he meets, by chance, a short time later. Gilly, "whose *clear, sensitive* eye gives the kaleidoscopic visions an intensity they had never had before him," according to Bernard Roger, also owes something, as we have seen, to the tutelary presence of Grace.‡

---

*Archer suggests "to make things simple, Vera symbolizes the century, and Grace eternal alchemy."

†Who in 1896 was one of the founding members of Alchemical Society of France with the hyperchemist François Jollivet-Castelot. [Hyperchemistry combines metaphysics with operative chemistry—*trans.*]

‡"It so happens that Grace," writes Khaitzine in the second volume of *La langue des oiseaux*, "is nothing other than the *Donum Dei*, the Gift of God."

In this regard, it is amusing to note, insofar as Irene Hillel-Erlanger depicts this child as "the salt of the earth, this makes the lady the *Godmother of Salt*!*

It is worth recalling here that in *The Dwellings of the Philosophers*, Fucanelli explains that "the *faithful servant* and *salt of the earth*, which Madame Hillel-Erlanger calls *Gilly* and which helps his master to triumph over the influence of Vera" is nothing other than the "*universal solvent*," in other words the *mercury of the Sages*, "the key without which no chemist will ever open the doors of the *Closed Palace of the King*."[10] Bernard Roger then puts the finishing touches on this (in his book *Paris and Alchemy*) when discussing the "seer" qualities of the very young man: "This is how this *universal solvent* will open to its master the sanctuary of nature, by restoring to him, through the pure and ingenuous vision of a child, a clear and relative vision of the interiority of the world behind the forms fixed by custom."

Regarding the name of this child, Jacques Simonelli suggests that "in accordance with the phonetic cabala, it must be heard as *j'y lis* [I read there], with the understanding that the place of this reading is the *mirror* in which the Cosmopolitan saw *all of nature naked*," "the *Mirror of Nature*, for which the kaleidoscope, the *Mirror of Truth*, is an exact equivalent."

André Coia-Gaité, who recalls that "it is thanks to Gilly that the kaleidoscopic visions become more intense and heart touching," is inclined "to see in this child's name a clue to the place where *Gît l'Y* [lies the Y], where the Y is located, that is to say the glass that holds the androgyne and whose clear and sensitive eye brings things into sharp focus." The allusion to the letter Y, the "letter of the Pythagoreans," refers us back to the androgyne which it often symbolizes.

La marraine du sel (*Godmother of Salt*) is the title of a novel by Maurice Fourré. In his article, "A la recherche de Fol-Yver," Jacques Simonelli mentions Fourré's own remarks explaining that it is, "in certain regions of the West, the assisting woman who presents the adorable catechumen at the moment the Celebrant of the Baptism blesses him with the symbol of the bitter salt!"

It may not be impossible to suggest another trail concerning this name and something in close proximity from a hypothesis voiced by Canseliet in his book on Swift. This hypothesis is based on the name of the traveler Gulliver, which he deconstructs into *Gulli* and *ver*, indicating that if "*ver* [worm] means the *spring*," "Gulli is the genitive of *Gullus* which, according to Du Cange, means *boat* or *vessel*," a word which, for the Alchemists, denotes "the matrix, the bearer of the stone, the vase of the art with which they perform certain operations."[11]

The fact remains that the man, rashly ignoring Grace's warning, which reminds him of the necessity of "anonymity," as Simonelli points out, and of "philosophical selflessness," therefore creates, with the child's help, an attraction, the *Guignol-Kaleido*, which is greeted "with such monstrous success that hundreds of spectators have to be turned away at each session," and they contemplate moving. This cannot help but bring to mind the affair of Rodolphe Salis's *Cabaret du chat noir* and his "Shadow Theater," which also attracted equally large audiences in the middle of the 1880s. This brilliant discovery, which brought fame and fortune to Salis, preceded all the techniques for projecting images that were invented at the time. About this, Khaitzine (in his book specifically entitled *Le cabaret du chat noir*) tells us that "all these inventions were based on a principle that could be defined as 'being the permutation of forms by light' and that this lapidary definition—in both senses of the word—is the same given to Alchemy by a certain Fulcanelli," when he said that it "is the permutation of forms by light, fire, or spirit." And of course, the Kaleidoscope bears a certain kinship, at least in appearance, with the various types of projectors manufactured at that time.

Joël Joze's enterprise aroused such enthusiasm that, a year later, it was present throughout the world, and each person connected near or far to the *Kaleido*—sometimes even personalized as the vision unfolded—should wear a "necessary insignia that is nothing other than a THERMOMÈTRE, a Standard Thermometer [that] presides over our hailing destinies," a "THERMO-MAÎTRE

[Thermo-Master] [that] saves us from ourselves," probably similar to the one drawn by Von Dongen—and which it would be much better to know how "to regulate . . . on the infallible level. Zero." In chapter VI of his book *Alchemy Explained through Its Classic Texts*, Canseliet writes that the thermometer is an "inestimable instrument of which I have no doubt that the alchemists had at their disposal and that they jealously scarcely scratched its arcane surface, its mystery." In an article titled "Mithraique alchimique," he makes "an important suggestion" when he proposes drawing a parallel between the kaleidoscopic thermometer and the (seven) regimes and reigns of the planets "in the *Open Entrance to the Closed Palace of the King* by Eirenaeus Philalethes." Patrick Rivière carries this suggestion further by pointing out that this measuring instrument "provides the temperature scale of the Great Work."[12] And Jacques Simonelli follows up on this by inviting us to study the chapter on "The Great Coction" in Canseliet's *L'Alchimie expliquée sur ses textes classiques*, in order to see "how the graduations of the thermometer drawn by Van Dongen can correspond to the weights, colors, and musical notes that are produced over the course of the third work!"[13] Then for his part, Bernard Roger says, "Have no doubt that the thermometer plays kabalistically with Master Therme or Master Hermes, the mercury of the philosophers called Trismegistus because it is all-powerful, according to the universal law of analogy, in the three kingdoms of nature in heaven, on earth, and in hell."* Thermometer, "the incomparable instrument of precision and decision," explains Irene Hillel-Erlanger, about which André Coia-Gatié, who incidentally corroborates Canseliet's remarks, confirms once again that the one drawn by Van Dongen "reveals to the seeker, the high level of knowledge attained" by the author.

However, this success, the extent of which displeased Grace, who reminded her lover that he owed his invention to "divine inspiration"—

---

*For his part, Richard Khaitzine writes (in vol. 2 of *La langue des oiseaux*) that this "strange thermometer [is] to be interpreted as *thermoMaître* or Master of alchemical heat."

which made it an authentic *Donum Dei**—and that out of a "Mirror of Truth," he was "making an instrument of vanity," at the risk of seeing his "visions . . . fade beyond recall," combined with the possibly unexpected return of the Countess Vera who, true to form, brings about the fall of the "Oculist of the Occult" and the destruction of the *Kaleido*, "forever." And it's Gilly, now eighteen years old, who tells us the final scene—"the battle of the two natures," says Bernard Roger—between the two hostile sisters,[†] because their bonds of kinship are now fully revealed, and the one he calls his Master, a scene that ends with the destruction of the device in the conflagration of Vera's mansion and even the entire neighborhood "up to Concorde." It is an indescribable pandemonium by which these few lines, by the very confusion they reveal, show its full scope:

> *Magnetic fluids with the currents*
> *of torrents of electricity*
> *Catastrophic crackling*
> *Night*
> *one hundred thousand window panes in splinters*
> *houses collapse.*

And then

> *. . . Victims*
> *thousands upon thousands*
> *carbonized*
> *asphyxiated*
> *torn to shreds . . .*

---

*"A spiritual light obtained through revelation," as Fulcanelli explains in the second volume of *The Dwellings of the Philosophers*. "The true secret lies elsewhere," writes André Coia-Gatié in *The Knighthood Errant*. "It is this 'Gift of God' that will allow this or that individual to experience the initiatory Quest in his or her body and mind!"
†This will also be the title of one of the scripts written by Hillel-Erlanger with Germaine Dulac.

This catastrophe, which cannot help but bring to mind the memory of the Bazar de la Charité fire* leaves the four main characters alive—the only survivors, in fact, since the others are only silhouettes in the background—in more or less good condition. Joël Joze, for example, ends up "half paralyzed": and more importantly, abandoned by grace, because the "fluids do not allow themselves to be harnessed a second time!" But all hope is not lost, for during a walk that Gilly takes with his Master, they find themselves back at *l'Étoile* (the Star),† which as Simonelli reminds us "is the visible sign of the canonical quality of the materials obtained from the first work and their final purification" and thus indicates that the artist is on the right path.

In the brilliant afterword "À la lueur de l'ourse" (In the glimmer of the she-bear, an allusion to the "Grande Ourse," the Big Dipper), which he published in the second edition of the novel and which readers would do well to read in detail,‡ Jacques Simonelli explains all that this short book owes "to the Kabbalah, to the science of cycles, and to alchemy."

---

*With its 125 dead and hundreds of injured, this catastrophe was the result of a fire, according to Khaitzine (in volume 2 of his *Language of the Birds*), which was caused "by a movie projector, an invention still in its infancy, due to the misuse of a highly flammable product."

†L'Étoile is the name of this major "crossroads" in Paris where the Arc de Triomphe stands.

‡Jacques Simonelli, "A la lueur de l'ourse," afterword to Hillel-Erlanger, *Voyages en kaléidoscope*. It goes without saying that I owe a great due to this particularly in-depth study. Concerning this title, borrowed from a verse of Hillel-Erlanger, "we know," writes Josane Charpentier, "that the bear is the hieroglyph of the pole star in the constellation of the Petite Ourse [Little Bear, the Little Dipper]. This is the star on which all sailors keep their eyes fixed, the one that guides them across the seas. And the alchemists sometimes compared themselves to sailors, and they spoke of the alchemical labor as a dangerous voyage where storms would sometimes be encountered." She goes on to say, "the bear is the *virgin mineral*, the *mercury of the sages*, the true craftsman of the Great Work." Bernard Roger recalls in his book on the Seville Cathedral that Canseliet believed, "in the language of the poets, which is also that of the Gods, the bear designates the pole, the north star along which the Artist must fix his route." It is the "image of the pole Star, in other words the spiritual core of matter, often called sulfur."

Among other seldom explored avenues, he emphasizes the obvious influence on the work, then very little-known, of René Guénon. He also aptly compares the two female characters with *Chessed* (grace) and *Geburah* (strictness), two of the Sephiroth on the Tree of Life dear to many surrealists, especially Brauner. He even draws a comparison between Grace, veiled in black, and the *Schekina*, which according to Gabrielle Sed-Tajna* is none other than the receptive and passive female principle of the divine world—the feminine part of God. He recalls that "the *Schekina* is traditionally located in *Malkuth* (the Kingdom), the tenth Sefiroth, and thus simultaneously receives the influences of the pillar of Grace and that of Rigor." This provides a luminous explanation for the scene in which the two sisters confront each other, and that it's "this last aspect that Grace displays when revealing her dazzling diamond, whose paralyzing effect immediately precedes the explosion of the Kaleidoscope." It would not be ridiculous to compare this "dazzling diamond" to the flame-colored carbuncle of Jean de Meung's *Roman de la Rose*, the very same precious stone that Fulcanelli (in *The Dwellings of the Philosophers*) presented as "the hermetic gem, the philosopher's stone of the Great Work or Medicine of the ancient sages, still called Absolute, Little Coal, or Precious Carbuncle (*carbunculus*), the shining sun of our microcosm and the star of eternal sapience." "The divine carbuncle of the Sages," says Flamand, "shines like a sun at the heart of this source of life that is the Fountain of Youth!"

In 1976, Canseliet wrote on the original cover of Hillel-Erlanger's book (in issue 286 of *Atlantis*) drawn by the painter Kees Van Dongen,† based on his personal reading of the text: "Circles in transmission, the principles, which are salt, mercury and sulfur, or body, mind and soul, interact. . . . But now let's turn to Van Dongen's main composition.

---

*Gabrielle Sed-Tajna is the former head of the Hebrew section of the Institute of the History and Study of Texts of the CNRS (Centre National de la Recherche Scientifique).
†Kees Van Dongen (1877–1968), a French painter of Dutch descent, was depicted by Picabia in his *Caravansérail* in 1924 this way: "Van Dongen, the little giant with a rapacious appetite for worldly women, and who paints like others do card tricks."

The triangles that we see there, sitting on their bases on the top left, and upside down on their tips on the right, represent, some of them, fire and sulfur, the others water and mercury. This is not as ordinary elements and minerals, but as the fire, sulfur, and mercury of the sages."

The linear drawing connects these triangular symbols quite closely, giving us to understand that sulfur and mercury are threefold at this level of alchemy, and that each is given the appropriate label, in the corresponding phase: vulgar, common, and philosophical.[14]

Simonelli, for his part, completes this analysis by showing in particular that this cover, especially through the double appearance of the word *Kali*, contains clear allusions to the Iron Age, the famous Kali Yuga, which "has no other seal but that of *Death*,"[15] dear to the author of *The Symbolism of the Cross*, René Guénon. He adds a word that Canseliet compares to *Kalen,* for *galena*, "the name of the metallic sulfur often taken to designate the primal matter of the alchemical work [among other things]," but which he clearly reads as *Kali*, "one of the salts that play a role in the crafting of the secret fire of the sages,* the inner left circle of which, bearing the name of Gilly, shows the spagyric symbol."

It is in his conclusion, which is also mine on this subject, of a brief text (in *Paris and Alchemy*) on Irene Hillel-Erlanger's little book that Bernard Roger best draws attention to the questions it raises, such as

---

*"This is an energy that activates all matter and keeps it always at the same temperature. It is also called the fifth fire" (Kamala-Jnana, *Dictionnaire de philosophie alchimique,* Argentières, France: Editions G. Charlet, 1961). Behind the pseudonym of Kamala-Jnana hides most likely Roger Caro (1911–1992) the founder, in the sixties, of the "Initiatory Alchemical Temple of Ajunta," which in the seventies became the "Elder Brothers of the Rose Cross," then the "Universal Church of the New Covenant." With respect to this man, Ithell Colquhoun writes (in *Sword of Wisdom*): "Roger Caro, author of *Pléiade alchimique* (1967) and *Concordances alchimiques* (1968) has also published a colored photographic record of the Great Work in its different stages and is associated with a fraternity known as *Frères ainés de la Rose Croix* which operates two temples, the *Ajunta* and its offshoot, the *Vrehappada*. Their members are European adepts, some of whom have taken magical names in Sanskrit." She states that their teachings seem to have some theosophical inspiration and that their members "engage in practical as well as theoretical alchemy."

when he notes: "The precise clues of this hermetic riddle could only have been provided by an educated practitioner. They bear the stamp of an authentic child of science who for the first time in the history of alchemical literature preferred to draw her metaphors not from ancient mythology but from the characteristic myth of her era, that of the high society life during the roaring twenties and the technological aspects of the first quarter of our [the twentieth] century."

5

ANDRÉ BRETON, ALCHEMIST?

Did André Breton not poetically transmute Paris?
RENÉ ALLEAU, "AU PERISCOPE DU TEMPS"

Clearly, Jacques Van Lennep was fully justified in emphasizing "the community of intention between [these] two great testimonies of human thought" and even in considering alchemy as "a gnosis that contains the seed of the spirit of surrealism." He even went so far as to write in his book *Art et alchimie*[1] (which didn't fail to catch the attention of some of Breton's friends*), "one of the most convincing proofs of alchemy's survival is undoubtedly its fundamental influence on this group, many artistic and philosophical designs of which it endorsed." He then went on to say, "The writings of André Breton reveal more than allusions to the hermetic art and on reading them, we are forced to conclude that the approaches of surrealism are in no way foreign to alchemical concerns." Richard Danier was even able to devote a book on *L'hermétisme alchimique chez André Breton*[2] in which he cites a letter of Canseliet dated December 1971 in which he wrote: "Alchemy, as you know, remains above all poetry, and it was inevitable that the ancient science of Hermes should deeply seduce

---

*But not the author of *Arcane 17*, as this book came out in the last trimester of 1966. (Breton died on September 28, 1966—*trans.*)

90

the author of *L'étoile scellée*," while René Alleau, in "Le mystérieux livre d'heure du rêve d'Elisa," indicates, "The influence of the classical texts of alchemy, already glimpsed in a perceptive stylistic analysis by Michel Beaujour (*André Breton et la transparence*[3]), is undeniable. This has been confirmed by S. Lamy,[4] as well as more recently in *André Breton, explorateur de la Mère Moire, Trois lectures d'Arcane 17, texte palimpseste* (Paris: P.U.F., 1986) by Pascaline Mourier-Casile."

I should not fail to note, in passing, that the Master of Savignies thought it worth mentioning in this letter the name of the small gallery opened on Sophie Babet's initiative at number 11 "on the friendly rue du Pré aux Clercs," in Saint Germain. Breton became the gallery's artistic advisor, which gave him full freedom to defend, in the rather tense postwar atmosphere of Paris, those painters who rejected "the realist regression in art" as well as the "danger of dissolving into an abstraction the authenticity of which was ever less verifiable."[5] It was René Alleau, with whom the Surrealists had recently joined forces, who proposed (as Renée Mabin points out) "to place the gallery under the sign of Alchemy," first of all [to] refer to all those extraordinary images that illustrated the treatises and posed a challenge to the interpreters of our time," but also to "evoke a secret language with analogies to poetry," not to mention the polysemy, not devoid of connections with the *language of the birds*, of this name that can also be read "*Ah, les toiles, c'est laid* [Ah, the canvases, that's ugly]," "which humorously reminds us that surrealism was not a cult of beauty."[6] In the context that interests us here, we should also mention the exhibition of Toyen's works that Breton organized there in 1953 especially as a number of them, perhaps in memory of Gold Alley in Hradčany, were inspired by the alchemical emblems of old Prague: *At the Gold Tree, At the Black Sun, At the Golden Wheel . . .*"

More anecdotally, but nonetheless significantly, we can note Breton's enduring interest, in connection with his fascination with the "admirable fourteenth century,"* in Nicolas Flamel, "one of the great accelerators

---

*"The golden century of Alchemy," Carrouges rightly notes when he quotes this phrase from the manifesto in his book, *André Breton et les données fondamentales du surréalisme*.

of the imagination,"* but who, as Frédéric Tristan said, "may" have "intrigued him. . . from a perspective that was more poetic than really hermetic,"† as well as his enduring attraction to that "great monument of the world of the unrevealed,"[7] the Tour Saint-Jacques, "that hotbed of alchemy to which we know that the millennial dream of transmutation was tied,"‡ as it was also tied to Prague, the "magical capital of old Europe,"[8] the city of Rudolph II , the emperor of the alchemists.

In this regard, Flamel and the Tour Saint-Jacques, this "staggering Tour Saint-Jacques," "the "veritable archetype of the tower of alchemical transmutations,"[9] whose ties with alchemy are beyond question, exercised a singular attraction on the surrealists and their close kin, beginning with Joris-Karl Huysmans. In his 1899 book *Gilles de Rais*, he had already noted that in the flamboyant fifteenth century, "the hermetic center of France was in Paris where the alchemists met beneath the vaults of Notre Dame and studied the hieroglyphs of the Charnel House of the Innocents and the portal of Saint-Jacques-de-la-Boucherie, on which Nicolas Flamel had written, in kabbalistic emblems, the preparation of the famous stone" (see plates 13 and 14). There was also Apollinaire, who had undoubtedly read the novel dedicated to the "son of science" by his friend Léo Larguier.[10] Breton himself even described "the two plates . . . which are said to have adorned the book of Abraham the Jew and which appeared in *Documents*."** He spoke of them at length in the *Second Manifesto*, told the story of a nocturnal stroll in *L'amour fou* (*Mad Love*) with "the ambassadress of saltpeter" around this monument

---

*Henri Béhar, ed., *Dictionnaire André Breton*. For Didier Kahn, however, in "Nicolas Flamel alchimiste?," his afterword to the republication of this individual's *Écrits alchimiques* (Paris: Les Belles Lettres, 2007), his status as an Adept would be merely a myth.

†In his interviews with Olivier Gissey in *Frédéric Tristan: L'appel de l'Orient intérieur*.

‡Jacques Van Lennep, *Art et alchimie*. He borrowed the expression "millennial dream of transmutation" from *Arcane 17*.

**But as Marguerite Bonnet, Etienne-Alain Hubert, and José Pierre, the authors of the critical apparatus on the *Second Manifesto* in the Pléiade edition, put it, "by cutting the end of the text about the first plate which refers to the *Massacre of the innocents*, he reinforces . . . the impression of mystery of the scene," dramatizes and suppresses "every alchemical interpretation of the figures."

and chose Brassai's famous photo (dating from 1932–1933) to illustrate it, then placed it at the very center of the "Ajours" of *Arcane 17*. We also have Michel Leiris who spoke of it in *Aurora*, as well as Elie-Charles Flamand who dedicated a small pamphlet to it in 1990.[11] Not to mention René Alleau, who titled his preface of the *Book of Hieroglyphic Figures* in his Bibliotheca Hermetica "Nicolas Flamel and Surrealism!" Or of course, Bernard Roger, who in *Paris and Alchemy* mentions this "last vestige of Saint-Jacques-de-la-Boucherie, against which the writer had his corner shop: the Tour Saint-Jacques, an immense sign for the eye and the ear, constructed between 1508 and 1522 at the crossroads of the Parisian *cardo* and the east-west overland route that mirrored the river's path. It was at the foot of this monument that generations of pilgrims would gather for their journey to Compostela!"

In any case, a quick glance at the titles in André Breton's library is particularly telling. There are some classics of alchemical literature, sometimes very old editions, such as a 1612 edition of *Le miroir d'alquimie de Jean de Mehun, philosophe très excellent*, Solomon Trismosin's *La toison d'or* (expanded French edition of 1612), and "Philippi Mulleri's" *Miracula chymica et mysteria medica* (1651). He also owned a rare edition of Michael Maier's *Scrutinium chymicum* (1687), and the *Histoire critique de Nicolas Flamel et de Pernelle, sa femme*, the monograph by Etienne-François Villain in the original 1761 edition published by G. Desprez. Others were translated and introduced or analyzed by more or less famous figures of the *Belle Epoque*, such as the *Histoire comique des états et empires de la lune et du soleil* by Cyrano de Bergerac published by Delagrave in 1886,* the *Étude sur Nicolas Flamel* by T. Calderon, published by Chastanier Printers in Nimes in 1888, *Cinq traités d'alchimie (Paracelse, Albert le Grand, Roger Bacon, R. Lulle, Arnaud de Villeneuve): Précédés de la table d'emeraude*, all in a translation by Alfred Poisson for Chacornac in 1890, and the translation by Louis Ménard of the writings attributed to Hermes Trismegistus, published by the Librarie

---

*A work for which Breton compiled six pages of manuscript notes that appear in it.

académique Perrin in 1910. After the war, we find *Le pimandre d'Hermès Trismégiste* (Paris: Editions Sirènes, 1920), and *La monade hiéroglyphique* by John Dee, in the translation by Grillot de Givry (Chacornac, 1925).* Another book by Grillot was also present, his *Musée des sorciers, mages et alchimistes* (Paris: Librairie de France, 1929).† He also owned *Les noces chymiques de Christian Rosencreutz* by "Jean-Valentin Andreae," "with a foreword and alchemical commentary by Aurifer," in other words Georges Richer! But he also had Paracelsus's *Prognostication* published in 1933 (again by Chacornac) with a study by Gaston Baissette, and the 1939 book by Robert Ambelain, *Dans l'ombre des cathédrales*, subtitled *Étude sur l'ésotérisme architectural et décoratif de Notre-Dame de Paris dans ses rapports avec le symbolisme hermétique, les doctrines secrètes, l'astrologie, la magie et l'alchimie* (Editions Adyar, connected to the Theosophical Society). After his return from the United States, Breton added to his library a *Trésor hermétique* published by Paul Derain in Lyon in 1942, a book containing the *Mutus Liber* with an introduction by Marc Haven (Dr. Emmanuel Delalande), one of the Compagnons of the Hiérophanie, as well as the *Traité symbolique de la pierre philosophale*, in sixty-eight figures on nineteen plates by Johann Conrad Barchusen‡ with a foreword by Paul Servant, to which the surrealist poet had made corrections. We also find *The Alchemists* by F. Sherwood Taylor (London: Heinemann, 1949), *Jacques Coeur* by Henri de Man (Paris, Bourges: Editions Tardy, 1951), and *Le codicille de Raymond Lulle,* in a translation of Léonce Bouyssou,

---

*In his book on René Alleau, Gilles Bucherie explains that this thinker had "an enigmatic relationship with the work of Grillot de Givry (1874–1929), taken as a source of intellectual and editorial inspiration."

†Which Breton discussed with Elie-Charles Flamand when they first met.

‡In this book, republished with an introduction by Dr. Marc Haven, under the title of *Trésor hermétique*, including the *Livre d'images sans paroles (Mutus Liber)*, are found descriptions and depictions of all the operations of Hermetic philosophy. Along with the *Traité symbolique de la pierre philosophale*, in seventy-eight figures, by Jean Conrad Barchusen, reissued for the first time with a note by Paul Servant, and a translation of his *Elementa Chimiae quibus subjuncta est confectura lapidis philosophici imaginibus repraesentata,* published in Leyden in 1718.

that was published by the Editions de la Haute Science in 1953, probably at the instigation of Amadou, who in the same year published his *Raymond Lulle et l'alchimie* with the same publisher. Breton's copy bears his dedication, which reads: "to Monsieur André Breton who seeks the Philosopher's Stone, with the admiration and deep respect of Robert Amadou!" An Amadou who was quite productive that year, as we also find on the author of *Nadja*'s bookshelves another book he published that year, *La poudre de sympathie* (Nizet) on "magnetic" medicine. Not to mention, of course, Fulcanelli's two books and his disciple's *Deux logis alchimiques*, in the 1945 Jean Schemit edition (with press clipping on Canseliet titled by Breton), the Edition de Minuit publication of Canseliet's translation of Basil Valentine's *Twelve Keys of Philosophy*, with a dedication, as well as *Alchimie—Études diverses de symbolisme hermétique et de pratique philosophale* (Paris: Jean-Jacques Pauvert, 1964). Finally, the *Anthologie de la poésie hermétique* by Claude d'Ygé (Paris: Editions Montbrun, 1948) completes the picture.

This influence of the Royal Art would only deepen over the years, and it is highly likely that when Breton wrote, in *Arcanum 17*, that "Osiris is a *black god*," he was clearly alluding to Fulcanelli, who also recalls this warning of the Egyptian priests to their new initiates. Fulcanelli went on saying the priests added: "This is the symbolical color of the shades and the *Cimmerian shadows*, the color of Satan, to whom *black roses* were offered. It is also the color of primitive *Chaos*, in which the seeds of all things are confused and mixed."[12] If this is the sentence the surrealist had in mind when he wrote his book in 1944, it also means that he knew the works of the Great Adept before he met Maurice Baskine, despite his claim that he introduced Fulcanelli's works to Breton. Patrick Rivière, for his part, asserts that it was in fact "Sarane Alexandrian who, in his *History of Occult Philosophy,* boasts of having introduced Fulcanelli's works . . . to André Breton who in his everyday magic verified the *alchemical perception* of the poet, as the good Master of Savignies stated in no uncertain terms."[13] But here again there is a small problem with the date because when Breton was writing *Arcanum 17* on the Gaspé peninsula, Alexandrian, according to his official biography, was in the Limousin region of France! In any case, it was still alchemy about which the author of the *Manifestos* spoke with the young Philippe Sollers during their first meeting on April 26, 1960. Van Lennep tells us that Breton owned a variant of the *Eighth Key of Basil Valentine*, printed on silk from the end of the eighteenth century.* Pierre Mabille, another high profile surrealist, also cites a passage from Basil Valentine, "the charitable cenobite of Erfut"† and "prestigious adept who did not scorn spagyric trials,"[14] in a presentation targeting the uninitiated in his *Mirror of the Marvelous*.[15] In the preface, "Draw Bridges," that he contributed to the book's posthumous republication in 1962 by Editions de Minuit, Breton, for whom Mabille was (in Hermetic matters) one of the principal initiators, stressed that fact that this disciple of the great Nostradamus expert,‡ occultist Pierre Vincenti Piobb (1874–1942),

---

*Jacques Van Lennep, "L'art alchimique et le surréel." It is worth asking if this might not be the same work that Canseliet spoke of in these words in his commentary on the "Ninth figure" and therefore ninth key of Basil Valentine that Van Lennep is in fact alluding to when he writes: "André Breton has pointed out a very beautiful reproduction of the mineral couple in the achieving of its philosophical and sensational acrobatics. It's a seventeenth-century painting on silk, in which the swirling, human hieroglyph, fixed for an instant above the circle, gives shape, with it, to the ball of the world, but in a magnificent countryside décor." And Fulcanelli's disciple continues, "The fourth issue of *Médium* (January 1955) offers an excellent snapshot of this exceptional work of art."

†Eugene Canseliet, "Philosophie universelle et spirituelle filiation," in *L'Alchimie* by E. J. Holmyard. According to Kurt Seligmann, however, the writings attributed to Basil Valentine are likely from the seventeenth century and "probably due to the hand of J. Thölde from Frankenhausen in Thuringia." However, Paul Sanda believes that "there were several authors not one writing under the pseudonym of Basil Valentine" and that "it was visibly German disciples of Paracelsus who invented this figure to compel others to believe that their Master's ideas about antimony and the occult properties of metals were already supported by a Benedictine." He added that "the detractors of Paracelsus concluded from this that he had plagiarized Basil Valentine" (Sanda, *Le Labyrinthe hermétique*).

‡When we know of the ties—at least intellectual ones—that existed between Pierre Mabille and René Alleau, it seems worth noting that the first printed work by Alleau was his 1947 study of Nostradamus. Both men, as Jean-Claude Bailly writes in a note on the public auction of Alleau's library, shared a strong interest in geomancy. In the same spirit, we can note that in the Pierre Mabille collection of the Jacques Doucet literary library, there is a *Treatise on Geomancy* (shelf mark MAB Ms 68), a sixty-seven-page manuscript in which a certain name crops up repeatedly, the name of Maurice Baskine (see chapter 14).

had "indicated several times [how much] he owed everything he said to alchemy, in which this scheme is inscribed like a watermark." This again strengthens the feeling that interest in the Art of Music was shared widely by surrealists of all generations.

Revisiting his text on Basil Valentine, which I think is worth citing at length, Mabille shares his specific vision of alchemy and the philosopher's stone:

For man, true conquest does not consist in establishing an ephemeral power over his fellows, but in mastering the elements. "Visit the Interior of the Earth to surprise its secrets." This is one of the basic precepts of the ancient masters. Let us go with them to discover the stone, which is at once the symbol of learning, the hidden scheme of the world, and the necessary material for the Great Work. What does that mean to the hermeticists? The Great Work is something that nature accomplishes every day when it draws various metals and species out of chaos. Each of the metals corresponds to a period of evolution, culminating in the most perfect among them: gold, immutable and precious. Each of the species is a step toward man, the perfect animal. Each individual represents a transitory form that is meant to resemble the prototypical man, who in turn resembles God, possessing His purity, power, and eternal nature. But whoever possesses the stone and its secret can make these slow processes happen at will. He can bring metals into being before their time and cure diseases that are only weaknesses and imperfections. This total science is what Brother Basil Valentine of the Order of Saint Benedict discusses in the *Twelve Keys of the Clavicle of the Precious Stone of the ancient philosophers*,* a work which he goes on to say in a footnote "is one of the most important in hermetic literature." Then in another footnote, Mabille (thus demonstrating the extent of his knowledge of esoteric matters), ventures a hypothesis about

---

*This is most likely the 1600 work *The Twelve Keys of Philosophy*.

Valentinius, the founder of one of the many second-century Gnostic cults in Egypt, concerning the name of this hermeticist that today in fact is considered to be a pseudonym "concealing collective works," born "from a timeless tradition." Nor does he neglect to mention that "Basil means king and that Valentine means the strength and potency of the universal medicine."*

To continue, weren't these Surrealists in fact inviting people to take an interest in the "Art of Music" when they wrote on one of their pamphlets that they distributed in the twenties: "You who have lead in your head, melt it down to make surrealist gold?"† In this regard, it is quite interesting to note that, testifying to a widely shared interest in the group for this subject, Robert Desnos, in 1929, as evidence of the group's widespread interest in this subject, published a well-known article on the *Book of Abraham the Jew*, attributed to Flamel,[16] in which he asks: "Wouldn't the rue Saint Martin, parallel to the Milky Way, be a fragment of the great road from Flanders to Compostela? Flamel's house on the rue des Escrivains was right next to it, and the Rues Flamel and Pernelle, which cut through its approximate location, not far from the Tour-Saint-Jacques-de-la-Boucherie, are the daughters of this route, which skirts the immense alchemical monument that is Notre Dame de Paris." For good measure, he continues: "You have to have lived in this part of Paris to experience the sulfurous smell of magic spells that emanates from its muddy streets and gutters!" Now 1929 is the exact year in which Breton, in his *Second Surrealist Manifesto*, at the same time that he proclaimed the necessity of occulting surrealism, explicitly

---

*In words very close to those used by Canseliet in his introduction to the *Twelve Keys*, Jacques Sadoul, in *Le trésor des alchimistes* (Editions Publications Premières, 1970), confirms: "It is obvious that Basil Valentine was a pseudonym. *Basileus* in Greek means king, *Valens* (*Valentis*) in Latin means powerful." Incidentally, like Flamel, Basil Valentine, "also" writes Canseliet, and these are his italics, "*owner and master of the star*," made the pilgrimage of Saint James of Compostela.

†This is an untranslatable play on words: *avoir du plomb dans la tête* ("to have lead in your head") means "to have a good head on one's shoulders"—*trans.*

stated, "I would appreciate your noting the remarkable analogy, insofar as their goals are concerned, between the Surrealist efforts and those of the alchemists: the philosopher's stone is nothing more or less than that which was to enable man's imagination to take a stunning revenge on all things, which brings us once again, after centuries of the mind's domestication and insane resignation, to the attempt to liberate once and for all the imagination by the 'long, immense, reasoned derangement of the senses,' and all the rest." Especially, when we consider with Van Lennep that this philosopher's stone is "nothing less than the soul of the world!"

If, according to this same author, it was Pierre Mabille, the surrealist most involved with esotericism, who was the first to take an interest in "the most original and the most admirable book of emblems of its time,"* Maier's *Atalanta Fugiens*, it's to Breton (who Canseliet described as "amazingly endowed with alchemical perception") that we owe a review of the "emblems engraved by Mathieu Merian" when he said they were "the most decisive touchstone of all one could wish for in art as a leap into understanding the mystery."[17] He would also cite this book in *L'art magique*. Then in the 1941 text, *On the Survival of Certain Myths and on Some Other Myths in Growth or Formation*, which carries the embryonic spirit of postwar surrealism, he dedicates a page to "the Philosopher's Stone." Here we can read the famous quote that ends the fifth part of *Mad Love*: "On the flank of the abyss, built from philosopher's stone, opens the Star Castle," placed between an "alchemical vignette, most certainly reproduced from Albert Poisson's anthology *Cinq traités d'alchimie des plus grands philosophes* [Five Alchemical Treatises of the Greatest Philosophers], (Chacornac, 1890, page 75), much used by Breton, where it figures at the beginning of the translation of Paracelsius's *The Treasure of Treasures for Alchemists*)" and a "composition on paper by Matta," entitled "on the other side: *La Pierre philosophale, Telesona du soleil et de la lune (foyers de peur)*."[18]

---

*Jörg Völlnagel, *Alchimie, l'art royal*. This author describes *L'Atalanta Fugiens* as "a total work of art before the fact."

The poetic beauty of this phrase could not conceal its esoteric meaning from Richard Danier. In the book[19] in which he unravels the alchemical thread running through Breton's three great narratives, he explains that the "Star Castle of Prague" to which this phrase directly alludes, and which appears as a caption on one of the photographs accompanying the text, is a representation of the Seal of Solomon, "two crossed equilateral triangles, one pointing upwards (fire, evolution) and the other pointing downwards (water, involution), symbolizing the union of the two principles, as well as that of the macrocosm and the microcosm." This "six-pointed star" in which "two elements are each represented by a triangle," when "correctly interpreted . . . yields the stone," because "the stone is the Star of Solomon," as Canseliet says in *Le feu du soleil* (The fire of the sun). Danier also sees in it "the symbol of the quintessence, the Star of the Mages," this "figure radiating in six points (*digamma*)" according to Fulcanelli, "which radiates on the surface of the compost," and stands as "proof of the poet's complete permeation by the Royal Art."

To show the whole picture, I must also point out that in order to illustrate in the same pamphlet (the main theme of which is the *Grands Transparents*), Breton uses a "figure of the wind borrowed from Michael Maier's classic *Atalanta Fugiens*." Etienne-Alain Hubert continues: "This emblem in Maier accompanies the commentary of a phrase from the *Emerald Tablet*, 'the wind has carried it in its belly' (hence the image of the child in the belly)," adding significantly, "Nothing here makes reference to the classic alchemical interpretation, discovering in this formulation the idea that sulfur is carried by quicksilver, in other words mercury, *silence that gives food for thought on the type of interest that Breton had in alchemy at the time*." (These are my italics!)

Nevertheless Canseliet still reveals that "André Breton certainly knew Alexandre-Toussaint Limojon de Saint-Didier's *Hermetic Triumph* well, from which he took the highly philosophical idea for his Surrealist exhibition [from 1947], especially that of forcing its visitors to trample through the sand of a narrow passage into a cavernous labyrinth. I deliberately repeat here Limojon's image: "Our practice is indeed a path through the sand, through which we must be guided by the North Star rather than by the traces whose marks can be seen there."*

An itinerary of initiatory inspiration," says Marie-Claire Dumas in her note on the subject of "Behind the Curtain."[20] No better illustration of alchemy's occult influence on Breton's thought could be highlighted!

We also know that in the 1948 text "Fronton virage" on Jean Ferry's study of Raymond Roussel, "an exegesis," which, according to Canseliet, is "magnificent, erudite, and decisive," Breton superimposes, as shown by Marie-Claire Dumas, "an esoteric interpretation broadly inspired by Fulcanelli," whom he mentions many times,† to his friend's analysis— while describing in passing the Adept as "the highest modern authority in this regard."

In this important text, Breton also refers to the *language of the birds* (or the *universal language*). This is the "Gay Sçavoir," according to Elie-Charles Flamand, the "hermetic Cabale" dear to the alchemists and updated by René Alleau in 1953. It is that "phonetic idiom based entirely on assonance" that Fulcanelli speaks about in both *The Mystery of the Cathedrals*‡ and in *The Dwellings of the Philosophers*—but also in

---

*Eugène Canseliet, *L'alchimie expliquée*. Limojon's quote, which is the subject of a footnote, comes from the "Lettre aux vrais disciples d'Hermès," which ends *Le triomphe hermétique*.

†No less than eleven direct citations from *The Dwellings of the Philosophers*.

‡In which he writes: "Finally I would add that *argot* (cant) is one of the forms derived from the *Language of the Birds*, parent and doyen of all other languages—the one spoken by philosophers and *diplomats*. . . . This is the language which teaches the mystery of things and unveils the most hidden truths. The ancient Incas called it the Court Language, because it was used by diplomats. To them it was the key to *a double science*, sacred and profane. In the Middle Ages it was called the *Gay Science* and the *Gay Knowledge, the Language of the Gods*, the *Dive-Bouteille*. Tradition assures us that men spoke it before the building of the Tower of Babel, which event caused this sacred language to be perverted and to be totally forgotten by the greater part of humanity." The italics and capital letters are Fulcanelli's.

his text on the cyclical Cross of Hendaye* in which he directly alludes to the rules of this famous "Diplomatique" dear to Grasset d'Orcet†—and about which he deemed wise to specify that "it's important to bear in mind that this language is essentially of kabbalistic necessity." He continues even more explicitly: "We have recourse to it in order to disguise such communication that we wish to reach certain privileged individuals while misleading the common mortal." He goes on to admit, "The cabala has indeed always been of great use to us. It has allowed us, without falsifying the truth, without falsifying expression, without falsifying science, and without perjuring ourselves, to say several things that one would seek in vain to find in the books of our predecessors."

While René Alleau, for whom "this 'language of the gods,' known to the ancients and unknown to the moderns, is essential for deciphering the riddles of pagan or Christian sacerdotal art," believes that "it was named like this from the Greek *diplomantiké tekné*" and assigns it "the task of discovering or rather divining a '*diplosemantos* or *diplosemos*' double meaning,"[21] for Vincent Bounoure it remains "the best style of teaching, the only one capable of making the attentive reader understand the chaos of the beginning." According to Elie-Charles Flamand, it's "a way of reading books that reveals hidden references of a hermetic

---

*This text was added by Canseliet to the second edition of *The Mystery of the Cathedrals,* and which would be, so it's said, an extract salvaged from the vanished manuscript, *Finis gloriae mundi.*

†Claude-Sosthène Grasset d'Orcet (1828–1900), a "scholar and ironic lexicographer," for Khaitzine, journalist, archaeologist, and important figure of French occultism, for whom "*Diplomatique*" was like the language of the birds. Fulcanelli, Canseliet, and some others cite him, and Peladan plagiarizes him. "One of the great merits of Grasset d'Orcet is that he decoded this diplomatic language, which until the nineteenth century was commonly used to transport these guarded truths. Unfortunately, while he gives us the main keys here and there, he doesn't hide the fact that this secret grimoire, based on puns, amphibologies and approximations in Old French [*langue d'oil*], is very difficult for the modern reader to unravel," says Jean-Pierre Deloux in "Grasset d'Orcet, l'hermétisme inconnu," his preface to *L'histoire secrète de l'Europe,* vol. 1 (Paris: Editions E-dite, 2000). Philippe G. Kerbellec, in his book *Comment lire Raymond Roussel, cryptanalyse* (Paris: Pauvert, 1988), claims that Grasset d'Orcet is Fulcanelli.

nature" and "in order to make their message emerge, we must have recourse in these texts to homophony, puns, anagrams, and other word games, and for the images, to decoding procedures similar to those applied to rebuses, emblems, allegories, logogriphs and other blazons, canting arms and old shop signs."[22] With regard to "Diplomatique", for which "the Sons of Science," according to him, "found the etymology in διπλοος, double, and μαθημα, science," he offers an explanation for it "as the procedure that makes it possible, in a conciliatory synthesis, to give two meanings—and often many more—to images and emblems." This lets us clearly see the proximity between the two notions! Bernard Roger, meanwhile, states (in the interview with Jacques Carletto cited earlier), "The language of the birds is something very important in the study of alchemy." "In fact," he adds, "we call it the language of the birds because birds fly from one tree to another. In the language of the birds, we leave one word, a sound that exists in the context of a grammar, but if that grammar is removed and the sound is kept and sent into another context, we have a completely different meaning!" He then warns, "This cannot go unrecognized by one who would profitably tread the paths of Hermes." So true is it that this *deeply moving* language, which has more than once eclipsed the *identity principle* upon which our overly proud logic rests," is the *"universal language,"* the *"horse tongue, cabala, language of the gods, argot"* which the adepts have used throughout the ages "in the writing of their works" and which "carries with it the essential, ever living elements of the *oral* teaching of alchemy." He also explains in this interview, "It is also called *argot, horse tongue, phonetic cabala* because the horse takes its rider somewhere else. In one jump it goes from one place to another. It's the same with language: we go from one mental place to another mental place. It is a way of taking the imagination on a journey." He concludes by saying: "As far removed from scientific discourse as the scientific language of our contemporaries," this *language of nature* "seems much closer to music, where the same note can take on very different values depending on the instrument that produces it, the chord, the melody or the rhythm."[23]

"This language, he says with his friend Camacho in their book on the Cathedral of Seville, "makes constant use of wordplay, puns, rebuses and words that are roughly phonetically similar, allowing us to perceive a hidden meaning when we hear a word or a phrase, where the word is pronounced but carried by the sound of syllables that are heard and linked differently." They then complete this presentation by comparing it to the alchemical process itself: A process in which the message sent by the literal sentence is simultaneously destroyed and a new message is reconstructed. We can translate this process by saying that "the body of the first message is evaporated in the spirit of the sound, while this spirit is fixed in the second message." "We therefore find," they conclude, "that the injunction concerning the central operation in the practice of the Great Work is thus applied to the realm of language."[24]

And "too bad," concludes Marie-Dominique Massoni in her afterword, "Le lai des étoiles" to Bernard Roger's *Demeures de l'invisible*, "for those who don't understand that cheap puns sometimes open the door to a yawning gap, to the absolute divergence, or that the language of birds is a coded language, because one does not enter the closed palace of the king without warning."

Notwithstanding the fact that, as Josane Carpentier reminds us, *"the language of the birds* is the real language of the Earthly Paradise, reached by those philosophers who found the stone,"* truly the "language of the Gods," *Nadja's* author suggests that practically all of Roussel's works, but also some texts of Jean-Pierre Brisset, Duchamp, the Desnos of *Rose Sélavy*, and the Leiris of *Glossaire: J'y serre mes gloses* are perhaps also tied to this "hermetic cabala" mentioned in general terms[25] in the second volume of Fulcanelli's *Dwellings*.† This

---

*"Garden of the Golden Age," Bernard Roger writes in "Le jour de l'etoile," "of which it was never said that it would remain inaccessible to humanity." It's also the *pardès* of Fulcanelli.

†Consider this passage in particular: "In addition to its purely alchemical role, the Cabala has been used in the creation of several literary masterpieces which many dilettantes can appreciate without suspecting what treasures they hide beneath the

is especially true if we keep in mind the definition given by Alleau in his *Aspects de l'alchimie traditionnelle* (where he also calls it "horse tongue"): "A chain of associations of notions implied in language itself, illuminating the unconscious and superconscious zones of language."[26] He completed this observation a few years later: "The 'language of the birds' of antiquity, the hermetic jargon of the initiates, taught by the coat of arms in its best, primarily in the thirteenth century, the medieval Enlightenment, which then came from the East."[27] But it is probably also helpful to cite this observation as a kind of warning: "It is virtually impossible not to take it into account when analyzing esoteric doctrines, which are expressed under the veil of a secret language, a veritable jargon that must be understood without being stopped by the letter of the texts. Of course, the great danger of the *phonetic cabala** remains delusional interpretations and the arbitrary nature of unwarranted comparisons, but, used prudently, it constitutes one of the most effective keys to an intuitive understanding of the meaning of the traditional teaching."

Not to be overlooked is what Bernard Roger said, using analogies about "The Day of the Star": "If the *horseman*, partially freed from the

---

(cont.d) attractiveness, the charm, the nobility of style. This is because the authors—whether their names are Homer, Virgil, Ovid, Plato, Dante, or Goethe—were all great initiates. They wrote their immortal works not so much to bequeath to posterity imperishable monuments of the human genius, but to instruct it in the sublime knowledge of which they were the repositories and which they had to transmit in their entirety. This is the way we should judge, in addition to the masters already mentioned, the marvelous artisans of chivalrous poems, jokes, etc., belonging to the cycle of the *Round Table* and of the *Grail*; the works of Francois Rabelais and the ones by De Cyrano Bergerac; *Don Quixote* by Miquel Cervantes; *Gulliver's Travels* by Swift; the *Dream of Polyphilus* by Francisco Colonna; the *Tales of Mother Goose* by Perrault; the *Songs of the King of Navarre* by Thibault de Champagne; *The Devil as a Predicator*, a curious Spanish book of which we do not know the author, and many other books which, albeit less famous, are not lesser in interest nor in knowledge."

*"The phonetic cabala," Canseliet writes in his "Introductory Thoughts" to *Héraldique alchimique nouvelle* "in which no rule counts, except the one that wants consonance to be as perfect as possible. There, in a few words, lies the whole secret of a key that is surely that of the universal language."

attraction that holds man to the ground, can quickly cross plains and hills, the *cabalist* can similarly transcend the logical rules of grammar and syntax and connect in a single line ideas and objects that are normally the most distant, salt [*sel*] with sky [*ciel*] and star [*étoile*] with the web [*toile*] spun by the spider with the cast-iron body." "'Dissolve and coagulate' advise the disciples of Hermes," he concludes, "this saying whose application in the mineral realm holds every promise, is no less important in that of language."[28] In addition to all this Canseliet himself makes the following remarks on "the edifying images of Hermetic philosophy": "Iconographic language is also the language spoken by the birds, which is the expression of the phonetic cabala and is no less described as *auditory* by Nicholas Flamel in his *Book of Hieroglyphic Figures*, in which he gives some details about his journey to Santiago de Compostela. This language was used by Rabelais, Francisco Colonna,* Cyrano Bergerac [*sic*],† Jonathan Swift, then revealed by Grasset d'Orcet and, finally practically popularized by the Adept Fulcanelli, who gave a brief definition."‡ The understanding shared by these last two individuals was moreover recalled by Canseliet in the chapter "Language and the Hermetic Cabala" in his *Alchemy Explained through its Classic Texts*, in which he states that "we should not be surprised at the extent to

---

*Regarding the relationship between Swift, Rabelais, and Colonna, Canseliet in chapter four of his book *L'alchimie expliquée sur ses textes classiques* suggests that while we cannot be certain that "the dean of Saint Patrick's was influenced by the *Lanternois* puns of François Rabelais," "it is . . . probable that the larger-than-life beneficiary of the Meudon vicarage was probably indebted to Francesco Colonna, the monk who wrote the famous *Dream of Poliphili*."

†Fulcanelli was the first to rebaptize the Adept Cyrano de Bergerac (the author of *The Other World or the States and Empires of Moon and Sun*) like this, the "libertine" (in the seventeenth-century sense of the word, meaning a kind of freethinker) and close friend of the philosopher Gassendi (1592–1655) to distinguish him from how Edmond Rostand portrayed him in his famous play.

‡Eugène Canseliet, "Propos luminaire," in Josane Charpentier, *La France des lieux et des demeures alchimiques*. Swift, "the singular dean of Saint Patrick's," said the Master Alchemist in his second preface to *The Mystery of the Cathedrals* about a man who "fully understood and practiced, in his own way," the language of the birds.

which the Master covers the *language of the birds*, for he knew Grasset d'Orcet!"

At this point, and after all these learned explanations, it is now easy to understand that between the alchemy of the word preached by Rimbaud and then by the surrealists and the language of the birds dear to the celestial farmers, there is only a step, the very small step that separates high poetry from the Art of Music.

But what is most striking in Breton's text is the postulate, based on the intuitions expressed by Jean Ferry in what would later become *A Study of Raymond Roussel* (Editions Arcanes, 1953), that he first formulates about *The Dust of Suns*.* Roussel was deliberately concealing something, "something profound and inestimable!" Showing evidence of a precise knowledge of what can and cannot be done in this field, unless he is benefiting from the opinion of a particularly well-informed advisor,† Breton, in fact, states, duly supported by the writings dictated by the Master Alchemist to Canseliet on "the secret teaching whose most sincere seekers have never attempted to reveal the elements" and which "the investigator" must "acquire" by "personal effort," "*that Raymond Roussel, at least in this case, endeavored to give us the rudiments necessary to the achievement of what the alchemists call the Great Work, and that he did so, after so many others, in the only way traditionally allowed.*" (Breton's italics.) Canseliet would later write (in the introductory remarks for *Two Alchemical Abodes*, though in words that

---

*In *Les méandres du sens*, Elie-Charles Flamand reminds us that "in Raymond Roussel's *La poussière des soleils*, in which André Breton found an alchemical framework beneath the fantasy story of a treasure hunt that served as its plot," appears in the eighth tableau of Act II, "an imaginary letter from Honoré d'Urfé . . . like a marker whose decoder admits not to have found the meaning." "As for me," Flamand continues, "I see here an allusion to the necessity of completing the Work when the *Astrea* reigns." "This noun," he adds, "forever associated with the name of Honoré d'Urfé also means, kabbalistically speaking, all the stars, those thousands of little *suns* that spread a *dust* that is none other than the *heavenly dew* that must be made to act on the latescent sea of the Sages."

†"It is true," Patrick Rivière notes in his "André Breton: Soleil noir et main de feu," that in hermetic matters, "André BRETON could not be any more prolix than he was in 'Fronton Virage.'"

might have disturbed Breton to some extent although they had the same opinion about the alchemical content of Raymond Roussel's book, *The Dust of Suns*): "Its title is singular, and expresses, in my opinion, the extreme division of the philosophical gold which is the star of the wise and of true poets, and of which each particle, like the host of the Latin Catholic mass of yesteryear, remains, despite every fracture, Christ and the Sun in their entirety."

In any case, with this "convincing survey of an unsuspected exegesis," Breton supported by *The Dwellings of the Philosophers*, enumerates everything evocative of alchemy in the play and shows Roussel "moving toward the crafting of the Great Work or at least toward its symbolic representation."[29] The result, to say the least, is edifying!* From the *skull* to the *dragon*, from the *subtle* to the *dense*, from *the work in the white phase* to the *powder of projection*, in passing by the *hermetic vessel*, the *rebis*, and the *philosopher's stone*, with liberal use of citations from Fulcanelli (no less than fifteen direct and indirect mentions altogether), Artephius,† Nicolas Flamel, Philalethes,‡ Basil Valentine, and Kunrath—which show the range of his at least *theoretical* knowledge of the subject—Breton suggests a rereading of the books by Roussel (now promoted to *Adept* of the hermetic tradition)[30] and "starting from there." Still in "Fronton Virage," doesn't Breton ask, "is it not more tempting to admit that Roussel, being an *Adept*, observes an imprescriptible ordinance? Or else that he transposes that ordinance from one sphere to another (as Rimbaud had started

---

*For more details, one may refer to "André Breton: Soleil noir et main de feu," Patrick Rivière's excellent preface to Richard Danier's book, *L'hermétisme alchimique chez André Breton*.

†About whom Bernard Roger wrote in *Les demeures de l'invisible*, "Tradition maintains that he lived for one thousand years."

‡At the beginning of *The Open Entrance to the Closed Palace of the King*, Eirenaeus Philalethes writes, "I am a Philosopher Adept, who will not name myself other than Philalethes, an anonymous name meaning *Lover of Truth*." As Jean Bies points out, there are, in the small world of the Artists, two Philalethes, an Eirenaeus and a Eugene, just as there are "two Trévisans (one from Trier, the other from Trévise)" and "two Cosmopolites (Sethon and Sendivogius)."

to do in *Alchemy of the Word*), which would imply in any case that he had to be aware of that ordinance and thus constitutes a far less satisfactory explanation" than the hypothesis of a "mental illness"? Marie-Claire Dumas herself concluded, "Who can say that the path opened by Breton has no exit?," thereby echoing a less-innocent-than-it-seems question of Michel Butor, who takes great care to leave it open: "Did Raymond Roussel throughout his entire life and in all his works pursue the recovery of this mental gold that came to him as an epiphany?"

But even if, as Jorge Camacho, Alain Gruger, and Bernard Roger show in their tract "Nadja trahie" (Nadja betrayed),* Breton never claimed to be working on making the "universal medicine," even if he "was not an initiate," because "the pursuit of alchemical knowledge would have meant prioritizing a particular path."[31] He never went to the "furnace" himself, as people usually say, even writing to René Alleau (a man we will come back to) in 1959, that he "kept stumbling over the necessity that he could not organically make his own of this 'practical work' of alchemy," adding he was aware that "understanding—this necessity—could only be the fruit of a very decisive enlightenment that he did not have" and that he "could not very easily tolerate the thought of being reduced to a purely poetic understanding of alchemical texts."† And Richard Danier[32] has clearly shown that "the description of an operative alchemy"—and, in parallel, of the poet's inner transformations—is an authentic common thread that runs through his three great poetic books, *Nadja*, *Mad Love*, and *Arcane 17*‡ especially.

---

*Tract published for the release of the book *Léona, héroine du surréalisme* by Hester Albach, which the three men violently condemned.

†Letter of October 11, 1952, cited by Hester Albach in *Léona*. According to Alain Joubert, however, who also quotes these phrases, the letter is from 1959. Bernard Roger, who was a close friend of his, confirmed for me Breton's interest in alchemy while stressing the fact that he "hadn't practiced it himself."

‡In "The Mysterious Book of Hours of Elisa's Dream," René Alleau also writes: "From a certain point of view, *Arcane 17* is linked (no less heretically and hermetically) to the 'gay science' or 'gay saber' of the 'trobar clus' or 'closed speech' of the 'Art of Love' and of 'the language of the birds.'"

Elie-Charles Flamand sums up things in the following somewhat curt words: "Breton borrows numerous elements from alchemy, uses the occultist theory of correspondences, speaks of the *Supreme Point*, but absolutely denies what is at the base of esotericism, thereby draining it of all substance. A disturbing ambivalence leading to a loss of coherence can be seen here."*

However, I believe that Danier is right when he states, "On the basis of magic thought Breton pursues an approach similar to that of the alchemists. The latter, starting from the postulates of High Magic, have no other aim than to restore life, to recreate on the scale of humanity and the microcosm, what God (or the 'engine of the world' in less religious terminology) did for the creation of the cosmos."† "This is no less than what the surrealists wanted," he continues, specifying that they "wanted to free man from his narrow world, to grant him the gift of clairvoyance, to help him penetrate the mysteries of the cosmos: to transform man and, through him, the world." A common thread, as I've said before, but we should still keep in mind the warning issued jointly by Roger, Camacho, and Gruger, who can legitimately be considered well-placed to speak on this topic: "Presenting the chronological development of his work as an alchemical process is at once a wretched example of marketing bait, an absurd undertaking to spread confusion, and an intellectual fraud."

But, even if Breton had discovered Fulcanelli's *Dwellings of the Philosophers* and its "extraordinary wealth of information and thought" in 1948, he still explained in a January 25 letter to Victor Brauner that he "did not succeed in lifting the veil," and that he was "lost between the literal and the figurative meanings," and "a certain necessary illu-

---

*Elie-Charles Flamand, *Les méandres du sens*. What Breton rejected, according to Flamand, who, as for him, did not scoff at the notion of transcendence, was quite simply—God!

†Bernard Roger notes in his book *Paris and Alchemy*, "All it takes is to open any classic work of alchemy to be assured that the masters of this art always presented the Great Work as an exact replica, on a human scale, of the creation of the world."

mination did not take place within him."[33] This is likely the "call" Canseliet spoke of earlier! But he would soon feel sufficiently comfortable with the subject to publish (in June 1953, in the last column of the eighth issue of *Médium*) a fairly sharp critique of the book by the former priest Pierre Geyraud, *L'occultisme à Paris*.[34] In it he notes, "we read with interest—but not without express reservations—what the chapter 'Alchemy' offers by way of a captivating elucidation on the origins of the *Dwellings of the Philosophers*, just as we regret that the chapter entitled 'Hermetic Cabala' is impossibly weak."

In fact, his interest in "philosophy by fire" only appeared publicly when he published (at the top of the fifth column in the November issue of *Médium* n°1), a short note (fourteen lines) with the title, "De la Crème du Lait de Vierge." It reads: "Every Sunday, at five o'clock, René Alleau presents a series of conferences on *The Classic Texts of Alchemy* at the Hall of Geography, 184 Boulevard Saint-Germain. From October 1952 to January 1953 we'll study the work of Eirenaeus Philalethes: *The Open Entrance of the Closed Palace of the King* (London, 1669). An impeccable presentation by a highly qualified speaker. The discussion which takes place at the end of each session, with an audience which is inevitably as mixed as can be imagined, is a model of how these things should be conducted." He invited his friends to join him, which Philippe Audoin and Jean-Louis Bédouin did, as did "our dear Benjamin Péret," as recalled by René Alleau in person in "Au périscope du temps."[35] According to David Nadeau,[36] citing a text by Marianne van Hirtum, Guy-René Doumayrou and Bernard Roger were the first to participate. Roger always stressed its importance as he did in the "notice," for example, of his book on the discovery of alchemy,[37] when he writes: "The cycle of lectures was like a signal. Alchemy and its texts would soon emerge from the shadows where they had been relegated for three centuries of disrepute." He then went on to say, "The *student of Science*, who until 1960 had to do his utmost to copy these unobtainable texts in the library, can now see them in the windows of bookstores. At this end of the twentieth century, he has much more theoretical material at his disposal than his seventeenth-century elders did at a time when alchemy was still held in high esteem," even if "both the [current] physical and mental environment" in which "the echoes of the *Word of Hermes*," "descended from the heavens and rising from the earth," are no longer perceived as clearly as they were then, is quite different to the extent that "in a world dominated by the tyrannical domination of the *syntheme*," the "*Word*, sole key to the *Garden of the Sages*" was lost and can only be found "under the revitalizing breath of symbol."

Between October 1952 and June 1953, a total of twenty-five conferences were held* on various topics such as "*The Reign of Saturn Transformed into an Age of Gold* According to Huginus à Barma," for example, on this short work on the dry path and its author, or "Alchemical Compost: The Mineral and Metallic Microbiology of *Celestial Agriculture*." There was even one on "The Alchemical Manuscripts of Newton," which explored the reasons for the embarrassed silence of historians of science on the subject. Also examined were Newton's annotations to *The Open Entrance to the Closed Castle of the King*, a question that the speaker must have—rightly—considered to be particularly important. Breton returned to this subject in the fourth issue of the same journal with another short text—this time, twenty-seven lines long. "Par la graisse de la rosée," announced both the continuation of these conferences, on the *Triomphe hermétique* by Limojon de Saint-Didier† this time, and the release of *Aspects de l'alchimie*

---

*The title of this short text by Breton, "De la Crème du Lait du Vierge" (Breton's capitalization) could easily refer to the *secret book of the very ancient philosopher Artephius dealing with the occult art and the philosopher's stone*, for example, cited by Alleau in *Aspects de l'alchimie traditionnelle*, in which can be read: "For you should know that all that is clear, pure, and spiritual rises high in the air and resembles white smoke and this is what we call the Milk of the Virgin." "The volatile, therefore the mercury of the Children of Hermes," specifies Bernard Roger, and Elie-Charles Flamand follows by saying, "the First Agent, the mercurial spirit, the Astral Fire, the Archaeus, the Gold of air or light . . . the milk of the stars also called the milk of the Virgin, *lac Virginis*, that brings life to the raw subject of the Work." The complete list of these conferences was published by Alleau in the *Cahier de l'Herne*, no. 72, on André Breton.

†The exact title of the conference is "Limojon de Saint-Didier et la Table d'Emeraude."

traditionnelle by Alleau himself, with a general table of alchemical symbols drawn and written in calligraphy by Canseliet (information that is NOT provided in the book), as well as an "important preface" by the same individual from which he quotes, quite significantly, the following passage: "His work seems to us all the more reliable, his authority all the greater because, convinced of the positive founding principles of alchemy . . . he has verified more deeply in this matter, the exactitude of the traditional teachings and thus communicated physically with the *Spirit.*"

As Fabrice Flahutez points out, "René Alleau's sessions were for Breton a way of understanding the functioning of images and modes of thought closely related to the processes of dream and fiction."[38] Because, as Richard Danier notes, in Breton, "alchemy came in only as the motor of a personal experience unique to the author, never as a revelation of knowledge for the reader, which somewhat charitable Masters would not miss doing." Alleau, moreover, says exactly the same thing about his friend (in the aforementioned interview with Robert Benayoun): "It wasn't the obscure as such that interested him, nor the occult. It was the possibility of extending the poetic experience into activities that were not literary, that had as little to do with literature as possible, and which, like alchemical literature, let's say, like alchemical texts, presented more luxurious images. Through this imagery of alchemical weddings, it's certain that everything that could possibly seduce Breton was gathered together!"

Alleau's "higher perspective," says Annie Le Brun, seduced Breton, who had long been interested in the *Ars Magna* and was always looking for allies in his battle against "existentialist rationalism" because it "allowed one to see, beyond the richness of the horizons, that the use of analogical thinking opened up, through and through, the depth of the similarities in which tradition and modernity, in their most acute manifestations, participated in the same quest, insofar as the intellectual and sensory stakes proved to be similarly inseparable."* And indeed

---

*In her guest post on Paul Jorion's blog, November 2, 2013.

it's Alleau who, in his preface to the new edition of Nicolas Flamel's *Book of Hieroglyphic Figures*, suggests, "It is therefore necessary to pay the full attention that is due to this unique attempt to reconcile these two tendencies of imagination and reason, of poetry and science, of desire and experience, of which traditional alchemy consists in its principle."

6

RENÉ ALLEAU, FULCANELLI'S OTHER DISCIPLE?

The sealed book of the universe does not allow itself to be read aloud. Nature flees the violation of evidence. She confides her mysteries only to murmurs, to half-light. . . . Knowing is not understanding; it is only savoring what we have glimpsed along the way.

RENÉ ALLEAU,
THE PRIMAL FORCE IN SYMBOLS

It was because of this cycle of conferences—which, as Gilles Bucherie tells us, had previously been the subject of exchanges with Eugène Canseliet,* all of which, "completely rewritten" still number, according to their author, "excluding the introduction and the presentation of the methodological problems . . . some 1400 pages that have never been published and will never be published ('at the request of Elisa

---

*Gilles Boucherie states that the René Alleau–Eugène Canseliet relationship began in 1945 with the exchange of letters on alchemy and its characteristics. As it continued it gradually became actual communications of a technical and strictly operative nature.

Breton'),"*—that René Alleau, himself an operative alchemist, joined†
the surrealist group at that time, or, to be more exact, because he
shared a close friendship with Breton. Alleau (see plate 6) began fre-
quenting the group, but he would later say despite all this that he had
committed himself to the quest for the Golden Fleece after discovering surrealism. "The dialogue and friendship between André Breton
and myself," he wrote in "Au périscope du temps," which began at that
time, "could be compared in its totality to that between Baudelaire
and Louis Ménard, the translator and interpreter of the then little-
known texts attributed to Hermès Trismegistus (1886). This would
be the transmission of a traditional doctrine and not some kind of
pedagogical 'philosophy of alchemy.'"‡ Henri Béhar, who elsewhere
describes René Alleau as an "esoteric scholar,"** also points out that
"his interest in Surrealism became apparent in the public sale of his
collection of books and manuscripts, and his correspondence with
Breton reveals the esteem and friendship they felt for each other."[1] As
Bedouin points out, this meeting between the two men "remarkably"
illustrates "the analogy between the goals Breton spoke of with regard
to surrealist research and to that of alchemy." Later, he speaks more

---

*First part of the quotation: René Alleau, "Les conférences hermétiques," in Michel
Murat, *André Breton: Cahier de l'Herne*; Second part of the quotation: Fabrice
Flahutez, "Quatre questions à René Alleau." In the list of the books published "by the
same author" that appears at the beginning of *La Science des symboles* (translated in
English as *The Primal Force in Symbols*) we find listed an *Introduction à la lecture des
textes alchimiques traditionnels* with these details "ed. Not for Sale, 1952–1953," which
might have something to do with these famous conferences! At the time I am writing
this, there is also a plan to publish these mythical texts.
†As Gilles Bucherie indicates, however, in his book *René Alleau et l'écriture philosophale*,
we can date his "encounter with surrealism" to the "beginning of his affiliation with
Antonin Artaud," "probably in 1936."
‡Louis Ménard (1822–1901), man of letters and chemist who was friends with Baudelaire
and who introduced him to hashish.
**In "D'un poème-objet," Béhar's preface to *André Breton: Arcane 17, le manuscrit
original*, in which he cites several times the text "Le mystérieux livre d'heures du rêve
d'Elisa," by René Alleau, which was published in *André Breton, la beauté convulsive*.

explicitly on this subject: "The fact that his [Alleau's] path would intersect many years later with that of the Surrealists from that time on would tend to show that the different paths taken by Alleau and other researchers of his kind, by Breton and the poets who shared the same concerns, all wind around the same axis, like the two snakes of the caduceus. From one end of their dual evolution to the other, the two paths never merge, although they do intersect and overlap at certain points."[2] There could be no better illustration of the two approaches, highlighted by the allusion to the two serpents of the caduceus.

Born in 1917 to a family of pharmacists and deceased in 2013, Alleau is one of the most eminent French experts of the history of symbolic thought and the so-called Hermetic sciences. In 1953, he was the author of *Aspects de l'alchimie traditionnelle*, the masterpiece that rekindled interest in this ancient science in the middle of the last century. Moreover, it bears on its cover a reproduction of the famous painting *Finis Gloriae Mundi* by Juan de Valdès Leal, which served as the title for Fucanelli's third but never published book. Alleau's book, according to Gilles Bucherie, was a study that "completes the works of Albert Poisson, Jolivert-Castelot, or even Gaston Bachelard, by inscribing them in a more open and practical composition." Also to his credit are his *De la nature des symboles* in 1958[3] and *La science des symboles: Contributions à l'étude des principes et des méthodes de la symbolique générale* in 1978.[*] In this last book, which is based on two propositions, "the existence of order in the universe" and "the probability of analogy . . . of structures between a partial order and a total order," he puts forward the idea that this same analogy, so dear to the surrealists, is the key to the general symbology under discussion, thus "implicitly establishing," as Annie Le Brun hammers home, "of what kind of mutilations result from what passes for thought today."

---

[*]He was also the author of *De la nature des symboles* mentioned by Audoin in his book on Bourges, and which Gilles Bucherie suggests "is a study if not a prefiguration of the future *Bibliotheca Hermetica* collection."

Although René Alleau did work on seventeenth-century alchemy, he didn't write his thesis on that subject under the guidance of Gaston Bachelard, as it has sometimes been suggested,* but he remained faithful throughout his life to "surrationalism" and, more generally, to the thought of this author—whom Canseliet on the other hand didn't like at all†—of *The Psychoanalysis of Fire*. Thus, on November 8, 1972 at the conference "Tradition and Invention" he was delivering at the Forty-Seventh Platonic Banquet of the Atlantis Association, whose members had asked him to preside, he launched himself into a violent denunciation of scientist and rationalistic dogma. He denounced this dogma as responsible for the "cultural and pedagogical segregation" that had led to the banishment of "the history and philosophy of the traditional disciplines, as well as the study of their language and symbolic logic" from the "universities, from their teaching, from their curricula, and even from any critical examination." "It is not with impunity, nor without the most serious individual and collective psychological consequences," he added, while sharply criticizing "contemporary myths and their humbug content," "that they exclude the surrational from a culture, that they deny all mystery, that they destroy all faith, even the faith of man in himself." In this same communication, he even ventures to say that in our time it has become necessary and even vital to "counterbalance education with initiation, the outer life by the inner life, the life of the body by the life of the spirit," because an "unprecedented imbalance has appeared between the uncontrolled expansion of our ability to invent and the natural environment over which our will to power is exerted externally, while our traditional abilities intended for our inner

---

*Information shared by Yann Lauthe.

†In an article from *L'Alchimie expliquée sur ses textes classiques* entitled "Sollicitations trompeuses ou insensées," Canseliet indeed deems it "opportune to seriously warn the student of alchemy" against Bachelard whose "psychoanalytical" approach visibly upset him—just like those of René Guénon and Carl Gustav Jung—who he considered to be "a speculative writer who has grasped so little of the Science that he wants to subjugate it to his psychological acrobatics while simply shrinking it to his fallacious conjectures and banal procedures!"

environment have been reduced," if not "become so dilapidated that we are not even fully aware of how much they have been impaired." And according to the lecturer, this imbalance poses a risk, if no action is taken, of "destroying the entire natural environment" of modern man, "and perhaps even his social environment."[4]

In the article, "Psychanalyse et alchimie," published in the third issue of Médium in 1954, in which he reviews an article on "Art et alchimie" by Serge Hutin in "the *Revue Métapsychique* of January–February 1954" on "the theories of C. G. Jung," Alleau follows in Canseliet's footsteps by implicitly taking a course opposed to the Swiss thinker—who in his eyes finds no more grace than Freud. He explains that the "intuitive reading" proposed by Jung "doesn't seem to correspond to the real process of decoding alchemical symbols, which, in order to be understood accurately, require not only the actual experience of the operations described, but also, and above all, a precise knowledge of the specific signs and terms of the vocabulary or 'jargon' of the 'chemical philosophers'" and suggests "instead to insist on the fact that these images are in many cases the product of a clear, attentive consciousness, capable of extreme premeditation and concerned with the preservation of the symbolic norms of a literary, philosophical and scientific culture, reserved for a limited number of seekers placed somewhat on the margins of human history." This is because, as he firmly states, "the pictorial and graphic representations of the Adepts testify to the vast erudition, the subtle intelligence, and sometimes the humor of their authors rather than to their surrender to the magical powers of the subconscious." Because it is from the "Holy Sun" and from the "crystalline place" of the "ultimate fulfillment" of the "true, essentially free consciousness" that "emanate from the symbols of the Adepts and the teachings of the Masters, as well as from the illuminations of Art and the flames of Nature." However, I could not help noticing that in his preface to the 1988 reprint of Grillot de Givry's *Musée des sorciers, mages, et alchimistes,* he refers to "this unique source of symbolic themes and *universal psychic* *archetypes* that make up the icoonography of magic, alchemy, and astrology." (Capitalization is Alleau's, italics are mine.)*

Nonetheless he remains convinced, as he shows in *Aspects de l'alchimie traditionnelle*, that "modern thought is a *conditioned thought,* for example, by the Western myth of reason, which is itself made up of numerous irrational elements that form those all-too-famous 'pieces of evidence' on which the 'principles of intelligibility' are based. In the end no one knows how to rationally explain or define them." "More than anyone else," Annie Le Brun says (in the November 2, 2013, article on Paul Jorion's blog that she dedicated to her recently deceased friend), "René Alleau saw how 'our modern sciences have concentrated their efforts on a process of increasing abstraction of phenomena in order to formalize them, axiomatize them and formulate them as general laws in mathematical language.'"

Mobilized in 1939 as a pharmacist, his path crossed with that of Breton who was also serving as an auxiliary military doctor. A Resistance fighter during the Occupation, he then worked (from 1948 to 1950) in West Africa, and during this seminal experience he seems to have come into contact with initiatory societies of blacksmiths, or more precisely, as he himself explains, with "*corporate* associations" used as a cover by "true *secret societies*" the tradition of which, only, "can be described with the word *alchemy*." (Italics are Alleau's.) Alleau remained rather mysterious about these contacts with African black-smiths, who could also be called "theurgists of fire,"† as Bernard Roger

---

*Canseliet, meanwhile, condemned Grillot de Givry for being hostile to Fulcanelli.

†These Greek peoples shared "Cabirian" initiations. Alleau listed their names in a very poetic manner: "the Idean Dactyls, the Phrygian Corybantes, the Cabiri of Samothrace, the Karkines and Sintians of Lemnos, the Telchines of Rhodes, and the Curetes of Crete." Caron and Hutin, citing Alleau, add that the Cabiri, who were theurgists of fire, "were the inhabitants of a Pelasgian island . . . the island of Samothrace, where, according to legend, Jason, the Argonauts, Pythagoras, and Orpheus were initiated." They go on saying, "it is this people of blacksmiths, these 'children of fire' . . . to whom we seem to owe a dominant influence on all the igneous arts and metallurgical rites from which the first notions of ancient alchemy emerged."

told me. Roger also recalls in the introduction to his book *Paris and Alchemy* that "we know from the studies of J. P. Rossignol during the last century that originally metallurgical techniques were inseparable from theurgical research of a priestly nature."* In an undated letter to Michel Carrouges, with whom he was close enough to close it with "an affectionate clasp of hands," he spells it out. He writes, "After Cameroon, Dahomey, Senegal, Mauritania, Morocco, ten thousand kilometers hypnotized, here I am again in 'Trance,'"† and in his book on the Art of Music, speaks as a connoisseur of the "important work of Marcel Griaule and Germaine Dieterlen on the Dogon, studies that clearly highlight the complex, initiatory role of the African blacksmith, who was feared and despised, admired and hated," as well as his own experience "of the metallurgists' influence" among the Bamun and the Bamikele of Cameroon, as well as among the "Sombas of northern Dahomey" whose blacksmiths "still today" pass on "secret teachings" "to warriors. And as Roger also recalled, Alleau showed in *Aspects de l'alchimie traditionnelle*, based on "his study of the Cabiri and the mysteries of Samothrace" (in which, incidentally, Sosthène Grasset d'Orcet also took a great interest, notably in a text published in *La Revue Britannique* in 1880, "Les cabires et la Vénus mutilée") that these techniques "were linked to initiations and mysteries and had indeed formed the foundations of operative alchemy in Antiquity."‡

These remarks, taken as a whole, are also confirmed by the definition of "the Art" given by Elie-Charles Flamand in his book *La tour*

---

*Allusion to Jean-Pierre Rossignol (1803–1893) and his book *Les métaux dans l'antiquité: origines religieuses de la métallurgie, ou les dieux de la Samothrace représentés comme métallurges d'après l'histoire et la géographie*, Paris: A. Durand, 1863. Reissue, Saint Chamond: Editions Abatos, 2009. These opinions referring again to the Cabiri are reiterated by Bernard Roger in *A la découverte de l'alchimie*.

†There is a pun here: "en Transe" sounds very much like "en France."

‡In a video interview on February 22, 2022, with Jacques Carletto, Bernard Renaud de la Faverie also speaks of the very thin limit between metallurgy and alchemy during certain operations.

Saint-Jacques. "Now, as we know, Alchemy, an initiatory method of spiritual realization based on material operations, is originally associated with the rites and mysteries of the metallurgists."* Flamand also revealed elsewhere that one of his paternal forbearers, "the augural ancestor," who died in 1937, was a blacksmith and farrier. In reference to this individual's forge, Flamand mentions the "alchemical cave," while emphasizing that like blacksmiths, alchemists "transformed matter, making it pass from one form into another." He then launched into a comparison between them, showing successively that "in primitive societies, blacksmithing involved an initiatory and ritual aspect" and that "the blacksmith, the master of the transformations of metal [is] also the master of fire who not only purifies by also confers spiritual Awakening."† He then concludes that their activities were closely related, writing "Alchemy could perhaps be considered as a sacralization of certain metallurgical operations."[5] In Alleau's opinion, it is crucial to keep in mind that "the artisanal techniques of metalworkers and goldsmiths concealed research of a theurgical and priestly nature, inspired by the secret teaching of the Mysteries of Antiquity."[6] In *Enigmas and Symbols of Mont Saint-Michel*, Alleau again mentions, in a footnote, these "priests-metallurgists of the island of Samothrace" and "the influence of the cult of the Cabiri that had spread from Greece to Ireland."

In this last book he examines the relationship between Saint Michel, the mountain consecrated to him, and alchemy, namely through the

---

*A footnote of Flamand's here refers back to the "book of Mircea Eliade, *Forgerons et alchimistes*, Paris: Flammarion, 1956."

†It might be helpful to recall here, when speaking of blacksmiths, that in some Masonic rituals, they speak of "Tubalcain, the son of Lamech" and therefore a descendant of Cain, "who invented the art of metalwork." Tubal-Cain was in fact, according to the *Zohar*, cited by Robert Ambelain, the descendant of Samael Iblis, the serpent of Eden, who had seduced his ancestor Eve. Moreover, Ambelain mentions a "tradition specific to the Caïnite smiths of the Sinaï," and in particular "the Tubal Kaïnites," who, "in the caste of blacksmiths form a specialized branch of casters of copper and bronze." According to Caron and Hutin, the famous seventeenth-century Danish chemist "Borrichius believed it certain that the true cradle of alchemy . . . was nevertheless to be found in the workshops of *Tubal-Caïn*, the formidable blacksmith of the Holy Scriptures."

creation of the Order of Saint Michel by Louis XI. The treasurer of this order was none other than his finance minister, Jean Bourré, master and builder of the castle of Plessis-Bourré in Equillé, in the département of Maine et Loire. This was one of the two alchemical dwellings about which Canseliet wrote (in a book of the same title: *Two Alchemical Abodes* [*Deux logis alchimiques*]). In the chapter entitled "The Golden Angel and Alchemy," after wondering "whether Joan of Arc's secret was purely spiritual or whether it involved the rediscovery, thanks to these revelations, of resources believed to have been lost" and therefore wondering about the nature of the revelations made by the "Maid" to Charles VII in order to obtain his support, and about their possible connection with the lost treasure of the Knights Templar, Alleau also cites Fulcanelli's *Dwellings of the Philosophers*, suggesting that the "'war treasure' of the Temple and of Joan was not necessarily silver or gold," but could have come "from heaven" and have something to do with the philosopher's stone.

In any case, Alleau considers the approach to the Art of Music to be most complex and explains that it would be futile to try to "reduce the meaning of alchemical treatises to arbitrary systems of interpretation." "The problems" it poses have "no chance of being solved, even partially, if we don't take into account the *secret* and *sacred* nature of this knowledge," since "this *secret* technique, which turns it into a *sacred* science," is based on "dissolution." They have no chance of being solved if we limit ourselves to a strictly "scientific" approach to things because, for example and to begin with, "all the 'chemical' interpretations of the 'primal matter' are false.* And this is all the more true since in order to make even a little progress, the reader, with no Ariadne's thread, must commit himself to a labyrinth in which everything has been *consciously and systematically prepared to throw the uninitiated into a state of inextricable mental confusion.*" (Italics are Alleau's.)

---

*Not to forget, Elie-Charles Flamand reminds us, that we mustn't confuse raw material, the natural sulfur of antimony already mentioned by Basil Valentine, and prime matter!

He then goes on to say that, to the extent that "alchemical manipulations serve as material support for a mental asceticism and in which the latter thereby testifies "to *the union of matter and consciousness* as the sovereign power of the *liberated mind*," "it is worth considering alchemy as an experimental, material religion, whose purpose is the illumination of consciousness, *the deliverance of mind and body*," and also an "attempt" to "*religiously* reconcile the fundamental logical contradictions that Greek physics was unable to resolve," "after the exuberant development of the rhetoric of the physicians"—in a word, a return to the "teaching of the Mysteries." (Italics are Alleau's.) In fact, alchemy is for him the inheritance of the knowledge handed down by ancient teachers such as "Zosimus the Panopolitan" or "Synesius"* who had taught from a "deep sense of universal unity that inspired them" as well as from "a sum of traditional knowledge that should never be underestimated." It is also the heir "of the teachings of the priestly colleges of High Antiquity" in which one sought to understand the conditions under which "the human aggregate and the mineral aggregate were able, *under the influence of a qualitative order of energy*, to free themselves from a rigorous phenomenal determinism," as well as the nature of this influence and the way in which this energy could be harnessed and used. (Italics are Alleau's.)

Further on, Alleau, repeating that "the most remarkable feature of alchemy was to make, from its beginnings, a definitive protest against dualism," speaks again of the original contents of this "experimental religion": "It has not been sufficiently noticed, in my opinion, how the affirmation of the unity of matter and of the possibility of transforming spirits into bodies and bodies into spirits clearly testifies to the loss of an ancient religious unity and to the desire to rediscover it." "Alchemy," he continues, "noting that '*everything that is observable is symbolic*,' asserts that '*everything that is symbolic is observable*.'

---

*Most likely Synesios of Cyrene (370–413), an alchemist and Neoplatonic philosopher of Alexandria and a student of Hypatia, who became a Christian bishop.

Consequently, the supreme Symbol of the symbol, namely unity, is observable and the *true man can contemplate the embodiment of the Logos in matter."* (Italics are Alleau's.)

However, "at no time" does the art separate "the transformations of the consciousness of the Operator from those of the material, so much so that in this mysterious union, a profound point of equilibrium is reached between an externalized inner world and an outer world that internalizes itself until illumination springs forth."* And we cannot fail to compare these final words with those of the concluding sentence in the text written by Bernard Roger for the booklet accompanying Camacho's exhibition *Le ton haut* "at Mathias Fels and Co. Gallery in the month of May 1969," concerning this "traveler" who "hears the fountain flowing three paces away in the high forest" and whose "approach leads to the transparent crossroads where *the inner world meets the world's interior.*" (Italics are mine.)

Be that as it may, inasmuch as the Great Work requires "ceaseless efforts" that seem to be "designed to produce, on the one hand, the *projection* of waking consciousness into a trans-rational state of waking, and, on the other hand, the *ascension* of the material to the igneous light that forms its boundary," the "one who can be initiated" must be armed with patience and demonstrate unwavering determination in order to be transported into an altered state of consciousness, it being then transported by the "philosopher's stone" "beyond the limits of the perishable *ego*, into a *new* world that is *normally* separated from our own by a *curtain of fire*."† This is because *"The disruption of the balance*

---

*In his introduction to the book by Crassellame, Bernard Roger speaks of the "operator's central position."

†It seems to me a good idea to compare these lines with this excerpt from Bernard Roger's *A la découverte de l'alchimie*: "He who wishes to pass from the labors of the first work to those of the second must pass through this curtain of fire, which in all points resembles the door of a temple at the end of the forecourt and beyond which begins the ritual domain of sacred practice. On this side of the door, time is in perpetual flight from an ungraspable present between what is no more and what will be, only to disappear as it appears. Beyond this door is rhythm and harmony between 'heaven' and 'earth.'"

of the logical mechanism of the uninitiated consciousness of the waking state seems . . . to constitute the dialectical principle of alchemy."

A very telling anecdote about Alleau's influence also gives us an idea of the esteem Eugène Canseliet had for the man he called his "longtime friend" and whose name he latinized in *L'alchimie expliquée sur ses textes classiques* into *Renati* Alleau! While he had always claimed to be the only disciple of "the Adept and thus Unknown Superior Fulcanelli, he let slip one day, when speaking of Alleau, that he was the *other* disciple—even if Elie-Charles Flamand is inclined to think that Alleau's Master was none other than the "ruril" of Savignies. And he wrote just as clearly (in his preface to Alleau's book *Aspects de l'alchimie traditionnelle*) on the one hand, "he is our friend, a disciple of Fulcanelli and a *son of science* like ourselves," while on the other hand he mentions a certain *narrow door* that can only be *the open entrance to the closed palace of the king.* Here he deems useful again to state explicitly that his alter ego "knew how to discover [it], sparing no effort and sacrifice, in the double domain of book study and laboratory experimentation." It is true that in matters of "book" knowledge or not, Alleau, for example, in his aforementioned article of the *Encyclopedia Universalis,* showed himself to be particularly well informed when discussing the "three main branches" of Western alchemy. "The first, Aristotelian and pre-chemistry" "developed the application of the ancient theory of the four elements to the transmutation of metals." The second branch, which he describes as being close to Geber's ideas, is based on "the Stoic's theories on the sympathy and antipathy of beings," and seeks "the relations between the life of metals and the universal soul." And above all the third "secret" branch is special *"and almost unknown, not only to historians but the majority of alchemists themselves."* (Italics are mine.) With reservations he describes it as "magical" and "as never leaving any trace" since it is only transmitted orally, but which he knows well enough to reveal that "its goal was symbolically the *Absolute* or the *Universal."* (Italics are Alleau's.) In any event, it was Canseliet who told Amadou during a 1978 interview, "How could I not agree with René Alleau, disciple of Fulcanelli, through the two books of the great Adept?"

The bond between the two men was so strong that René Alleau paid homage to Canseliet (in *Atlantis*) in these words, "For more than forty years, I have known his sacrifices, trials, and labors fraternally enough to be able to testify to my admiration for his unwavering obstinacy and his patience and perseverance capable of resisting and overcoming everything. Courage of steel forged in the fires of a true passion, what life could be more beautiful and more worthy of *a true man*?" (Italics are Alleau's.) And, even if we must remain cautious about their content, the Maître de Savignies, in his interviews with Robert Amadou, *Le feu du soleil,** says again of the author of *Aspects de l'alchimie traditionnelle* that he "is an all the more authentic alchemist because he possesses the solid fundamentals of an academic," moreover emphasizing that "his attachment to the positive practice of fire is undeniable, which makes him the surest kind of physico-chemical artist." The word of a goldsmith, we can all agree, and perhaps it is even permitted to see in him "the young child beneath the old man," this "alchemist beneath the engineer" that Bachelard mentions at the beginning of *The Psychoanalysis of Fire*!

Throughout his life, Alleau, according to Annie Le Brun, "was always working on this synthesis between what he called the 'external sciences' and the 'internal sciences,'" still fully desirous of "restoring the occult to culture," as Amadou put it,† but also of fighting "the rationalist ban that weighs on all traditional disciplines."[7] Strengthened "by thirty years of experience" in the field of "the authenticity of

---

*Robert Amadou, *Le feu du soleil*. Amadou published this book of interviews without giving Canseliet the opportunity to reread them, causing a definitive rupture between the two men. Canseliet felt that Amadou had revealed without his consent things that should not have been made public.

†Gilles Bucherie recalls that Amadou, in *Occident, Orient*, writes: "In 1950, with René Alleau, we undertook the task of bringing Occultism to the existing culture. I immediately published *Occultism*, the magazine *La tour Saint-Jacques* right behind." The editorial board of this magazine, which devoted a large space to alchemy, notably included René Alleau, Michel Carrouges, Henri Hunwald, and Claude d'Ygé.

alchemical works and the historical identification of their authors,"[8] he became, after having initiated the "Quintessences" Collection for Editions Caractères* at the end of the fifties, the director between 1970 and 1977 of the *Bibliotheca Hermetica* at Editions Denoël then Retz after 1975. This collection contained twenty-two titles, among which were *The Book of Hieroglyphic Figures* by Nicolas Flamel, *Alchemy and Alchemists* by Louis Figuier, *The Open Entrance to the Closed Palace of the King* by Eirenaeus Philalethes, *The Light Leaving on Its Own from the Darkness* by "Fra Marc-Antonio Crassellame Chinese," *The Most Holy Trinosophia* by the Comte de Saint-Germain, *The Hermetic Triumph* by Limojon de Saint-Didier, *The Treatise on the Philosopher's Stone* by Lambsprinck, *The Secret Work of the Philosophy of Hermes* by Jean d'Espagnet, the *Mytho-Hermetic Dictionary* by Dom Pernety, *The Hermetic Visions* by Clovis Hesteau de Nuysement, *The Key to the Secret of Secrets* by Nicolas Valois, and *The Treasure of Treasures* by Nicolas Gosparmy, these last two being members of the Cénacle de Flers. Also appearing were Solomon Trismosin's *Golden Fleece,* the Cosmopolite's *New Chemical Light,* and *The Triumphal Chariot of Antimony* or *The Last Testament* of Basil Valentine. Dedicated to the publication or republication of the great classics of magic, astrology, and alchemy, this mythical collection, "thought" as Gilles Bucherie described it, "as the initial basis of a . . . work" of building a critical European alchemical corpus, has the merit, moreover, of renewing the approach of traditional knowledge, which in passing reveals what I have elsewhere called an "underground route" of Hermeticism,† "in the constructive perspective of a new history of ideas." To sum up the spirit of the project, we can perfectly use the phrases Alleau used several times in the prospectuses announcing the conferences at the Hall of Geography, because the aim is the same: "To present to the

---

*Whose orientation he presented in a very Fulcanneli-like fashion in his preface to the new edition of a book by Jean-Baptiste Le Breton, *Les clefs de la philosophie spagyrique,* cited by Fulcanelli and Canseliet.

†For which surrealism is in certain regards, as I see it, one of the outcomes.

educated public texts selected from among the best and rarely found in bookstores, to transmit them in their original form to scholars and students of all ages, while explaining and analyzing this traditional doctrine." It is also, to some extent, a way of fighting, as Annie Le Brun says,* against "the *cultural repression* of a colonialist and imperialist industrial society which in this way washes away its unconscious fantasies of guilt toward the traditional societies it has destroyed." Another "lover of Science," Bernard Roger, became one of the experts in charge of preparing and revising the books to be published by comparing the different versions of the old editions. He also made a major contribution as a translator and writer of prefaces, notably signing his name to introductions to the books of Nicolas Valois (*The Five Books or the Key to the Secret of Secrets*), Nicolas Gospamy (*The Treasure of Treasures*), the Cosmopolite (*New Chemical Light*), and Mathurin Eyquem du Martineau (*The Pilot of the Living Wave*). He also wrote one for *The Light Leaving on its Own from the Darkness*, and translated Lambsprinck's *Treatise on the Philosopher's Stone*.

In order to explain the nature of their work, Roger explained that "although it doesn't depend at all on the profane and temporal limits in which the vicissitudes of institutions and the changes of society are located," "it is no less legitimate to consider and study historically the *external manifestations* and *material expressions* of alchemy in the different civilizations, according to the domains in which the appearance of these influences can be observed." This includes painting and sculpture as well as the novel and poetry but also architecture, since cathedrals in particular "still bear sufficient evidence of the presence of the myths and symbols of hermetic esotericism, for which there is no need to prove their importance in medieval society up to the early years of the sixteenth century." It is also to be found "in the rites and sacred signs of initiations, at the heart of which is Alchemy. Long before it was known in the West, it cast its mysterious gleam in

---

*In the previously cited article on Paul Jorion's blog.

the East and Far East, in the darkness of tombs and in the shadows of ancient temples." From this perspective, the seventeenth century, the century of transition, appears to the author of *Paris and Alchemy* as the era in which, in a last attempt to avoid entering into "a process of solidification and materialization of an irreversible historical cycle that would have to be followed into its final consequences and the unprecedented crises of contemporary civilization," the Adepts, also known as the *Noble Travelers*, by carrying out numerous public transmutations* of which memories and even material traces have been preserved, revealed themselves before, it is said, leaving Europe at the beginning of the eighteenth century and disappearing forever— leaving us to grapple with "modern thought" and the "intellectual mirages" it produces.†

For his part, René Alleau, who believes that "any ideological, philosophical, or religious system, based on being, having, or doing, represents and *can only represent* an *exoteric* modality of knowledge" so that "there is therefore no reason to oppose *essence* to *existence* or *being* to *becoming* because, from the level of esotericism, these questions do not arise," advocates "a return to the sources of the traditional hermetic arts" whose "teachings . . . bear no relation to the confusion and errors of modern *occultism* and *scientism*." In the general preface to the books of his collection, he writes in a programmatic and highly significant way,

---

*"Realized," he adds in *A la découverte de l'alchimie*, "under the control of individuals whose scientific authority, social standing, critical sense, or philosophical intelligence form so many guarantees as to the credibility of their testimony"—sometimes accompanied by signed and countersigned statements!

†Bernard Roger, introduction to Marc-Antonio Crasselame, *La lumière sortant par soi-même des ténèbres*. Roger also said of this treatise that it was one of the "works published in this time," the seventeenth century, in which the Adepts taught "in a clearer way than before, the source of their knowledge and the principles of their works." In the same cautionary spirit, it can prove helpful, in the light of current climate events, for example, to remember that Fulcanelli, almost a century ago, wrote in *The Dwellings of the Philosophers*, "To all philosophers, to educated people, whoever they may be, to specialized scientists, as well as to simple observers, we pose the question: 'Have you ever thought about the inevitable consequences which are to result from unlimited progress?'"

"The concept of *false science* is now being replaced by the essentially esoteric and symbolic concept of a *traditional knowledge* that manifests itself in arts and practices, a language and pictures whose poetic value frees us from arbitrary and inadequate scientific criticism about their aims."

To sum up the meaning Alleau wished to give his approach, which he believed should culminate in a synthesis between the real data of modern reason and the true foundations of ancient faith,[9] we need only quote his own words, which echo those of Breton in "Before the Curtain": "By rejecting traditional disciplines, by excluding them from our teaching, academic rationalism has been the main culprit responsible for a cultural repression that is currently anarchically liberating itself in the waves of confused and regressive 'occultism' and 'mysticism' that bear witness to the profound paleo-psychic malaise of our contemporaries."[10] This is something Gilles Bucherie emphasizes most aptly when he writes in his essay on Alleau: "The timeliness of René Alleau's work and thought allows us to see beyond the crisis we are living today—behind the entropy of History—that people are still, discreetly, trying to complete the Great Work."[11]

Moreover, as he said in a conference on March 9, 1953, cited by Guy-René Doumayrou in April 1989, in "Surréalisme, ésotérisme," the eighth issue of *DOCSUR*, alchemy always offered Alleau "a frame of reference: nature, which ceaselessly changes its productions without changing its laws. The knowledge of nature should allow us to expel the *cherubim* who guard the garden where the Tree of Life grows.[12] This is the true revolt."

Frédérick Tristan (Jean-Paul Baron, 1931–2022), author of many books of an initiatory nature (including one that won the Goncourt Prize in 1983, *Les égarés*) and a close friend of Alleau since 1964, in the preface to his own book, *L'obsédante,* published in 1991,[13] spoke of his first contacts with surrealism and the author of *The Primal Force of Symbol* toward the end of the 1950s: "I would say that my admiration for André Breton was unambiguous at that time, but that, while Georges Bataille continued to fascinate me in a cruel way, I did not belong to the clan of young surrealists. *Nadja* and *Mad Love* had thrown me for a loop. . . . Nevertheless, I was closer to the magazine *La tour Saint-Jacques* and René Alleau than to *Le Surréalisme même* and Jean Schuster." And he continued: "As proof, I can only cite the article that appeared in *Structure** n°1 in March 1957, and which is being republished here, because it situates precisely the intellectual position that was mine at the time."

And this position is in fact quite critical, although he takes great pains to present Breton as "an admirable man, one of the most sovereignly luminous of our time,"† since Tristan, claiming that the first issue of *Le Surréalisme même* did not meet any of his requirements, wrote that he had the feeling of "wandering through a museum of medical oddities, whose jars all seemed empty." He justified the severity of his judgment with these few lines about a text dedicated to the heroine of the beautiful novella published by Wilhelm Jensen in 1903, which had attracted Jung and Freud—who saw in it "delusion and dream"—as well as the surrealists:

> We would like something like that prestigious Gradiva that René Alleau told us about, that woman in a hurry in Pompeii who crosses our gaze like a singular flash of understanding (but where is she going?). Gradiva Rediviva, that's fine, (but where does she come from?) and we are ready in turn to follow her luminous steps. For she comes from and returns to our greatest mystery. Because she is ours (oh, how much!), as well as this initiatory degree of which the

---

*In 1957 and 1958, Pierre Renaud published in Paris the periodical *Structure*, in which could be heard the new voices of Yvonne Caroutch (his daughter, future interviewer of Mandiargues), François Augiéras, and of course, Frédérick Tristan.

†As he recalls in his interviews with Olivier Gissey, it was Malcolm de Chazal who "through an exchange of letters (he lived in Mauritius) was able to put him in contact with Breton, who asked him for various articles, including one on magics for his 'Art magique,' a collective article that in the end didn't appear."

surrealist movement will never know what to do, because it has forbidden itself to enter the temple. The temple from which Gradiva comes. To which she returns. To which we follow her. Where she reaches complete fulfillment like a resurrection, like a rediscovered loyalty, like a necessary lesson.

Tristan's complaints are primarily, and mistakenly, focused on the fact that "surrealism has closed the door to the sacred!"*

It seems that a word should be said here, of course, about this "Gradiva rediviva" published by Alleau in 1956. In it he curtly questions the—inadequate—reading of Jensen's book by a Freud guilty of not having seen that the German philosopher whose hero, Norbert, "travels in the atmosphere of a 'nuptial journey' reminiscent of 'the chemical wedding' of the ancient authors" "used [a] code" "intended only for initiates" that "places all its novelty under the sign of [a] mysterious language," "the language of the birds" or "phonetic cabala." We find ourselves once again in the presence of the " veritable 'jargon' and 'closed speech' or *'trobar clus'* of the lovers of the 'Gaye Science' or 'Gay Saber.'" He makes it clear that Gradiva takes her name from a certain *Gradivus Mars,* "associated by the Salii or Salians, priests of Ancient Rome, with the same gods worshipped by the Cabiri of Samothrace," and points out that a "search for the philosophical or double Mercury of the mysterious 'Rebis,' starting from a 'common or simple Mercury,' is clearly indicated by Jensen." Alleau also detects his allusion to Maier's *Atalanta Fugiens* and glimpses in the novella's conclusion "a message of consolation and hope with a universal scope." He offers an alchemical interpretation suggested by the "material and

---

*In fact, as he confided to this same Olivier Gissey, Tristan, who had become quite close to the Grand Mason Jean Tourniac (Jean Granger), would more or less come around to sharing Tourniac's opinion about Breton and the surrealists: "What this man and his disciples are missing is the understanding that poetry is the royal path for approaching the only reality that exists: transcendence. He could not reach an understanding with Daumal and that's really a pity." A notion the surrealists would find totally unacceptable!

positive experimental problem" posed by the opening lines: *"How to give life to the stone, how to pass from the mineral to the vegetable kingdom, how to revive the dead?"*[14]

Yet, this same Alleau, whose "Gradiva rediviva" squarely places the emphasis on the fact that Jensen "belonged to circles whose members held knowledge and experiences corresponding to the dimensions of another reality" (to quote Gilles Bucherie), who would mention Tristan and his text to André Breton. Breton happily opened the doors of his rue Fontaine studio to the young man and even asked him, it seems, if he was "one of the potential initiates mentioned by Alleau."

Reflecting on René Alleau's last days and death, "which almost went unnoticed by the intellectuals of his time," his close friend Frédérick Tristan said again in 2013, "How not to think of the particular state René Alleau was in when he was in Uzès, where he had retired with his wife, Denise? He shut his office door behind him once and for all, abandoned his precious library and studio, and still alive and well, seemed to forget the world. The extremely harsh struggle, leading to a complete exhaustion of all logical contradictions, was completed by entering into satori! He had become the 'sealed Star.'" And he went on to say, "Now, the author of *Aspects de l'alchimie traditionnelle* wrote, 'The triggering of satori doesn't present a purely intellectual aspect. It concerns the totality of the life of an individual who is engaged in a passionate confrontation with the unknown. . . . Nevertheless, access to satori constitutes only a preliminary inner revolution, a transition to a different logic on which a physics of the waking state, the experimental foundation of traditional cosmology, is built.'"[15]

It was once again the faithful Tristan, a year after his friend's death, who, while resuming his analysis (in his interview with Olivier Gissey), recalled that "the decisive articles that René Alleau contributed to the *Encyclopedia Universalis* for the entries on Alchemy, Astrology, and Magic remain, in fact, invaluably relevant at a time when a pseudo-initiatory decadence tends to use these traditional techniques inappropriately."

However, we should finally note with the greatest interest what his friend, the surrealist poet Jean-Pierre Lassalle, wrote in conclusion of the article dedicated to Alleau after his death in 2013 (in the fifty-third issue of *Les cahiers d'Occitanie*).* "René Alleau has gone to join Basil Valentine, Nicolas Flamel, Fulcanelli, Eugène Canseliet in the empyrean realm of the masters of the philosopher's stone. They are all everlasting diamonds that diffract the purest and most invigorating light."

---

*December 2013.

7

THE MYSTERIOUS
DOCTOR HUNWALD AND
THE HERMES CIRCLE

*I knew Doctor H—too well to be able to tell the color of his
eyes; I had not studied him enough to be able to paint them.*

MICHEL BUTOR,
PORTRAIT OF THE ARTIST AS A YOUNG APE

To create an atmosphere, let's say that the author of *Nadja* probably
met Alleau at one of the aforementioned "philosophical agapes" at the
home of Doctor Henri Hunwald (see plate 7), "a small apartment on
rue du Val-de-Grâce, in the same building that today houses the con-
sulate of the People's Republic of Hungary, crammed with books on
alchemy, English ghost stories, and science fiction novels."[1] It was here
that Eugène Canseliet, a friend of the householder since the middle of
the forties, Gaston Sauvage, Claude d'Ygé, himself one of Canseliet's
"oldest disciples," as well as Jean Palou, surrealist and historian of
Freemasonry, would meet. René Alleau was then the person who played
a decisive role in bringing together surrealists and "alchemists."*

---

*Based on what Bernard Roger told me, "to speak of surrealism and alchemy, it is

If we have already discussed—or if we are going to discuss at length—the majority of the men whose names I have just quoted, it will probably be helpful to point out that Gaston Sauvage was a chemist by training who had had the privilege of participating, along with Jean-Julien Champagne, and Eugène Canseliet, in the famous transmutation performed by the adept Fulcanelli in Sarcelles in 1922, "in the factory of the Georgi company and in the small room on the second floor," he says, "where our father had just died, in front of the hall of the purifiers." Claude Lablatinière, also known as Claude d'Ygé (1912–1964), also boasted of having received from Fulcanelli a regular transmission, thanks to Canseliet, whom he had met at the end of the thirties through Jules Boucher. D'Ygé was, we are told in the preface to the new edition of his anthology, *Nouvelle assemblée des philosophes chymiques: Aperçus sur le Grand Œuvre des Alchimistes*, by a certain C.—J. F., "one of the very close friends" of Dr. Hunwald as well as the writer Michel Butor. At the end of the forties and early fifties, Butor participated in surrealist activities and even sent a copy of his book *L'emploi du temps* (*Passing Time*) to Breton in 1956 as "a token of friendship and admiration."[*] René Alleau was also an avid visitor to the rue du Val-du-Grace, where they enthusiastically compared the results of their research. The complicity alluded to here, moreover, is quite clear when, in a note of his address "to the researchers" at the beginning of *Nouvelle assemblée des philosophes chymiques,* d'Ygé[†] compliments Butor for the great flair of his review "L'alchimie et son langage" of Alleau's book, *Aspects de l'alchimie traditionnelle,*

(cont.d) necessary to mention the figures of Alleau, Jorge Camacho, and Alain Gruger." Not to mention that of Bernard Roger himself! A list to which I would personally add Philippe Audoin, Elie-Charles Flamand, and Maurice Baskine, not to overlook, of course, the unclassifiable Ithell Colquhoun.

[*]But also, *La modification* (*A Change of heart*. Simon and Schuster. 1959) in 1957, *Génie du lieu* (*The Spirit of Mediterranean Places*. Marlboro press. 1986) in 1958, and *Répertoire II* in 1964.

[†]In the previously mentioned entry "Alchemy," René Alleau, in 1968, was just as complimentary.

published in the journal *Critique* in 1953. D'Ygé writes: "This article shows the author's rare understanding and 'accurate intuition' of the difficult alchemical problem. We recommend that the average reader, who does not know what is precisely alchemy, read this article and think about it. This is the first time that we find in a literary review a critical study on Alchemy that could teach many 'necessary things' to the self-proclaimed alchemists of the group of contemporary 'symbolico-hermeticist' writers." This certainly puts the putative father of the Nouveau Roman* in a completely different light! I should add that D'Ygé's masterwork, published in 1954 with a preface by Canseliet and a banner with the inscription "Charitable Guide for the Lovers of Science," seemed important enough to Philippe Audoin and Vincent Bounoure for them to mention it in, respectively, *Bourges cité première*, and "Preface to a Treatise on Matrices." However, according to the Master of Savignies himself (in a text "*In Memoriam* Claude Lablatinière d'Ygé," published in issue 227 of *Atlantis*), "Although Claude d'Ygé never raised his quest to the operative level, it was still determined and persistent, and he wrote two books which sufficiently illustrated his work to earn him a place in the forefront of the hermetic sciences as well as the most excellent reputation."[2] Canseliet is in an even better position to recall this second book, an *Anthology of Hermetic Poetry* (1948), printed in 150 copies and dedicated to "La Fraternité d'Héliopolis, which goes back to the beginning of time," as he wrote the preface again. Author of *Les alchimistes* with Michel Caron, Serge Hutin, who had also written in *Gouvernants invisibles et sociétés secrètes* (J'ai Lu, 1971) that he had "good reason to think that the Templars knew the secret of metal transmutation" and believed that "many of today's practitioners of alchemy owe much of their knowledge to him." In the thirties Claude d'Ygé was also a member of Maria de Naglowska's Confrérie de la Flèche d'Or, which practiced a kind of sex magic.

---

*A paternity Butor didn't want at any price!

These meetings in which "alchemy and hermeticism were the primary themes of study" are mentioned in the first part of Michel's Butor's early book *Portrait of the Artist as a Young Ape*. Butor thus underwent, through contact with this group, "a kind of initiatory course marked by alchemy and which forced the Adept to make a descent into hell before he could know illumination,"* an experience that leaves persistent traces through all his books. This is recalled by Robert Amadou at the beginning of his book of interviews with Canseliet (*Le feu du soleil*), who doesn't allow even a shred of doubt to survive as he even describes the *capriccio* of the future author of *Passage de Milan* to be initiatory in a precisely alchemical understanding, and says that "Butor was interested in alchemy and not only speculatively (although he did not work at the furnace)."

As recalled by Henri Desoubeaux, in this *capriccio*, which is more "autobiographical" than it seems, and whose title contains two words evocative of alchemy—*artist*, one of the names used in the Middle Ages for alchemists,† then perceived as *"apes* of nature"‡ (see plate 11)—a book in which the daughter of the "great Fulcanelli,** Rector of the University of Figures, so called because of the precious enigmas she so generously produced," also appears as a prisoner in a philosophical "abode," Butor is one of the rare individuals who speaks of Dr. H.††
He endeavors to describe him as follows, providing what is probably

---

*This is at least what Jacques Van Lennep, in his book *Une pierre en tête,* retained of Jennifer Waelti-Walter's dissertation at Victoria University in British Columbia, who consulted him during the preparation of her work.

†According to Canseliet, while the word "artist" is commonly used to mean alchemists, "Adept," and thereby " Unknown Superior," applies exclusively to someone who has completed the Great Work.

‡In this regard, Philippe Audoin writes in his *Bourges cité première*, "Alchemists, as we have seen, claimed to imitate Nature, to literally be *apes*—in other words *sages* and, through antiphrasis, madmen." (Audoin's italics.)

**A close kin to Elie-Charles Flamand's "daughter of the sun"?

††In his novel, the author only speaks of Hunwald as Dr. H., but in her essay, Jennifer Waelti-Walter indicated in a footnote that "the identity of the characters and place names was provided [to her] by Michel Butor on June 20, 1970.

the only portrait of him that we have: "He had a high forehead. I'm tempted to say that his hair was greying, but upon reflection, I don't think that was the case; perhaps I saw it graying later, or maybe only now that he is dead I imagine him older than he actually was." As a reminder, the doctor died in 1961, while Butor's book dates from 1967.

Hunwald, whom Jean-Pierre Lassalle swears was Butor's "mentor,"* is therefore depicted as a man who *could be no more than forty years old*," but who the narrator made older and older and whom he later compared, simply because he was Hungarian, to "the old man of Basil Valentine, already identified with the alchemists' lead and sulfur"—in other words with "Saturn, who eats his own children so they can be reborn," "the lead that fixes the mercury by cutting its feet off with his scythe, the philosopher's stone, the father of metals."† This description fits the "man of great age of the alchemical theater,"‡ in whose mouth Basil Valentine placed the following words in *The Twelve Keys of Philosophy*: "Hungary first begot me, the sky and the stars fed me, the earth nursed me. Though I must die and be buried, yet Vulcan causes me to be born anew. Therefore, Hungary is my native land, and the earth which contains everything is my mother." And also this ambivalent presentation of the benefits—of which I've barely spoken yet—of the "precious stone of the ancient philosophers": "This our stone not only has power to cure leprous and imperfect metallic bodies and to regenerate them by reducing and converting them into a totally achieved

---

*Lassalle, "Témoignage d'un ami de longue date." Lassalle's previous quote is from the same article.

†Jennifer Waelti-Walter, *Alchimie et littérature*. Furthermore, as Fulcanelli writes in the *Mystery of the Cathedrals*: "The Philosopher's Stone and the Philosophic Stone are, then, two things similar in kind and origin, but the first is raw, while the second, which is derived from it, is perfectly cooked and digested."

‡Henri Desoubeaux, "Portrait de l'artiste en jeune singe ou Butor et l'autobiographie: Entre Sartre et Breton." Perhaps this "man of great age of the alchemical theater" is he whose face figures on the back of that of the young girl who personifies Prudence, the statue that stands to the northeast of the splendid dwelling of the philosophers that is Francois II's tomb in Nantes Cathedral.

nature; but also preserving men's health, and procuring them a long life: and by its celestial virtue it has led me to such an old age that weary of such a long life, I would now like to leave this world."

Born in 1908 to a Jewish family in Hungary, this discreet individual was a political refugee who, after crossing through Switzerland in 1942, probably arrived in France after the war since it was into his house that Mircea Eliade (as he says in the second volume of his memoirs, *Exile's Odyssey [1937–1960]*) moved in September 1945 when he decided not to return to Romania. Again, according to Butor, Hunwald, in order to practice medicine in France, "had to write a new dissertation on Paracelsus"* on whom he was "a great expert," an obligation he fulfilled in 1948. Enrolled into the Ordre des Médecins de la Seine in October 1949, he worked as a general practitioner and homeopath. Incidentally, under "Origine et destinée de la médecine hermétique," one of the rare texts we have from him published as an appendix in Eric J. Holmyard's book on alchemy, we can see beneath Hunwald's signature a mention of him as a "professor at the School of Anthropology."† Here is where this Hermetic scholar, as Flamand described him, taught "biological thought" and ethnography, with courses focusing primarily on "Sun and Moon, the physio-pathological tendencies," as shown by a manuscript held by the Monaco multimedia library. His name also appears, next to that of Pierre Mabille ("Principes planétaires"), in a text titled "Tendances physio-astrologiques" in the book *Jupiter et Saturne: Typologie astrologique de Jupiter et Saturne* published in 1982 by Editions Traditionnelles under the direction of André Barbault,

---

*Phillippus Theophrastus Bombast von Hohenheim, a.k.a. Paracelsus (1493–1541), was a doctor, alchemist, and lay theologian from German Switzerland. The exact title of Hunwald's dissertation is *Paracelse et les débuts de la chimie médicale*.

†Founded in 1875 by Paul Broca, Louis-Adolphe Bertillon, and Jean-Louis Armand de Quatrefages de Bréau, and in 1889 given recognition as an institution useful to the public, the School of Anthropology, as Khaitzine shows, "long included a number of freemasons, like the Free University of Brussels"—for example, Pierre Mabille as of 1948.

founder and presenter of the International Center of Astrology in the fifties, as well as in Robert Amadou's periodical, *La tour Saint-Jacques*, on which he also collaborated. Particularly notable is an article he contributed to the first issue (November–December 1955) with the title "Paracelse, le médecin à la croisée des chemins,"* followed by a second article in the next issue. He was also a member of this review's editorial board. We can also find Henri Hunwald in a 1985 issue of the *Cahiers de l'Hermétisme* dedicated to astrology in which one of his earlier texts, "Paracelse et l'astrologie médicale" was republished. Gilles Bucherie also claims that Hunwald presented a series of lectures, whose subject he doesn't identify, in 1954 "at the academic society hall," which André Breton attended as well, which seems to show the two men had a friendly relationship.

Jean-Pierre Lassalle, another surrealist, also claims that this "doctor who treated Breton" was the "translator of *Alchemy and Medicine* by the spagyrist-alchemist† von Bernus." This book, for which he also wrote the preface,[3] was published in France in 1960. He writes here that in this "major work" "for the first time since the end of the eighteenth century . . . an alchemist who has been preparing and applying Paracelsian remedies for forty years agrees to speak." In his *Portrait of the Artist as a Young Ape*, in which he also appears, Michel Butor confirms this information by presenting Baron Alexander von Bernus (1880–1965), who was also a fan of occultism and alchemy, and a friend of Rudolf Steiner, like this: "Alexander von B., poet, storyteller,‡ who

---

*In the same issue, René Alleau published an article entitled, "Le livre d'heures de Jehan Lallemant."

†However, alchemy and spagyrics are not the same thing, even if both have "a material starting point . . . the use of a mineral material, because the latter, as Bernard Roger tells us in *Paris et l'alchimie,* is nothing other than ancient chemistry," "a set of exoteric techniques," whereas the former "was and remains a traditional esoteric science and a sacred art."

‡Jennifer Waelti-Walter also states that in addition to *Alchimie et médecine*, "his best poems were published under the title: *De l'or à minuit*" in 1948 and "his stories, *Les fleurs du magicien*" in 1951 and translated into French in 1960.

long ago in Vienna had been a close friend of Hofmannsthal and his whole circle, but also a leading practitioner of spagyric medicine, [prepares] in his dispensary, according to ancient recipes, those of Paracelsus in particular, electuaries, balms, salves, and tinctures which he sent to numerous correspondents under the Sol-Luna Laboratory label." He founded this laboratory, which still exists today, in 1921. Butor then gives this description in which it would be hard not to see a little surrealist touch: "Alexander von B. was an old German of great elegance, whose features reminded me of Max Ernst, [with] an aquiline nose, pale blue eyes, white hair swept back from both sides of a high forehead."

In July 1953, Hunwald, clearly showing the nature of his relationship with the baron, dedicated the copy of *Aspects de l'alchimie traditionnelle* he sent him as follows: "In the hope that all four of us (you, dear Baron, the author [René Alleau], the preface writer [Eugène Canseliet] of this book, and my own small self) can meet very soon for a hermetic colloquium in four voices!" Through a closer examination of the page* on which this document appears, we see that around this same time, Eugène Canseliet, René Alleau, and Claude d'Ygé also sent him their books, which, if we add Butor to the list, at least testifies to the existence of a small discreet circle of friends sharing the same passion. In 1955, for example, Canseliet sent him, via Hunwald, a copy of *Deux logis alchimiques* for his seventy-fifth birthday, dedicated to the "philosopher by fire, he too a son of Alchemy for which the Germany of the Princes was the cradle." This was followed in 1956 by his edition of Basil Valentine's *Twelve Keys of Philosophy*, accompanied by a message in Latin! In January 1955, Claude d'Ygé sent him his *Nouvelle assemblée des philosophes chymiques* with this dedication: "To the poet Von Bernus, to the alchemist who knows *from experience* that the mystery of the Stable in Bethlehem is the wondrous Christian summary of the Great Work. To the learned son of Hermes who knows the secret of the 'salty and sticky

---

Archiv dell' Ermetismo. These documents are presented as coming from the Alexander von Bernus archives kept at the Baden State Library in Karlsruhe.

silt of the Genesis.' Fraternally." René Alleau, meanwhile sent him a copy
of his book *De la nature des symboles* with this dedication on August 3,
1960: "To Monsieur le Baron Alexander von Bernus, as a token of my sincere admiration for his work and with respectful homage." On August 9
of that same year, he sent him a card depicting the Schloss Donaumünster
(Donaumünster Castle) where the baron lived "with the expression of my
grateful respect," and, on it, the following short poem, which could give
the impression that he had personally stayed there:

> *Strangers and wanderers on the earth*
> *Thus were the Masters and the poor*
> *Though they possessed all the holy riches*
> *Of the World;*
> *Hunted everywhere by the curse of Cain,*
> *But if they had known*
> *The castle of Donaumünster*
> *That he who is a King of Peace*
> *Has blessed thrice*
> *Then their spirits come*
> *Like the storks from the unknown East*
> *They would have chosen to alight upon this high place*
> *And there in the darkness keep watch*
> *Over the immortal Fire of the Sanctuary . . .*

As a good disciple of von Bernus, it seems that Hunwald was indeed
interested in Hermeticism only from the perspective of medicine in its
connections with astrology and alchemy.* He sought to evaluate the
contribution of "Paracelsus, unsurpassed model of hermetic medicine"
to his art, namely by explaining his "great revolutionary idea: *Defeat*

---

*In his foreword to the republication of Flamel's *Book of Hieroglyphic Figures*, René
Alleau explains that since antiquity, "Alchemy was closely tied to Medicine, its object
remaining the 'healing of imperfect metals' with the 'Philosopher's Stone' or 'Universal
Medicine.'" The uppercase letters and quotes are Alleau's.

astrological determinism with the help of alchemical remedies." He also endeavored to rediscover the trace of his successors, among whom Alexander von Bernus, whose name appears prominently in the "family tree suggesting the evolution of medicine." This "excessively schematic representation" accompanies the article instead of the never-written entire volume, which "the history of hermetic medicine"* calls for. It's easy to note in passing the allusion to the anthroposophical movement founded by Rudolf Steiner, whose "medicine and pharmacy" Hunwald presented as "deeply permeated by hermetic and Paracelsian thought, including the Doctrine of Signatures." He thus quite clearly fits into the lineage of those who Mircea Eliade calls "philosopher-chemists."

"The surrealist writers Arpad Mezei and Marcel Jean," the Quebecois writer David Nadeau writes in his book *L'Arche utopique: Le surréalisme et la loge maçonnique Thébah,* "sent him their thanks in the book *Genèse de la pensée moderne dans la littérature française* (1950) for providing documentation on the subject of the 'successive ages of humanity' and the Great Year of 25,790 solar years." "Bernard Roger," he continues, "sent me a copy of an unpublished text by Hunwald, *Les origines cosmiques du pentagramme,* which seems never to have been intended for publication, and in which the author explains that this astronomical figure illustrates the five synodic revolutions of each of the two sidereal revolutions of Venus. Around three thousand B.C., Mesopotamian astronomers succeeded in accurately determining these motions: *Coïncidence curieuse ou hasard objectif, les tablettes de Djomet-Nasr, aux pentagrammes parfaits, font partie de la collection Herbert Wald, à l'Ashmolean Museum d'Oxford, qui doit son origine au grand Elias Ashmole, dont le rôle de chaînon entre les Rose-Croix et la Maçonnerie est bien connu"†*—an unpublished text that may have been

---

*Hunwald took this opportunity to provide the elements of a bibliography for this topic.

†Odd coincidence or objective chance, the Djomet Nasr tablets with their perfect pentagrams form part of the Herbert Wald Collection at the Ashmolean Museum, which owes its origin to the great Elias Ashmole, whose role as a link between the Rosicrucians and Masonry is well known.

written for the members of the Hermes Circle or more certainly for those of the Thebah Lodge.

In spite of all this, we have, to put it briefly, very little information about this rather discreet and mysterious, yet influential, individual— "an individual of transmission and revelation," as Jean-Claude Bailly* puts it. In addition to the very rare German edition of the *Chemical Writings of the Brother Valentine of the Order of Saint Benedict* published in Hamburg in 1717† and mentioned by Canseliet in his introduction to the new edition of Valentine's *Twelve Keys* for Editions de Minuit in 1956, he "naturally possessed all the works of Jacob Böhme." He knew quite a lot of things about ghosts. Nadeau notes that his ex-libris "depicts in a sun framed by the four elements a glass sphere surrounded by a winged, crowned Ouroboros, within which a raven stands on a skull": *Caput mortuum.*‡

Hunwald was "admired by both Breton and Butor," and was "very close friends with Maryse Sandoz who was a member of the surrealist group,"** but also with Michel Carrouges, to whom he sent a postcard from a German museum depicting a medieval alchemist's laboratory and on which he simply wrote, "Alchemy, I have everything." There was also the esotericist Paul Vulliaud who dedicated his last book[4] to him "with

---

*In the sale catalog for the Alleau collection in 2009.

†Canseliet didn't fail to "emphasize," about this translation of Valentine's work, "the tireless courtesy of Doctor Hunwald, who is well known to the *enthusiasts* of the Art" as well as his great knowledge, or more precisely, his erudition. (Italics and capitalization are Canseliet's.)

‡This *caput mortuum*, also called "the raven's head, the Moor's head, the dark jacket, John's blackbird," writes Flamand in his *Les méandres du sens*, stands for what "the alchemists called *ashes*"—in other words, "the powdered and very fertile matter resulting from the work in Black" from which "one will be able to extract the philosophical Sulfur or mineral Light." This is confirmed by Canseliet in these words: "Previously subjected to the delitescent action of lunar rays, the *caput mortuum* becomes, when exposed to fire, an ash or rather a powdery, aromatic compost, both vital and fertile, which is now ready to yield its sulfur to mercury" (*L'alchimie expliquée sur ses textes classiques*)!

**Richard Khaitzine, *La langue des oiseaux*, vol. 3. This would be Maryse Sandoz, of the Sandoz laboratories, who was then the wife of Michel Zimbacca.

tenderness." Hunwald died in 1964 after suffering a heart attack while performing his duties as Senior Warden during a Masonic meeting. I don't know if Jennifer Waelti-Walter, who gives us a valuable clue about him by writing that "he symbolizes the guide and the adept, the one who invites the disciple to follow him on the path of work," was aware of this detail of importance, but "Doctor H." was received as an entered apprentice on April 26, 1956, in the Thebah Lodge of the Grand Lodge of France, the lodge that had once been that of René Guénon. Hunwald was "the most notable brother" in this lodge "during the decade of 1950–1960" as well as the sponsor of some of his surrealist friends—everything is connected—namely Bernard Roger, René Alleau, Elie-Charles Flamand, Guy-René Doumayrou, Roger Van Hecke, and Jean Palou.

First and foremost he played a decisive role in the founding of the very discreet Hermes Circle, "a philosophical and historical study group"* one of whose objectives was to identify the alchemical signs on Parisian buildings (see plate 16). This may well be related to the aborted plan to create a "Cercle de la Rose du Livre" with Breton around the same time. The Hermes Circle was officially presided over by Eugène Canseliet, at the time when he had just published *The Twelve Keys of Philosophy*, and its vice president was Henri Hunwald. It is clear that they met in the latter's new home at 11 Boulevard Saint-Germain, which also served as their headquarters. It was founded "as an organization based on law of 1901" during a constituting session facilitated by René Alleau, who seems to have played a role as secretary, at least some of the time. The meeting took place on Thursday, December 20, 1956, during which were discussed its goals as well as the place and frequency of meetings, its financial resources, its organization, with possible branches "in the provinces and abroad," the "composition of its administrative board and the leadership of research groups," the "work program . . . and the distribution of tasks to be carried out."

---

*Very little has been written about this organization, practically all of whose members have died.

They decided to form nine working groups, the first on the "Philosophy of Hermeticism" under the direction of René Alleau, and the second on "Christian Symbology," under Robert Amadou. A third group to study "Iconographical Symbolism" would be led by M. André. The fourth on "Hermetic Symbolism" would be led by Eugéne Canseliet. Marie-Madeleine Davy, a philosopher specializing in medieval mysticism and theology and author, in particular, of the "remarkable *Initiation à la symbolique romane*"* should have been asked to lead a group on "medieval philosophy," while Claude d'Ygé would have been entrusted with that on "Hermetic Literature" and Mircea Eliade with that on the "History of Religions." The Egyptian Mounir Hafez, a leading thinker on Sufism who in his youth had published texts in surrealist magazines, would have been asked to lead the work on "Eastern Symbolism," while Dr. Hunwald would have led the group devoted to the "History of Hermeticism." According to the documents in my possession, which I enclose as an appendix, all the group leaders with the exception of M. M. Davy and a certain M. Ranque† should have been members of the association's Board of Directors, as well as, at least initially as guests, Elie-Charles Flamand‡ and Bernard Roger, in particular, who both confirmed this to me, and Guy-René Doumayrou,

---

*René Alleau shows evidence of the esteem he bears (in his *Énigmes et symboles du Mont Saint-Michel*) for M. M. Davy's book, which he cites on several occasions. He also includes her (in the introduction to *The Primal Force of Symbols*) among those whose "books and works" definitely influenced him, and in the bibliography he again cites her *Clefs de l'art roman: la symbolique romane* (Paris: Berg, 1973). Frédérick Tristan, who managed the "Spiritualités vivantes" collection at Albin Michel with Davy, speaks of her in these terms in his interview with Olivier Gissey: "The literary and philosophical attachment of Marie-Madeleine Davy to medieval Germanic thought particularly inspired her enamored awareness of the divine. In it she found a living source of meditation founded on the inner path connected to the universal order." And he goes on to say, "Marie-Madeleine Davy would immerse herself in this mystical life while remaining an intellectual keen on interrogating and admiring some of her contemporaries like Gabriel Marcel, Nicolas Berdiaev, Jules Monchanin, and Hervé le Saux."

†This is probably Georges Ranque, born in 1898 in Ambérieu en Bugey and who died in 1973. In 1972 he published *La pierre philosophale* with the publisher Robert Laffont.

‡Elie-Charles Flamand only became a member in 1957.

the unrecognized author of such important works as *Géographie sidérale* and *Cinq paradigmes de la géometrie sacrée et leur signature monumentale*.

Before proceeding, it seems helpful to discuss Doumayrou in more detail. A member of the surrealist group since 1950, plus a Freemason, heraldry expert, architect, and specialist of sacred geometry, Doumayrou (who died in 2011) is known as the author of his remarkable *Géographie sidérale* (Sidereal geography) (Union générale d'éditions, 1975), *Cinq paradigmes de la géométrie sacrée et leur signature monumentale* (Five paradigms of sacred geometry and their monumental signature) (Arma Artis, 1997) as well as *Évocations de l'esprit des lieux: Les jalons d'un espace-temps poétique autour du Languedoc* (Evocation of the spirit of places: The landmarks of a poetic time/space around Languedoc) (Centre international de documentation occitane, 1987). Not to mention *L'abrégé de symbolisme pratique* (Abridged practical symbolism), subtitled *évocation de l'esprit des lieux* (evoking the spirit of places) in 1985. Only a few copies were distributed for friends, "with the name and date of the publication *Lunate septimaniae 1985*." In an autobiographical note, written on June 2, 1990, and cited by Patrick Fréchet, he introduces himself as follows: "Born in Béziers, 1925. Architect, but always on the margins of professional achievement. Active participation in the Surrealist group in the 1950s. Explored the possibility of subjecting the institutions of urban civilization to the poetic impulse. Discovered elements of an answer in archaeology, in the form of a symbolic geography underlined by the inscription of data from traditional philosophy (astrology, alchemy). Lives in retirement in Languedoc." Architect, in fact, Guy-René Doumayrou had, like Bernard Roger, "conceived" very early on, as Didier Deroeux notes, "plans for surrealist architecture and urban environments, drawing up blueprints for 'future cities' inspired by the sacred sciences (the metaphysics of numbers, geomancy) and the traditional symbology of ancient civilizations." It is in this capacity that, thanks to the kind intervention of Adrien Dax, he was able to exhibit the model of his "Garden of Wonder," with its "domes of immortality" and its "egg of transmutations," where "ritual perfor-mances" could be given, at the Daniel Cordier Gallery in 1959–1960, as part of the Exposition inteRnatiOnale du Surréalisme.

All the names mentioned above, especially those of Henri Hunwald, as we've seen, Eugéne Canseliet, René Alleau, Elie-Charles Flamand, Marie-Madeleine Davy, and Mounir Hafez, can be found on the contents pages of the issues of Robert Amadou's magazine, *La tour Saint-Jacques*, next to those of Amadou himself, André Breton, Michel Carrouges, Jean Palou, Joë Bousquet, Malcolm de Chazal, René Nelli, Mircea Eliade, and Lise Deharme. These names are also those of most of the contributors to Holmyard's book on alchemy, the editor having chosen to "give a voice to those writers and artists who have devoted a significant part of their lives to alchemy, whether they actually practiced it or whether they had solely sought to penetrate the arcana through the study of texts, or whether they had discov-ered the analogous connection between alchemy and their own kind of artistic creation, in other words, the purifying action of matter and the concentration of spirit that tends to transform them into a single living body of extreme life."[5] And in fact, the said contributors, qualified individuals if there ever were any, are none other than René Alleau, Eugène Canseliet, Claude d'Ygé, Mircea Eliade, and Henri Hunwald. Joining them are Jacques Van Lennep, Serge Hutin, and Michel Carrouges, as well as the dramatist Romain Weingarten, who claimed to be close to the surrealists, and Alexandre Labzine, best known as author of a biography of Guénon but also the translator and adaptor of Edward Bulwer Lytton's *Zanoni*.

This cenacle, which was short-lived and had only an embryonic organization, can probably be considered, as Gilles Bucherie suggests, as a forerunner of the "Institut des Sciences Traditionnelles" imagined by Alleau and Hunwald, which never saw the light of day. It was appar-ently engaged in theoretical work, listening to oral communications (similar to oral lectures on Masonic matters delivered in the Lodge), based on the particular expertise and interests of its members, such as that of Elie-Charles Flamand for the *Tabula Smaragdina*, thought to have had some influence on the content of Doumayrou's later works on sacred geography or that of Alleau. Among the other activities of the group are the strolls through the streets of Paris in search of the alchemical symbols decorating old buildings—walks that undoubtedly left their mark on Bernard Roger's *Paris and Alchemy*, dedicated "to the memory of Dr. Henri Hunwald."

For example, the minutes of the second meeting of the group, chaired by Hunwald, which mentions "presentations . . . given by Mr. Alleau, Mr. Amadou, Mr. André, Mr. Bouillier, Mr. Flamand, Mr. Roger," give a good idea of the organization's activities. René Alleau presented a statement on the need to develop "a new methodology, more suitable for the study of symbols," which in all likelihood was directly related to the research that would culminate in 1976 with the publication of his masterpiece, *The Science of Symbols: Contribution to the Study of Symbology's Principles and Methods* (Paris: Payot). "Mr. Amadou and Mr. Bouillier* [explained] the interpretation of Notre-Dame de Paris in contemporary literature and [indicated] the detectable traces of its symbolism in Huysmans's *La Cathédrale*, and Hugo's *Notre-Dame de Paris*, in particular. Finally, Mr. André, Mr. Flamand, and Mr. Roger [presented] the first part of an iconographical study of Notre-Dame de Paris," by striving to "show the original appearance of the Work† of art before its restorations." The minutes also state that the three men "established a parallel between the interpretations of the sculptures on the portals referring to Viollet-le-Duc, de Guilhermy,‡ and Queyron** and the hermetic interpretation, particularly that of Fulcanelli in *The Mystery of*

---

*Likely the bibliophile, Henry Bouillier.

†"Minutes of the meeting of January 31, 1957." (Capitalization in original.)

‡Ferdinand de Guilhermy (1809–1878), French historian and archaeologist, author with Eugène Viollet-le-Duc of a *Description de Notre-Dame, cathédrale de Paris*.

**Pierre-Emile Queyron (1821–1878) was, starting in 1852, the first works inspector of Notre-Dame in Paris.

the Cathedrals"—a work that, as we will see, was later continued by Bernard Roger.

Moreover, these works by André, Flamand, and Roger on "the iconography of Notre-Dame" were at the heart of the following meetings, apparently strongly based on this building and things related to it, since the reports associated with it focus on "The Cathedral: Its Importance in Social Life, Its Social Value, Its Symbolic Value" on March 21, 1957, and "The Hermetic Philosophy and Symbolism of the Virgin" on May 16. It is true, Josane Charpentier points out, that in the Middle Ages, Notre-Dame was "the philosophical church" "and, as Victor Hugo said, 'the most satisfying summary of the hermetic science' of which the church of Saint-Jacques-la-Boucherie (sic) was a complete hieroglyph,"[6] but also the place where the alchemists used to meet once a week on Saturdays, "on the day of Saturn," says Fulcanelli. In all these cases, the meeting ended with a general discussion—such as that of May 16, which seems to have been the last according to Bernard Roger and Jorge Camacho.

In any case, beyond the various calculations about the possible renaissance of occultism that these activities could have brought about, it is more than likely that the increased interest in alchemy that stands out in the seventies via the books on general symbology, sacred geography, and the esoteric content of tales and legends, all of a rare quality, that were later presented to the public—or not*—by those who had taken part in the Hermes Circle meetings, owed much to what had been introduced of the essential then, and contributed greatly to the surrealist project of "totally remodeling human understanding," which Breton had borrowed from Charles Fourier.

---

*I'm mainly thinking here of *L'abrégé de symbolisme pratique, évocation de l'esprit des lieux* by Guy-René Doumayrou.

8

ART AND ALCHEMY

Every artist has to resume the pursuit of the Golden Fleece by himself.

ANDRÉ BRETON, *PROLEGOMENA TO A THIRD SURREALIST MANIFESTO OR NOT*

Defined, as Bernard Roger reminds us in *A la découverte de l'alchimie*, as, according to Zosimos the Panopolitan, "a sacred and divine art of making gold and silver," and according to Pelagius the philosopher, a "divine and sacred art," and according to Olympiodorus, a "sacred art" and even *sacerdotal*, alchemy therefore clearly reflects "practices of a sacred nature on an appropriate material used as a support, *as required for any artistic activity.*"[1]

Now, one of the specific features of the sacred art, according to Jörg Völlnagel, is that "alchemy tells its stories best in images rather than words; it is through images that they are most compelling." Most often they take the form of a "narrative of extraordinary stories, as magnificent, exuberant, cruel, magical, and surreal as the tales of the *Thousand and One Nights*, expressed through fantastic, never-before-seen images." This is one way of putting your finger on the inseparable importance of image and word, which adequately support each other in the construction of the alchemical imagination according to the reading made of it by the one who discovers them, sometimes at the price of ambiguity.

Following in the footsteps of Serge Hutin in his preface to Jacques Van Lennep's book, *Art and Alchemy*,[2] it is worth noting that it is hard not to be struck by "the existence in the West of numerous artworks whose hermetic esotericism is their sole reason for being." Probably "created by the alchemists themselves or under their supervision," these works may illustrate the precept taken from *The Secret Work of Hermetic Philosophy*: "the Philosophers speak more freely and clearly through enigmatic figures and characters, as if through a silent language, than through words." Canseliet cites this as an epigraph in his introduction to the *Mutus Liber*, that *Mute Book* that specifically lacks any explanatory text. Klossowski de Rola echoes this when he writes, "Hermetic iconography reveals what the texts have carefully left unsaid. The Philosophers gladly admit this. For example, we can read after the word 'end' in the Arsenal Library's manuscript 973, 'All that remains to be done is the oral teaching of the primal matter and the second matter; The authors never named them in their writings, but only depicted them in their hieroglyphic figures.'"[3] Especially when it's a question of transmitting "universal symbols," in all their expressive purity, whose roots go back to the dawn of time and "reveal fundamental aspects of the human mentality and unconscious" that moreover "still live within us."*

And yet words have much to say and Van Lennep, who does not miss the opportunity to note that the art of Hermes is "first and foremost functional" and "sustained by a poetic imagination that draws constant vitality from that nature of which the alchemist was the most assiduous lover," recalls that this art, the only one closely linked to a science, philosophy, and "ethics," "was also the only one since the Middle Ages that used images as words and assembled them into allegorical *texts* defending [said] philosophy or retracing mystical operations," thus

---

*Jacques Van Lennep, *Art et alchimie*. And speaking of the *Mutus Liber*, how can we not recall the little-known Roland Sig, a postwar surrealist, who also made his own version, which has practically never been exhibited.

reviving "one of the very oldest functions of the arts perceived as languages." Knowing that "no image of hermetic art is the gratuitous product of the imagination" and that "each is incorporated into a complex system of a philosophy that gives it meaning."

But he also reminds us that "alchemical art is . . . an esoteric art for initiates," because only initiation provides access to "the particular meaning of a certain number of symbols that belong exclusively to the alchemists' legacy." And he lists several beautiful images that are pregnant with meaning, like that "of the red lion or the green lion, royal couples, two stones, inhabited vessels, the wolf that symbolizes antimony or the chicken that corresponds to compost."[4]

For his part, Michel Carrouges was fully justified in underscoring (as we saw earlier) the "clearly pre-surrealist" nature of their writings and in reminding us that Breton at the time of the *Manifestos* correctly pointed out "that the famous *figures* of Nicolas Flamel are astonishing precursors of surrealist paintings." Much later in *L'art magique,* Breton again deplores "the irreparable loss of the paintings created under Flamel's direction at the Charnel House of the Innocents, paintings of which *The Book of Abraham the Jew* only leaves us a crudely executed memory." Similarly he spoke of his taste for "the reproductions of it provided in Givrot de Givry's *Picture Museum of Sorcery, Magic, and Alchemy,*" and the illustrations by Robert Fludd or Basil Valentine, which could also be found there. He owned a copy of this book with his ex libris, which ended up in René Alleau's library when Breton's library was dispersed.[5]

This is implicitly confirmed by Van Lennep in his article in Holmyard's book, in which he makes special mention of the surrealist painter and alchemist Baskine, even going so far as to write "that the surrealist revolution restored absolute validity to alchemical art!" From this perspective, despite some reservations, we must agree with him, that surrealism "like alchemy, sublimated the minerals, performed transformations of kingdoms, spoke the language of the elements" and even used the "language of the birds."

But Bernard Roger is equally justified in saying, in the same spirit, that "the art of Hermes has inspired painting and sculpture as deeply as it has inspired the novel or the poem," and adding, probably with the writings of Canseliet and Fulcanelli in mind, that "in the plastic arts as well as in architecture, our cathedrals and castles bear sufficient evidence of the presence of myths and symbols of hermetic esotericism that there is no need to prove its importance in medieval civilization and beyond into the sixteenth century."[6]

Following in the footsteps of Breton, who, as I've shown, was drawn to esotericism and Hermeticism early on and believed that the expression "alchemy of the word" had to be taken "literally," a number of their companions, "Dali, Ernst, Tanguy, Fini,* and Magritte bathed in the same springs as Bosch and Breughel,"[7] Van Lennep tells us, just as, Carrouges adds "de Chirico . . . , Masson and sometimes even Picasso" or Paalen, "a William Blake who unites the two eras." Not to mention Victor Brauner, many of whose works, beginning with the *Philosopher's Stone* in 1940, with its sleepwalker irresistibly drawn to a fabulous crystal, bear the mark of the Art of Music, and whose last studio he dubbed the Athanor!

Surrealist in spite of everything, Salvador Dali had already confided in 1968 in *The Passions According to Dali* that "by making his whole life an alchemical object he happily believed himself to be a descendant of the Catalan Ramon Lull," the presumed author of the *Opera Chemica* codex, "the visionary doctor" who was credited with introducing the word *alchemy* into Catalan. This same Dali, who is said to have stayed at the Castle of Dampierre-sur-Boutonne† in the 1970s, created with René Alleau's assistance (whose expertise is once again on display here) a mag-

---

*In this regard, in *Les alchimistes*, Hutin and Caron show that "alchemical symbols are archetypes belonging to humanity's collective unconscious, which is why they are found in countless legends and why they reappear in some 'automatic' paintings of contemporary surrealist painters (Leonor Fini, for example)."

†Paradoxically, while the anonymous author of the small introductory brochure sold at the chateau constantly minimizes the alchemical aspect of the gallery of the same name, and uses the conditional when mentioning Dali's stay there, several of Dali's lithographs from *L'alchimie des philosophes* are exhibited in the tower.

nificent artist's book on classic alchemical texts of both East and West, *The Alchemy of the Philosophers*, published by the Gala-Salvador Dali Foundation on the occasion of the exhibition of the same name, in 1976. The edition was limited to 275 copies! René Alleau, with the help of a crew of nine experts, including Marie-Madeleine Davy (also Geneviève Javary, an expert on the Christian Kabbalah, the eminent Indologists Jean Filliozat and Guy Mazars, the equally eminent Sinologists Max Kaltenmark and Kristopher Shipper, the Hellenist Henri-Dominique Saffrey, the Orientalist Vincent Monteil, and Arab philosophy expert Yves Marquet, author of the book *Alchimie, astrologie et mystique en Islam: autour des Frères de la Pureté*), trace through a selection of texts that "form a set of very old and highly poetic writings,"[8] "the path followed by alchemical philosophy from a universal perspective." Most taken from prestigious libraries, "the texts and alchemical manuscripts were printed in facsimile" and accompanied by "original translations in French and English" "offering a universal vision of mystical knowledge and wisdom through the prism of different cultures." Given who the members of the scientific team are, it comes as no surprise to see that, covering a period extending from the third to eleventh centuries, they "go back to the origins of Chinese alchemical thought, and include the most illustrious texts of Indian, Greek, Arab, Hebrew, and Western alchemy." Two Chinese texts, "The Elixir of Immortality" and "On Yin and Yang," both taken from the "*Tao-Tsang* book" and respectively signed Ko Hung and Tchang Kieou-kai,* are complemented by an Indian work written by Madhava, "The System of Mercury."† Greek alchemy is represented by three texts. The first, "The Dream of an Alchemist"

---

*The Daozang or Tao-Tsang is the "Taoist Canon," consisting of 1400 texts collected from 400 CE on. Ko Hung or Ge Hong (283–343 CE) is a philosopher and alchemist from the Jin Era and a native of southern China. Tchang Kieou-kai lived in the eighth century.

†This is a fourteenth-century Indian philosopher named Madhavacharya, the author of the *Sarvadarsanasangraha*, in other words the *Summary of all the philosophical systems*, from which comes the text proposed by the authors.

is from the *Visions of Zosimos* (the Panopolitan whose path we have crossed before); the second, "The Serpent Ouroboros," is borrowed from an anonymous manuscript in the National Library of France; and the third, "Solomon's Labyrinth," is from the Marciana National Library in Venice. Despite the significant Arab role in the transmission of these texts, namely the Greek, translated at the behest of Prince Khalid ibn Yaz, Alleau and his team only kept one of the Arab alchemical texts: "The Emerald Tablet" (*Lawh az-zumurrud*), whose importance has long been established. A text entitled "On the Colors of Angels and Metals," taken from chapter XXV of the *Sefer Ha Zohar*, the *Book of Splendor*, strongly influenced by the Kabbalah, serves as a reminder of the important role of alchemy in the Hebrew tradition—and I will not fail to mention here the figure of Maitre Canches who accompanied Nicolas Flamel on his return from Compostela. Three names, finally, are singled out to represent the medieval Western alchemy which often owes much to the Jews and Arabs: Arnaud de Villeneuve, with a text entitled "The Secret Preparation of the Great Work," a passage from the *Epistola missa a Rainaldo de Villanova Papæ Bonifacio*; Jehan de Meung (1280–1315), with an extract from the *Romance of the Rose*, "The Resurrection of the Phoenix"; and to pay homage where homage is due, Ramon Lull with "The King and the Queen," a passage from the *Le codicille* manuscript in the Arsenal Library in Paris. Dali, for his part, created "ten original color plates on parchment, lithography, serigraphy, and engraving," ten plates sometimes enhanced with gold to illustrate the universal nature of the Art of Music and the particularities of the different cultural approaches to what would come to be called "the Sacred Science." The ten plates are *Immortality*, *The Yin and the Yang*, *The Dream of an Alchemist or the Tree of Life*, *The Ouroboros*, *The Labyrinth*, *The Emerald Tablet*, *The Angel of Alchemy*, *The Philosophical Crucible*, *The Phoenix*, and finally *The King and Queen*. These were accompanied by six serigraphs introducing the various chapters. All of this was placed in a magnificent leather, parchment, and resin box measuring 83x64x20 centimeters.

As for the Belgians, Magritte did acknowledge, shortly before his death, in a letter to Van Lennep—Van Lennep, when he was a young art historian, had given a lecture on his paintings in which he drew a parallel between one of his paintings, *L'homme du large*, and Breton's use of the famous phrase "Osiris is a dark god" in *Arcane 17*—some "interest" in the Art of Music, to which he had probably been introduced by his friend Marcel Lecomte.* Another surrealist "with a passion for alchemy and esotericism" is Jacques Lacomblez, kingpin of the magazine *Edda* and the *Phases* group in Belgium, whose works, such as *The Alchemical Ladder* (2013) refer directly to it. Although he "considered it, like Breton, as a philosophical materialism, comparable to the artistic work of transforming matter" and "opposed all idealistic ideas at the source of a degenerate imagery, the paraphernalia of a worn-out esotericism,"[9] the painter—and poet—showed great "interest in Ibn Arabi, author of *The Alchemy of Perfect Happiness*, an initiatory path toward perfection." And Van Lennep adds, "This treatise, which belongs to the important Arabic alchemical tradition, magnifies the original language of the birds, that cabala knowledge of which is recommended by the Koran. Like the alchemists and Cyrano de Bergerac, Lacomblez practiced this language in its forms and colors as well as its musicality and in its word!"[10] Nor did he overlook the painter's participation in the 1986

---

*In an email of September 7, 2022, Jacques Van Lennep writes me: "From 1965, I spent time with Lecomte, an employee like me at the MRBAB (Musées Royaux des Beaux-Arts de Belgique). He was very knowledgeable about esotericism and had been a friend and influencer of Magritte since the beginning. Cf. my articles "Marcel Lecomte, cet alchimiste . . ." and "Une baignoire comme ultime bibliothèque" in *Fantasmagie*, May 1967, n° 25, and April 1968, n° 26. This is why I devoted a lecture to Magritte's *L'homme du large* [Man of the sea)] (1927), whose subject and title had been suggested by Lecomte. I discussed this painting from the standpoint of occultism. Magritte could not attend this lecture because his dog Loulou wasn't allowed in the MRBAB so he asked me for the text. Cf. my article "L'Homme du large" in *Fantasmagie*, September 1968, n° 28. This earned me his last important letter (dated May 9, 1967) in which he says: 'You see a kind of marriage that doesn't besmirch common decency between the alchemists' hope and my own despair and lack of hope. I can't deduce anything from mystery, which would be to misunderstand its essence.'" Van Lennep's conclusion: "Magritte never displayed any interest in the occult sciences but we cannot rule out Lecomte's influence in the case of the painting in question."

Biennale de Venise, on the theme of *Art and Science—Art and Alchemy, Arte e alchimia*, organized by the art historian Arturo Schwarz. He also cited the article he had written "on the relationship between Hermetic philosophy and his work," even quoting the first sentences of the text, which he had seen early and which speak volumes: "The liaison between art and alchemy seems to me to be based on something obvious; to the extent that I cannot consider the artistic gesture as a human mode of expression, but really as a vector of knowledge, it is normal that a relationship with alchemy would be woven in this sense."

In his contribution to the catalog *Perahim 1914–2008*, with the very explicit title "L'oeuvre de Perahim ou l'athanor du merveilleux,"[11] Michel Remy emphasizes the importance in this Romanian painter's work—especially after 1980—of the references to the Art of Music and its accompanying Language of the Birds. He even goes so far as to say that "the language of Perahim's images is alchemical in nature" and that it is an "alchemical painting/writing." Perahim personally confirmed his long-held interest in celestial agriculture. In his response to a questionnaire that Schwarz gave to all the artists participating in the *Arte e alchemia* exhibition, he says he had spent "days in the tiny streets of the alchemists and following the tracks of the Golem" during his stay in Prague in 1938. He adds that, after his arrival in Paris in 1969, he read Gershom Scholem's book on the Kabbalah, Fulcanelli's *Mystery of the Cathedrals*, and Alleau's *Aspects de l'alchimie traditionnelle*. "While Perahim," Remy clarifies, "did not present himself as a direct heir to the alchemists, alchemical knowledge nevertheless is visible in his work like a subtext, an underground current that irrigates his imagination." He then lingers over two canvases, *Twenty-Eight Visibles* from 1977 and *Metamorphosis in Red* from 1983. A chief feature of the first painting is a palm tree, also a symbol of immortality, "which the Ancients called *phoinix,* the same word they used to designate the color red and the phoenix"*—Φοινιξ—while the red background of the second paint-

---

*Here in fact Michel Remy quotes Dan Stanciu and his article "L'air Perahim" (*Perahim, la parade sauvage*, Strasburg, 2014).

ing, "the famous *rubedo,* color of sulfur and the phoenix," again and "of the sun and the fire that transmute the vile body, the last stage of the alchemical operation," "correspond to the phase when the body dissolves and the spirit solidifies, the first becoming the second," in "this world at a boil," according to the very words of the one Remy calls an "alchipainter." This world in which "transmutations take place according to the play of analogies and correspondences that the individual manages without really knowing how." These are "chemical weddings," a miracle that therefore smacks of the *Donum Dei.**

Another friend of Arturo Schwarz, who wrote several texts about him, published thirteen of his ready-mades, and most importantly, created the catalogue raisonné of his works. The same Duchamp who told Robert Lebel,[12] *"If* I have ever practiced *alchemy,* it *was* in the only way it *can* be done now, that is to say, without knowing it," seems to have held an attitude toward the Art of Music that was quite unique, starting with the beginning of his work on *The Bride Stripped Bare by Her Bachelors Even* directly after meeting Kandinsky and reading his book *On the Spiritual in Art.* So unique that Nadia Choucha, in her book *Surrealism and the Occult,*[13] who bases her claims on two eighteenth-century parables borrowed from Albert Poisson's *Théories et symboles des alchimistes,* "which Duchamp must have used as the starting point of his work," points out that "the male and female elements in the *Large Glass* tend to unite and thus reach a sense of 'wholeness,'" a "sense of perfection and wholeness," she says, that "was symbolized in alchemy by the androgyne, a divine and unified being that is both male and female." She then goes on to say that it's "the symbol of the undifferentiated consciousness sought by the alchemists when all opposites are reconciled. Duchamp was a modern alchemist and the *Large Glass,* his Great Work."

But we must also add Wifredo Lam to this list, who had "magnificent knowledge," as Ann Tronche tells us, of "alchemical heraldry," and

---

*Remember that *Donum Dei* is the title of a still-anonymous alchemical treatise from the second half of the fifteenth century.

whose "interest in alchemy is probably explained by his urge to give status to the presence of the invisible within the visible, a form of the intensity of thought restored to its true inner light !"[14] There is also Toyen, who in addition to her paintings dedicated to Gold Street, the famous *Zlàtka ulička* in Prague Castle, after her definitive move to France, did a portrait of André Breton "in the center of three superimposed triangles," "surrounded by allusions to the four elements (flames representing fire; swallows, the air; minerals, the earth; and a pond, water)," which would, according to Philippe Audoin, induce an alchemical reading!

Toyen (Maria Cerminova) was a Czech artist and cofounder of the surrealist group in Prague in 1934. She is a good representative of the interest that her friends then and now, perhaps because of the special atmosphere that reigned in the capital of Bohemia, had and still have for the Ars Magna. It was on the initiative of Jan and Eva Svankmajer, as well as Martin Stejskal, Ivo Purs, and Karol Baron, for example, that the texts of Fulcanelli and Canseliet, as well as Alleau's *Aspects de l'alchimie traditionnelle*, were translated into Czech. It was Stejskal, moreover, who organized, in 1989, with the collaboration of Stanislav Zadrobilek, the exhibition *Opus Magnum* that focused, somewhat similarly to Arturo Schwarz's exhibition in Venice, on the relations that could be maintained between art and the celestial agriculture. Thanks to the efforts of Jan Svankmajer, an ancient alchemist's laboratory was reconstructed in this exhibition and Eva Svankmajerova shared her interpretations of the plates from the *Mutus Liber*.

What then can we say about Josef Sima, the Czech member of the Grand Jeu who gave the following explanation concerning his brilliant watercolors of a seer: "It's the light and unity of all things that form the subject of my paintings, it's the unity of matter of which light is the most sublime manifestation, light perceived not as a mysterious fluid that illuminates objects, but as a force that creates the existence of objects."[15]

It is also from alchemy that Ludwig Zeller and Suzanna Wald, two Chilean surrealists associated with the *Phases* Group of Edouard Jaguer, borrowed the title of the magazine they founded in Toronto in 1974. This is *The Philosophical Egg*, the second series of which their daughter Beatriz Hausner has been publishing with Peter Dubé since 2021. Now, in so far as the *philosophical egg*, "which gathers the four elements, gives birth to the chick, the fifth being, that is to say the quintessence— another principle central to alchemy,"[16] the choice of this title can't be considered as mere coincidence.

Written in 1966, Van Lennep's *Art and Alchemy** obviously couldn't take into account the work of Jorge Camacho, who was then still a young painter whose talent was just beginning to blossom. And yet, he was already an artist for whom, as Juan Manuel Bonet† puts it in such pretty alchemical terms, "the central fire of poetry was so important," which reminds us that one of the most famous alchemical maxims is none other than the *I.N.R.I.* (*Igne Natura Renovatur Integra*) found on the Cross, which translates as *All of Nature Is Renewed by Fire*! With his "unique and dual painting, a wondrous and terrifying mystery that resists decoding,"[17] he is without a doubt one of the surrealists, like René Alleau, Bernard Roger, Elie-Charles Flamand, and Maurice Baskine, who clearly and openly showed a deep interest in the Science of Hermes, which, incidentally, he very quickly identified with his idea of freedom.

---

*In his article "Jacques Lacomblez" he emphasizes, however, that Camacho was "entirely inspired by this alchemy"!

†In the booklet *Feu central—Jorge Camacho dans ses tours*, published on the occasion of his February–March 2013 exhibition at the Cervantes Institute in Paris.

9

THE PARIS OF BERNARD ROGER

In the steps of Gobineau de Montluisant, Cambriel, and all the rest, we shall undertake the pious pilgrimage, speak to the stones, and question them.

FULCANELLI, *THE MYSTERY OF THE CATHEDRALS*

While I've already spoken of the role played by René Alleau and his principal books, I must also say a few words before going further about Camacho's other great accomplice, Bernard Roger. Although his name has already appeared, it will continue to do so throughout this entire book thanks to his discreet but influential presence, especially through his prefaces, commentaries, translations, and other written contributions. If Gilles Bucherie* is entitled to claim in his book on Alleau that "the study of alchemical texts and the reading of hermetic symbolism opens up access to multiple fields, such as architecture, but also, more generally, the history of art," just as he had good reason to claim that "this will require a methodology" when concluding that "this part of René Alleau's work remains up in the air," we have good reason to point out to him that this is because his accomplice and friend Bernard Roger

---

*Even if I don't overlook the contributions in this domain by the author of *Énigmes et symboles du Mont Saint-Michel*.

(an architect by training, let's not forget) would take charge of this particular aspect of things. This includes the methodology undoubtedly inspired by Fulcanelli's books and to a (much) lesser extent "a careful reading of the explanations of the symbolism present in the Guénon opus," but in the light that undeniably shines from the works of Henri Dontenville and his *French Mythology*.

Born in 1924, Bernard Roger, architect and disciple of Auguste Perret,* but a poet at heart, first championed surrealist architecture, proposing in particular to "transform Notre-Dame into a palace of love,"† after, probably, its purification by fire, as he writes: "From the ashes will emerge a sparkling jewel, and on the stone will be woven the lives of men."‡ Later he proposed the construction of "a cinema at the bottom of a lake," Lake Pavin, "an ancient crater in which, for the moment, water takes the place of fire."[1] This cannot help but bring to mind Rimbaud's "living room at the bottom of a lake."

As Richard Khaitzne recalls, "from 1970–1980, he was Worshipful Master of the Tebah [*sic*] Lodge of the Grand Lodge of France,"[2] in which, as we have seen, he had been received thanks to Henri Hunwald. In the same interview with Jacques Carletto quoted above, he said that he "had come to Freemasonry through alchemy." This is probably why, in his introduction to *The Light Emerging by Itself from the Darkness*, he mentioned the *Blazing Star* from an expert's point of view. This Hermetical-Masonic ritual of the alchemical grades** was published in 1766 by the Baron Theodore-Henry de Tschoudy and "expounds all the essential principles of the great work in a form so clear and complete that a person must be absolutely lacking in the quality of occult understanding if he does not succeed in obtaining

---

*Auguste Perret (1874–1954) is the "rebuilder of Le Havre," a French harbor that had been destroyed during WWII.

†Suggestion made on the occasion of the Eighth International Exhibition of Surrealism, EROS, at Cordier Gallery in 1959–1960.

‡A remark that assumes a particular resonance after the fire of spring 2019.

**Including that, really, of Supreme Commander of the stars!

the absolute truth by studying it."[3] In its final pages it repeats part of the work attributed to the enigmatic Fra Marc-Antonio Crasselame in the "curious Catechism or Instruction for the grade of Adept or Apprentice Philosopher, sublime and unknown." In passing, Roger recalls that Tschoudy explicitly considered alchemy to be "the trunk, the essential tree of masonry"* before wondering in his conclusion about "the direct influence that [this traditional science] had in the first years of the eighteenth century on the elaboration of Masonic rituals and even on the formation of the Order itself." It is worth saying a word about Baron Tschoudy here, whom Jean Solis describes as an "adventurer," "Swiss through his father," "Lorrain . . . for a good portion of his life, with a post in the Metz Parliament," who "died at forty-nine after a turbulent life with many facets." Solis adds that "wherever he went, he created, restored, or revived Masonic lodges, often with high grades that are sometimes of his own invention, but not always." Continuing, he says, "we know little of his alchemical frequentations but we still have to note his proximity to Mediterranean hermeticists like Sansevero, Di Sangro, and Gualdo† who played a role in another no less curious figure's entrance on the stage: Cagliostro."[4] Tschoudy's ritual, which quotes Valentine, Flamel, Lull, and above all the Cosmopolite and Sendivogius, smacks much more of alchemy to Jean Solis than of "a Masonic rite to be performed scrupulously." Bernard Roger, meanwhile, alludes again to Baron Tschoudy and his book, *The Blazing Star or the Society of Freemasons Considered in All its Aspects* "published in *The East in the Home of Silence*," in *Paris and*

---

*To such an extent that an "Instruction for doing the Great Work" figures prominently in the ritual.

†This is likely Raimondo di Sangro, prince of San Severo (1710–1771), an important figure of the Enlightenment in Italy, freethinker, alchemist, and Freemason. Gualdo, who Guénon nicknames "the alchemist of Venice," is in fact known as Federico Gualdi. Master of Cagliostro and personal friend of Saint Germain, this German was reputed to have produced an alchemical transmutation for King Frederick August II of Poland. He was considered to be an adept who possessed the "divine secret" and the elixir of long life.

Alchemy,* then in the book on Seville Cathedral that he wrote with Camacho.

Thus alerted, Bernard Roger soon took an interest in the alchemical representations appearing on some Parisian buildings, as shown by the text "The Emblems of Rue Monbel," published in *L'archibras,*† which he concluded by invoking "the sacred time to which belongs the immortal chain of the Sons of Science," undoubtedly close kin to the Widow's Sons! This text would be reprinted in his formidable *Paris and Alchemy,* which I should not forget to point out is dedicated to Doctor Hunwald and illustrated with photographs of the monuments—taken by Jorge Camacho!

"Reflecting on the relationship between Paris and alchemy is as much a matter of rediscovering facets of the *City of Light* that have shone in a discreet shadow since its origins as it is of finding a route through the tangled undergrowth of Sleeping Beauty's Park." It's precisely this, in the author's own words, that is the subject of this dazzling, erudite book in which Bernard Roger sets out to study "the parallelism between the crafting of the luminous material known as the Philosopher's Stone and the evolution of the *City of Light* from its origins," "a city that is a model of excellence in this regard," on a par with Prague and Bourges. All three cities are built atop an inextricable network of cellars and underground passages.

Divided into three parts, dedicated to respectively "Before Yesterday," "Yesterday," and "Today," that is to the *myths,* to the *Children of Hermes in Paris,* and to the *alchemical Emblems of Paris,* the book, from the introduction on, present the French capital as "a labyrinth that attracts the traveler to a center where one can feel the intense presence of *keys,*

---

*Bernard Roger, *Paris et l'alchimie.* In the same book Roger mentions "the symbolic age" and certain practices of the grade of "Grand Elect of the Sacred Vault, 14th degree of the Ancient and Accepted Scottish Rite."

†"Les emblèmes de la rue Monbel." As Bernard Roger recalls, Fulcanelli had already mentioned this large sculpture, which he had seen being installed, in the part of *The Mystery of the Cathedrals* devoted to Paris.

of which certain encounters appear as shadows cast on everyday life." Since the author gives some of those keys with great finesse, it seems to me particularly interesting to look with some attention at the first of these parts and at the keys the author reveals—especially since one might well find among them some that give access to the *Open Entrance to the Closed Palace of the King* that Philalethes speaks of.

Among them we see that the city was placed under the dual rulership of a divine couple formed by Mercury—with his caduceus—and a Gallic Venus, Rosmerta—with her cornucopia—who in fact is none other than the imposing Hecate, she "who in ancient Greece . . . also guarded the crossroads"! Another key is provided by the existence in Roman-era Lutece of a temple dedicated to Isis, its occult patroness. Very poetically, Bernard Roger points out that this city "is probably the place in Europe where the greatest concentration of Black Madonnas can be seen, images of the female *omnipotence* that gives birth to worlds, the night in which hides the day that is destined to be born, the darkness in which all light rests before its manifestation." This reminds us of "the priority of darkness over light," but it also brings us back to "the raw material of all that exists," "*black* because, as in black, all colors are hidden in it," "*virgin* because it is not subject to the yoke of formal determination, and yet *on the verge of giving birth* because it contains all promises," because it is that "Nothing in which Everything lies," the "mother" of the Great Work, the "*chaos* in which is contained in potential all that is necessary for its realization."

Roger goes on to explain that "one tradition establishes a striking analogy between the *founding* of Paris and the *Foundations* of the Great Work: so the root of Parisis would be Isis, just as the root of the Philosopher's Stone is the primordial Earth, represented in the form of the Black Madonna." Some other discreet keys appear like this legend, which mentions the founding of Lutece by fleeing Trojans or the other "tradition" that seeks to "push the city's origin back to a Greek colony," one associated with Hercules when he crossed through Gaul toward the garden of the Hesperides to fulfill his eleventh task and pick the famous

Golden Apples. This expedition appears "in classical alchemical texts" as a "synonym for the implementation of the Great Work," "the harvesting of the fruits illustrating the happy conclusion of the labors." "It's as if one wanted to emphasize," says Roger, "from a time that is impossible to define, the importance of Paris as an initiatory center where Hermetic philosophy was taught, and that the origin and destiny of the city were closely linked to the activity of this center." Through the joint presence of Hermes and Isis-Aphrodite, the city of Paris was placed "under the sign of the *Hermaphrodite*," which for the alchemists means the "Philosophical Mercury," the goal of the Second Work, the attainment of which is the necessary condition for the "coction of the Third Work." This coction was often compared to a navigation, and the "Mercury" was called the "Vessel of the Great Work." This brings us to "another piece of evidence for the hermetic vocation of Paris," which is displayed "for all to see on monuments and municipal posters—it's the *vessel on the coat of arms of Paris*"!*

In the following passage, "La nef des armes de Paris," the author speaks at length of the Cabiri dear to both Grasset d'Orcet and Alleau, to whom belonged the Dioscuri-Castor and Pollux—both Argonauts and members of Jason's crew. "Metallurgists but also . . . officiants who ritually celebrated the birth of metals," the Cabiri, honored as gods in Samothrace as in the other islands of the Sea of Thrace, were there the subject of a cult (linked, incidentally, to that of the Great Goddess), the famous *mysteries of Samothrace*, linked to "the teachings of a *sarcerdotal art* inseparable from techniques related to the fusion of metals, which very probably introduced *practical alchemy* to the Mediterranean world." Coincidentally, a Roman monument discovered "in the most *sacred* place on the island, under the choir of Notre Dame," depicting the Dioscuri at the side of Vulcan can't help but bring to mind another

---

*Which, as a reminder, reads: "Gules, the ship equipped and dressed in argent sailing on waves of the same, moving from the point, on chief azure sown with golden fleur-de-lys"—a silver sailing ship on waves of the sea in a red field, with a chief showing the royal emblem of gold-on-blue fleur-de-lis.

legend, one that makes the Argonauts the founders of Paris! But this boat depicted on the coat of arms for the capital of France especially recalls the "*hermetic vessel*" or "*vase*" that "contains the natural *fire* necessary for the development of the Work." "Lutece," he concludes, "*the place of marshes*, could have no better location than in the Parisis or place of Isis: the marshy water and the magnet that has the ability to attract, from the depths of the sky, the *universal spirit*. . . . Just as in the practice of the mineral Great Work the stone is born from a vile and chaotic soil, Paris has flourished on top of muddy ground, a shifting earth mixed with water, close kin to the 'black earth' of the Nile, the *Kemit* of the ancient Egyptians, to soon become the 'pearl' of the Western world!"

Bernard Roger goes on to point out that during the Renaissance, three very likely legendary "lives of saints" created between the third and sixth centuries, "in other words, between the debut of evangelization [and] the birth of the French monarchy," specifically those of Saint Denis, Saint Marcel, and Sainte Geneviève, helped to direct people's minds "toward the perspective of a relationship between the mysteries of Antiquity and the founding of Paris," concealing authentic Hermetic content between an exoteric façade.

The author links the myth of the death of Saint Denis/Dionysus first with the Orphic myths, then with that of Osiris, and finally, back to Paris, with the myth of Adam and Eve as presented by Fulcanelli in in *The Dwellings of the Philosophers*. He reminds us that for the traditional authors, Dionysus represented "the Mercury of the Wise" (see plate 8) who had to die and be reborn so that the stone may appear. The fact that it is necessary, as the adept teaches, "*to kill the living in order to resurrect the dead*," encourages us to look differently at the tortured Saint Denis, "going deep into his own death, carrying his *head* in his hands, to a place that would become the Mecca of the French monarchy: the Basilica of Saint Denis."

Referring to Saint Marcel, Bishop of Paris in the first half of the fifth century CE, "who is said to have subdued and expelled from the city "a much larger dragon" that was about to open the tomb of a great sinner, the author explains in the same way that it is, in short, that kind of "victory" that "the operator must obtain at the end of the first operation of the labors of the Great Work," which ends with the birth of "a new body, of a double nature, the *double thing* or the *rebis*."

According to Roger, Saint Marcel, whose name "can be read in the Language of the Birds, *Mars-Helios*," "achieves his *martial action* by going toward the *south*," whereas Saint Denis "submits to his *mercurial passion* by going toward the *North* or *Pole Star*." "Justified as it may be," he adds, "by applying the principle of analogy, to compare the elaboration of the *City of Light* with that of 'chemical light,' we can say that Saint Denis possesses qualities that make him play the role of 'Mercury' in this process, and Saint Marcel that of 'sulfur.'" And yet, to these two essential "natures" must be added a third, pacifying one, that of *salt*, which "history and legend nourish in the graceful form of a woman, the third of the titular patrons of Paris," Sainte Geneviève.

Born in Nanterre at the beginning of the fifth century, Saint Geneviève (incidentally founder of the Basilica of Saint Denis) owes her status to several miracles that saved the city during several sieges, the first by Attila and the second by Clovis before his conversion, two "delaying" actions that the author calls "*rescues*." (Italics are Roger's). After a brilliant demonstration based on the life of the saint and a small painting kept at Saint-Merry, Roger concludes that "behind Geneviève there is a living material and spiritual, mineral body known as the *Salt of the Wise*," "the *great secret* of hermetic art, which no text ever reveals, since it belongs to the realm of the sacred, the *Gift of God*, as some authors call it," which "can only be revealed to those who have *crossed the bridge*, in other words, beyond our clear consciousness, into a twilight region at the edge of the night, where the spirit of the 'laborer' runs a great risk of falling and getting lost if he is not guided by his *good star*." (Italics are Roger's.) Logically following the reasoning about the movements of Saint Denis and Saint Marcel that I summarized in the previous paragraph, the author stresses that, since Geneviève "circled from the *West* to the *East* and from *East* to *West*, the course of the three saints forms "a cross whose center is found on Ile de la Cité." "Thus," he concludes, "in the geographical structure of Paris as in the composition of all natural bodies, the 'formal or mercurial' principle is joined at the halfway point to the 'luminous or sulphurous' principle by means of the 'harmonizing energy of salt'" represented by Geneviève.

Since Paris proved to be "one of the most important centers for the teaching and practice of the art of Hermes," even if, "for lack of documents, we cannot trace the period before the twelfth century, in other words to the earliest Western manifestation of the chemical quest of the Great Work," Bernard Roger endeavors, in the second part of his book, to introduce the great figures of alchemy, from Alain de Lisle, the "Universal Doctor," to Fulcanelli.

Thus, the main figures of the Middle Ages, many of whom passed through the University of Montpellier, are paraded: Thomas Aquinas, the "angelic doctor"; Roger Bacon, the "admirable doctor"; Arnaud de Villeneuve, harassed by the Inquisition; his friend Ramon Lull, the "enlightened doctor"; Jean de Meung, and the *Romance of the Rose*; and of course, Nicolas Flamel and his *Book of Hieroglyphic Figures*, to which no less than eight pages are devoted. Here is a Flamel whose life "appears as the perfect example of that of a 'Son of Hermes' who knows that the gifts he has received from fortune are worthy of higher use than that of exalting the power of a temporary self-hood!"

There follow several references to the artists of the sixteenth, seventeenth, and eighteenth centuries, beginning with Denis Zacaire, and then, a few years after the publication of their *Manifestoes* in Germany, to the "Rosicrucians in Paris," of whom Fulcanelli wrote: "the Adepts bearing this title are only *brothers through knowledge* and the success of their work." "The true and powerful initiate," Savinien de Cyrano de Bergerac, to whom the author of the *Mystery of the Cathedrals* was the first to draw attention, followed in this regard by his disciple Canseliet, is the subject of a short study that emphasizes the importance of his message whose "scope can only be suspected." The masterpiece of this former student of Gassendi, "*The Other World*, consisting of the *States and Empires of the Moon* and the *States and Empires of the Sun*, belongs," says Roger, "to the category of coded books that cannot be penetrated by the intelligence trained in school alone if not accompanied by the instruments that make them understandable," among which, first and foremost, is "the knowledge of the *language of the birds* of which Cyrano had full mastery." His writings, "including a full explanation of the Great Work (which makes it difficult to believe that the author was not himself a practitioner or at least had witnessed its preliminary operations)," as well as his scientific works, "reveal an audacious style of reasoning and methodical enthusiasm that, in some respects, make him the greatest and most illustrious of his contemporaries!"

After recounting the tragic misadventures of the Baron[5] and Baroness of Beausoleil and Etienne Vinache, who were imprisoned in the Bastille until the end of their days, by Richelieu and Louis XIV respectively, perhaps because their activities undermined "international monetary agreements," the author introduces Esprit Gobineau de Montluisant. He was a man "perfectly informed about the theory of the Great Work" who was "the first to give a systematic critical analysis of the iconography of Notre-Dame in accordance with the hermetic doctrine," especially that of the "triple Western portal"—an activity to which Bernard Roger and his friend Jorge Camacho would devote themselves in another time and place with their book on *The Cathedral of Seville and the Hermetic Bestiary of the Portal of Saint Christopher and the Immaculate Conception*.[6]

All honor to whom honor is due, no less than five pages—enlivened by one of his portraits, which belonged to the Marquise d'Urfé,* whose salon he frequented—are then devoted to the author of *The Most Holy Trinosophy*, the Comte de Saint Germain. He was "a mysterious gentleman . . . whose conduct and financial means

---

*Of the family that owned the Bastie d'Urfé of which Elie-Charles Flamand speaks in *Les méandres du sens*. See chapter 15.

suggested a great lord, but who never seems to have revealed his origins to anyone," and "friendly and generous, of high rectitude and impeccable integrity, skilled in all the arts." "By the extent of his knowledge, which always amazed those who spoke with him," this aristocrat "who probably alarmed his contemporaries because of the mystery always surrounding his origins, his real name, and the source of his revenues," seems to have been an exceptional chemist specializing in dyes. But Roger implies that this may well be "only one particular application in the field of an embryonic industry of the result of works with a more universal scope." In any event, he ends his entry on the Comte by suggesting that he was an Adept, in other words one of those individuals "freed of the *individual* condition of subjugation to a limited time span . . . that make up the heart of humanity" and "old as it . . . have recovered his memory."

Quite logically, next comes Jean-Baptiste Alliette, self-proclaimed disciple of the individual just discussed by the author, "a quite unique character," who under the name of Etteila would write several books on divination, but especially *Les sept nuances de l'oeuvre philosophique hermétique*, in which "he gives the results of his labors on the Great Work." While he obviously doesn't take the cartomancer completely seriously, Roger on the other hand seems to give more credit to the supposed "son of science," even going so far as to write: "Etteila seems to have been an educated and industrious artist, who in his own way obeyed the traditional law of silence."

Bernard Roger then mentions "two of the most important works of alchemical literature," both of which appeared in "the second half of the nineteenth century, the splendid period of Romanticism." The first, *Hermès dévoilé*, "written by an Adept, the last to have appeared before Fulcanelli" is attributed to a certain Cyliani about whom we know nothing else. It's rather a short text, quite autobiographical in nature, a "link in the long traditional chain of *inspired* works." We know even less about the second book, *Récréations hermétiques*, except that it was also the work of an Adept!

Another important nineteenth-century figure is Louis-Paul-François Cambriel, who may well have received the *Donum Dei*. He innovatively sought financial resources for his work through the press and wrote a *Cours de philosophie hermétique en dix-neuf leçons* and was, "according to Gobineau de Montluisant, the second author to have provided an alchemical interpretation of Notre Dame de Paris." The analysis of his work's reception by several scientists of the time gives Bernard Roger another opportunity to describe the difference that exists between alchemy and chemistry: "One belongs to the sacred realm of living causes, the other rewards only the observation of phenomena concerning the reactions of a matter considered to be devoid of life."

On Albert Poisson, whom, as we've seen, Breton particularly appreciated, but who died prematurely at the age of twenty-five, Roger, while criticizing that late-nineteenth-century "occult school" "that only filled the landscape with smoke and participated in the devaluation of the ancient science of Hermes," points out that this author was quite precocious, and expresses his surprise that he was able, despite his youth, to produce this "methodical approach to the theory of the Great Work" in "his treatise on the *Théories et symboles des alchimistes*," published in 1891.

Before bringing up Irène Hillel-Erlanger (whom I have already discussed in detail), Bernard Roger devotes a page to the controversial figure of Alphonse Jobert,* whose experiments seemed to him to smack less of alchemy than of *archimy*—"similar in its aims, but limited to metallic transmutation based on strictly chemical means and materials."

He concludes his portrait gallery with Fulcanelli as he appeared through his books and the legend that his disciple, Canseliet,† largely

---

*According to Khaitzine, Alphone Jobert, whose real name was Alphonse Dousson, and who was convicted of fraud in 1912, would be none other than Fulcanelli.

†And a little bit backward, it should be said, of the portrait he gives of him in his preface to the second edition of *The Mystery of the Cathedrals*: "this man from another age [who] through his strange appearance, his old-fashioned manners, and unusual activities, attracted, without wanting to, the attention of the lazy, the curious, and the stupid, much less, however, than was to enact the total obliteration of his public personality a little later."

contributed to constructing around him. Roger reminds us that *The Mystery of the Cathedrals*, written by the latter as dictated by his Master, appeared posthumously in 1926, two years after André Breton published *The First Surrealist Manifesto*, and he examines the various hypotheses concerning the Adept's identity before concluding that there will certainly never be an answer to this question. He reiterates that "the teaching" transmitted in Fulcanelli's two books "is complete therein, based on the tradition bequeathed by the Adepts who succeeded one another through time, but also and above all on the practical results of the experiments at the furnace." He also confesses his admiration for the "marvelous archeology"—to be understood as "the knowledge of the Archaeus, in other words the principle of all life in nature and, in the specific field of the Great Work, that of 'the compound, *rebis,* mixture . . . the igneous material that is the basis of the philosopher's stone.'" "This is what the adept invites us to do by deciphering the messages left in the monuments by so many unknown teachers," Bernard Roger explains, adding that "we can't recommend enough the reading and rereading of the *Mystery of the Cathedrals* and *The Dwellings of the Philosophers* for those who wish to find their bearings," especially since Fulcanelli was more *charitable* than many of his colleagues, being the first to point out, in particular, the vital role played by *the language of birds* in the "teaching the art."

However, today, in Paris and its suburbs, there are still many unknown "students of science" who will reveal themselves if they want and who work "in silence," "with as much fervor and hope as those of the fourteenth century," despite the context of "universal dissolution, as threatening and unstoppable in the realm of intelligence as in that of material life!"

Opening with a map identifying fifty-one "alchemical sites" throughout the City of Light, the third part of *Paris and Alchemy* offers a long, labyrinthine stroll devoted to the search for "still living traces of their passage" sown by the "Children of Hermes" on "monuments where they discreetly left (for the enlightened seeker) their most precious teachings, often with more candor and precision than in their texts." This is a concentric promenade starting from the sacred center, the Cité, to the town, the right bank, and then to the University, the left bank.

From the oldest monuments, located on Ile de la Cité, such as Notre-Dame and the Sainte Chapelle, to the most recent, such as the "emblematic grouping," on an apartment building on rue Monbel* that was unfortunately destroyed in the summer of 1968 in the seventeenth arrondissement (this building had been "built in Art Nouveau style at the beginning of the twentieth century" by an "unknown Adept" "animated by the same spirit as those of past centuries"), while passing by symbol-charged sites like the Hôtel de Cluny, the Marais, the Louvre, and Ile Saint-Louis, Bernard Roger masterfully guides us through the arcana of the French capital. This is how I became interested in "an emblem that is among the most important and rare, of hermetic philosophy," "the Serpente of the rue d'Hautefeuille." This emblem "reveals that Mélusine and the 'mother' of the Great Work, the *stone* in its first state, are one and the same thing" which twice shows that the *Sons of Science* see the *mother of light* as none other than the *stone of the philosophers*, the concrete, mineral and metal base that is the starting point of their work."(Italics and capitalization are Roger's.) There is also the *Baphomet* of Saint-Merry Church that, although it dates from the 1842 restoration, is nothing other for the author than a "perfectly orthodox figure of the 'double mercury' of the alchemists who also called it Hermaphrodite or *Rebis*, the 'twofold thing'"—in other words, the "bisexual being born of the love of an old man and a young virgin, fixed and volatile, the polar principle of the Work doomed to destruction and whose death should give birth to the *phoenix, young king*, or triumphant philosopher's stone."[7]

---

*Already the subject of an article, "Les Emblèmes de la rue Monbel," in the second issue of *L'archibras* in October 1967.

And at the end of this erudite stroll, we can think, with no great risk, that the new look Roger casts over these new mysteries of Paris is the result of an approach that aims to "participate in the transmission of essential elements of an ancient memory in which shines an *Orient*, without which humanity runs the risk of losing itself." And it owes much to the wanderings and meditations of some, at least, of the members of the Hermes Circle, for these images "testify to the existence" of a "'time' when the notion of duration is abolished, in which persist only the rhythms marked, in the skies of the large as of the small world, in the complex movement of the luminaries"—in other words, the "sacred time to which belongs the undying chain of the Children of Hermes."

10

BERNARD ROGER AND THE LADY OF THE WORK

The "sole desire" of the Sons of Hermes is directed toward the lady of his Work, often called by the name of Nature, sometimes humanized with the features of a nymph who opens to the good artist access to the luminous world of the Adeptat.

BERNARD ROGER, *PARIS ET L'ALCHIMIE*

At the end of the sixties, without completely breaking with surrealism, Bernard Roger took some distance in order to devote himself to alchemy with some friends. In addition to *Paris and Alchemy*, several other high-quality works, written solo and from which I've drawn much, mark his later course. There is *A la découverte de l'alchimie* (Discovering alchemy), for example, in 1988, to "point out to those who are thirsty the existence of a clear and wondrous spring, at the heart of a palace in the forest where the Sleeping Beauty lies and to provide them with an accurate compass that can lead them to her." Then there is *Initiation et contes de fées* (released in English as *The Initiatory Path in Fairy Tales*) in 2013. This is a stroll through the folk tales of Europe, "stories of bygone days," that "tell in their own way and without revealing too much to those who tell them than to those who listen to them of a traditional initiation whose principles can be found as much in alchemical practice as in Freemasonry" and thus reflect some of its highest concerns.* Finally, in 2022, a new book, *Les demeures de l'invisible* (The dwellings of the invisible), was published by Editions Venus d'Ailleurs.

With a very short text entitled "Melius spe licebat" that appeared in *L'archibras* (issue no. 6) in December 1968, Bernard Roger offered his own version of the events of May 1968, and it is alchemical! He fact he believed that the young rebels in whom "was the water of life" (but he could just as easily be called *secret fire*) were comparable to the "morning star, [to the] madmen dressed in green leaf, [to the] green vitriol,† [to the] mysterious site where vibration becomes body." Apart from the allusion to the "green king," close to the *Green Man*‡ dear to our British friends, and to the *madman*, of whom I spoke earlier, who also symbolizes "the mercury itself, the unique and proper material of the wise," we can only note the irony of the author's use of a maxim that appears on one of the ninety-six caissons that adorn the ceiling of the upper gallery in the Château of Dampierre-sur-Boutonne, in the Charente. Sixty-one of these caissons (which are divided into eight series) have an alchemical content. This is truly a philosophical dwelling if ever there was one—one to which Fulcanelli personally devoted several famous pages in his second book. Josane Charpentier tells us we can see "a pennant sur-

---

*Concerning these tales and in a similar spirit, René Alleau writes in his foreword to Nicolas Flamel's *Book of Hieroglyphic Figures*: "Their obscure and symbolic formulation is adapted to the language of the unconscious and of its dreams but not to rational critical intelligence, and even less to the herd commonsensical instinct of freethinkers and adults."

†Green in alchemy is the color of beginning.

‡Fulcanelli writes of this Green Man in *The Dwellings of the Philosophers* as follows: "This simple man with abundant, disheveled hair, and unkempt beard, this man of nature whose traditional knowledge leads him to despise the vain frivolity of the poor fools who think they are wise, stands head and shoulders above other men, just as he stands above the mound of stones which he tramples underfoot. He is the Enlightened one, for he has received the light, spiritual enlightenment."

rounding a tree trunk covered with leaves and fruits [which] bears the inscription MELIUS SPE LICEBAT on the fourth caisson of the third series. 'We could have hoped for better.'"[1] And she adds, "Here is the first sulfur, which is *the gold of the wise*, the as of yet unripe fruit on the *arbor scientae*"!

In the next issue of the same journal, in March 1969, Bernard Roger squarely places alchemy, in an article with the most appropriate title, "Le jour de l'étoile," under the sign of Rimbaud, at the same rank of several of the principal values of surrealism, Revolution and Poetry. We know the importance of the Star for the philosophers by fire that it guides and to whom it indicates, in the crucible, that the Work is on the right path.* He writes, "It is possible to consider the liberation of the *Artist* from the perspective of a prefiguration of that of humanity as a whole, a goal he silently works toward. Like every authentic revolutionary, like every poet, the Son of Art must first be a *seer*."

With Eliade, Roger condemns those for whom alchemy "appears to be an early form of chemistry,"[2] and explains that from his standpoint, alchemy is "that esoteric discipline [that] constitutes . . . in its essence and in accordance with the traditional expression of the Adepts, the Sacred Art, which means that it is not dependent upon the profane and temporal limits on which the vicissitudes of institutions and the changes in societies are founded." An "initiatory ideal whose basis [is] the *will to the presence* of a universal harmony, an Art of Love in accordance with the teaching of the *Romance of the Rose*, a learned allegory of the labors of the Great Work,"† it fits in "the ancient esoteric tradition of the 'High Science' that saw in the scholar the preeminent initiate and hero engaged in a chivalrous and aristocratic quest." It is therefore incompatible with "a scientific approach based on the *will to power*," for example, that rationalism which in the hands of the bourgeoisie is

---

*This also brings to mind what Jacques Simonelli wrote in "A la lueur de l'ourse."
†Elie-Charles Flamand (*Les méandres du sens*) believes "a didactic explanation of the science of Hermes" appears in this book.

nothing but "the theoretical instrument of its conquest of power and its struggle against the aristocracy."[3] This rationalism born out of a Cartesianism* whose "Dutch aspect"† shouldn't be overlooked is destined to enjoy "permanent success" "in a mercantile capitalist society or in a bureaucratic police state where it is important not to confuse hierarchies and index cards, so that order prevails, regardless of the means used to impose it on individuals."

For Bernard Roger, Cartesianism, the extension of Renaissance humanism and the foundation of modern thought, imprisoned by its own "ontological errors" and "intellectual illusions and subject to the rule of numbers and the tyranny of the multitude," completed the "divorce that was to separate and oppose man and nature." It emptied "the *spiritual function of the scholar*, his initiatory mastery as an artist engaged by the spirit in the operations of harmonious improvement of matter, and as a *man accountable* for the beauty of the world through the subjective meaning he alone is capable of giving to phenomena of all living, that is to say essentially poetic, content solely for the abstract benefit of an alleged and never concretely accessible objectivity." And in order to transmit this essential message, he emphasized "the mission that the Hermetic tradition entrusts, in every age, the *Artist*, who must be first and foremost a poet, etymologically speaking a creator," adding that "only he who brings the world into being and recreates it as himself can give meaning to what would be absurd without him."[4]

---

*It is interesting in this regard to note that the translator—and commentator—of Crasselame's poem, introduced as Bruno de Lansac, bewails "to one of his friends," in an otherwise admirable letter preceding the text, the fact that given "the taste of the century," "one would much prefer seeing a treatise of philosophy according to Descartes than according to Hermes!"

†In other words, according to Roger, everything connected to "the need for order, clarity, exact measure, values that are easily exchanged through the full extent of the intellectual, moral, and social universe," everything that "transparently expresses the practical requirements for stock-keeping, market control, currency circulation, traffic monitoring, and earnings stability."

Finally, I cannot fail to ask about the identity, or *nature*, if I dare say so* of "this lady of the Work" to whom he dedicates a full-page text in the fourth issue of the *Bulletin de liaison surréaliste* (July 1971), from which I cannot resist quoting this extract:

> She is the ocean in which the world swims, a feline
> running through the forest, the gentle dew upon the
>   ground,
> the fire that devours it. She is nothing, and everything
> comes from her. She was before the first stone
> She is always younger than the present second!

And then this:

> Her abode is nowhere. She dwells there between
> darkness and light, between earth and fire.
> There at the time foretold for all time she takes he
> who seeks her with love. She is the earth that contains
> all fire, the darkness that contains all light, North
> Star, hope of the traveler. She herself is
> the journey, herself the traveler, she that no place can
>   hold down,
> that no link can fulfill, unsettling
> and mad in the eyes of the world: the only real one.[5]

Perhaps it is the "very great Lady" whom Canseliet (in *Alchemy Explained through its Classic Texts*) said he "had the singular pleasure of meeting and who is none other than Nature herself," she whom he had "admired on the forty-second emblem of Michael Maier and who is in reality, the Lady who occupies every thought of the *Knight Errant*, of the *cavalier* to or rather *cabalier* [cabalist], who sets out on

---

*The italics, in no way gratuitous, are Canseliet's.

an adventure, the most extraordinary type of which is *the ingenious Don Quixote of La Mancha.*" Roger also wrote about Emblem XLII (the forty-second emblem of Michael Maier in his book *Atalanta Fugiens*), which he considered to be "a limpid image of every initiatory path," in a text entitled "Alchimie, voie initiatique": "The emblem XLII . . . depicts a night scene weakly lit by the moon. On a winding country road, a woman burdened with fruits and flowers walks with a firm step. An elderly man follows behind her at some distance, a staff in his right hand and a pair of glasses on his nose. Illuminating his path with the help of a lantern, he walks in the deep footprints left in the ground by the woman who precedes him as a guide." Of course, it is easy to see here the obvious kinship between this "elderly man" and the Hermit of the tarot, but it's the rest of the commentary that's particularly interesting. Roger continues as follows: "The text of the epigram," which customarily accompanies this kind of work, "specifies that the woman is none other than Nature, bearing all her riches, and the man who takes great pains to place his steps within those she left is a wise alchemist walking on the right path." Perhaps this "Lady of the Work" is the "most-sweet Mother Nature / The most perfect creature, who God made after the Angels," "Mother and Mistress / Ruler of the macrocosm / Who was created for the microcosm," to whom Jean de Meung "pays honors and homages in *The Romance of the Rose,* or else again, but it's all one, this crowned winged woman who, in Jean Perréal's painting *Nature's Remonstrances to the Wandering Alchemist* (1516), personifies her."

Everything indicates that, under her carnal veil, she maintains a certain kinship with the "Woman Blessed Among All—*Benedicta in mulieribus,*"[6] the beautiful lady, "naked, with a star on her brow, in a glass ball containing a mixture of mercury and gold"* represented in the famous painting Jean-Julien Champagne made in 1910 at

---

*Richard Khaitzine, *La langue de oiseaux*, vol. 3. Elsewhere Khaitzine writes "emerging from a flask."

Fulcanelli's request, *The Vessel of the Great Work*, whose model (opinions vary) seems to have been either that friend of Irène Hillel-Erlanger I mentioned earlier,* the famous Louise Barbe, or the famous actress "Victorine Josephine Roger, whose stage name was Henriette Roggers."† She was a woman with whom the author of *The Capital of Pain* seems to have had a brief affair, which sheds light on the confidence made by Canseliet to Breton, which was reported by Khaitzine: "The poet Paul Eluard, whose real name was Eugene Grindel, if he were still alive would not be able to look at [this canvas] without feeling the deepest emotion." Canseliet's property, this painting would not be shown until 1979 on the occasion of the republication by Pauvert of *Two Alchemical Abodes*, where it appears as a color plate frontispiece accompanied by the following remark: "The exquisite and pure creation embodied by this young woman, in other words the Stone or the Philosophical Medicine, comes into being, frees itself and rises out of the vitreous mass that is the flask of the final coction, according to the Adepts inscribed in gold letters on the two pillars, inside and on either side of the composition."

---

*Canseliet asserts that "this young Lady" (capitalization is his), "the person who, on earth, became for this instance the painter's model, belonged to the best society and was a frequent visitor to Madame Erlanger's home."

†Other Fulcanelli specialists, namely Jean Artéro, shared this opinion. According to Khaitzine, Henriette Roggers also "frequented Irène Erlanger's home." Wife of the academician Claude Farrère, she made a brief appearance at the side of this latter in *Caravanserail*, a Dadaist novel written in 1924 by Francis Picabia but only published posthumously in 1974.

11

JORGE CAMACHO AND ALAIN GRUGER, SURREALISTS AND OPERATIVES

Our star is single and yet it is double.

FULCANELLI, CITED BY CANSELIET IN THE
SECOND PREFACE TO *THE MYSTERY OF THE CATHEDRALS*

The egg with transparent wings / Perched on a sulfur skull.

OHCAMAC, *L'ARBRE ACIDE*

The author of a work that René Alleau has described "as already among the most enduring phosphorescences of contemporary painting,"[1] Jorge Camacho (see plates 1 and 2) was born in Havana in 1934 and died in Paris in 2011. He was a Cuban native, therefore, "and consequently of Latin culture," to use Canseliet's words, like Wifredo Lam, who initially had a certain influence on his work. He is one of the last painters to whom Breton dedicated a text in *Surrealism and Painting*. In 1950, a poet friend introduced him to the writings of Breton, Péret, and Lautréamont as well as reproductions of paintings by Tanguy, de

Chirico, and Miro. He abandoned his law studies in 1952 after decid-
ing to devote his time exclusively to painting, more or less as an autodidact, and it soon became clear that his work would be born "from his
desire to paint everything in reality that is enigmatic and paradoxical."
A long stay in Mexico permitted him to acquaint himself with "the
Pre-Columbians, their myths, their art," as noted by Marie-Dominique
Massoni* in her text "Camacho, archer de l'invisible,"† which was a decisive encounter, as shown by his first one-man show in 1955 in Havana.
He then spent time in Martinique where he met Aimé Césaire, and
then, when in the United States for an exhibition, he discovered the
Amerindian works of the Hopi and Zuni at the Smithsonian Institute.
He immediately perceived them, as Anne Tronche notes in her book
on the painter, "as crystallized objects of poetic energy, capable with
their symbolic charge to offer access to another system of consciousness."[2] Jorge Camacho moved to Paris in 1959. After visiting his studio,
Breton invited him to join the surrealist group in 1961. He was perhaps seduced by his paintings, "which depict signs, or ersatz signs, as if,
whether magic art or the magic of art, their mere representation could
give access to the sacredness of existence."[3]

Camacho then had a flurry of exhibitions, almost all of them the-
matic. Following *The Immaculate Conception of Popes: Homage to Oscar
Panizza* (the sulfurous author of *The Council of Love*),‡ an homage
paid at a one-man show at the Raymond Cordier Gallery in Paris in
1962, came an exhibition of "canvases" at the gallery of Matthias Fels
that were, according to Marie-Dominique Massoni, "inspired by his
encounter with Sade." This exhibition in 1964 took its name from the

---

*Marie-Dominique Massoni, who co-led the Paris group for a time, formed a connection
with the surrealists "around the seventies." It was Camacho in person who "encouraged
[her] approach to alchemy" and who "several years after introduced her to Doumayrou
and Bernard Roger." "Jorge Camacho," she goes on to say in "Le lai des étoiles," "Bernard
Roger, and other surrealist friends long labored in the fields of alchemy."
†This text appeared on the *Ouvaton* site of the surrealist group of Paris, then in the
Czech surrealist review, *Analogon*.
‡To whom Breton devoted a text in 1959.

article that Breton had written about this painter: "Brousse au-devant de Camacho" (Bushland in front of Camacho). In this document, the leader of the movement underscores the artist's concern about "making clear his moral and social position," but is determined however to show that Camacho, "he who sets traps," "has always been careful to not allow his deepest and absolutely individual impulses to become estranged, or the resources which have accrued to him in his own right to be compromised, or the revelation of everything inside him that is UNIQUE be hidden from us."[4] He had thus refused abdicating his full freedom of creation. Breton adds, "It is exactly because he is able to comply unhesitatingly to these two demands that Jorge Camacho qualifies in the highest degree as a *surrealist* artist." (As in all the other cases, capitalization and italics are the author's.) Camacho had already been taking part in group activities for three years at this time and would participate in the Eleventh International Exhibition of Surrealism, *L'écart absolu*, in 1965, for which he created, based on seven preparatory drawings entitled *Hantise de la virginité*,* a "handsome Sadian reliquary," to use the words of Christian Nicaise, which he called *La Souveraine*. Following a show in Caracas whose theme was George Bataille's *Story of the Eye* in 1965, and then an *Hommage à Jean-Pierre Duprey*, "*l'oiseau d'ombre-passage*,"† in Brussels in 1966, he participated in *HARR: Hommage à Raymond Roussel*, in Paris in 1967. All of these exhibitions offer a good idea of the international recognition this painter's work was beginning to enjoy, as well as the nature of the universe in which he was evolving—and also the mounting evidence of his great freedom in tone and selection. "His pictorial space," as the mysterious Archer wrote quite appropriately, "approaches torturous worlds in which the most sophisticated

---

*Dedicated to his wife Marguerita, the "nine draft pages from the manuscript" given to Breton were reproduced in a small pamphlet of which Christian Nicaise "printed seventy-seven copies for friends as homage to the painter who had died on March 20, 2011"—one month after his death (Jorge Camacho, *Hantise de la virginité*).
†Jean-Pierre Duprey, surrealist poet and artist, best known for *La forêt sacrilège*. He died in 1959.

esotericism coexists with the most surprising shamanism." Philippe Audoin wrote, with regard to *HARR*, in his contribution to the *Princip Slasti* (Pleasure Principle) catalog, "The Fountain of Fortune" (with an impressive demonstration to support it), that with one of the display windows created for this occasion the Cuban "unknowingly created a complete alchemical paradigm," mainly because "the three colors of the *Last Work*—black, white, red—are arranged here in their proper order and acceptance." But was it really "unknowingly"? By working on Roussel, whose last play, *The Dust of Suns*, "that acroamatic work of theater," Breton thought was a metaphor for the Great Work,* Camacho had in fact become familiar with the "phonetic cabala," the language of the birds, "the mother and eldest of all the others," "the art of saying stupidities in everyday speech in order to communicate truths to those who alone know the language necessary to understand the true meaning," to cite Jean-Luc Caradeau,[5] the language that "the Adept who has attained the final revelation"[6] possesses perfectly, that "which teaches the mystery of things and reveals the most hidden truths."[7] This analysis is confirmed by Laurent Albarracin,[8] who reminds us that Raymond Roussel made extensive use of techniques—"puns, quasi-homonyms, phrases with metagrams, assonances between two statements whose meaning he stretches in order to fill in the semantic distortion through narration," or the "dislocation of any sentence to break it up into new words"—all more or less comparable to a language of birds, which aims to give words a secondary meaning (and reveal a hidden meaning) by playing with their phonetic proximity. Albarracin then goes on to note that he believes we can speak in this instance of a, "let's say,

---

*Breton was able to persuade René Alleau to share his analysis, thus demonstrating that he had not only mastered basic alchemical knowledge, but also had at least some intuition in this field. The term *acroamatic*, etymologically meaning "that which is received by the ear," applies perfectly to a teaching transmitted exclusively orally, notoriously that of the alchemists ("the word of mouth indispensable to all hermetic knowledge"). It is also used by Canseliet in his preface to Alleau's *Aspects de l'alchimie traditionnelle*, which seems to indicate that he shared Breton's analysis.

magical-oneiric use of the language of the birds or phonetic cabala, similar to what can be seen among various precursors or companions of surrealism: Jean-Pierre Brisset, Grasset d'Orcet, Michel Leiris, and Ghérasim Luca." He takes this opportunity to say that "Camacho's painting can be akin . . . in certain regards . . . to the making of rebuses," which cannot be considered as foreign to alchemy.

In 1967, at the invitation of the government through Wifredo Lam and Carlos Franqui, he went to Cuba to have an exhibition based on *Mr. K* (Kafka) and to participate in several events organized by the authorities. However, after staying there for a few months, he discovered the totalitarian reality of Castroism, which, like many other surrealists, he had initially sympathized with. He harbored real fears that he would not be allowed to leave the country because of his Cuban nationality, and after this experience he developed a deep hostility toward the regime that many of his friends could not understand. It was also during this time that he met the writer Reinaldo Arenas, a homosexual and political dissident who had been persecuted and imprisoned by the regime. They became friends, for Camacho a "brother forever" whom he tried to help by any and all means, mainly by getting his books published directly in France. They remained friends until Arenas, in exile and ill, decided to commit suicide in 1990. In 1988, the two men issued a letter-petition, *Un plebiscito a Fidel*, that was signed by more than two hundred intellectuals and scientists, including eighteen Nobel Prize winners. In it they called for a referendum and free elections to be held in the island.

In the text he wrote on the painter's connection with the writings of Raymond Roussel, "Comment Jorge Camacho a écrit un certain *Harr*,"[9] Laurent Albarracin, inspired by the contribution that his friend François-René Simon had published about Camacho in the *International Encyclopedia of Surrealism*,[10] showed that the painter "was a complete and accomplished individual" whose "work and life" would be better placed in a context of research that went far beyond mere pictorial productions: his surrealist commitment, alchemy heraldry, Hermetic sciences, ornithology, and translation (Mallarmé)." A "traveler," says Bernard Roger, for those who get his meaning,[11] in his foreword to his friend's study on *The Myth of Isis and Osiris and Its Relation to Hermetic Symbolism.*[12]

Camacho—like his friend Bernard Roger, who at the time provided the alchemical reading of May '68 with his magnificent text "Melius spe licelat" in *L'Archibras*, which I mentioned above—participated in his own way in the beautiful month of May. This is because, according to Anne Tronche, "above all, he understood that the repeated calls for freedom" of the youth of that time "could also be understood as a protest against the daily threat that weighed heavily on the marvelous." However, it was not until "around 1968," to quote his own words,[13] in other words the exact time when he went to Prague with his surrealist friends for the *Princip Slasti* exhibition, that he became close friends with Bernard Roger, a long-time member of the group who introduced him to alchemy and then to René Alleau.* It is necessary to add Canseliet to these two men, for it was who allowed him (as he told Gérard Durozoi) to "enter without any detours into the path of traditional alchemy, thus removing from (his) path all speculations of an occultist nature or other pseudo-mystical doctrines, which, like parasites, graft themselves onto the admirable body of this science and adulterate it." "I can place my interest for alchemy to around the year 1968," he explained, before going on to say, "It goes without saying that the hermetic science, which began to interest me at this time, fits quite well into the context of the revolt, this time of a philosophical nature, against all dogmatic and academic notions of Nature." Alchemy, after the three political disappointments spawned by the disillusionment caused by his trip to Cuba, the crushing of the Prague Spring, and the failure of May '68, would therefore merge with his very idea of freedom. "He recognized himself," says François-René Simon, "in a way of

---

*While Bernard Roger was a full member of the group, Alleau was more specifically connected with Breton on a personal basis.

thinking and acting that repairs the mutilating rationalism of our civilization. It reunites man and the world with the ribbon of analogy."

"Alchemy," he clarified, in his response to the aforementioned investigation by the Milanese surrealist Arturo Schwarz, *Arte e alchemia*, "is an *autonomous science*" that "since its origins, many centuries ago . . . has demonstrated its independence from Religion, Philosophy, Art, and official Science." (Capitalization and italics are Camacho's.) André Coia-Gatié described this official science as founded "on the assertion of hypotheses, quickly elevated to the rank of certainties, then relegated to the shelf of accessories while new theories secure the ephemeral fame of their authors."

From phonetic cabala to high science, and "the alchemical cabal (being) shrouded in its own methodical deciphering," says Marie Dominique Massoni, Jorge Camacho is one of the few members of the group who, beyond the interest of *Arcanum 17*'s author for the Art of Science, would venture into the practice of operative alchemy in friendship with Fulcanelli's disciple, Eugène Canseliet, who also had close ties with his "dear friend, André Breton." Speaking of his friend's stays "in the land of the *Black Earth, Kemit*, as it was once called by its own inhabitants," Bernard Roger would later write, "in the *black earth*, from the highly recondite *subject of the wise*, he made further journeys to the center of the tiny and immense kingdom where the tomb of the ruler of the Great Work lies buried beneath the burning sands," adding, in a blatant allusion to the Breton of *Arcane 17*, this time, that "in both cases, the quest is similar, since it leads the pilgrim, on different but parallel levels, to the tomb of the black god Osiris, who, in the realm of operative alchemy, is none other than the 'sulfur' of the philosophers."* After coming into contact with Canseliet, the Cuban painter visited him in Savignies, where he lived, and they became quite close—alchemical initiation implies belonging to a chain of initiates. Camacho,

---

*Foreword to Camacho's *Le mythe d'Isis et d'Osiris et sa relation avec le symbolisme hermétique*. A blatant allusion to Breton as well as to Fulcanelli himself.

who "truly practiced alchemy, both speculative and operative," confirms Roger,* and "showed evidence of real talent for it," would have two laboratories in succession. One was in Ronquerolles near Paris, on a property lent to him by his friend Jean Dausset, winner of the Nobel Prize for medicine, and the other was in Spain. This latter was in a turret of his house in Los Pajaros, near Almonte, where he would work at the furnace, "for there are things to be discovered through fire," with "his inseparable friend," Alain Gruger—who had copied unpublished texts from libraries—and it seems, according to Marguerita Camacho,† that the two men at least succeeded at the "first work," Cyliani's "magic marriage of Venus and Mars"—before terminating their work " because their lives were organized differently." "At that time," Alain Joubert conformed shortly before his death, in the introduction to the exhibition dedicated to the painter Torgia—a.k.a. Marguerita Camacho—by the Sophie Scheidecker Gallery in June 2021, "Jorge Camacho, in the company of Alain Gruger, was working on very elaborate alchemical research, which involved frequent and discreet contacts with Eugène Canseliet or René Alleau." Nor does he fail to remind us, very delicately that "the presence of the feminine plays its part in the orchestration of the alchemical work in the same obvious way as the morning dew, through a subtle analogical shift."[14]

Before proceeding, a word is called for on Alain Gruger, the other close friend whom Camacho met in 1962. According to Canseliet he was "inseparable" from Camacho. Gruger was also probably the most discreet of these already very discreet men, so discreet that he seemed to participate in a collective exhibition under the pseudonym of Vesoul in "assumed secrecy." Although Gruger was never a regular member of the group he sometimes took part in the "café" meetings, which his wife,

---

*A close friend of Jorge Camacho, Roger confirmed to me in an interview on October 26, 2014, that they had "worked together."
†The quotes before and after this one are from Marguerita Camacho, collected during the interview of November 26, 2014.

Marie-Jo, attended more often than he did. It's worth noting that she, who was like him a chemist by training, often worked with both men, notwithstanding the necessity to forget chemistry in order to practice alchemy. At the end of 2019, in the "polyphonic monologue" introduced as a dialogue, "Les Très Riches Heures du sieur Gruger," which Joubert wrote about him in the preface to the catalogue of the first exhibition of his works by the Sophie Scheidecker Gallery,* the author, putting these words in his artist's mouth, offers some keys to his character: "A poet to whom we are very attached, you and I . . . André Breton, since it is him, in seeking *the gold of time*, hasn't he come close to a purely poetic inter-pretation of the alchemical quest, and isn't analogy the key to the world that opens the door to all the secrets that lie within man and only ask to sparkle before his dazzled eyes?" Then, in response to his sidekick's question about what he knows about him, Joubert, obliquely revealing what he knows by establishing certain facts for the first time in a way that is both clear and sibylline in appearance, continues in these terms: "For example, with your favorite accomplice, Jorge Camacho, you liked *to caress the stones with philosophy*, you *had more often than one too many irons in the fire*,† and you knew how *to decipher the conversation of the birds* while mixing in your own grain of salt, I believe. Moreover, you were *a clandestine passenger of surrealism*, which, without anyone claim-ing it, led you to surround yourself with friends who were all marked by this sign." (My italics.) "In this enchanting place," writes Surpik Angelini about Los Parajos, Jorge Camacho "managed to rediscover alchemical alloys that opened the doors to certain processes that Eugène Canseliet, the Adept who was closest to the great Master, the enigmatic Fulcanelli, passed on to him personally." "From this," she continues, "the movement of the sun and moon, the winds, the dunes, the dew and

---

*Referring to the Alain Gruger exhibition of December 11, 2019, to February 22, 2020, at the Sophie Scheidecker Gallery, Paris.

†The pun here resists translation. *Plus souvent au four qu'au Moulin* (which translates literally as "more often at the oven than the mill") is a variation on the French saying *être au four et au Moulin*, which means "having too many irons in the fire."—*trans.*

the underground waters, the insects and the birds cease to be fragments in his inner language and become superb initiatory testimonies."[15] It should not be forgotten that alchemical practice—which requires constant work and availability and is likely to discourage anyone not willing or able to devote himself to it wholeheartedly—is based on the impossibility of separating the operative from the speculative, *ora et labora*—or as the *Mutus Liber* precisely states, "*Ora, lege, lege, lege, relege, labora et invenies*"*—clearly being the two facets (plus) of the Artist's *quest*. Furthermore, as it is a traditional science with an initiatory dimension, whose symbols can only be deciphered if someone has given you the key, the transmission from master to disciple, "but only among an elite,"[16] is of fundamental importance. Camacho confirms this in his *Myth of Isis and Osiris*, when, deploring that "this 'aristocratic' attitude of the Adepts has earned alchemy relentless detractors, too impatient to reach the goal or too ignorant to find the way, despite long years of study and reflection," he insists "on the importance of the role the Master should play in the study and practice of the Art of Hermes," for "often he can guide the neophyte—through a few words whispered in his ear—on the nature of a sign, on the obstacle to overcome in order to achieve success in an operation." Michel Butor plows the same furrow when he writes, "There is no classic text in which the author writes that he discovered everything by himself. He claims he only repeats, at best improves, what others have done before him. But he does tell us that he relied on ancient texts, and often their study alone wouldn't have been enough if a Master hadn't wanted to enlighten him. It is a knowledge that everyone can find only to the extent that the essential part has been bequeathed to him." And he adds, "The alchemist considers this

---

*Or according to the words of Artephius in *Three Treatises on Natural Philosophy*: "Work hard then, my son, put up thy supplications to God almighty; be diligent in searching the books of the learned in this science; for one book openeth another; think and meditate of these things profoundly; and avoid all things which vanish in or will not endure the fire, because from these adjustable, perishing, or consuming things, you can never attain to the perfect matter . . ."

difficulty in getting access essential, because it is a question of transforming the mentality of the reader in order to make him capable of seeing the meaning of the actions described."[17] "The fragmentation," says Canseliet, "that transforms the Magister into a philosophical puzzle is unlikely to frighten the educated investigator, but it will quickly discourage the layman who is unable to find his way through this different kind of labyrinth and won't be able to restore the order of the manipulations." But unlike Breton, whose books, Richard Danier has shown, in which "alchemy appears only as the engine of a personal experience unique to the author, never as a revelation of knowledge for the reader," "never lead the reader to unsuspected occult truths or open initiatory horizons, contrary to what more charitable Masters do!"

From the time of his *Ton Haut* exhibition in 1969, Jorge Camacho seems to have become set on *transmitting* this teaching "with a series of paintings inspired by alchemical science"*—even though Breton, with a nicely put phrase playing on the dual sense of the word "artist"—which completes, in passing, Butor's observation cited earlier, as emphasized in his *Prolegomena to a Third Manifesto of Surrealism or Not*, that "every Artist has to resume the pursuit of the Golden Fleece by himself." On the other hand, Camacho answered Arturo Schwarz's 1986 inquiry quite clearly when he said that "an 'alchemical vision' of the world is too individual and unique an experience to be communicated to the outside world by someone who has been initiated into the Hermetic Science. . . . This 'alchemical vision' is personal and belongs to the one who has ventured inside the labyrinth of Alchemical research." And in 1989 Guy-René Doumayrou wrote about this exhibition, "Then as never happened before, the paintings, signed Jorge Camacho, instead of borrowing images suggested by an allegorical vocabulary, created a poetic

---

*In the list of his one-man shows in the catalog for *Le livre des fleurs* for his exhibition at Thessa Hérold Gallery in 2003. Camacho, moreover, doesn't seem to be only "eager to transmit" by means of his drawings and paintings. Alone or with friends he took part in the publication or republication of no less than six books—and two catalogs—with specifically alchemical content.

language based on concrete experience whose allusions could only be deciphered by the initiated."[18] However, I should not overlook the small fly in the ointment introduced by François-René Simon who contradicts these definitive statements by pointing out that "even the emblem of 'Ton Haut' . . . and all this while remaining faithful to alchemical symbolism, Camacho's images—like the *Acte en or* (1967) which the language of the birds would gladly see born from the athanor—cannot be read as the 'operative' images of the old grimoires; he introduces his own personal dimension, in particular this taste for the perpetual transmutation of life by the hands of death." This is what Gilles Bucherie, in his aforementioned book on René Alleau, explains in these words: "The reading of alchemy and its imagery would lead the painter Jorge Camacho to combine pictorial art and poetic analogy from an alchemical imaginary realm"—which he concludes with this fine observation: "There is a veritable fusion and transmutation of the natural elements: water, air, earth, and fire, in all of Camacho's paintings." Curiously, in this exhibition catalog (which is nevertheless highly original), with illustrations taken from ancient treatises dealing exclusively with the Hermetic initiatory tradition and the symbology of the Great Work, all we see of Camacho's work are two engravings—Camacho, who as Bernard Roger, writes, "only draws and paints because he is first and foremost a poet." We should not forget what, after Fulcanelli who considers it as highly important, Canseliet, mentioning his friend Phileas Lebesgue, says about the Greek word ποιησις, "poeisis meaning action, creation, efficacy," an observation that he would repeat word for word about Elie-Charles Flamand. Bernard Roger's text from this catalog, stamped with a green seal evocative of *the moon's saliva*, therefore of the color that the salt becomes during the first stage of the work,* speaks in the sibylline manner of a traveler whose "joyful approach . . . has led

---

*In *L'hermétisme dans la vie de Swift et dans ses voyages*, Canseliet writes, "The universal spirit is green and imparts its color to the green in which it rises as the first phenomenon of sublimation."

to the transparent crossroads where the inner world meets the world's interior." The title alone, which is also based on a play on words, is quite meaningful in this respect. According to the rules of the language of the birds, which is omnipresent in alchemical texts to the great intellectual delight of the surrealists, the "Ton Haut" (High Pitch) is an allusion to Latona, in other words the *materia prima*. Bernard Roger writes of this in his book *On the Discovery of Alchemy*, as he told me in person, "As for Latona, the Adepts liked to play on her name using *tun* or barrel, *tonneau* or *tonne*, to speak about *Latone* [French spelling of the name of the goddess], which they accordingly often represented as an oak cask or even a hollow oak."[19] He revisits this in *Paris and Alchemy*, citing Fulcanelli who, in *The Dwellings of the Philosophers*, speaks of the "identical function held by the mythological princess Latona, mother of the sun and moon, and the cask or *tun*, which the cabalists teach is the vessel in which fermentation should take place, which they call the hollow oak." "The Greeks called her *Leto* which comes from *letos*, or *leitos*, with the Ionic meaning of common good, common possession, common house (*tô lêiton*), that is, the protective envelope, common to the double embryo." She can also be found in the Latin inscription of the phylactery that accompanies the fourteenth emblem of *New Alchemical Heraldry*, "*Dealbata Latona*," which can be translated *as Latona whitened*. Bernard Roger describes this operation: "*To Whiten Latona*, a constant order among Western Adepts which is both to clean a mineral considered as primal matter that were provided by nature from its 'accidents' or 'wastes,' in order to let it attain a higher condition and also facilitate the goddess's luminous delivery, bringing to life two astral bodies, the solar Apollo, father of all the arts, and Artemis the nocturnal mistress of the wild universe in which all possibilities are hidden, a reflection in the sky of the most distant stars."[20] In 1970, "choosing as his personal motto Michael Maier's phrase, '*Silentium post clamores*,' which accompanies his coat of arms at the end of *New Alchemical Heraldry*, Jorge Camacho decided to no longer participate in collective activities, without, however, abandoning his attachment to surrealism."* But as Gilles Bucherie suggests—and this is based on all the cross-collaborations, at least the public ones, whose frequency is visible—it seems that a sort of *compagnonnage* was established at that time, informally, but quite genuinely, and despite the "different sensibilities" of the protagonists, "who all exchanged ideas to perfect the phases of the Great Work." Thus a "kind of *compagnonnage* would be forged between Jorge Camacho, Alain Gruger, Bernard Roger, René Alleau, and Eugène Canseliet"—a kind of informal group† whose members' work would implicitly influence and echo each other! After the *Ascendant Licorne* (Ascendant Unicorn) exhibition, with a preface by Vincent Bounoure in 1973 at the Galerie deSeine, he presented a series of paintings entitled *The Dance of Death* at the same venue in 1976. This exhibition had a preface by René Alleau who placed it under the patronage of the Italian painter Giulio Campagnola and his 1509 engraving, "the hermetic philosopher in the countryside,"‡ explaining that his painter friend "has faithfully followed the traditional rule that the philosopher must endeavor to show the multiple aspects of a single point of the 'High Science' rather than claiming to analyze all the arcana." He specifies that "what is essentially at stake here is the *Caput Mortuum* in operational practice, hence the emblematic significance of the 'skull' in all these paintings," before adding that "we know that 'dissolution,' which is equivalent to Death in the alchemical treatises, is the

*Camacho, "Repères biographiques." *Silentium post clamores* is more specifically the title of a book published in 1617 by Michael Maier, author of *Atalanta Fugiens*, in defense of the Rosicrucian brotherhood.

†In the interview with the title "Du héron vert à la caverne," which particularly features René Alleau, which he granted to Yoan Armand Gil and me on June 17, 2022. Bernard Roger explains, however, "I cannot say that I was truly friends with Canseliet, we saw each other several times, we had esteem for each other and got along well. We had exchanges, he recommended things to read, I met him several times at the national library. . . . He was quite funny."

‡And thus also of the "Church of John," "the inner church of this mysterious Pre-Masonry to which belonged the majority of philosophers, artists, and scholars of Europe of this time," Alleau adds.

key to all the operations of the Work and that without it, no transformation is possible"—"dissolution or Death is the central point of the mysteries of the Great Work."[21]

"Son of light, flowing stream, crossing through, surfacing from bodies, dismembered skeletons, death seizes the living flesh but life is in the heart of the bone," doubles down Marie-Dominique Massoni.

12
THE OPEN BOOKS
OF THE ARTISTS

Could you read a closed book?
Break the chain of our matter by means of this torch.
When the cage is open, the bird can fly away.
The fire is beneath the smoke.

BERNARD ROGER AND JORGE CAMACHO,
TYPUS MUNDI

. . . the two books of which I spoke earlier. I will add that
one is closed and symbolizes the crude subject, and that the
other is open, and depicts the same passive matter after it
has undergone penetration by the spirit.

EUGÈNE CANSELIET,
L'ALCHIMIE EXPLIQUÉE SUR LES TEXTES CLASSIQUES

Your books are sealed, like the book of the Apocalypse; they
are sealed with cabalistic seals. You must break them, one
by one.

FULCANELLI, *THE MYSTERY OF THE CATHEDRALS*

Here is the first secret, the one which the philosophers
do not reveal and which they keep under the enigmatic
expression of the Path of St. James.

FULCANELLI, THE DWELLINGS
OF THE PHILOSOPHERS

As further evidence of his sustained interest—inherited from Breton—
in alchemy, in 1978 Camacho, together with Alain Gruger and Eugène
Canseliet, published the book *New Alchemical Heraldry*, for which he
provided the illustrations. This book has the appearance of a synthesis of
alchemical and surrealist researches, a book from which, to use Bernard
Roger's words, "radiates the intense beauty of an experience in which one's
entire being is engaged."* All of Camacho's work, "like all authentically
'traditional' works, in other words not 'classic,' but connected to a true
esoteric and initiatory tradition," in accordance with terms used elsewhere
by Alleau, appears in fact like "a remarkable synthesis between traditional
inspiration and the original expression of modernity."[1]

In 1982, the painter began managing a collection of books on
alchemy for Fata Morgana editions and published *Hermeticism in the
Life of Swift and His Travels* by Eugène Canseliet,† which he illustrated
with nine emblematic drawings. The catalogue for his 1984 exhibition
at the Loeb Gallery in Paris, titled, with a wink to René Alleau, *La
philosophie dans le paysage*, opened with a poem by his good friend Joyce
Mansour and focused on shamanism, another of his main interests. The
same may have been true of another exhibition held that same year at

---

*But the "closed book" is also the symbol of the raw primal matter just as it comes out of
the ore: "At the end of the first labors, or preparation of the soil," Bernard Roger writes
in *A la découverte de l'alchimie*, "the *closed book*, or passive subject of the work, is opened
thanks to the intervention of a spark of sidereal light that penetrates it and finds a fire of
the same nature within and combines with it."

†An offprint of *Cahiers du sud*, *L'hermétisme dans la vie de Swift et dans ses voyages* by
Eugène Canseliet was published in the Little Library of Traditional Alchemy by Fata
Morgana editions in 1983.

the Jacqueline Storme Gallery in Lille, which Camacho had visited several years earlier at the invitation of Roger Frézin and the Atelier de la Monnaie. In his text "Insular Challenge," Arenas wrote of his friend's work that "violence here reaches its most unusual and glorious union with alchemy."

In 1986, during the Forty-Second International Exhibition of Art in Venice, *Arte e alchimia*, to which he had been invited by Arturo Schwarz, he met Pol Lambert of the Epsilon Gallery in Brussels, who would then begin publishing his books on alchemy. As a result, in 1991, the painter published *The Philosophical Owl* in Brussels,[2] a collection of fifteen eighteenth-century maxims with commentary by Camacho, taken from a book of the same century dedicated to the Virgin Mary, *Mater Amoris et Dolori, quam Christus in cruce moriens omnibus ac singulis suis fidelibus in matrem legavit: ECCE MATER TUA** that the painter found in Prague in 1968. It has an introduction by Bernard Roger and a frontispiece by Mimi Parent depicting an owl, that "handsome nocturnal adventurer of silent flight [who] brings to mind an activity that cannot take place until the sun has set beneath the horizon," as the same Roger emphasizes in *The Cathedral of Seville*, before clarifying that "in the sense of an interpretation on the level of operative alchemy, this bird that only awakes at night, who can only see in darkness, bears a message often passed on in the history of this science, albeit generally in a discreet way." Now, even though the large X symbolizing the "secret fire" of the Adepts is missing from its chest, this owl philosophizing on the threshold of Camacho and Roger's book—but also on the sill of a labyrinth—is wearing glasses, like the one Henry Kunrath placed "at the beginning of the boards of his Amphitheater of Eternal Wisdom" accompanied by the motto: "WAS HELLFEN FALKEN LICHT ODER BRILN, SO DIE LEVT NICHT SEHEN WOLLEN" ("What good are torches or glasses if men do not wish to see").[3]

**The mother of love and sorrow, who Christ dying on the cross bequeathed to his faithful as mother: Here is your mother*, a 1726 book by Antonius Ginther (1679–1725).

In his six-page introduction to this collection of engravings (incidentally dedicated to "Eugène Canseliet, F.C.H.") Bernard Roger, emphasizing from the outset, following Nicolas Flamel, "the two levels of intelligence of the images," the "two degrees of interpretation," one "theological" and the other "philosophical according to the magisterium of Hermes," that generally overlays alchemical representations, recalls the importance of "phylacteries" (to which Fulcanelli had already drawn attention), "by spelling out their function in the iconography in general as guardians of some hidden meaning." He then explains that they "form the soul of each of the fifteen devices whose bodies are the emblems newly analyzed by Camacho."

In fact, these fifteen "devices," whose inspiration at first glance seems to be an impeccably orthodox Catholicism, could well be the subject of an alchemical reading, thus possessing a hidden alchemical meaning that is distilled for us, as Roger tells us, "in his commentaries based on experiments at the firebox." This would be Jorge Camacho, more charitable than ever, "following the same star as the pilgrims on the Way of Compostela."

In 1993, with the Parisian exhibition *Histoire de Chaman*,* which even shook up Claude Levi-Strauss, he bore witness to another initiatory experience that could be fundamentally the same as the earlier one. "The painter," writes Surpik Angelini, "sheds light on the sublime experiences of the journey into the depths of the soul after crossing through the veils of appearance and gaining access to the spirits that obscure the light, in order to reveal the mysterious enchantment of the *mediums* that establish contact between us and natural forces."

In 1995, the painter wrote a valuable booklet on the *Myth of Isis and Osiris and Its Relationship with Hermetic Symbolism*,[4] naturally accompanied by a short preface by Bernard Roger! Starting with the first page of the book, we find ourselves at the very heart of the matter, insofar as it is dedicated, quite specifically, "To Fulcanelli, F.C.H., *in*

---

*Again accompanied by a text by Bernard Roger.

the Gold of Time." We immediately notice the title of *Brother Knight of Heliopolis* attached to the name of the author of *The Mystery of the Cathedrals*, as well as the direct allusion to the inscription on Breton's tomb in the cemetery of Batignolles.

Knowing that, as "Pierre Dujols de Valois under the pseudonym of Magophon" said in his "Hypotypose" to the *Mutus Liber*, there is a "positive substratum that is the foundation of the sanctuaries of every form of worship spread across the globe," Camacho presents here, in Bernard Roger's words, nothing less than the first "exegesis" of the myth of Isis and Osiris, "that has been attempted to date based on the original tales, as best as they can be translated in the present day." This myth, which is "centered on the mystery of the space-time passages where life plays out until the unknown realm of death, and from the invisible domain of death to the light of life, is also found at the very heart of alchemy's true secret." The main aim of this secret is therefore obviously not the production of gold or any other precious metal—but in correspondence with calcination, it is no less directly related to "the motif of 'dying and becoming'" and therefore plays "a central philosophical role"![5] The author of the preface takes advantage of this to remind us of the immense importance that the ancient Egyptians, just like the Sons of Science today, attached to the journey "in the *world of doubles*," evoking "the *Duat* (or *Tuat*),* a twilight world of passages marked at a short distance from the horizon as on the surface of the worked material by the presence of the brilliant star that astronomy recognizes as the planet Venus, called *Lucifer* or *vesper* depending on whether it precedes the rising of the sun or accompanies its setting." He adds that "all those who have taken their first steps on the practice of the Art of Hermes know that this star is perceived in the 'Mirror of the Art,' in which no one can reach it, however, without having, like Cyliani, crossed through the door of the Temple."

---

*The lower heaven, both the site of Ra's passage during the hours of night and the beyond where the dead dwell.

Camacho begins his book questioning the importance that Fulcanelli must have granted to Egyptian civilization in general and "to the Egyptian myth in its connections with the Great Work," in particular, to choose to dedicate his two books "to the Brethren of Heliopolis, the solar city of ancient Egypt," of which practically nothing remains—but which was once "the birthplace of the hermetic philosophy of Greco-Roman Egypt." He then devotes himself to an analysis as detailed as it is persuasive, or at least seems so to an uninitiated like me, of the myth of Isis and Osiris as presented by the "Heliopolitan tradition" in the light of classical alchemical texts as well as his personal operative experience, as he alludes to his *philosophical Owl*!

At the end of this brief study, Camacho also mentions the individual I have previously identified as the *Green Man*, that "Man of the Woods" whom Fulcanelli identifies as the person the alchemist should take as his model. This *"Natural Man"* would be a "scholar of simple mind, an attentive and critical examiner of nature, which he should always strive to imitate as the monkey imitates man." This is why he is "the absolute master of the Work, the obscure and never lazy worker, the secret agent and the *faithful or loyal servant of the Philosopher"*— whom we have already met earlier. Comparing him to the "Egyptian BES" he concludes that the alchemist, like this deity, "must find his way through the dense jungle of an imaginary adventure. For he must often be more a poet than a man of science." Perhaps even a surrealist poet.

He collaborated again with Bernard Roger, but this time simply as commentator, in the 1997 publication of *Typus Mundi*, "a very rare small volume that Fulcanelli himself held in high esteem."* It was written in the eighteenth century by "nine fathers of the Society of Jesus," a collection of moral emblems to which the two men, with a wink to the "other students of Science [their] Brethren" added "new and brief com-

---

*Eugéne Canseliet, in his second preface for *The Dwellings of the Philosophers*, cited by Bernard Roger in a prefatory note to *Typus Mundi*, "the little book of the Rhetoricians of the College of Jesus in Anvers" (Huelva, Spain: Editions du Tenuel, 1977). He also wrote the three following observations.

mentaries from another perspective than that intended by the scholarly *rhéteurs* [rhetoricians]"* before giving them clearly different alchemical interpretations that now accompanied the "mystical-moral" quatrains of their Jesuit predecessors.

In the same year, Pierre d'Alun Editions offered a reprint dedicated to "René Alleau, philosopher of nature," consisting of "several extracts from the seven chapters of Basil Valentine's *Revelation of the Mysteries of the Tinctures of the Seven Metals*, entitled for this occasion *On the Nature of Things.* It was accompanied by eight extremely precise emblematic drawings by Jorge Camacho and a text by Bernard Roger in which he notes that "Camacho awakens, in a contemporary context, this cabalistic art in which the drawn or painted image simultaneously opens to word play and the tangible domain of experimentation at the furnace." He also invites us to recognize "in the septenary of its aspects the 'Fountain of the Lovers of Science' who, according to Jean de la Fontaine de Valenciennes [*sic*]" "is the mother of the seven metals."† He emphasizes the far-from-ordinary nature of the "vertiginous encounter, over several great valleys of time, of the fifteenth-century Adept and the twentieth-century Artist, the perfect legitimacy of which should not surprise us but rather amaze us, since it takes place at the center of the circle." He also takes this opportunity to remind us again that Camacho is above all a poet‡ who paints. Once again Roger explains

---

*"Rhéteur can be said in the etymological sense of the word," the two surrealists subsequently observed, "he who has received the word and knows how to transmit it."

†It may come as a surprise that the author says "septenary" but the first of the eight illustrated plates serves as a frontispiece, while each of the other seven accompanies a short text by Valentine.

‡He actually is, as he is the author, under the transparent pseudonym of Ohcamac, "born November 29, 1959, in the spot known as Gare Saint Lazare in Paris," of an impossible to find short collection of poems, *L'arbre acide* (published 1968 and reprinted in Huelva in 2002). Alain-Valery Aelberts and Jean-Jacques Auquier specify in a brief note in their book *Poètes singuliers du surréalisme et autres lieux* that it "can [then] be considered as all his writings." But only if we leave out *Semen contra* followed by *Harr*, a collection of forty poems accompanied by twenty watercolors published by Pierre Mainard editions in May 2019.

that "if alchemy and poetry . . . share the common goal of recreating the created, they also find common motivating cause in the fire that burns secretly in the heart of all beings of nature and through which, every second, Nature renews itself." Here we will recall that alchemy, according to René Alleau, is a theurgy of fire, this fire "ceaselessly descending from 'heaven' and climbing from the earth," which the rebel Prometheus stole from the gods and gave to humanity. This "igneous fluid, . . . *Secret Fire*, the mystery of which lies in the heart of Alchemy" is "none other than an image of the spiritual substance that emanates from the Principle and contains the property of giving life to the beings of the three kingdoms in our sublunary world."[6]

Perhaps it is worth noting here, in passing, with Jennifer Waelti-Waters that "Brother Basil Valentine was probably a German monk of Saint Benedict's Order in the fifteenth or sixteenth century," unless he is purely imaginary since "no trace of his life can be found in this Order's records." He then would be a simple "personification," as Sabine Stuart de Chevalier said (according to Canseliet) "of the hermetic gem and its miraculous virtues." A "precursor to Paracelsus," and "experienced chemist," "his works describe his experiments in the form of mythological allegories *without any reference to Christianity*" (my italics) and there can be no doubt that this fact was found particularly striking by the surrealists who studied his work, which had already been analyzed with "as much science as discernment"* by the same Canseliet. "It seems," adds Waelti-Waters, "that in him the material and spiritual aspects of the hermetic art, which are always one with Flamel, are separated."

Also in 1998, the Cuban painter, who had explicitly stated in his response to Arturo Schwartz's inquiry that "it goes without saying that all true alchemical iconography is based on the fundamental principles of Natural Philosophy" (the uppercase letters are Camacho's), provided illustrations for the emblems in *Arcanes de la philosophie naturelle*

---

*Séverin Batfroi, in "Aspects d'une mission," his contribution to a special issue of *Atlantis* in homage to Canseliet.

published by Editions Pol François Lambert with an introduction by Bernard Roger. In it, the author notes, "It is in a spirit of great sincerity, based on five lusters of study and work at the furnace, and for the least without 'real desire,' that Jorge Camacho has composed, to show the actors and different scenes of the Chemical Theater that he describes with extreme precision, the frontispiece and fifteen plates of this new *Mute Book*."

Finally, in 2011, the two men created, with the same publisher, *The Cathedral of Seville and the Hermetic Bestiary of the Portal of Saint Christopher and the Immaculate Conception*. Marie Dominique Massoni wrote about this book in the fifth issue of *S.U.R.R.*: "With Jorge Camacho and Bernard Roger as light bearers, alchemy and freemasonry form a morning star and an evening star, and the Pole Star of poetry comes as the language of Nature." Equipped with a historical overview by Edouardo Fernandez Sanchez, this book is illustrated with numerous photos* by Camacho in which, by analyzing the series of sculptures of a major Catholic site that still carry "elements of hermetic science," in other words, a "philosophical dwelling," the two men continue, to some extent, the work initiated by Fulcanelli with *The Mystery of the Cathedrals*.† They also continue, in a broader sense, the task already suggested by Roger on the last page of *Paris and Alchemy* when he expressed his wish that the quest begun in his book for this considerable heritage, which unfortunately "is diminishing day by day," "be continued by the Lovers of Science‡ of today and tomorrow not only in Paris but in all the towns and cities of France, Europe, and numerous

---

*The photos of this book, which was published in Spain, are in black and white. According to Bernard Roger there is a much better set in color that could not be used.

†Anne Tronche, *Jorge Camacho, vue imprenable*. The two authors don't refrain from citing Fulcanelli to support their remarks.

‡These "Lovers of Science," about which he writes elsewhere: "Who are they if not the disciples of the Science of Love, based on the natural law of analogy through which communicate all the kingdoms and levels of existence" (*Introduction to De la Nature des Métaux* [On the Nature of Metals]).

places throughout the world." And although to write this work, Bernard Roger confided to me that he had never been to Andalusia, we cannot fail to remember that Los Pajaros, Camacho's property in Spain, is very close to Almonte and the National Park of Doñana, almost halfway between Huelva and Seville. Nor should we forget that the book raises the question of "the existence of alchemical activity if not of an initiatory center in the region at the end of the nineteenth and beginning of the twentieth centuries." Moreover, as Roger and Camacho remind us, it was in a villa near Seville "where time does not seem to be the same as that in which the rest of humanity is active," that Canseliet claims he met his Master Fulcanelli, who is believed to have died in 1925—after 1950.* This villa located about ten miles from the city is one around which, the two authors reveal, strange phenomena have actually been witnessed and even been reported in the local newspapers. In *Le feu du soleil*, his interviews with Robert Amadou, Eugène Canseliet, who was convinced that there was an "entire society on earth, a category of individuals who lived on a different plane from ours,"† spoke of 1952 and states he met his Master for the last time, on two separate occasions during his stay, "on the banks of the Guadalquivir," as Khaitzine put it. He continues:

> There were contemporaries of Philip II in the mansion where I saw Fulcanelli again. Right away, I didn't get it. I was forbidden to look out the windows; I saw this staircase with a succession of very beautiful planes and children playing. I thought these were the children of some guests, spoiled children playing dress-up. But no! They belonged to another age. No, this was not a "vision." All the people had kept their old clothing. . . . There were also many young women

---

*Jacques Bergier said he talked with Fulcanelli in 1937 while Louis Pauwels always claimed that he met him in 1953 at Le Procope on rue de l'Ancienne Comédie in Paris. But we know how little credit the surrealists gave to the authors of *Morning of the Magicians*!
†This irresistibly brings to mind some of the observations Breton made in 1942 in *Prolegomena to a Third Manifesto of Surrealism or Not*, mainly about the Great Transparents.

who looked like they had stepped straight out of a Velasquez painting, wearing the necklace of the Golden Fleece.

He alluded to this encounter again in 1979 in a show hosted by
Jacques Chancel on France Inter in which he made clear that the Adept,
who would then be one hundred and thirteen years old, looked like he
was fifty. For his part, Richard Khaitzine suggested that "the first allusion to a trip to Castille by Canseliet was made by Claude Seignolle
in 1969 in his book, *Invitation au château de l'étrange*, published by
Maisonneuve et Larose." He completed the anecdote with the revelation
that again "in 1966, Eugène Canseliet would have stayed with a strange
Spanish family who possessed alchemical knowledge and lived as if time
had stopped in the eighteenth century."[7] But during this second journey, there was no longer any question of meeting Fulcanelli.

The Gothic construction of the "new" Cathedral of Seville,
begun in 1400 on the site of the "former mosque, which had been
Christianized since the thirteenth century," was interrupted in 1580,
"leaving unfinished," Edouardo Fernandez Sanchez says in his introduction, "the north and south portals of the transept, which were
sealed up with brick walls." "This significant place of worship," Roger
and Camacho thought it wise to establish right at the outset, thus
making it clear to the *students of science*, "was a vessel that overcame
many storms and dominated abysses, carrying the immutable spirit
above the waters."

Under the direction of Adolfo Fernandez Casanova,* liberal anti-
clerical and Freemason disciple of a Spanish disciple of Viollet le Duc,
Juan Madrazo Kuntz, the construction for the completion and layout
of the building, begun in 1888, began with the south portal, known
then as "Saint Christopher's," then continued in 1895 with that of

---

*When he speaks of it again in *Les demeures de l'invisible*—published in 2022—Bernard
Roger points out that the "work of architects like Viollet Le Duc in France or Fernandez
Casanova in Andalusia permits a glimpse of these builders' certain knowledge of this
domain," in other words the domain of the Art of Music!

the north portal of the "Immaculate Conception," dominated by the Pole Star, which was completed in 1927. The sculptures that adorn it were created by the master stonecutter Francisco Montenegro based on "the original drawings of Fernandez Casanova, who thus proved to be the true creator of this admirable grouping that forms the bestiary of the Seville Cathedral." This grouping is of "high quality inspiration and exceptional workmanship," so exceptional that "studying the flora and fauna" depicted there, "the impression that a message was left here by some 'charitable' and noble traveler quickly becomes a conviction"! The authors also point out, in the opening lines of their work, that, in conformance with Fulcanelli's observation, if "in all medieval cathedrals . . . the south rose and the north rose respectively correspond to the white and black colors of the Great Work, in Seville the symbol is reasserted by the arrangement of the two portals of the transept, one opening onto the activity of the city, the other onto the shady garden of a vanished world," the "patio of Los Naranjos, an enclosure of freshness and a remnant of the Moorish civilization."

Simply by raising one's gaze above the portal of St. Christopher, that "giant ferryman whom the Christian world" made into "the *Christophoros*, 'who carries Christ' or the *Chrysophorus* 'who carries the gold' (in other words the sun, heart, and origin of light)," "the giant Χριστοφόρος, 'Christophoros,' who carries the Christ on his shoulders," as Elie-Charles Flamand says, and who "corresponds to the primal matter, Χρυσοφόρος, 'Chrysophoros,' virtually the carrier of the philosopher's gold," we cannot help but be struck by "the seal of Solomon, a graphic sign of the philosopher's stone that seems to spread around its site on the gable the igneous energy with which it is overflowing" and seems to place the porch "under the sign of Hermes!"

The other portal, that of the Immaculate Conception, is decorated with "a terracotta composition" created in 1917 by Adolfo Lopez Rodriguez in which the Virgin Mary stands majestically, her appearance conforming to the images that flourished in Catholic iconography from the fifteenth century. What is less in conformity with the standard representation are the two figures surrounding her, Saint Michael and Saint John. Saint John, on the left, has an eagle behind him holding in its beak a ribbon from which hangs a cubic stone unfolding a *phylactery**—which as Fulcanelli taught, invites us to search for a hermetic meaning. This scene, which illustrates "the first operation of the alchemical work," the authors advise should be considered as "the title of the great lapidary book that opens at the portal of the Conception, and faces the observer, whose attention should from now on be directed toward the sculptures that make up its pages." A great book that, from capital to capital, but also on other supports, describes the various stages of the work with the coded precision that characterizes the work of "artists who," as Bernard Roger says, "are spiritually engaged in the operations of the harmonic perfection of matter and are responsible for the beauty of the world through the subjective meaning they were able to give to phenomena," and eventually reminds us of "the inalienable unity of spirit and matter that the teaching of alchemy has always proclaimed." A great book of which Jorge Camacho and Bernard Roger, as kindly as in *Le hibou philosophe* (The philosopher owl), help us to decipher several images that smack of a tradition that is both Masonic and linked to the Art of Music. But that's another story.

---

*In art history, this refers to a pennant or banner with furled ends carrying the words spoken by an individual or the caption of the subject depicted. It was often used by the artists of the Middle Ages and Renaissance. "Whether it bears an epigraph or not, it suffices to find a phylactery on any subject to be assured that the image conceals a hidden meaning, a secret signification marked by its mere presence as intended for researchers," writes Fulcanelli in *The Dwellings of the Philosophers*.

13
THE NEW ALCHEMICAL HERALDRY

For is not this "ars cabalistica" or a secret and a hidden art? Is it not an art full of secrets? And believest thou O fool that we plainly teach this secret of secrets, taking our words according to their literal signification?

THE SECRET BOOK OF THE MOST ANCIENT PHILOSOPHER
ARTEPHIUS CONCERNING THE HIDDEN ART
AND THE PHILOSOPHER'S STONE

As I wrote earlier, quoting Bernard Roger's preface to Basil Valentine's book "illustrated" by the artist, "it is from a three-hundred-year slumber that Camacho awakens, in a contemporary context, the kabbalistic art in which the drawn or painted image spontaneously opens to the play of words and to the tangible domain of experimentation at the furnace." This is because, as René Alleau (another accomplice) points out, "the West today is further away than ever before" from "the primordial tradition,"* the one whose disappearance condemns a civilization cut off from it "to spiritual decadence and material

---

*The Guénonian tone of this can't be missed!

214

destruction." But the fact remains that it has never been entirely lost nor will it ever be.

In the same manner as Julien Champagne illustrating Fulcanelli's books,* Camacho, as Roger told me, was very fond of emblems,† emblems that Canseliet described as "a small world formed by coats of arms that sing through their images and speak through their maxims." Camacho, who stated loud and clear that what "interested him personally in alchemical art was the decoding of the secret and sacred aspect of the message concealed within the symbolic image," and thought "that all artistic speculation centered on this theme that fails to transmit a fair and true hermetic knowledge remains inoperative,"‡ reconnects in this last book—as well as *Hermeticism in Swift's Life and Travels*, *Le hibou philosophe*, *Arcana of Natural Philosophy*, and especially *New Alchemical Heraldry*—with the tradition of the *emblemata*. These emblematic treatises were particularly popular between the sixteenth and eighteenth centuries, born in the wake of Francesco Colonna's *Hypnerotomachia poliphili* (*Dream of Poliphili*) the last of these treatises being, as Bernard Roger reminds us, "that of Barchusen: *Elementa chemica,* published in 1718."[1]

These works would gradually assume a Hermetic dimension, a very fine example of which is Maier's *Atalanta Fugiens*, "the hermetic epic about a heroine from Greek mythology that introduced the alchemical quest into the realm of the book of emblems,"** whose subtitle is

---

*This was in particular the opinion of the Hermeticist Archer who even went so far as to consider Camacho to be "a continuer, almost an heir, to Julien Champagne, at least in some of the works he produced." This Julien Champagne was someone that some people, Sarane Alexandrian for example, thought was Fulcanelli himself, but it's likely more complicated than that, as emphasized by Richard Khaitzine when writing, "Eugène Canseliet . . . in addition to the fact he did not have the maturity required—which he acknowledged—always denied that he was the author of these texts."

†Definition of the emblem by René Alleau in *The Primal Force in Symbol*: "The body allows the soul to be seen entirely, without veils."

‡In his response to Arturo Schwartz's inquiry.

**The museum label for the work in the exhibition, *La Franc-maçonnerie*, Bibliothèque nationale de France, Paris, April–September 2016.

Emblemata nova de secretis naturae chymica. These are transversal works whose ternary structure is immutable and which generally consist of emblems, coded images, and rebuses, accompanied by sayings, proverbs, or maxims, the words of the wise (here Artists or "Lovers of Science"), moral precepts, or skillfully analyzed verses. Bernard Roger writes (in his text entitled "Alchemy, Initiatory Path") "that each emblem [in Michael Maier's book] is accompanied by a Latin epigram in the form of a sextet, with a three-voice fugue taking up the last two lines." Thus, there are three levels of information, the epigrammatic title, the *motto* or *titulus* that carries the emblem's meaning, the ever-active image, the *symbolon* that specifically illustrates it and makes it possible to be memorized (as Canseliet says, "a small symbolic scene that is different each time"), and finally an explanatory text that, in the case that interests us, is directly related to the process of realizing the Great Work.

As a token of friendship, at least, *New Alchemical Heraldry* by Jorge Camacho and Alain Gruger, published by Le Soleil Noir, "that *black sun* that is the non-accidental logo of the publisher,"[*] and which smacks of this type of book, is preceded by some "preliminary thoughts" and followed by an epilogue signed by Canseliet. He doesn't hesitate to add, as was his habit, the initials F. C. H. to his name (as is the case on his tombstone), and he takes the trouble to explain the implications of the work of his two friends (which seem particularly interesting to me as they form, as I said earlier, a kind of synthesis of the alchemical and surrealist researches, and therefore of the "discreet collaboration of painter and chemist"). "They transformed many of their discoveries, out of love and charity, into emblems and devices on escutcheons and pennants." We should remember that those Adepts who leave clues are said *charitable.*

The "album," as Camacho called it, this "magnificent album over which hovers the shadow of the wise and scrupulous author of 'Fronton Virage' [Breton—*trans.*]" consists of forty-three maxims

---

[*]Eugène Canseliet, Epilogue in Camacho and Gruger, *Héraldique alchimique nouvelle.*

rather than emblems,*[2] the main bodies of which are all Camacho's work. At the same time the phylacteries that form their souls, with the exception of the first one, harbor Latin expressions while the accompanying commentaries "have been selected from the philosophical or poetic works of a variety of ancient and modern authors," whose identification is left to the reader. Moreover, as is often intentionally the case with the surrealists—and in a more accidental way with the alchemists—"the image enters into analogous poetic relationship with the text," as Alain Joubert noted in an interview with Claire Boustani. Speaking of the importance of the phylacteries, whose presence should "attract the visitor's attention," we should not overlook here that according to Bernard Roger's observations in both *Paris and Alchemy* and *Le hibou philosophe*, "they always indicate the existence of a secret meaning in the compositions in which they appear, as we are taught by Fulcanelli." This latter wrote specifically in *The Dwellings of the Philosophers* that "whether it bears an epigraph or not, it is enough to find a phylactery on any subject to be certain that the image contains a hidden meaning, a secret signification offered to the seeker and marked by its mere presence." Three other emblems—as frontispiece, "Paradigm of the Great Work," in other words "Vitriol" in Basil Valentine's *Azoth of the Philosophers*, then "The chemical man or the hidden gold of the wise," preceding Canseliet's "preliminary thoughts," and finally "The lone black eye"† as a kind of opening to the same author's epilogue—complete the set, giving us then a total

---

*According to René Alleau, contrary to emblems, maxims—and this seems to me to be the case here—"always impose upon us a subtle detour, a singular and indirect allusion, a voluntary divergence between that which is shown and that which is signified. In other words, it is not enough to see the maxim in order to understand it immediately; we must also guess its resonances and its inner music, sometimes hardly perceptible upon first examination."

†Allusion to Nerval's "Black Sun" but also to the publisher, François di Dio. There is a pun, here, between "le Soleil Noir" (The Black Sun), the name of Di Dio's publishing house borrowed from Gérard de Nerval and "Le seul oeil noir" (The lone black eye) which both sound very similar when read aloud.

of fifty illustrations. The three more or less complete coats of arms bear the "arms" of the authors that "speak or sing all or part of the Work," that of Fulcanelli's disciple, with "his iron helm adorned with feathers," these "feathered crests showing the superfluous quantity of the volatile spirit that emerges from the tightly sealed *iron* helmet and evaporates in the air,"* accompanied by the famous device "*Quand Sel Y Est*" (When Salt Is There).

Flamand analyzed Canseliet's motto as follows: "This is the kind of kabbalistic wordplay to which he lent his name. He was incontestably a worthy bearer of the *Salt of Sapience* and he knew how to dispense fragments of it with discernment and by degrees to those who were predestined and prepared to receive them!"[3] He also provided the explanation of Camacho and Gruger's title, making it clear that heraldry, which "falls under the jurisdiction of that language that the great initiates wanted to be that of the birds and consequently that of the 'gay science or gay scavoir,'" "forms an integral part of alchemy for which it is the initial and hieroglyphic expression."[4] "Not one of these coats of arms," Canseliet says again, "exists without the word." "They are like small windows that open onto an immense, unknown word that is accessible only to every true poet"—but "the coat of arms speaks only to those who are capable of grasping its indistinct language." In this context, it is well worth recalling what Elie-Charles Flamand said in his very beautiful book, *Les méandres du sens*: "It is certain that heraldry, an emanation of the initiatory nature of the chivalric order, was inseparable from alchemical gnosis, for both drink from the same traditional spring. Thus the customary symbolism of the coat of arms is often analogically linked to various stages of the processes of the Work." It would be difficult to state this better!

Now, as in the texts of Fulcanelli or Canseliet, the authors are "pas-

---

*This quote comes from the article "Le blason, creuset alchimique," published with no author name in issue 281 of the magazine *Atlantis, héraldique et alchimie ou de l'origine hermétique du blason.*

sionate about" Cervantes,* Colonna, Rabelais,† Cyrano de Bergerac, Swift, Perrault, and several others. Poets are quite prominent in the texts chosen to convey the accompanying message in Camacho and Gruger's book, as we can find quotations taken from the works of those the surrealists appreciated most highly. Alfred Jarry—*Days and Nights* and *Absolute Love*—for example, is directly cited no less than nine times, while Xavier Forneret, "the black man with the white face" rediscovered by Breton appears five times. The work of Edgar Allen Poe is represented three times directly and once indirectly—through the inscription of a work of Crebillon. Gérard de Nerval, Villiers de L'Isle-Adam (who cites Byron), and Saint-Pol Roux—notably with an excerpt from *Les Reposoirs de la procession*—appear three times each, before Aloysius Bertrand, Rimbaud, and Raymond Roussel, whose texts are mentioned twice each, specifically, in the case of the latter, his famous play *The Dust of Suns*. The fabulist Florian (because he is quoted by Jarry), Rabelais, Swift (about whom Canseliet wrote), Sade, Béranger, and Fourier are quoted once each, as are Breton, Duchamp (in a play on words), and Michaux (an old friend of Canseliet's) for contemporaries. Heraclitus, the sole pre-Socratic philosopher to appear, is quoted twice—once perhaps because of the title of an aquatint by Joan Miró, *Without the Sun and Despite the Other Stars, We Would Have Night*. Callimachus of Cyrene, Lucretius, and Cicero (for the authors of antiquity), and the thirteenth-century Persian mystic poet Jalāl al-Dīn Muḥammad Rūmī, complete the list. Two biblical texts are called on, the Book of Job and the Song of Songs—without absolute certainty for the second case. On the other hand it comes as a surprise to note that writings

---

*It will be noted that André Coia-Gatié is also the author of a "hermetic reading of the work of Cervantes," entitled "Don Quichotte, le chevalier errant," published after his book *La Chevalerie errante*.

†Rabelais of whom Fulcanelli openly wrote in *The Mystery of the Cathedrals*, "*The Life of Gargantua and Pantagruel* by François Rabelais is an esoteric work, a novel in cant. The good curé of Meudon reveals himself in it as a great initiate, as well as a first-class cabalist."

directly related to alchemy are proportionately much less represented, although Camacho constantly quotes alchemical engravings in his own works. While Michael Maier—and especially *Atalanta Fugiens* (a turn of phrase from XXXI of this book, for example, is reused in emblem XXXVII)—appears twice among quoted authors, like Jung (although once indirectly) Paracelsus appears only indirectly, mainly through the mention of the "Archaea." Stephan Michelspacher (*Cabala, Mirror of Art and Nature in Alchymia*, 1615), Pierre Jean Fabre (*Anatomia totius universi*, 1646), Johann Ehrard Neithold, alias Naxagoras (*Alchymia denudate*, 1715) and Dom Pernety (*Mytho-Hermetic Dictionary*, 1758) are the only other alchemical authors cited. For his part, Jerome Cardan appears only thanks to a quote from René Alleau. Regarding the penultimate author listed, all we can state is that the second text cited, in the commentary to Camacho's forty-fourth drawing, appears in the second volume of Fulcanelli's *Dwellings of the Philosophers*. After expressing a "wish that the son of science discovers there the manner of interpreting the sealed books, and knows how to take advantage of a so little veiled teaching," the Adept provides a "French version in a clear language of an original cabalistic text of Naxagoras,"* a version worth transcribing as it is simply the "Very Detailed Description of the manner of extracting, and releasing, the Spirit from Gold, enclosed in the vile mineral matter, so as to build the sacred Temple of Light and to discover other analogous secrets"! "The sacred Temple of Light," Fulcanelli explains in a footnote, "is the name given to the philosopher's stone—our microcosm, in relationship to the temple of Jerusalem, the image of the universe or of the macrocosm."

Without going deeper into a necessarily technical and complicated explanation of the emblems drawn by Camacho and knowing that, as Canseliet reminds us, "*the Philosophers express themselves more freely and*

---

*In the second preface to *The Dwellings of the Philosophers*, Canseliet also mentions "Naxagoras of whom we read, at the side of the Master, *Alchemy Unveiled* [*Alchymia Denudata*] in the very faithful manuscript translation of the eighteenth century."

clearly through characters and enigmatic figures, as if by a mute language, than through words,[5] it is still worth examining several of them more closely, because they show us the extent to which the painter adheres to alchemical tradition. Above all, however, we must ask ourselves if Camacho and his friend Gruger were not playing a little game with their readers, by surreptitiously introducing an additional element into their composition, color, which plays a major role in this armorial science that this painter knew intimately—but also in alchemy. Certainly, if looked at distractedly, the coats of arms appearing in the *New Alchemical Heraldry* are in black and white, but when studied closely, it will be seen that the authors resorted to a system of crosshatchings and interlacing curved lines used in the carving of coats of arms in stone, especially in funerary monuments. In this way red, *gueules*, is represented by parallel vertical lines; blue, *azur*, by horizontal crosshatching; green, *sinople*, by diagonal parallel lines going from the viewer's left to the right;* violet, *pourpre*, "color," writes Khaitzine, "of the Holy Spirit and thus the *mercury* of the alchemists,"[6] by diagonal lines going this time from the viewer's right to left; white, *argent*, being only the absence of color, by an absence of crosshatching; black, *sable*, by closely crossed vertical and horizontal lines; and yellow, *or*, by a scattering of little dots.

Some of these reading keys are also used by Bernard Roger in his introduction to the new edition of Basil Valentine's book *On the Nature of the Metals*, when he points out, for example, that in one of the plates, fire "falls from the stars in drops of *sinople* to give life to the material of the work."

But let's return to the forty-first emblem as an example. Its title is "the Wooden Horse," in which the use of the famous and truthfully magnificent verse of Rimbaud—"It has been found again. What? Eternity. It is the sea mingled with the sun"—compels Hermeticist Archer to wonder outright if it might not validate the conclusion that "the distinction between the dry way and the wet way is partly

---

*We should not forget that the direction of coats of arms is reversed in heraldry.

a sophistry"! He then rightly points out that the kite with which the *chemical child* with the sun for a head is playing in Camacho's drawing reminds us that the "wooden horse . . . takes us back of course to children's games, of which the kite is another illustration," whereas the maxim, *Ludus Puerorum*, in the phylactery beneath the coat of arms, is a direct allusion to the anonymous *Treatise said of the Work of Women and the Play of Children*, an expression echoed by "*Operis processio dicitur omne opus mulierum* and *ludus pueroroum*" in the first words of a treatise on the *Artis auriferae* from 1593. And I cannot resist the pleasure of quoting a few passages from these treatises. First this one:

> This thing from which the stone is extracted, the poor as well as the rich possess it. It is Women's Work, and Child's Play, and the stone is its flower.

Then there are these, employed by Canseliet in his commentary of *Mutus Liber*:

> Now the triple play of children should precede the work of the women. For the children often are playing with three things. In the first place, often with very old walls. Secondly with urine. And thirdly with embers.

And finally:

> The first game procures the material of the stone. The second game increases the soul. The third game prepares the body for life.

More prosaically, Jörg Völlnagel, commenting on two of the illuminated illustrations of *Splendor Solis*, *Children's Game and Women's Work*, explains that the *Ludus Puerorum* corresponds to the *coagulatio*, the operation during which "sulfur becomes the active agent that binds and fixes the mercury," an "exchange of roles between the two substances" that the author compares to "an exchange of roles between the two substances of a children's game during which 'the one that was on top becomes the one that is below.'" However, in the second case, it is "the sublimation" that "allows the state of perfect whiteness to be achieved: the *albedo*, the penultimate degree of the work" that is compared "to the women's work of washing to whiten, of cooking for as long as needed . . ."

In his *Bourges cité première*, Philippe Audoin also speaks of these children's games and women's work whose presence he detects in a bas-relief in the former town hall of this city about which he says, quoting Philalethes, "At the time the Adept was writing, this expression had to have been long a cliché. Flamel in particular made it clear that Perrenelle, his wife, would not have found herself facing great difficulties in the final operations." Then he mentions more specifically the *Ludus Puerorum* with regard to a "cherub riding a wooden horse" at the Hotel Lallemant:* "A very similar scene is illustrated in a treatise by S. Trismosin, *Aureum Vellus* (1598): here we see the wooden horse again. . . . In another book by the same author, *Splendor Solis*,† it's the pinwheel that appears—but an adjacent panel shows women engaged in various domestic tasks.

Finally, he adds, "the famous *Mutus Liber* contains a similar image: the child is working at the furnace without abandoning his shuttlecock and racket, and a woman, similarly occupied, keeps hold of her distaff." "Salomon Trismosin," says Bernard Joly (quoting Van Lennep) in his book *La rationalité de l'alchimie au XVIIᵉ siècle*, "sees in this a symbol of two alchemical operations: coagulation, in which the quicksilver that was formerly the agent becomes the patient, and this is why this art is

---

*On one of the caissons decorating the ceiling of the chapel.

†*Splendor Solis* is a sixteenth-century German manuscript written by Salomon Trismosin and inspired by the *Aurora Consurgens*, decorated with twenty-two miniatures, attributed to the Augsburg painter Jörg Breu the Elder, that figure among the most beautiful alchemical illustrations. *La toison d'or* (The golden fleece) is a French version.

compared to a game played by children, inasmuch as what was above is now below; and the sublimation, or whitening, and this is why we compare this art to the work of women, which is to clean in order to make white, and to cook for all the time required."

In the same way in his "epilogue," Canseliet offers his own symbolic explanation for emblem XL, in which (in accordance with a principle of which Camacho and Gruger are also fond), he combines, with the names of two of the most eminent surrealists, the names of Maier, of "the noble Lambspring,"* of Altus,† of Savinien de Cyrano de Bergerac or further on of "the Adept Cosmopolite," and also, to "this famous *fish* that André Breton, in his poem to Antonin Artaud of the year 1924 . . . said was *soluble*,"‡ "the hermetic fish, whether the *dolphin* of the *Mute Book* or the *remora* of the great Cyrano [that] should be grilled so that it can enter into dissolution!"** All this in the light, "as an outer crest and in the manner of a seal," of a "sable sun," "a rather cold sun but [whose] move-

---

*Cabalistic pseudonym designating the author, a certain Abraham Lambspring, of an alchemical poem in German accompanied by fifteen emblems later translated into Latin under the title *De lapide philosophico*.

†"The *Mute Book*," Canseliet translates, "in which, however, all hermetic philosophy is represented in hieroglyphic figures, consecrated to the thrice good and most great merciful God, and dedicated to the sons of the Art only by the author whose name is Altus." As an explanation about Altus's identity, the name of the Protestant Isaac Baulot, "expert pharmacist of New Rochelle," has been brought up, but Khaitzine disagrees, clearly suggesting this would rather be "Jacobus Sulot" (alias Jacob Saulat) "Sire des Marez," who received royal privilege for his book in 1676.

‡I have not found any trace of a connection, one which even Marguerite Bonnet doesn't speak of either, between Artaud and Breton's *Soluble Fish*.

**In *The Dwelling of the Philosophers*, Fulcanelli writes, "We had several times the opportunity to note the important role played by the fish on the alchemical scene. Under the name of dolphin, echeneis, or remora, it characterizes the humid and cold principle of the Work which is our mercury, and which gradually coagulates in contact with and by the effect of the sulfur, an agent of desiccation and of fixity." "Vitriol, in particular," Canseliet adds in his introduction to *Douze Clefs*, "forms *the vessel of nature, the philosophical egg,* within which the *remora* or, more clearly, the little *dolphin,* during the course of an extremely delicate coction, will become the all-powerful *King* described by the chromo vignettes of Solomon Trismosin." (Canseliet's italics.) [In French the word *dauphin* means both dauphin (as in crown prince), and dolphin—trans.]

ments are heated." Now this "fish that swims in the *Philosophical Sea*,"* this "fish that the fisherman of the *Mutus Liber* caught with a net from the pontic water," is none other than the "*echineis* [*sic*] *remora,* which has the full power 'to stop the vessel,'" as Phillipe Audoin says. It is also the one that Roger and Camacho[7] present in *The Cathedral of Seville* under the name of εχενηις, described by Aristotle as a little sea fish capable of holding back the largest vessels, to which Latin gave the name *remora,* kin to the verb *remoror,* meaning to delay or to detain.† Also appearing in emblem XXXVIII, entitled "The Harvest," but also *Picatrix,*‡ and outright called by Bernard Roger "the fishing of the remora,"** it is a representation of what the alchemists named the *Rebis,* the *Androgynous One,* the philosophical mercury that indissolubly "combines the two principles at their highest level of activity within itself."[8]

The catching of the remora, practiced with the help of a small net "with intercrossing links or macles,"†† irresistibly brings to mind Guy Béatrice's observation about Geoffrey Plantagenet's tombstone (now in the Museum of Le Mans) that the "four-pointed ray of the escarbun-cle"‡‡ (which incidentally are green) is "emblem of the terrestrial sky, of the hermetic sea [mother]*** from which will soon be born the emerald

---

*"Remora," writes Bernard Roger as well in his *Paris and Alchemy,* "a fish who swims, the Cosmopolite says, 'in our hermetic sea.'"

†"The echeneis," writes Fulcanelli in *The Dwellings of the Philosophers,* "is the pilot of the running waters, our mercury, the faithful friend of the alchemist, the one which has to absorb the secret fire, the igneous energy of the Salamander and finally, remain stable, permanent, always victorious, under the safekeeping and protection of his master."

‡This can be translated as "anglerfish."

**In *A la découverte de l'alchimie.* Although *remora* is a masculine noun in French, here Roger uses it in the feminine.

††Audoin, *Bourges cité première.* In a footnote, Audoin indicates, moreover, that "macle" (alteration, or pattern created by different fabrics sewn together) most likely means, as a synecdoche, a kind of fishing net.

‡‡About this, André Coia-Gatié refers "to the analysis by Robert Viel on the macles and rays of escarbuncles as other symbols of the universal life force" in his book *Les origines symboliques du blason.*

***The homophony between mer/sea and mère/mother has to be kept in mind.

of the philosophers." This sounds as "*rets*" (net) of the escarbuncle, in other word escarbuncle net, a net helpful at catching the escarbuncle, a net that makes it possible, in particular, to catch the little hermetic fish.[9]

Elie-Charles Flamand seems to be offering "Patient ships reefs / Held fast by the Remora" as commentary in "Lambeaux d'un portu-lan de l'internelle navigation" (Tatters of a portolan chart for internel navigation,) one of the texts in his 1968 collection *La lune feuillée* (The leafed moon).

Once again it's Bernard Roger, who throughout his book on the discovery of alchemy sowed clues, who gave the title of "the House of Gold" to emblem XXIII ("the Eclipse"), which is accompanied by the word *corvus*, "crow" or "raven," in its phylactery. This is the symbol of the alchemical *Putrefaction*, that death of the material body necessary for the rebirth in a higher state of its Spirit.[10] Through its black color, initial appearance of the decomposition following the perfect mixtion of the materials of the Egg, in the cooking of the Rebis—which, according to Fulcanelli, is the "canonical seal of the Work"—the "*magical seal*" reveals to the artist that he has followed the right path and that the philosophical mixtion has been prepared *canonically*.

14

MAURICE BASKINE, FANTASOPHER

At what door shall I finally meet friend Saturn?

MICHEL BUTOR,
"FANTASOPHAL PHYLACTERY"

Three or four other names are summoned to appear in this small constellation of surrealist alchemists, first and foremost that of the painter
Maurice Baskine, the bulk of whose work is now housed at the Museum
of Modern and Contemporary Art in Cordes-sur-Ciel, donated by Jean
and Monique Saucet. A close friend of the painter, Jean Saucet, also
emphasizes the anti-conformist nature of the individual, as he describes
him in the short, emotionally charged text, "Ami présent," which
appears on the last page of the catalog for the exhibition shown from
July 1 to September 15, 1990, at the Grenier du Chapitre in Cahors.*
The text sets the stage perfectly with its share of mystery:

> I will always see you, Maurice, with your prophet's mane of hair, your
> wind-blown cape, like a great night bird colliding into the lights of
> Montparnasse from Raspail Vert to la Rotonde. Every evening, you

---

*Jean Saucet in *Maurice Baskine: Peintre, Sculpteur, Alchimiste*, catalog of the exhibition.
Jean Saucet was the primary collector of Baskine's work. Monique Escat, whose name
appears later, was the exhibition curator.

would disembark from what you called your "balloon basket," a miserable attic dwelling* where you spent twenty years of your life, until your death, lurking among pots of multicolored powders, brushes, frames, paintings, that were even stored under the bed and, impervious, the athanor. For you have delved into the innermost depths of your *fantasophy*, the innermost depths of your soul, according to the codes of an alchemy drawing from the most remote past and the most distant future. An art that goes beyond the daily routine, but limited to the human. An art in which the tortures of volumes and aggressive impastos spawn gorgons, suns, ophelias, explosions, bedazzlements that mark off this uncontrollable crest of constant, anguished interrogation. And then one day, you came up to me and said, "I've finished my work." A week later, Maurice, you were no more.

Born in 1901 in Kharkiv to a family of six children, five of whom were boys and two of whom, Etienne Ruhaud tells us, "died at an early age, [along with] a daughter who died in Auschwitz,"[1] Miron Maurice Baskine, of whom Sarane Alexandrian wrote that his "work illustrates in striking fashion that combination of Eros and Hermes for finding the secrets of transforming lead into gold and common love into Sublime Love,"[2] arrived in Paris in 1905 with his parents. They were fleeing the antisemitic pogroms of the time. Again, according to Ruhaud, they lived in a "Hausmannian apartment building on avenue Ledru-Rollin. The father, Élie Idel Baskine (1873–1921), a native of Kremenchuk on the Dnieper, sold a variety of goods, including slippers, and died prematurely in the Villejuif hospital. We know little about his wife, Hacia Tchoudnowski (1875–1943), except that she died in the Rothschild Hospital in the 12th arrondissement after being imprisoned in Drancy." A philosophical hobo, he described himself as the "last alchemist, first fantasopher,"† explaining this last term as follows: "Only he can take

---

*At no. 1 Boulevard Edgar Quinet.
†The words *fantasophe*, *fantasophie*, or *fantasophal* are regularly used by Paul Sanda to label his own *works*.

pride in the name fantasopher who has projected his fluid onto a valid support. This support, after calcination, will allow the appearance of clusters of heads, the heads of the body-beautiful,* representation of the stone at black [first state of the philosopher's stone], and this stone I give the name of Fantasopher's Stone. Whoever achieves it is a fantasopher."†

Sarane Alexandrian, who was also his friend, says nothing different when he evokes his memory in these words:

> I had a high regard for Maurice Baskine, the phantasopher with the big round glasses (he called his philosophy of life phantasophy)‡ who searched for the philosopher's stone in the athanor of his house in Fontenay-sous-Bois, and who left us magnificent alchemical paintings, a new Tarot deck, a triptych of the Great Work, and a magical object, the Photoron with mirror.

First a bookkeeper, than a traveling salesman from 1923 to 1937, it was during the thirties that this "seeker who confronted the telluric," as Paul Sanda puts it, had a kind of revelation. After reading a book on dreams that showed him a new world, another reality, he began to study astrology, tarot, magic, and alchemy through the work of the Cosmopolite, Latin Greek, and Hebrew—with a particular reference to Nostradamus (as Saucet again indicates): "Nostradamus. First quest, first enigma, first challenge, for he who was still stumbling on the long rocky road to his promised Thebes. Closely studying the photocopies of

---

*"Corps-beau" in French phonetically sounds like *corbeau*, meaning raven. "Têtes de corps-beaux" (Heads of beautiful bodies) sounds like "Têtes de corbeaux" (Heads of ravens). In alchemical symbology, the "head of the raven" is used to symbolize the end of the First Work.

†Jean Saucet, "Maurice Baskine," in *Maurice Baskine (1901–1968) Rétrospective*. This exhibition catalog is presented by the author of its preface, Paul Quillès, as intended to become a "reference work."

‡It will be noted that the spelling of the word *fantasophie* varies depending upon the author.

the original edition of the *Centuries*, he questioned the quatrains, imagining grids, magic squares, from which, from one spell of lassitude to the next, would blossom courtesy of an unconscious hand, his achievement, this painted work, a Message and not an illustration."

Although, according to Paul Sanda, it was rather speculative in nature, it was shortly after he had begun his search for the philosopher's stone in the kitchen of the villa at 84 avenue de Neuilly, in Fontenay-sous-Bois, where he lived, that he began to paint in parallel as an "occultist," as Aimé Patri put it in a 1952 text, "for the artists, as an artist for the occultists," categories he escaped because "he was not a man of our times but a medieval artisan, like those who built the cathedrals."* But Patri continues, "He disappointed the *occultists* when he revealed to them, for example, that the famous quatrains did not contain the *prophecies* their clientele hoped for but were only a *game*. He also disconcerted the artists by teaching them that this *game* was serious because it contained a science!" Didn't this self-taught painter and sculptor, if not himself a "magician of matter," who would go so far as to invent his own material, which he called "Fantasophal," say, "Three times, in the Anima, the Corpus, and the Spiritus, I have traveled through the hermetic labyrinth† and my work is the message collected over the course of my threefold pilgrimage"?[3]

Despite his age he joined an artillery unit as a volunteer in May 1940, and demobilized at the end of July. Three years later, he was imprisoned in the Noé Camp of Haute Garonne, then in the camp of the Todt Organization in Martigues, but resisting the S.T.O. (the forced labor program imposed by the German occupation), he joined the Maquis and became a French Resistance fighter (F.F.I.) in 1944. After the war, his first exhibition, which ran from March 24 to April 12, 1945, at the Katia

---

*Aimé Patri, "Apologie" in *Maurice Baskine (1901–1968) Rétrospective*. A professor of philosophy who was close to Boris Souvarine before the war, Aimé Patri (1904–1983) was one of the figures solicited by Breton to answer the preliminary inquiry for his book *L'art magique*. He also interviewed him for the magazine *Paru* in 1948.
†It will be noted in passing that *Le labyrinthe hermétique* is the title of one of the main books Paul Sanda has dedicated to alchemy.

Granoff Gallery, *Le temple du mas*, inspired by Nostradamus's *Centuries*, came to the attention of Dubuffet, who saw him as an outsider artist—as well as Van Lennep, who also described him in the same way! Baskine, meanwhile spoke of "*atomic art* in reference to the H-Bomb, to describe his metallic colored sculptures of painted plaster, covered with fragments that looked like the result of explosions. They generally disconcerted the public, but attracted the attention of Dubuffet, Paulhan, and even André Breton," adds Ruhaud. As a natural consequence the artist joined the surrealist group in 1946 and participated in the strange, international exhibition at the Maeght Gallery in 1947 under the sign of Fulcanelli and Rosenkreutz,* using a Godin furnace to create a thirteenth altar,† *l'Athanor*, over which a queen towered. In the same year, "he who reveals wholeheartedly," as Breton wrote in his dedication to him of a copy of the *Second Manifesto*, also produced, at his request, three original etchings for the deluxe French edition of *Arcanum 17*, representing, according to Van Lennep, salt, sulfur, and mercury. Throughout his life, he continued to illustrate the books—those with strong esoteric content—of the writers with whom he felt close, such as Rabelais, of whom Elie-Charles Flamand wrote that his "satirical verve mocked the *puffers*" and who "knew how to hide in many places with such ingenuity, among the burlesque joys and vitriolic outbursts of his *Pantagruel*, several of the most important points of the esoteric doctrine,"‡ or Charles Perrault, whose Mother Goose tales

---

*According to Van Lennep, "L'art alchimique et le surréel." Christian Rosenkreutz is the mythical founder of the Rosy Cross.

†Although there were originally only supposed to be twelve, Baskine was associated with a "chest" at the altar created by Wifredo Lam in homage to Lautréamont, *La chevelure de Falmer*.

‡Elie-Charles Flamand, *Les méandres du sens*. In the same spirit, Canseliet states that in the title of the book of "the abstractor of the quinte essence," *La vie très horrifique du grand Gargantua*, the third term should be read as aurific, as it is so true, as he says again in his introduction to the *Twelve Keys* "that it would be hard to find among the immense number of alchemical books . . . a treatise that was more prolix and more meticulous on the place of the Quintessence or Entelechy, and especially on the *matras* (matrix) that would make its elaboration possible, than the *Fifth and Final Book of the Good Pantagruel*." (Capitalization and italics are Canseliet's.)

may not be exactly what they seem to be.* "This solitary autodidact," Monique Escat also points out, "considered himself to be particularly the interpreter of Gérard de Nerval, Baudelaire, and Nostradamus—in his work the Centuries, the Temple of the Mas, the Goose Game. These different creations he regarded as only various stages of his research."[4] As Etienne Ruhaud points out, "a personal, Nervalian mythology can be read between the lines" in his work, "especially when Baskine paints his own father with the features of the King of Dough† (the one who brings money back home), and his mother with the features of the Queen of the Sabbath (she who organizes the sacred ceremony)."

It's in the same way in 1947 that the painter, who at the time was giving lectures on Nostradamus and the tarot, of which we know since *The Dwellings of the Philosophers* that being "the complete hieroglyph of the Great Work, it contains the twenty-one operations or stages through which the philosophical mercury must pass before it reaches the final perfection of the Elixir," would have introduced Breton to Fulcanelli's writings, although he doesn't claim this honor alone. "It is certain," Van Lennep writes, "that Baskine, for whom art was a privileged means of transmutation, taught André Breton something." In 1948, he met Pierre Demarne and Francis Meunier, the surrealist painter of Cordes-sur-Ciel, during the exhibition *Comme* (How), which he had organized at the Jean Bard Gallery in Paris. However, he violently broke from the group after the Carrouges affair in a letter written on June 2, 1951, to Breton in which he said : "Obviously the work is completely simple: Solve e [*sic*] coagula, but all these dissolutions and all these coagulations are far too lacking in exaltation. So allow me to stay away from the manipulations of a puffer, which don't ennoble lead but do debase gold. . . . For me, the work is a renunciation, with all its obligations, which is activity. I

---

*"*La rose hermétique*, the *Don de Dieu*, finally the *Pierre philosophale*, whose fanciful *Contes de ma Mère Loye* [*sic*], keepers of the most ancient traditions," Canseliet states, "develop with so much wisdom the millennial arcana."

†"Roi de Thune" was the name of the King of the Beggars, the boss of the Court of Miracles in Paris in the Middle-Ages—at least in *Les Misérables* by Victor Hugo.

walk, I go forward. Alone."* Breton never seems to have forgiven him, since in a 1964 letter to André Parinaud, he scornfully states, in a final settling of accounts, "for a very short time, he made up the numbers (in the group) as a Sunday Surrealist."

But even if the use of the word "puffer" with its strong pejorative connotations was to create a lasting rift between Baskine, who was also separating from his wife at this time, and most of his former friends, he nevertheless remained, at least intellectually, within the surrealist sphere of influence, developing the idea of *fantasophical* alchemy, the motivation of which is easily seen in his painting *The Doors of Heaven*. Dominated, as Jean-Gabriel Jonin says in the film Jean Desvilles made about Baskine in 2004, by the "blue night and radiant yellow," it depicts seven faces at the top of the painting, the seven planets connected by a rope held by a lion on the right and a unicorn on the left, which in this case represent sulfur and mercury, "the emerging light of mercury." In the center, "twelve couples shining with light" capped by a phoenix remind us that the alchemical process does not take place at just any old time; the months of the year have their role to play in it. Based on a few select themes, the Hebrew Kabbalah, in particular the Tree of the Sephiroth, the Goose Game, and, as we have seen, astrology and alchemy, Baskine, as shown by this maxim that sounds like a motto—"*Dive into yourself, pass from the Real to the Surreal, enter the depths of the unknown*"†—seems to be then in fact beginning an initiatory kind of descent within himself of the kind Breton spoke of in the *Second Manifesto* when he wrote: "Recall that the idea of Surrealism tends simply to the total recuperation of our psychic forces by a means which is no other than a vertiginous descent within ourselves, the systematic illumination of hidden places, the progressive darkening of all other places."

---

*I found out about the text of this letter in Jean Desville's film, *Maurice Baskine* (Résonance, 2004).
†In *Maurice Baskine (1901–1968) Rétrospective*.

In 1952, Breton's first wife, Simone Collinet, organized an exhibition for Baskine at the Furstenberg Gallery. This was followed by a one-day presentation of his altarpiece, *La Mère folle* (on October 6, 1954), housed at the National Museum of Modern Art in Paris, the title of which can't help but evoke the "aqueous fire" or "igneous fire," of mercury.* This is the "universal solvent," "the alchemical symbol of death in the three kingdoms," whose "defining characteristic . . . is," according to René Alleau, "to cause the *death* of the *metals* in order to enable the operator to extract their *virtues* or *cores* by *corporealizing the spirits and by spiritualizing the bodies*, which constitutes the definition of the magister's basic operation"[5]—but also enables, more prosaically, as Elie-Charles Flamand reminds us, "to extract from vulgar gold its components in order to obtain the *powder of projection*, thanks to which transmutation will be possible."[6]

In the meantime, on June 9, 1953, he took part in an event organized at the Geography Hall in Paris, *Premier bilan de l'art actuel*, at which the artists Bryen, Hérold, Lam, Serpan, and Lapicque were also present, as well as Mathieu, Atlan, Bazaine, Bizière, Schneider, and Fougeron. The critics Duthuit, Jaguer, Estienne, Lebel, Tapié, and Waldberg were also present. During his intervention in the heated debate, Baskine is quoted as saying, according to Jean-Gabriel Jonin:

> Between stays in Heaven, in the clouds, and others in Hell, where he frequented Asmodeus and Astaroth among others, Maurice Baskine lived most often in the Labyrinth. The Minotaur taught him how to undertake the Great Work. He showed him the difference between two seemingly similar works, one of which contains a message and the other of which is mute. Because the work of art, the Minotaur told him, should say something. It has a mission to fulfill. It should, challenging Space and Time, carry a message to the one who must

---

*Still called *marotte* or *mérotte*, the Mad Mother (Mère folle) also represents "the hermetic science itself, considered in the variety and extent of its teaching" (Fulcanelli, *The Dwellings of the Philosophers*).

know. The Minotaur then gave him the keys to three Doors: that of magic which leads to Matter, that of astrology which leads to Style, and that of alchemy which leads to the Subject. He taught him again the Language of the Birds that makes it possible to read the works that are seven times sealed.[7]

And we should recall here that the labyrinth is, among other things, the "symbol for the labor of the Alchemical Work," as writes Josane Charpentier.

It was also at this time, around 1953, that he began work on the *Tarot of Consciousness*, whose most unconventional cards are executed, most likely with a pen, on a scratched black ink wash in a style that is very similar to the more colorful work that can be seen in Cordes-sur-Ciel. The deck, which can of course be used for divination, is accompanied by a small collection of dense spiritual texts that provide an initiatory kind of teaching, *Le dessous des cartes de Maître Mât* (The underside of Master Fool's cards), in which he presents the quintessence of his alchemical and Hermetic research in order to, as he says, "provide clarity in all things." The Arcana, which don't bear any of the denominations that characterize the Tarot of Marseilles, for example, are simply associated with two concepts generally, which do not fully cover the values traditionally associated with them. For example, there are only two words at the bottom of the first card, the Juggler or Magician: *will* and *creation*. Arcanum IX, the Hermit, has only three: *prudence, reserve,* and *wisdom*. Card XII, the Hanged Man, has *sacrifice* and *atonement* while card XVI, the Tower, has *fall* and *ruin,* which conforms to its standard meaning. Card XVII, the Star, is *faith* and *hope* while the "numberless Arcanum" falls under the Janus-like symbol of *madness* and *wisdom*! Aimé Patri* sees it as the work of a good "student of Nature, who knows how to draw from the darkest matter

---

*Aimé Patri, also a trade-unionist and militant Trotskyist then socialist, wrote on Malcolm de Chazal and Mallarmé, and contributed texts to *La tour Saint-Jacques, Les cahiers du Sud,* and *Le surréalisme même.*

the fire incubating within it that gets back its vigor when it comes into contact with a mind that is still in possession of its original gift." This deck, published long after the death of its creator, thanks to his nephew Henri Baskine, unfortunately went inexplicably unnoticed despite its mystical content and its undeniable artistic qualities.

In 1956, another surrealist, Robert Lebel, organized a *Parafestation fantasophale* in his home at 14 avenue du President Wilson in Baskine's honor, to which the ghosts of Hieronymus Bosch and Gustave Moreau were also summoned. It was at this time that in addition to *Solve et Coagula*, his sealed paintings, illustrating another phase of the Work, the *Chemical Wedding*, the *Coniuctio oppositorum*, and the three bas-reliefs entitled *The Work at Black*, *The Work at White*, and *The Work at Red*, as well as sculptures like *The Ship or the Chariot of Antimony*, were first exhibited.

In 1957, again at the Furstenberg Gallery, he presented his large trip-tych "Fantasophe-Roc or the erection of the stone of Fantasophopolis," which measures two and a half meters by two meters when closed, and nearly five meters by two meters when open. Created between 1952 and 1957, it's a veritable synopsis of his research. On the right part, a brick wall with twenty-one ogival doors that must be crossed through repre-sent the twenty-one phases that one must go through. In the center, a pyramid flanked by two supporting piece, a lion and a unicorn, repre-senting red sulfur and white sulfur, and crowned by a phoenix, resume the twenty-one labors that must be performed in order to achieve the Great Work. Finally, on the left stands a Sephirotic Tree borrowed from the Kabbalah with its ten Sephiroths commingled, according to Jean-Gabriel Jonin, with the "geese from the goose game, which Baskine called the *geese-seals*,* sealing a truth that it is necessary to pierce"—and here the phonetic cabala makes its return.

---

*"Geese" is "oies," in French, and "sceau" is "seal." That's how we come to "oies-sceaux," which sounds like "oiseaux," "birds." All this is a perfect illustration of what the language of the birds is.

In 1964, he also participated in the famous so-called surrealist exhibition organized by Patrick Waldberg at the Charpentier Gallery, an exhibition that was harshly attacked by Breton and his friends. On the first page of the catalog, we can read these lines, which look like remarks Baskine might have made: "'Surrealism has come into its fifth hermetic phase. In alchemy the peacock's tail, which is the iris, is also the fifth phase of color. It symbolizes purification and multiplication. We have draped our walls with it.' The walls of the exhibition were draped in red."[8] In 1967, he was again invited to the exhibition *Treasures of Surrealism* in Knokke-le-Zoute, Belgium.

Jacques Van Lennep again, in his 1979 text on alchemical art and the surreal,[9] cited among the representatives of this "tremendous art to which the surrealist revolution has restored its absolute validity," "the Frenchman Maurice Baskine, one of the pioneers passed away recently." And in his 2007 book *A Stone in the Head: Alchemical Works*,[10] he recalled their meeting, at the painter's request, at the café La Palette in Saint-Germain-des-Près, shortly after the publication of *Art and Alchemy*. He described his interlocutor as an "impressive" man, "a kind of wizard straight out of a horror movie or comic book" before adding that the works he had made "expressed the outlandish theory of Fantasophy that alchemy had inspired him" to adopt.*

In a manner that shows significantly how challenging is any approach of the artist's work, Monique Escat, in the catalogue of the Cahors exhibition, while emphasizing the "magnetic beauty" of Baskine's works, explains that it was very difficult, although they had been "analyzed by experts in occultism," to "decipher" them and "to attribute a meaning to pieces whose titles did not come to us," because "for Maurice Baskine, his pictorial and sculptural work was not a commentary on alchemical themes, but the expression of an alchemy that he had rethought for his own purposes, thus achieving his great work."

---

*Currently, Paul Sanda in Cordes-sur-Ciel—and it is no coincidence—claims in turn to be a fantasopher.

This is likely why Bernard Roger, when Yoan Armand Gil and I met him, told us, that while he found him "impressive," he considered him to be "totally overestimated" in the domain of alchemy, saying, "He had a box of matches that he would take out and tell us that he had the Philosopher's Stone! And then, when he painted, and someone asked him how he did it, he answered, 'The Philosopher's Stone.'"

Maurice Baskine died in the Lariboisière Hospital in Paris on July 8, 1968. "Baskine's works," Jean-Gabriel Jonin sums up perfectly, "like all alchemical iconography are the expression of a realization that cannot be translated into other terms. They can only be apprehended through a contemplation that is prolonged until they illuminate themselves from within"! And like a leitmotif, we can see the recurrence in his paintings and sculptures, particularly *The Athanor*, of a pair of dice, a six and a three. Which makes nine!* Nine, the expression of perfection, harmony, and fulfillment, as well as for Parmenides the symbol of the totality of being. In short, the number of the initiate.

During the first exhibition of his work to be organized after his death at the Cathedral of Cahors, in the summer of 1990, Monique Escat described his work as follows: "His production is diverse: paintings in which colors and unknown materials collide, sculptures, and gouaches: strange, sometimes inaccessible art, but whose poetic force transcends the artist's gesture through a powerful, luminous work in which every element has the strength of a symbol."

And Michel Butor, again and above all, who claims he only knew the painter as a bridge partner, writes a short text *in memoriam* in the catalog with the title "Phantasophal Phylactery,† which ends as follows:

---

*It should be noted that Lucien Rigaud, in his *Dictionnaire d'argot moderne* published by Paul Ollendorf on Paris in 1881, claimed that the slang expression "six and three make nine" designates a *lame person*, through "allusion to the uneven appearance of the lame whose steps appear to show different numbers." And it is well known that traditionally, the lame person is an initiate.

†It seems a slightly different version appears in the Cordes-sur-Ciel exhibition.

. . . and antechambers after porches and from miseries to vestibules, skylights, windows and crossings;

and new scoriae and gravels become stamens and buds; I thank you all pilots, messengers, and fairies who save me; will I really thanks to you reach Mercury's windows, force Mars's crossings, insinuate myself into the Moon's ogival windows and blossom in the openings of the Sun? And all through time without time the dead without death . . .

15

ELIE-CHARLES FLAMAND

*So, right here was one of the marks of this art of Hermes
that would, later, radiate over my entire being.*
ELIE-CHARLES FLAMAND, *LES MÉANDRES DU SENS*

Let us "give honor where honor is due" to one last figure of this group
of individuals close to Breton—and not a lesser one that we have yet
to summon. This would be Elie-Charles Flamand (see plates 3 and 4),
who "came close to creating symbiosis between surrealism and occultism," as Jean-Clarence Lambert said,[1] who believed that "the world is
in reality only an illusory form in which the Absolute can appear," who
thought of poetic practice like a progression toward the inner Light, if
not truly a spiritual exercise, while considering that a person could have
"access to the true, living values and strip the Tradition of the shams
of traditionalism." We could easily be persuaded of this by reading the
following passage taken from the poem "À un oiseau de houille perché
sur la plus haute branche de feu," written in 1953 and published in 1957
with illustrations by Toyen,* in which we are "in the presence of a form
of verbal alchemy," as Michel Passelergue says.[2] He goes on to say that

---

*To whom he dedicated the poem "En proie à leurs regards" in his collection *La lune
feuillée.*

"alchemy will soon become one of the domains explored by Elie-Charles Flamand in his esoteric quest."

> *I have wandered through deserts of crushed bones of*
> > *cold lava*
> *Long have I sought footprints beneath the ashes*
> *I thought I saw the extinction of the flame that flickers*
> *In the deepest depths of the enclosed darkness*
> *Hermit at last*
> *Inhabiting the lofty remnants of a leaning tower*
> *On the side of suffering*
> *Having banished my fears my angers*
> *Drunk with patience I waited*
> *In the primordial moisture of silence.*

Nor should it come as any surprise that Elie-Charles Flamand began to take an interest in the musicalism of Henry Valensi, even writing a text in the small catalog of the *First Retrospective of the Musicalist Salons (1932–1960)* organized (through his efforts) at the Hexagram Gallery of Paris from June to September 1973. This is the same gallery that hosted the twenty-three salons that mark out the history of this movement. Now, the founder of *Musicalism*, the painter Valensi, who considered Mallarmé to be the first "musicalist" for having "musicalized" the word and given it, as Thibaudet says, "new symbolic meanings," thought of color-matter as vibration just like sound and believed it was time to introduce movement, rhythm, and space-time into art, to give them true plasticity, which would ultimately lead him to "pure abstraction."

So the position adopted by Flamand in 1970 on the Art of Music in his *Érotique de l'alchimie* (The eroticism of alchemy) should come as no surprise. This was a book in which, according to Canseliet, who wrote the preface, he "sought to satisfy both the legitimate desire for knowledge and simple curiosity" in a way that could not be any more clear. "Alchemy," he wrote, "asserts the necessity of a material basis for the construction of a spiritual work. According to its notions, the transformations created by the alchemist are analogous to the initiatory process that takes place spiritually within himself. By means of Involution, matter appears to be what remains farthest from the Divine. However, it's in the depths of the fallen natural mass that the operator will find the spark of the uncreated Fire and will then be able to spiritually transmute himself through communion with transcendence."

By his own admission, "the existing analogy between Poetry and Alchemy" led Flamand to study the latter, and "his master in the Art of Hermes," and to a certain extent, his life teacher, is none other than Eugène Canseliet, whom he met in 1954 thanks to René Alleau and André Breton.* He mentions Canseliet's "noble figure" in *Les méandres du sens*, a book that is a "look back at his life," whose first part, on the castle of la Bastie d'Urfé, comes right in the wake of *The Dwellings of the Philosophers* and *Two Alchemical Abodes*, and for good reason:

I can still remember the moments of initiatory serenity that I spent at his side in the laboratory where glowed [*ardait*] his athanor. With the meticulous meditative gravitas, and solemn gestures of one performing a sacred rite, he skillfully measured out the substances after weighing them with a precision scales, handled tongs and crucible, adjusted the fires and, to both my amazement and my spiritual awakening, he showed me the rising of the Magi's Star over the Philosopher's Sea, followed by many other operations applied to the maternal material and the saving Spirit it reveals. In this way he generously extended to me Ariadne's thread, and inspired my desire to work on my own.

---

*In the bibliographical bio that appears in the book *Elie-Charles Flamand* (Paris: Editions Renée Jeanne, 1982), his friend Alain Mercier also writes that the poet became friends with Canseliet in 1954 and was initiated by him into the Art of Hermes, "in its theory and practice." In fact, it was Breton who introduced Flamand to Alleau and Alleau who introduced him to Canseliet, which clearly shows just how long the three men knew each other.

"In 2004," he added, "I find myself cruelly missing his presence as a guide in my quest." And again in a later interview with Gwen Garnier-Duguy, published in June 2013 in the online journal *Recours au poème*, Flamand speaks again of the fascination he felt for "the alchemy whose theory and practice the admirable Master, Fulcanelli's disciple, Canseliet had passed on to him."

"I used to meditate at length on the commentaries," he writes in *Les méandres du sens* (which seems to lend credit to the idea that he was more a speculative than an operative alchemist) "that the Adept Fulcanelli and his disciple Eugène Canseliet, my most generous Master, devoted to these anthologies of hermetic iconography." I would contemplate "the lofty, silent words of Tradition, urging me to put them into practice, and their intense harmonies continue endlessly, regenerating the depths of my being."

Canseliet did know "the poet Elie-Charles Flamand" quite well as a man "deeply smitten with the alchemical mystery"* and also esteemed him highly as "the author of the text casting light on the magnificent illustrations of the three volumes . . . devoted to the pictorial schools of the Renaissance and . . . published . . . by Editions Rencontre of Lausanne," that "generous trilogy" that he considered to be "an open mine that provides great resources for the untiring efforts of the hermeticist."† And the same Canseliet does state in his preface to *Érotique de l'alchimie* that his friend has never "worked at the furnace," nor

---

*Eugène Canseliet, introduction to *Mutus Liber*. In this text, Canseliet tells how "during an equally helpful and pleasant exploration" of the Saint-Ouen flea market Flamand discovered "two graceful intaglios" depicting "the little scenes of the *Mutus Liber*" (plates 6 and 7) and had made him a "gift of the engraving thus doubly spared from the most threatening of fates."

†Eugène Canseliet, introduction to *Mutus Liber*. Here Canseliet alludes to the three books on Renaissance painting published in 1966 by Flamand at Editions Rencontre, the first on the Italian fifteenth century, with a preface by Jean-Clarence Lambert, the second on the Italian sixteenth century, with a preface by Robert Lebel, and the last on "the painting in France, Germany, Switzerland, and Flanders in the sixteenth century, with a preface by André Pieyre de Mandiargues."

practiced the "alchemical labor at the heart of the athanor."[3] And yet, it was likely not so foreign to him, although never crowned with success, as certain clues would indicate, as well as Flamand himself, when he confides that "the secrets of transmutation, which set into motion the comic forces of death and regeneration" are the "arcana whose quest was one of the constants in his life,"[4] or when he evokes with great realism "the sparkling white metal surface of the bath grown cold again [which shows] then this major sign: the imprint of a five-pointed star." He also told Isabelle Roche in 2006, "Alchemical practice poses substantial practical problems and I, alas, could not devote myself to it as much as I would have liked: it is not enough to read the classic texts, you have to be able to work in the laboratory because contact with the material is fundamental. Now you need a lot of space to set up a laboratory, and that is hardly possible in the city." He then goes on to say, "In spite of all this, I have not given up my search for alchemical instruction. I have a well-stocked library on the subject, and one of my friends has a laboratory. I hope soon to be able to make use of his equipment and to work again, as they say, 'at the furnace,' as I was once able to do."[5] Or again when he seems to deliver part of his truth with these verses taken from the poem "Le chemineau de l'improbable" (The vagabond of the improbable),* subtitled "Attempt at a Lyrical Autobiography," published in 2009 in *Les strates de l'instant* by one "who knowing the mother aspires to make his way to the cradle of the son for the star of the magi":†

> *The universal panacea: man, animal, plant, mineral*
> *Perfect remedy of the entire cosmos*
> *Yes he made Sulfur gush out of Mercury*
> *But unfortunately the odds were not in his favor*
> *Cruelly, the Donum Dei did not appear . . .*

---

*A title that suits him quite well!

†Text of a dedication from Eugène Canseliet to Elie-Charles Flamand.

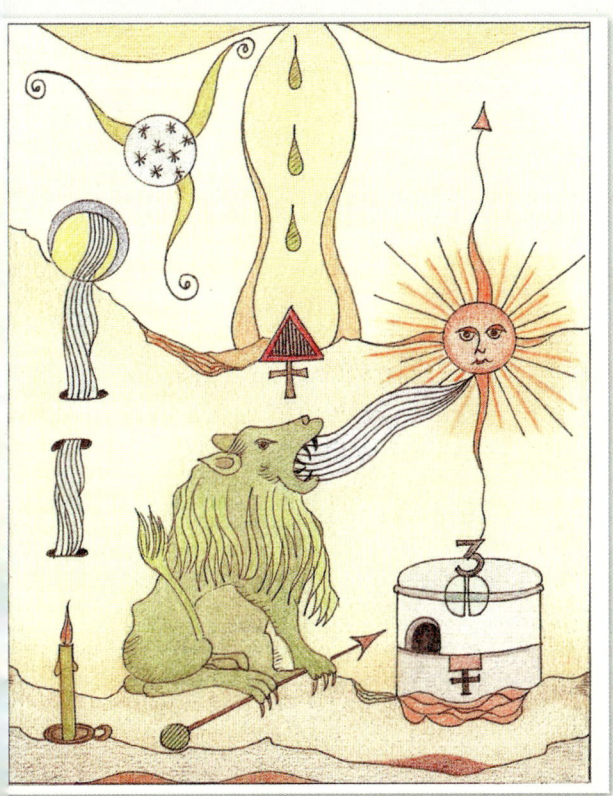

Plate 1. Cuban painter Jorge Camacho's alchemical work *Esmerelda* illustrates the stage of the Work in which salt from the sea meets the dew of heaven.
Jorge Camacho Estate

Plate 2. Jorge Camacho's *Hermetic Fish* represents another stage of the Great Work.
Jorge Camacho Estate

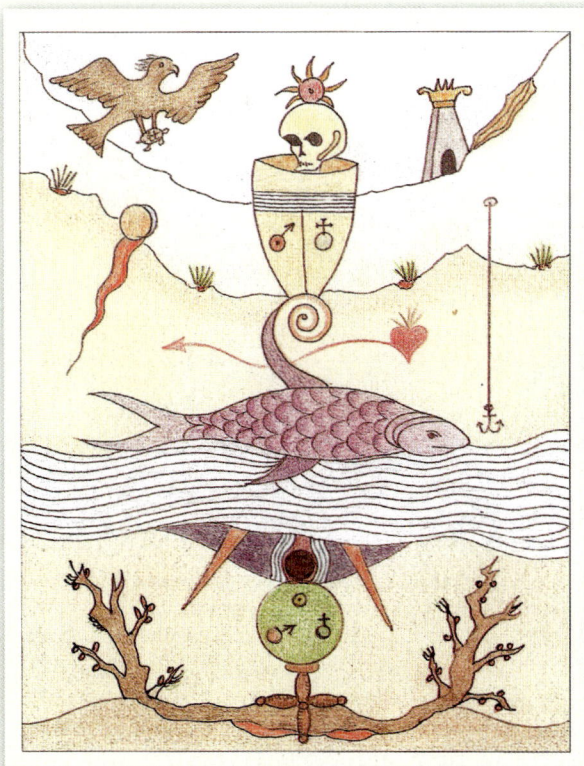

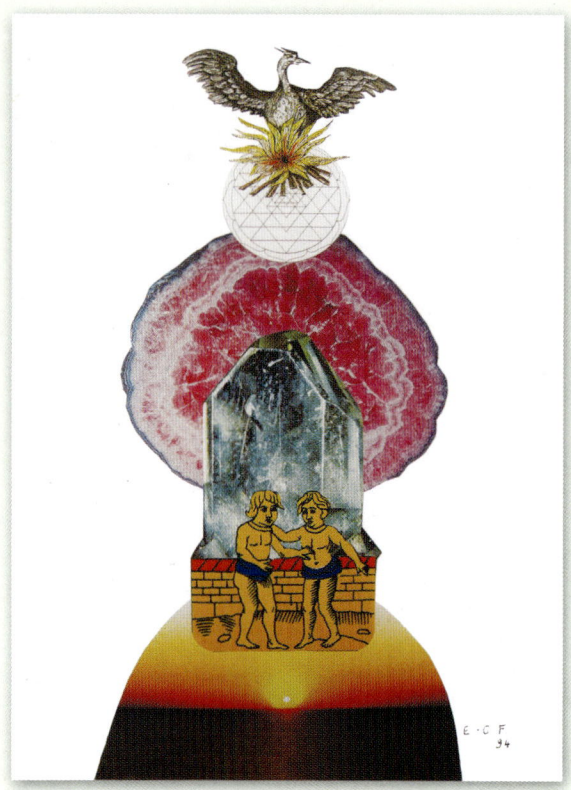

Plate 3. A collage by
Elie-Charles Flamand.
Elie-Charles Flamand Estate

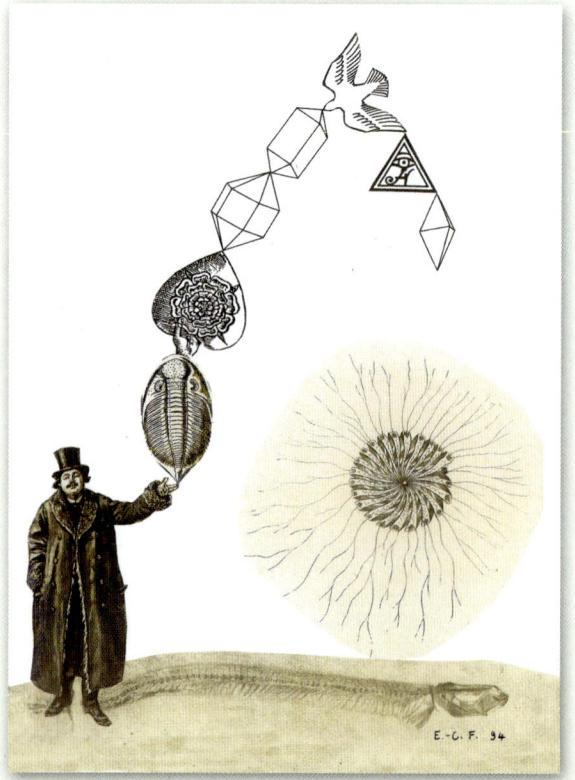

Plate 4. A self-portrait
collage by Elie-Charles
Flamand.
Elie-Charles Flamand Estate

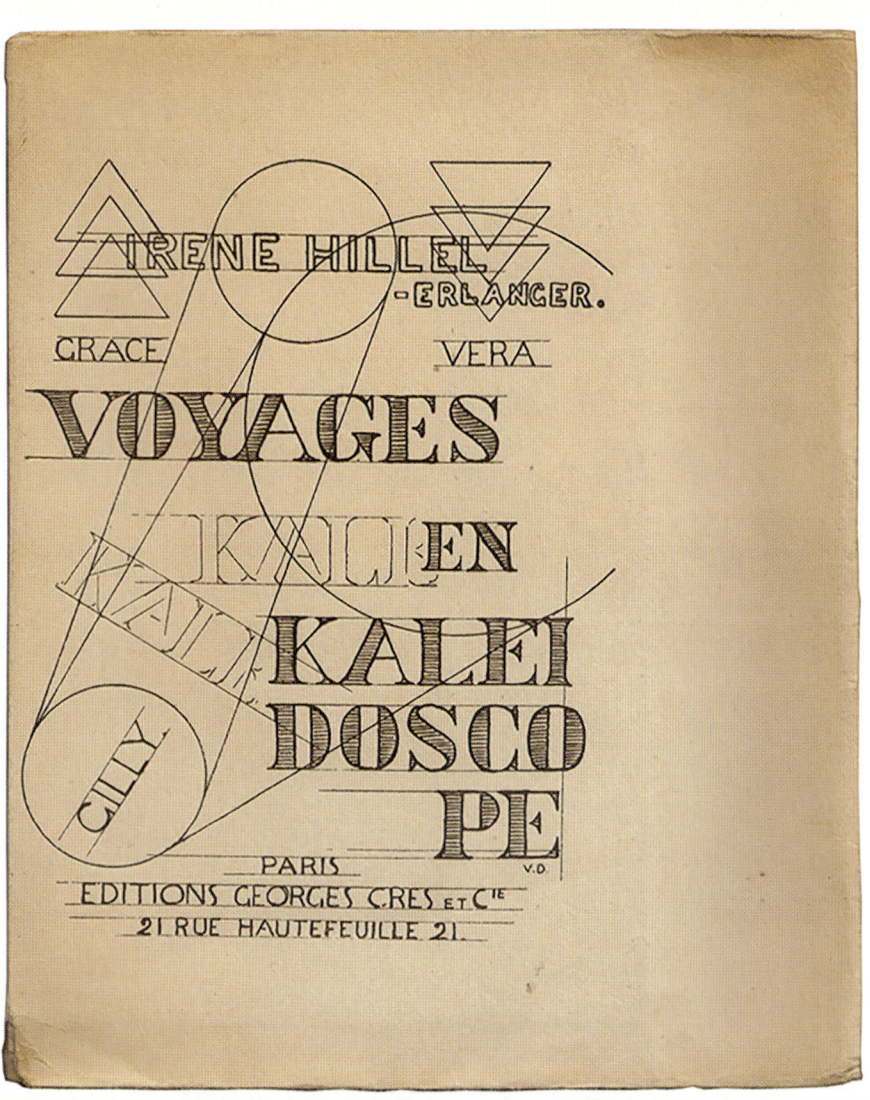

Plate 5. The original cover of Irene Hillel-Erlanger's *Voyages en Kaleidoscope* (*Kaleidescopic Journeys*).

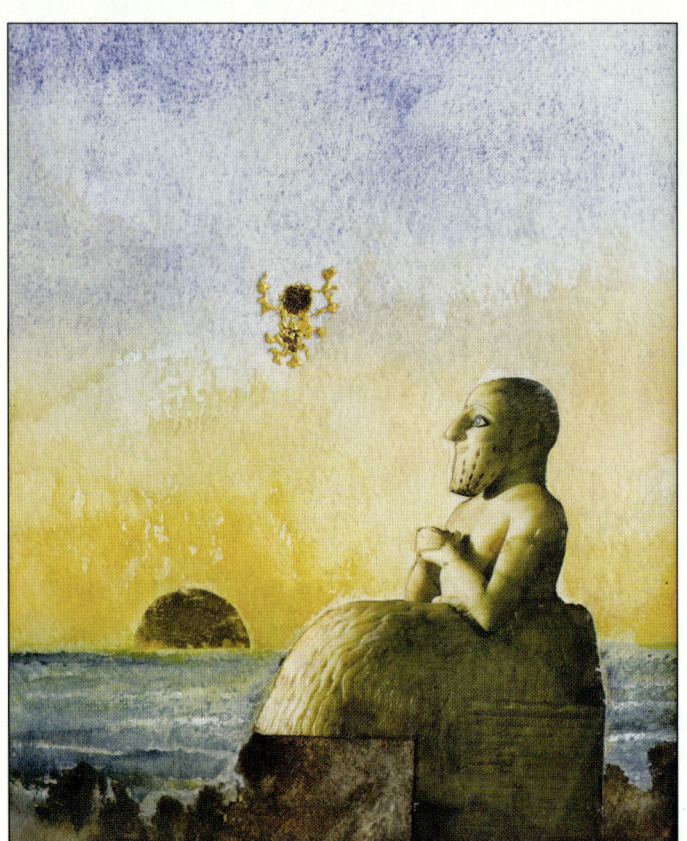

Plate 6.
*La prière
philosophale*
(The prayer of the
philosophers) by
René Alleau.
René Alleau Estate

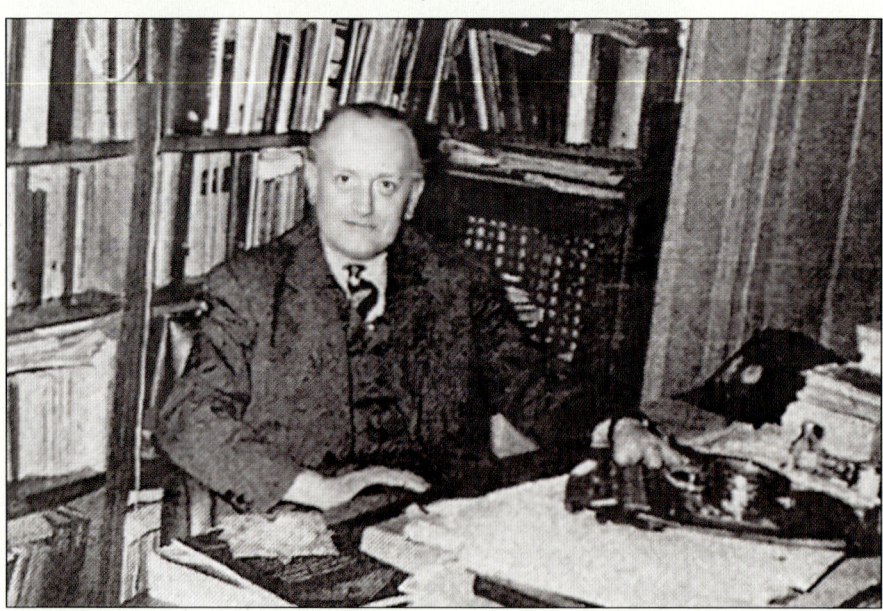

Plate 7. The only known portrait of Henri Hunwald.

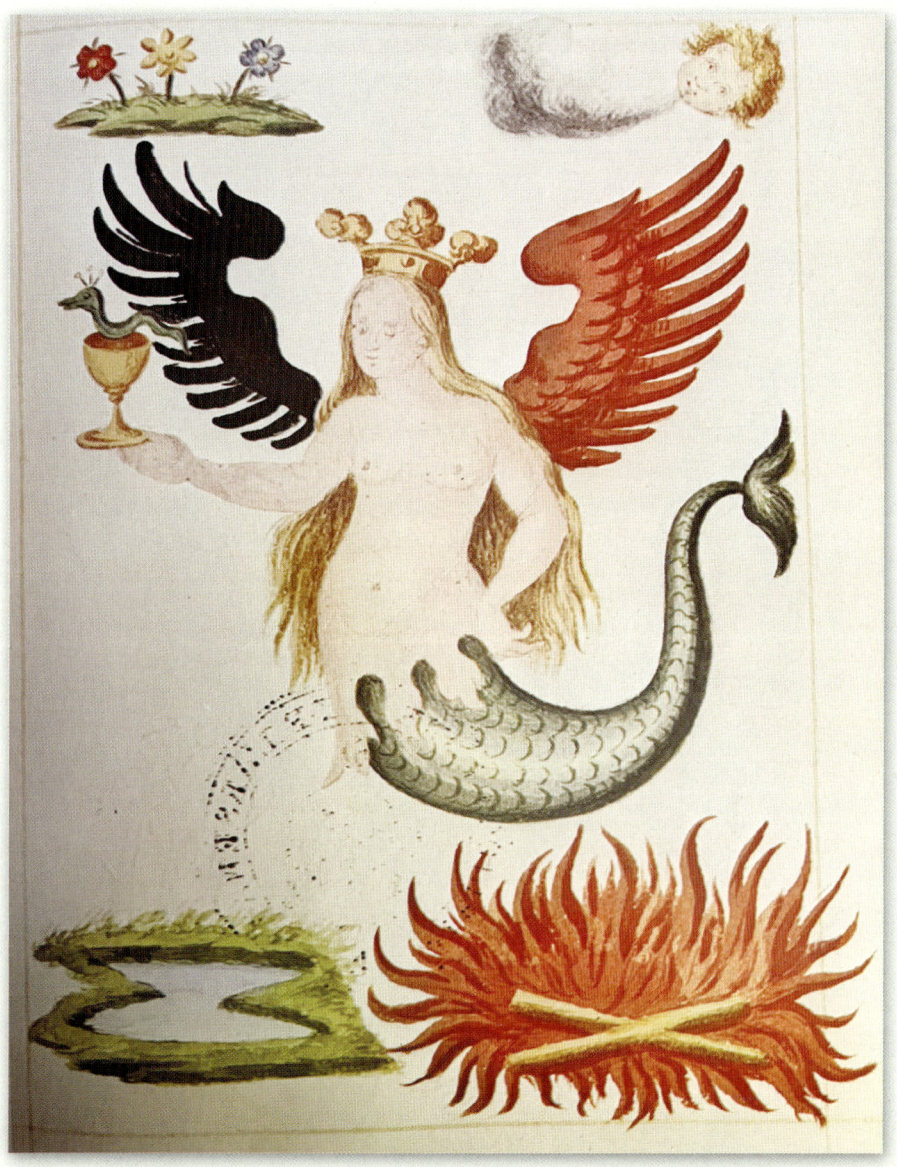

Plate 8. The siren as a representation of Mercury the Wise
in the eighteenth century alchemical text *Solidonius Philosophus*,
attributed to Nicholas Barnaud.

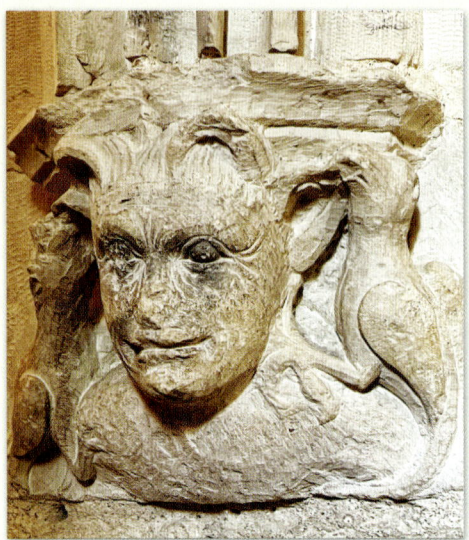

Plate 9. Symbolic depiction of the language of the birds in the Bourges Cathedral in France.
Photo by Jon E. Graham

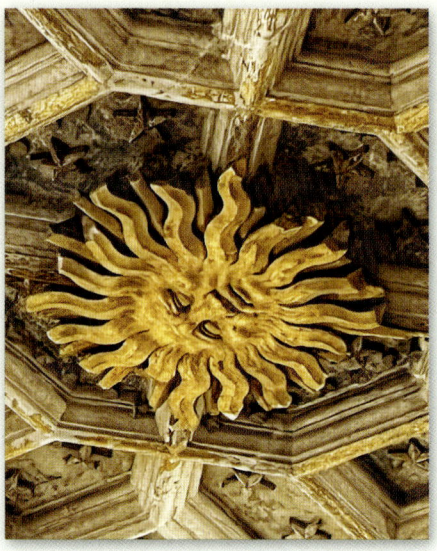

Plate 10. The alchemical sun featured on the ceiling of Bourges Cathedral.
Photo by Jon E. Graham

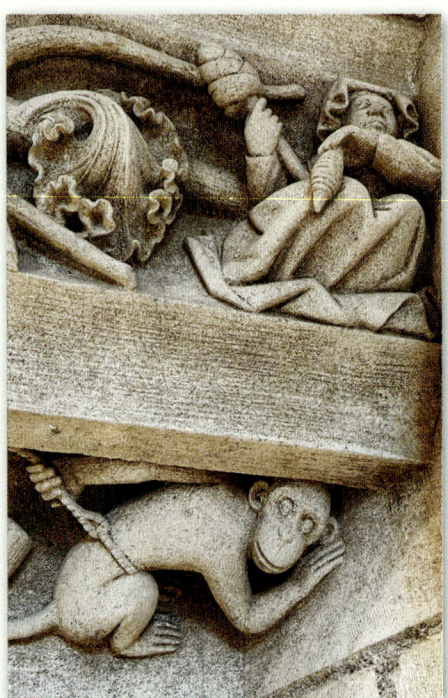

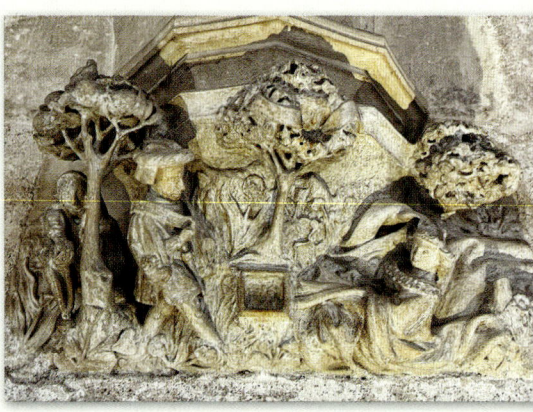

Plate 12. Depiction of alchemical parable Tristan and Iseult in the palace of finance minister and alleged alchemist Jacques Coeur.
Photo by Jon E. Graham

Plate 11. Monkey detail in the palace of Jacques Coeur. The alchemists viewed themselves as "apes of nature."
Photo by Jon E. Graham

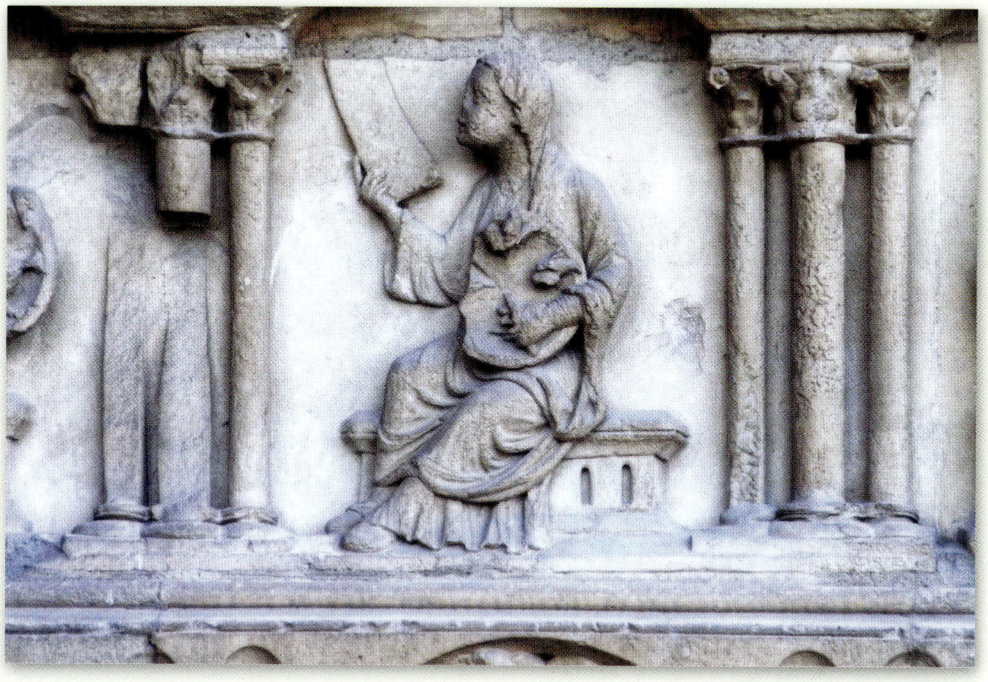

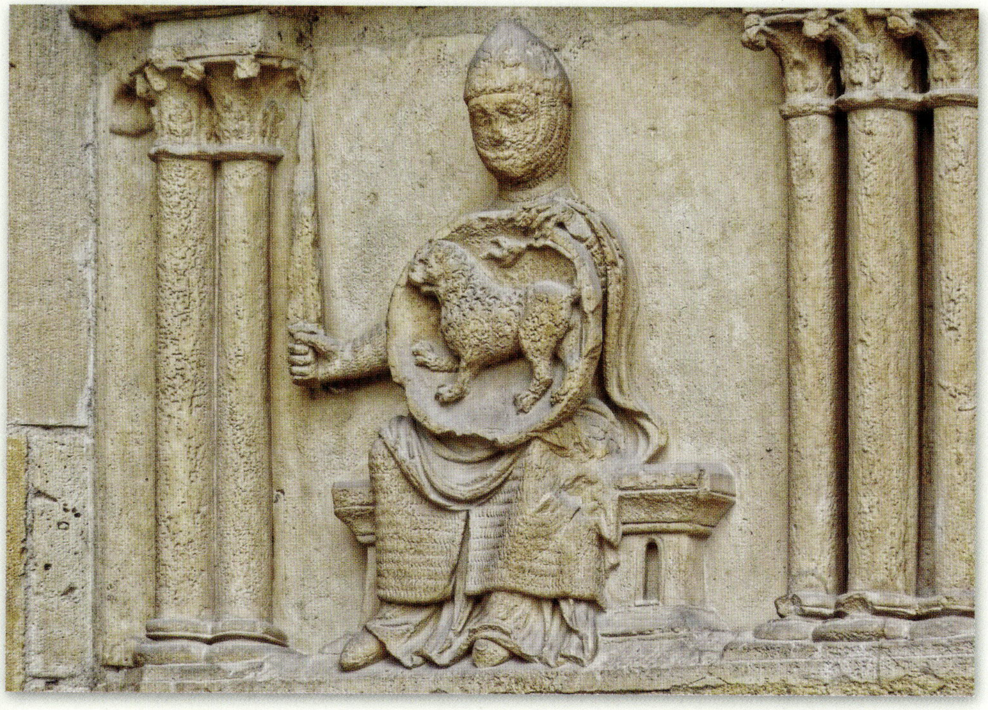

Plates 13–14. The Great Work of alchemy
depicted in the Notre Dame cathedral in Paris.
Photos by Jon E. Graham

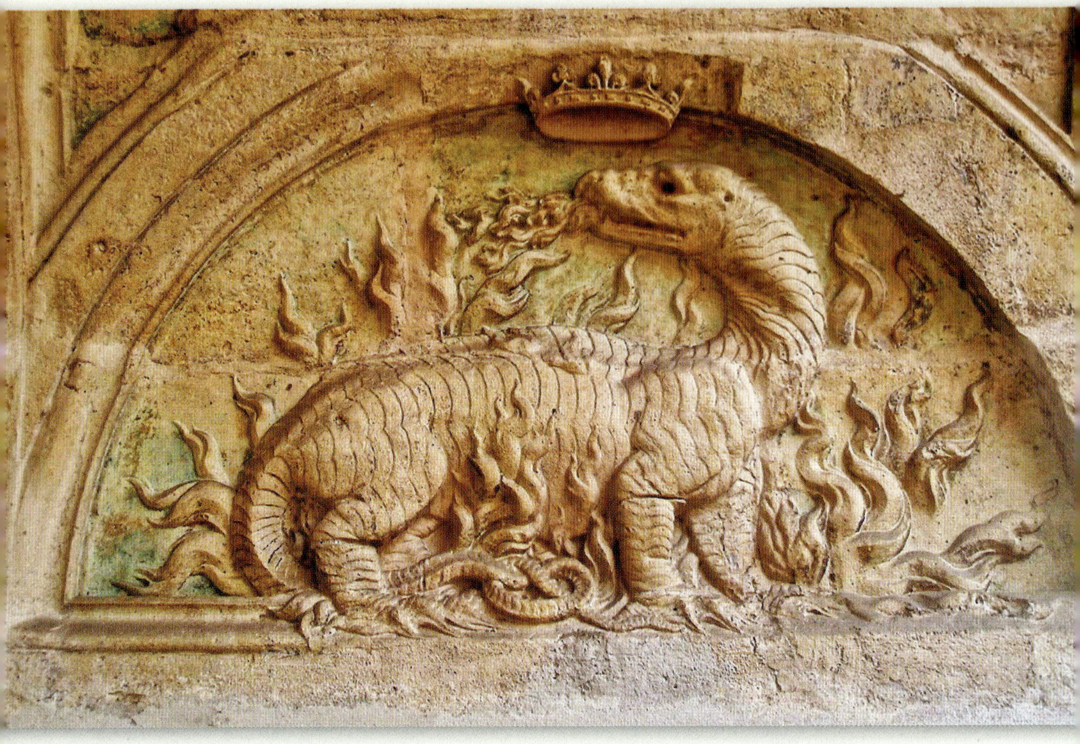

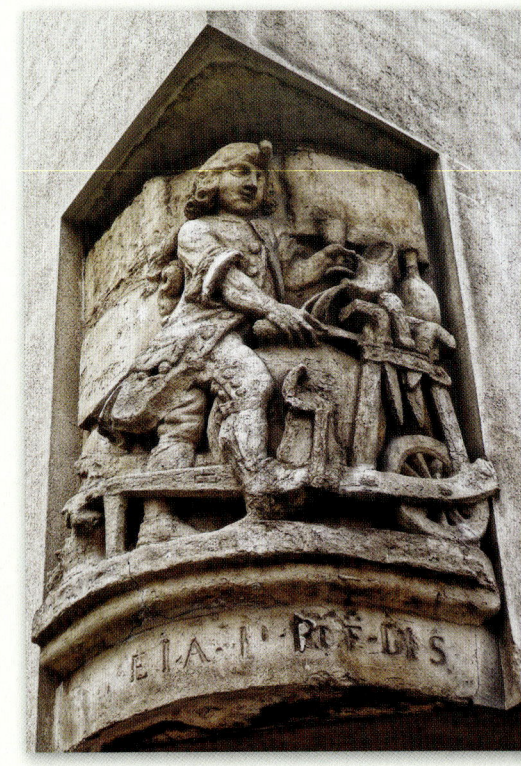

Plate 15. The secret fire of the alchemists, an alchemical symbol discussed in Bernard Roger's book on Paris and Alchemy. The love knot in the salamander's tail is a key to its hidden symbolism.
Photo by Jon E. Graham

Plate 16. *Le rémouleur,* depiction of a knife-grinder in the Marais quarter of Paris.
Photo by Jon E. Graham

In his interview with Gwen Garnier-Duguy, Flamand states explicitly:

> The transmission of the Art of Hermes occurs orally. The master verifies that the disciple meditates with sufficient application on the numerous classic texts that are cryptic. . . .* The student sometimes succeeds, at the cost of many hardships, to find Ariadne's thread and to first identify the *Materia prima*. He is then guided through long, complex manipulations in the laboratory once he has grasped their meaning and exact sequence. In this way he can hope, if he proves worthy of receiving the *Donum Dei* (unfortunately, I wasn't) to achieve the transmutation. Obviously, all of this takes place in secret.

But he didn't fail to clarify: "I label as cryptic alchemical texts, which are puzzles to solve. Those of poetry cannot be called such for they work differently."

With respect to this *Donum Dei*,† which puts in an appearance here, if I may put it that way, and of which Flamand also says "it is traditionally said of the Philosopher's Stone that the Almighty only grants to a very few elect" while Khaitzine sees it above all as "the *sine qua non* condition in alchemical matters,"[6] and considers it the "necessary illumination" Breton expected in vain. It is not superfluous to recall what Bernard Roger says about it in his book on Paris and alchemy: "This 'great secret' of the hermetic art, which no text would ever reveal for it belongs to the domain of the sacred," no surprise it can "only be revealed to one who has *crossed the bridge*, in other words is *beyond* clear consciousness."‡

---

*In all cases, though, as he writes in *Les meandres du sens*, "the intercession of magisterial texts is necessary to help the alchemist during his tireless quest."

†Of which Canseliet said that it "transformed the simple alchemist into a Sage and philosopher into a proven Adept."

‡As Fulcanelli says in *The Dwellings of the Philosophers*, "Let us add that during the Middle Ages the *Gift of God* applied to the *Secretum secretorum* [Secret of secrets], which precisely signifies the secret par excellence, that of the universal *spirit*."

Elie-Charles Flamand, whose approach is clearly his own, makes clear in his book *Les méandres du sens* that "for the Alchemists," the "*mineral Light*, that of bursting mercury that will enable the ardent sulfurous seed to develop," is "hidden" "at the core of this dark material." It is the "primitive soil of the raw stone that is the *subject of the art*" whose "emblem" is nothing other than "the Black Madonna, Our Lady Underground in her retreat."* He adds that "the symbolism of the cave housing the precious ore containing the *Secret Fire* as well as the Stone of the Wise in potential is depicted in other forms in certain treatises and illustrations." As an example, he cites "one of [his] favorite books of the alchemical discipline, in which the underlying humor found in a large number of writings due to the Sons of Science is given free rein in places," "*The Hermetical Triumph or the Victorious Philosophical Stone* (1699) by Limojon de Saint Didier," adorned with an engraved frontispiece depicting a fire in a cavern with the aphorism attributed to Hermes: *De cavernis metallorum occultus est, qui lapis est venerabilis. It's found hidden in the caverns of the metals, that which is the true stone.*"[7]

The fact remains that we still find, in *Les méandres du sens*, the "tale of a journey—that in this instance can with good reason be labeled initiatory"—and which a perspicacious journalist compared to the "construction of a novel by Butor, *Portrait of the Artist as a Young Ape*" that Flamand had not read before writing his text, the confession of an authentic illumination:

> When I opened my eyes again, I realized, not without surprise, that the vision had lasted only a few seconds. All I could do was acquiesce fully and gratefully to the mystery. *What we should undoubtedly consider to be the major operation of the* Ars Magna *had appeared to me, translated into suggestive images.* This experience also brought me a spiritual ferment that boded well for a subtle and fortunate development. [My italics.]

---

*And the close kinship of the Black Madonnas and Isis is well known!

Paul Sanda, who knew Flamand well and happily says that "the first work he read in this field of research" was the *Érotique de l'alchimie*, writes, however, in his preface, "Alchemical Eroticism, Symbolic Alchemy" for the text published of a short lecture given by Sarane Alexandrian at Cordes-sur-Ciel in 2003: "While both Elie-Charles Flamand and Sarane Alexandrian were not operatives and did not come to know this great secret, they at least had the merit to grasp its speculative essence, and I could say the deity's intention in matter, which can only reveal itself to creators of the *highest sensibility*."[8]

Born in 1928, in the former capital of the Gauls and deceased in Paris in 2016, "poet of the High Margins, of the Quest, and the Mysteries of the Light," according to Jacques Simonomis, Charles Flamand would add, with no afterthoughts, he said, Elie, to his first name, in 1959, to distinguish himself from a Belgian with the same name. He probably had no reason to do so to become, by following a "moral trajectory," as Marc Kober puts it so well,[9] this remarkable "metaphysical poet," "living and true," to quote Julien Starck[10] And here we are almost back to that "moral truth" mentioned by Breton I mentioned earlier. This should come as no surprise insofar as, to borrow the words of Yves-Alain Favre,[11] "poetry often takes the appearance of a spiritual approach, as an ascetic practice aiming for an inner transformation of the individual," thereby having "the same goal and proceeding in the same way as alchemy." He goes on to say that "the manipulation of language and the quest for the absolute, remaining deeply bound to each other," "the poet like the alchemist thereby performs a dual operation: poetic creation transforms him internally and the spiritual transformation directly influences the writing of the poem."

In fact, as shown by a response to André Lagrange in 1993, published in the text "Entrée du médium,"[12] the goals the poet set for himself testify to the strength of his requirements:

to meet the unforeseeable, to attempt to incarnate eternity in an instant; to grasp real reality by finding the harmonic laws of correspondences between the Material plane and the Spiritual plane; to receive the fecund energies of the Word; to transform my being by drawing from the vast reservoir of Sacred Knowledge that the alchemists called the *Universal Spirit* to experience through poetry Goethe's *stirb und werde*, "die and become";* to strive to share with others the best one has discovered within oneself, giving them either a bit of serenity or else disturbing them by revealing the personal conflicts dwelling within . . .

But it is also, as he shared with Roger Otahi, "to impose the most complete silence on the Ego, so that the impersonal Self that is located well beyond the conscious mind can make itself heard!" This is also close to what Yves-Alain Favre states when he points out, "Poetry for Elie-Charles Flamand possesses an essential analogy with alchemy. It sees no division between work on the language of the quest and that of inner transformation."

Elie-Charles Flamand was recently made a bit easier to find by the publication of *Braise de l'unité*,† a collection of all his anthologized works published up to 2015, which constitutes the authentic "logbook of the inner traveler" set upon "reanimating the threefold star of being." After beginning his studies in geology, mineralogy, and paleontology under the tutelage of Jean Viret, Flamand decided to follow the poet's path, "which demands that one devote their life to it." He joined the surrealist group in 1952 thanks to Jean-Louis Bédouin, to whom he had been introduced by Pierre Seghers. At this time already Breton, according to his own statements, quite symbolically appreciated the "so harmonious performance offshore" of the young poet, similar "to those of a dolphin,"—and here again how can we avoid thinking of the one in the *Mutus Liber?* This cannot help but remind us that Fulcanelli, whose works Breton, as is well known, knew perfectly, presented this

---

*A reference to Goethe's poem, "Blessed Desire," in *West-Eastern Divan.*
†Electronic version by Recours au poème éditeur and paper version by La Lucarne Ovale, 2015. The latter publishes the bulk of Elie-Charles Flamand's poetic work.

"mysterious fish" as the "preeminent royal fish" in *The Mystery of the Cathedrals*. He said even more explicitly that "this is our precious sulfur, the newborn child, the little king." An anonymous author added its description as "the living quintessence concealed in the water," in his article, "Le blason, creuset alchimique."[13]

Breton undoubtedly liked Flamand's collections of poetry, the first of which, *A un Oiseau de houille perché sur la plus haute branche du feu* (To a bird of coal perched in the highest branch of fire), the author sent him with the following dedication: "To André Breton, this poem written at a time when the fiery rose of his friendship was, together with *the pyre of birdlight*, one of the two flames burning at either end of my fog-shrouded night. For all that his heart and mind gave me with such generosity and still gives me inexhaustibly. As a token of intense affection." (My italics.)

Nevertheless, he did not object to Flamand's expulsion from the group "by letter of May 11, 1960,"[14] a "definite occultation without appeal" for "ruiniform esotericism," a "path on which he [Breton] had eagerly urged him to follow," as Flamand said to Lagrange. To the extent that Breton had welcomed the short narrative with the explicit title *Sur les pas de la fille du soleil* (In the steps of the daughter of the sun), written in August 1952 in Saint-Cirq Lapopie but unpublished until 2002, he had been the first one to read this text. In a short text published in his posthumous book *Propos mosaïqué*, Flamand, who rightly considered it a privilege to have had the opportunity to "enjoy [Breton's] radiant presence almost every day for eight years," reaffirmed "the veneration [he] had for the memory" of one he viewed as a man of "extreme sensitivity and generosity" who radiated "an intense human warmth," a "radiant presence" whose "daily frequentation inspired surpassing oneself, defiance of all conventions, and creative audacity" and who knew "with impeccable tact and concern [how] to encourage his embryonic gifts and strengthen his poetic vocation." And yet, he was opposed to a certain "spirit of negation" and eventually confessed that "an ever-expanding receptivity to spirituality and a commitment to the spiritual quest gradually pulled him away from a certain number of the notions held by the man who founded surrealism."[15] In the 1968 interview with Roger Otahi mentioned in chapter 1, he said (and the italics and uppercase letters are his): "What I consider to be Surrealism's mistake is to believe that this voice that speaks within is the subconscious or unconscious mind of the psychoanalysts. On the contrary, the latter consists only of psychic residues that we need to steer clear of. The Native Word that crosses through the poet, when he is truly *in a state of grace*, and uses him like an instrument, is the *Universal Spirit* of the alchemists."

However, unlike what happened a dozen years earlier with Maurice Baskine, Breton kept his friendship. Flamand, who says he retained from "this surrealist adventure" the idea that "poetic creation is not a gratuitous literary exercise, but something that compels the entire being," again notes in *Les méandres du sens*: "Dear André, you are undoubtedly the man I have loved most and the very robust mental bond formed between us has not been broken, I'm convinced of that. In the Eternal Present, you remain close to me." And thirty years later, reflecting again on how Breton had been, "as far as his intellectual course was concerned, the *Great Awakener*," he went on to say, "Whatever our differences of opinion, I don't think I ever betrayed the best aspect of your message, as you reminded me one day, which was to not compromise with these three causes: poetry, love, freedom." He explained it this way in his interview with André Lagrange: "He taught me, among many other things, that poetry is no literary amusement but a means of liberation and regeneration, a search for the *supreme point*, and that it is necessary to react against rationalism, stifling and solidified norms, and stupid conventions in order to break through appearances, to perceive the hidden truths, to truly attain a form of illumination." A word— *illumination*—he has a habit of directly connecting to the virtues of the philosopher's stone!

"It is obvious," says Kober, that "this poetry is initiation and alchemy. It is an alchemical journey, 'initiatory lattice of finisterres' in the poet's image. It's the poetry of the labyrinth and of voyages to distant lands, of getting lost in the twists and turns before arriving safely at the port." This opinion is shared by Matthieu Baumier, who turns a pretty phrase saying: "Flamand's poetry is an alchemist's step toward the star," and "reading it, we hear the distant sound of André Breton's footsteps on his way to René Alleau's in the company of Eugène Canseliet." But while Elie-Charles Flamand nevertheless refutes an exclusively alchemical reading of his texts,* as his friend André Pieyre de Mandiargues† had already said in the preface he wrote for *La Lune feuillée* in 1968. (Mandiargues, Dominique Rabourdin tells us, "was a great admirer of his erudite poetry and the refinement of his vocabulary that lent it such a particular tone.")[16] And Flamand refutes this interpretation of his poetry because he considers that, if he accepted such an opinion, "it would be a didactic poetry that teaches recipes for performing the Great Work," which it is not. Speaking of his third collection and of the "verbal alchemy that sparkles so brilliantly therein," Canseliet, as for him, deemed it worth mentioning, in an article published in *Atlantis* at the end of 1969:

> Let's make clear that the earth of the leaves,‡ during the white stage of the Work, becomes the leafed Moon, which is the phase of the Great Work in which spirituality reigns all powerful. Alas!

---

*But I think it is important to say that Flamand thought it wise to recall, in *Les méandres du sens*, that Mandiargues had "mentioned that his interest in alchemy had a certain impact on the themes of his poetry."

†To whom he dedicated, in his collection *La lune feuillée*, the text "Interrègne," which begins with these lines:
  In the orchards of the salamander
  My alley of triumphal waters vaporized
  In which the hand shucked its pearls of oblivion . . .

‡"EARTH OF THE LEAVES. Hermes gave this name to the matter of the work in putrefaction; but its proper name, Flamel says, is *Laton* or *Laton that should be whitened*," as can be read in Dom Antoine-Joseph Pernety's *Mytho-Hermetic Dictionary*. "Laton" is "brass"—there is a pun with laton/brass on the one hand and *La Tonne/Latone* on the other, as explained in chapter 11.

Nothing is less designated as a factor of success than the elevation of the spirit in the present era in which cybernetics and immorality share between them, in general favor, all glory and profit. The *leafed Moon** designates this other world of the immaculate doves of Diana† of which Eirenaeus Philalethes speaks in his *Open Entrance to the Closed Palace of the King*, which clearly seems to have inspired Elie-Charles Flamand with the most perfect felicity.[17]

"An author who belies the preconceived notion according to which the surrealists would be less erudite than others,"[18] he is the first to remind us that in "all poetry worthy of the name," it "is obviously not a matter of taking from the Philosopher's Art a certain number of its most specific symbols . . . then arranging them in some pseudo-hermetic way," nor "attempting to create a coded writing in which knowledge of the Art of Hermes is expressed didactically," but "essentially" the "Purification and Sublimation of Language." "Even if," he continues in his interview with Lagrange, "concepts borrowed from an age-old Wisdom and initiatory experience are incorporated into my work and can therefore give it esoteric extensions, my poems are not made up of cryptograms concealing precepts, a hermetic teaching, as some critics have, alas, mistakenly imagined."

After spelling out how he sees "the poetry of Elie-Charles Flamand as perfectly showing us the bonds that can be established between

---

*The "leafed moon whose number is 27," we read in an extract from *Magical Venus*, published by Flamand in *Érotique de l'alchimie*. It also appears in the long list of names provided by the students of science to the first material reproduced in Pernety's *Mytho-Hermetic Dictionary*. Elsewhere in this same book, it is defined as the White Stone. It is interesting to recall here that the gallery *À l'étoile scellée*, for which Breton was the artistic advisor, was almost named *À la lune feuillée*, as he said himself in the December 1952 issue of *Arts*.

†This is an allusion to this passage in *The Open Entrance to the Closed Palace of the King* by Eirenaeus Philalethes: "But in the grove of Diana are two doves that soothe its rabid madness (of our chaos) if applied by the art of the nymph Mercury. To prevent this hydrophobia to start again, take it and plunge it under water till it perish therein; then the rabid and black dog will appear panting and half suffocated—drive him down with vigorous blows, and the darkness will be dispelled" (London, 1669).

alchemy and poetry," Yves-Alain Favre describes its nature in detail: "First of all his poetry draws its inspiration from alchemy, borrowing from it images and symbols, which, even before the poet employed them, have already received a strong charge of meaning and are thus overdetermined: phases of the Work, precious stones, cameos,* and Rose-Cross, make it possible through their symbology to shed a stronger light on the poet's experience."

But he takes great pains to explain his remarks by adding that, despite "its essential analogy with alchemy," "we cannot speak of alchemical poetry, for Elie-Charles Flamand does not transmit any doctrine and his poems contain no consistent hermetic knowledge that it would be their task to communicate to initiates." "Let's say," he ends, "that the ritual and images used by the alchemists enable him to better realize his itinerary and his own inner experience."

The most the poet can bring himself to acknowledge (again in his interview with André Lagrange), is that his "poetry borrows most specifically from alchemy its principle of both verbal and spiritual Transmutation in its various phases." Nonetheless it remains true, as Kober points out, "that behind the accumulation of 'scoria' in the stream, the poet with a gold pan still perceives chips of sapience." In a February 1979 text from *Attiser la rose cruciale*,† "The Quest for the Word," subtitled "Essay on Hierophanic Poetry," which he would even label a "quasi-manifesto,"‡ Flamand, wishing "to show that poetry is a

---

*Stanislas de Guaïta speaks of it this way: "Gaffarel (seventeenth-century writer) called Gamahaez or cameo stones that had been spontaneously imprinted with certain hieroglyphs to which he attributed admirable virtues, and which he ranked as natural talismans. According to his theory, these marks, often wondrously clear and sharp, are the signatures of the elementary Forces that manifest in the three lower kingdoms" (*Le serpent de la Genèse*). For Flamand, in *Sur les pas de la fille du soleil*, they are "those mysterious 'games of nature' whose study is scorned in the present day."

†A collection whose title alludes discreetly but clearly to the Rosicrucians. It provides a perfect illustration of Yves-Alain Favre's remarks about the "images and symbols" that are powerfully charged with the "meaning" and "overdetermination" contained by Flamand's texts.

‡In the interview with Gwen Garnier-Duguy published online at *Recours au poème*.

spiritual experience very close to an initiatory or mystical approach" "setting off on the path of Light," provides several of the key principles for reading his work. "The vital energy of the Logos," he explains first:

> exerts itself in nature by means of the Universal Spirit,* the mediator between the Uncreated and gross matter. This half-material, half-spiritual agent disseminates itself throughout the universe whose harmony it maintains. It establishes communication between beings and things; it is also a link between the human being and the powers of the subtle planes. It is through its intervention that everything has meaning and everything speaks to the poet's soul, on the condition that he has known, through feeling and intuition, to find harmony with the vibratory state of that ocean of etheric strength, which ebbs and flows beneath the crust of appearances.

He goes on to say: "The work of expression consists of stripping language of its impurities so that the spiritual charge it conceals in its depths may flow out. There is a resemblance here to the Hermetic Great Work in which the alchemist opens the vile and crude primal matter, because a passive mercurial substance there imprisons the pure and active Sulfur, which is nothing other than the divine spark."

In conclusion, Flamand, who told Roger Otahi, "I never doubted that the paths of poetry lead to the *supreme point* of which Breton speaks, although he has never gone to the bottom of the metaphysical meaning of such a term," said that "through poetry an ascent to the Principle can be achieved," because "the Word" is "one of the modalities of the Uncreated Light." And "the poet . . . strives to collect the igneous blood of the dragon of the word. He dissolves the common idiom then

---

*In *Les méandres du sens*, Flamand also indicates that "alchemically the Paraclete represents that mysterious agent called by the Adepts the Universal Spirit that, according to them, breathes life into the three kingdoms of nature."

slightly coagulates the essential Word that contains this shadowy mass, thus spiritualizing the matter of language, so that it can better material-ize its Spirit." We can read, at the end of his poem "Solve et Coagula" in the collection *Jouvence d'un soleil terminal*:

> *Salamander he highlights*
> *At the end the lake of Hermes*

16

ELIE-CHARLES FLAMAND IN THE STEPS OF THE DAUGHTER OF THE SUN

Gradually, the poet emerges from the lair of limbo. Coming into view in the distance he sees serene glimmers until then unsuspected. The black work, without which no transfiguration is possible, has been achieved. The "dark night" opens on "the golden dawn." Here is the threshold of the spiritual world. We presently are celebrating here the marriage of heaven and hell.

ELIE-CHARLES FLAMAND, "LA QUÊTE DU VERBE,
ESSAI SUR LA POÉSIE HIÉROPHANIQUE"
IN *ATTISER LA ROSE CRUCIALE*

One text holds a special place in Flamand's work, because it seems to describe specifically a progression toward the Great Work, and raises the question of how far we can follow him when he says that he does not transmit anything, at least on the initiatory level. I am referring of course to the short book I briefly mentioned earlier, *Sur les pas de la fille du soleil*, which bears the following dedication: "To the memory of André Breton who encouraged me to write this story and was its first reader." It ends with the note: "Paris/Saint-Cirq-Lapopie, August 1958." The author explained to Isabelle Roche that the idea for the book came to him during a stay in Saint-Cirq with Breton, who "encouraged [him] to work on it" and which he "finished writing after his return to Paris."

This thirty-eight-page booklet, divided into five chapters, is preceded, besides the dedication to Breton, by the device *"Solus, per solum, ad solem,"* which Flamand translated elsewhere[1] as "Alone, from the interior of the earth, toward the sun." It's the story of a certain René Sol, whom we quickly realize is the main character, and we recall here that in the fifteenth century treatise of *Donum Dei*, it's from the union of Sol and Luna,* the King and Queen of the kingdom of Alchemy, that the Red King will be born, the "sovereign power that commands the alchemical and cosmic agents"—and who embodies the Great Work.

Each chapter, illustrated by a work of Obeline Flamand, is introduced by a poetic quote, similar to the emblems of Camacho and Gruger's *New Alchemical Heraldry*. The first chapter is thus placed under the sign of an isolated fragment by Arthur Rimbaud: *"Take heed, O my absent life!"* The epigraph for the second chapter is a quote by the Dadaist and surrealist Jean Arp: "He who awakens his soul causes the empires of silence to grow. He rests like the sky over the voice of death." The third part is introduced by the last verse of Gerard de Nerval's "Vers dorés":

> *Often in the dark being dwells a hidden God;*
> *and like a nascent eye covered by its eyelids,*
> *a pure spirit grows beneath the bark of stones.*

---

*There is also an alchemical poem written in old German from the very beginning of the fifteenth century whose title is "Sol et Luna"!

Opening the fourth chapter of Flamand's book, we find the German romantic poet Novalis,* with no less than eight lines taken from the "Song of the Dead" that Ludwig Tieck quotes in the afterword written for his friend's unfinished novel *Heinrich von Ofterdingen*,† an admirable meditation on the relationship between dream and reality:

Now for us, to love is to live!
Like the elements, we intimately
Blend the streams of existence,
Bubbling, heart to heart.
Lustfully, the currents part,
Because the battle of the elements
Is the most intense moment of love
And the heart of our heart.

Lastly, the final passage opens with a citation in Greek of an extract from the twentieth hour of Apollonius of Thyana's *Nuctemeron*, which literally means *The Day of the Night*, accompanied by the translation made in the nineteenth century by l'Abbé Constant, the great initiate known as Éliphas Lévi: "Here achieved by fire the works of the eternal light."

To sum up, the various parts of the book are placed under the sign of four poets—Rimbaud, the surrealist Jean Arp, and two Romantics, the Frenchman de Nerval and the German Novalis—along with that of the first-century thaumaturge and Neo-Pythagorean philosopher Apollonius—or Apollonios—of Thyana, translated by one of the most

---

*There is nothing gratuitous about this choice. Michael Löwy, in his book *La comète incandescente*, cites in this regard a phrase by Albert Béguin emphasizing the kinship between alchemy and the romantic aspiration: "For Novalis . . . perfect consciousness, obtained through inner transformation would by the same token transform the world."

†Novalis (Friedrich von Hardenberg), *Henri d'Ofterdingen* (Paris: UGE 10/18, 1967). It's Armand Guerne who gives this title to the quoted poem in *Les disciples à Sais, Hymnes à la nuit, Chants religieux* (Paris: Gallimard, Poésie, 1975). The translation here is different from those of Rovini in the 10/18 edition or Guerne's Gallimard edition.

important French esotericists of the nineteenth century, Éliphas Lévi, whose influence on the poets of his time is well known, starting with Hugo, Baudelaire, and Nerval, and even later on Breton.

But what does this little book say, one whose argument seems to be more or less present—and by means of the same images and same keywords—in *Les méandres du sens* when Elie-Charles Flamand brings up this "same manifestation of the hidden, infinite, and omnipresent dynamism" of "the vital current that gushes from the central cosmic point" capable of "igniting the divine spark that watches at the core of the human being and causing it to expand into a radiant sun, on the condition that the philosopher committed to the path that leads to the reintegration of original innocence knew beforehand to master and reduce the shadow zones, to pierce the dense mists of evil that surround like a gangue the sanctuary where lies the igneous seed of the inner gold"? After passing through a door, "made entirely of black, gleaming wood, decorated with barbarian designs whose provenance no archeologist could date or identify," adorned on its lower part with "a large heraldic sun radiating a darkened light"* and on the upper panel a high relief depicting "a group of sphinxes inextricably engaged in combat, wings beating, breasts erect, eyes maddened, ferociously rending with their leonine claws"—a clear allusion to the struggle between the two natures—the hero René Sol's journey begins in "chaos, in the lair where the mysteries are celebrated" at the "limits of himself," in front of the "fossilized sponge of his own old body," "a geode of dead flesh," which he destroys by launching his "enclosed soul" into the "lukewarm ball of his breath." In passing, we can recall here that the "'chaos of sages' or philosophers, in which the four elements are imprisoned, but confused and disorganized"[2] is nothing other than the *Prima Materia*. This is because, as Roger and Camacho wrote in *The Cathedral of Seville*, "the way in which the artist begins his work is a chaos that he must

---

*This also brings to mind Victor Hugo's verse in "Ce que dit la bouche d'ombre": "A frightful black sun from which the night radiates."

organize in accordance with his intention, and which the Adepts have often taken as a model of the state of confusion in which the *elements* are found before they are organized into the different bodies of the large Cosmos." It is then that he sees the birth of "a tutelary star whose sparkling guides him" and that we readers are rewarded with typically alchemical notation, in italics, definitely worthy of the sixteenth- or seventeenth-century treatises such as this one: "The morning star has flushed out its cursed sister and reigns over the new heavens. From his green eye falls a ray that caused a drop of dew to coagulate in me, crystal of a true wisdom, a promise of a limpid universe that will house the vertebral oak. From the crucible to the abyss slowly rises the carbuncle of the first day."

And it is probably the "Rebis or amalgam of the philosopher, the Androgyne, the *Royal Child* more perfect than his parents, which is nothing other than the matter that's attained the white stage, the first stage of the Philosopher's stone."[3] This is true if we take Philippe Audoin at his word, who writes that the star, the she-bear, "seals (in both senses of the word)" the end of the first stage since "its appearance indicates the birth of the fruit of the *philosophical Marriage*: the *double Mercury*, the *Hermaphrodite*, the *Androgyne*, also called REBIS (two-things), which combines within itself the two principles in the highest degree of activity," because "the *Rebis* must first die to be resuscitated within the glorious body that is the Stone," the "funeral passage, known as *putrefaction* or *crow* (being) marked by the color black."[4]

With regard to this ray coming out of a green eye, we can also probably see here an allusion to that *nostoc*, the moon's spit or saliva, "which is something that is born at night, that needs the night in order to develop, and can be worked only at night." Fulcanelli speaks of this in *The Mystery of the Cathedrals** as does André Breton in "Permanence

---

*"This cryptogram known to all peasants," "this algae" that the Philosophers have taken "as a hieroglyphic type of their material" "is also that something *born at night*, which needs the night in order to develop and can work only at night."

of Gallic Art." But we can also recall that, as Richard Khaitzine aptly points out, "in the process of the work, and this information is rarely provided by the texts, it's the color green that follows the black and heralds the white."[5]

Similarly, later in Flamand's text, still italicized we read: *"Here rolls the rosette of Isis; in its course, it adds a jewel-like sparkle to the light of liberation. From on high, she has just set the seal of union upon me. A budding stem curls in the multi-colored wind."* Now, in the alchemical texts, the wheel or rosette that appears after the death of the Crown, *Caput corvi* or *Putrefaction forum*—which represents the *Nigredo* or first stage of the transformation of the primal matter—consists of eight compartments, seven of which correspond to the metals and colors of the work. *Black*, for example, is associated with Saturn, while *ash grey* corresponds to Jupiter and *white* to the Moon. Venus has a *bluish green* that fades to a *pale red*, while a *deep reddish yellow* represents Mars, and the Sun is a *light yellow* moving into the *intense purple* of daybreak. All of these colors form the palette known as the Peacock's tail* and correspond to the phase called *iridescence*, in reference to the nymph Iris and of course to the colors of the rainbow. To master the colors is to master the fire of the Alchemists to obtain the philosopher's stone.

And what can we say that I have not yet said in one way or another of a phrase like this—"Their battle has caused the pillars of earth and heaven to cross into an X"—or again one in which Flamand writes: "Plucked are the shales of night, wafted beyond the ramparts of Being, the pilot bird of your destiny."

Sometimes these maxims are more directly gnomic in nature, as shown by this one: "A sign comes forth and the path is illuminated, the consumed life renews itself like a phoenix, inertia can germinate in the palm of your hand." "Like a phoenix," the fiery bird that is reborn out of putrefaction, which "is the last . . . emblem of the Philosopher's Stone," as

---

*The "peacock's tail," Jörg Völlnagel writes, "describes the changing play of color inside" the *vas hermeticum*.

Canseliet reminds us, before adding: "It is red, like the fabled bird whose Greek name is also precisely that of the royal color: φοινιξ, phoinix, red"!*

However, the continuation of René Sol's journey and the challenges he confronts, illustrated by the phrase "I crossed over and my double, weighed down by his gangue, remained nailed to the sterile reef of the other shore," clearly seems to correspond to this expression of a "personal progression toward the Absolute" using alchemy as "an already formed symbology that allowed him to mark out his itinerary," which as I indicated earlier was representative of Flamand's work.

At the beginning of the third chapter, the "too violent brightness" that forces the hero to shield his eyes at the end of the second chapter is echoed by the evocation of the "splendor of the day," a subtle allusion to the *Splendor solis*† so dear to the children of Art. But this third chapter detailing René Sol's arrival "at the threshold of a neglected curiosity cabinet" with its collections "arranged according to the method adopted by the old naturalists," an "extinct world . . . molded from the canonically prepared earth of a disintegrated self" (the "Adamic Earth"?), is also a reminder that Flamand himself was originally trained as a naturalist. Especially since, a few lines later, the character finds himself (in another striking coincidence), in a "place outside of time" that greatly resembles an alchemist's laboratory—like Eugène Canseliet's, which Flamand visited frequently at the time. Next, following a mediation likely intended as a reminder that *the door is inside,* having found his key in a hearth sporting a salamander,‡ (see plate 15) he makes his way

---

*Eugène Canseliet, *Trois anciens traités d'alchimie*. This quote appears as a commentary of the "frontispiece of a valuable old manuscript that," as the Master tells us, "he received as a gift from Mr. and Mrs. Michel Renaud de la Faverie."

†I have already mentioned this very famous German alchemical treatise from the first half of the sixteenth century, a work, as Van Lennep says, "of a German alchemist hidden beneath the pseudonym of Solomon Trismosin," in which we find, for example, a splendid illustration of the *Donum Dei*.

‡"This fabulous lizard stands for nothing else but the incombustible and fixed central salt, which preserves its nature even in the ashes of the calcinated metals and which the ancients called metallic seed" (Fulcanelli, *The Dwellings of the Philosophers*).

to a vast rotunda. This brings to mind "the very magnificent one" in Grace's home in *Kaleidoscopic Journeys*, illuminated by "a glass roof cut into a six-branched star," the famous seal of Solomon that is "the symbol of the union of the four elements, which represents, as we know," Flamand writes "the purpose of the work, the Red Stone, in its supreme and radiant harmony."[6] This symbol which is "drawn without lifting the pen . . . is the recognition sign of a certain category of Adepts,"[7] "the shining star of the macrocosm," Éliphas Lévi says, "hieroglyph" and "conventional sign," according to Bernard Roger, "of the perfect Philosopher's Stone," materializing the harmonious union of the opposites, the four principles, for example—hot, cold, wet, and dry—coming from the four primordial elements, fire, air, earth, and water. It materializes "in a new body, so filled with light it is on the verge of becoming luminous, also called 'crown of the wise' because it brings to its 'inventor' the *crown* of the Adeptat."*

In this theater bathed in a blue-green light, René finally finds himself in the presence of a "woman draped in a flowing, shimmering dress of blue shot silk," wearing a "green gem with dazzling reflections," and "*en ferronnière* on her brow."† She was the one "he'd been pursuing for so long, from tormented dreams to impassioned wakefulness, without ever managing to embrace her." And if we take the opportunity to recall here, Flamand, in his book on alchemical eroticism, presented the *Philosophical Discourse on the Stone of the Sages and Its Wondrous Birth*, which tells us that the heavenly and powerfully desirable lady, the "fully naked nymph of admirable beauty" who, in the text, "appears to Philotechne‡ is she who brings

---

*Bernard Roger, *Paris et l'alchimie*. Canseliet, in his commentary on Basil Valentine's *Twelve Keys*, speaks of "the philosopher's stone, whose symbol—the six-branched star—is formed by the two superimposed triangles of water and fire."

†A ferronnière is a headband with a small jewel suspended in the center that encircles the wearer's forehead.

‡The abbreviated pseudonym of the author of this "German treatise from the beginning of the sixteenth century," *Ein Philosophischer Discurs*, Philotechnium Tyronem Halolithium.

revelation to the human beings predestined to achieve the Great Work." The "Lady of the Great Work"? "We find her," he continues, "at the beginning of the *Chemical Wedding*. It is she who invites Christian Rosenkreutz to come to the hermetic ceremony and his description of this gracious messenger follows: 'a wonderfully beautiful female figure, dressed all in blue, spangled like the heavens with golden stars.'" We have already seen her in Bernard Roger's work! Flamand describes her as a "voluptuous goddess" who "is none other than the embodied Spiritus Mundi."[8]

> Queen of the primal rhythm, from before the beginning of time, for mirrors she uses nocturnal lakes, for palace the center of transformation with agate fingers where memory goes astray; she suddenly opens her doors to trembling forms in order to clothe them in insubstantial lives, veils of fog from which she weaves her whims.

Writes Bernard Roger in his prose poem, "The Lady of the Work."

With respect to the splendid emerald that adorns the brow of this woman, can we fail to think of the "Emerald of the Philosophers"? According to Flamand, this is what the unknown author—perhaps Sédir—speaks of, in the "singular and very rare little book entitled: *Vénus magique contenant les théories secrètes et les pratiques de la Science des sexes*," that "Emerald of the Philosophers [which] serves to veil the 'philosophical vitriol' whose green colors—with its many symbolic implications—has always inspired the enthusiasm of the teachers."*

Flamand also says, in fact quoting one of Canseliet's footnotes in his commentary on Georges Aurach's *Most Precious Gift of God* (1415): "O blessed viridity! says Kunrath [*sic*] in his *Amphitheatrum*

---

*And how can't the radiance of the gems, despite the difference of the stone, not bring to mind the diamond worn by Grace in *Voyages en kaléidoscope* (see chapter 4) or the fiery red gem of the *Roman de la Rose* by Jean de Meung, which Bernard Roger discusses in *Paris et l'alchimie*?

Sapientiae Aeternae,* learn, O Theosopher, to contemplate the viridity Ruah Elohim; you Kabbalist, the green line, the revolving world; Mage, nature, Physio-chemist, the Green Lion, *Duenegh viride Adrop,* the Quintessence!"† This "blessed viridity that makes all things germinate" Flamand again speaks about in *Les méandres du sens,* adding that it symbolizes regeneration and that "it's the very color of the Universal Spirit when it takes on corporeal substance in a precious salt, the philosophical Vitriol." Similarly commenting on the fifth of Basil Valentine's *Twelve Keys* in the Michael Maier edition,[9] Flamand writes, "This engraving is devoted to the exaltation of the Universal Mind, the *green lion* of solar essence . . . Kunrath calls this Spirit 'the pre-material sperm of the great world' and compares it to the *Ruach Elohim* of Genesis."‡

---

*In fact, *Amphitheatrum Sapientiae Aeternae* (The theater of eternal wisdom) by the German "fan of theosophy and doctor of the other medicine," Heinrich Khunrath (1560–1605), to whom Rudolph II granted his "privilege" in 1598, includes nine illustrations, four circular and five rectangular, to one of which—"The (Alchemical) Citadel" or fortress—René Alleau devoted a study published in April 1953 in the first issue of Franz Hellens's review, *Le Disque Vert.* In this study he explains, according to Gilles Bucherie that it is "one of the most luminous attempts at synthesis of sacred and secret knowledge ever attempted in Europe by the genius of an era marked as profoundly by the founding of the first scientific and literary academies as by the banning of festivals and the assemblies of Madmen."

†Elie-Charles Flamand, *Érotique de l'alchimie.* In a footnote, Canseliet adds, "According to Rulandus, in his *Lexicon Alchemiae:* Adrop id est lapis ipse, *it's the very stone.* . . . For Dom Pernety, green Duenech or Antimony is also named Brass (*Mytho-Hermetic Dictionary*)." It will be noted that the Khunrath quote is lacking, after the first three words, what follows: "that makes all things germinate."

‡Elie-Charles Flamand, *Érotique de l'alchimie.* Flamand spelled *Ruah/Ruach* two different ways. In *Les méandres du sens,* he writes: "Many other words have designated (this force). The Hindus call it Prana, the Chinese Ch'i, the Hebrews Ruach, the Greeks, nous, Paracelsus and Van Helmont, Archaea; other hermetic philosophers, Azoth, green lion, Spiritus Mundi, sidereal Light," and further on, he adds "the all-powerful cosmic energy, the life force." Nor can we fail to note that Bernard Roger also mentions the *Ruach Elohim* in his description of the "Wheel" of Notre Dame of Paris (*Paris et l'alchimie*). Canseliet, in *L'alchimie expliquée sur ses textes classiques* (chapter 9), recalls that Rabelais, "through Pantagruel," speaks of "the island ruled by the winds and for which the name *Ruach* means in Hebrew soul, breath, or spirit."

The last part, finally, recounts how René Sol, at the end of an authentic initiatory process that has witnessed "the illumination of the most obscure nooks and crannies of his being . . . for he has drunk the milk of the moon,"* likely that "liquor of heavenly origin" that spurted from the breast of the celestial messenger, "that *dry water* that the authors also call *Virginal Milk*,"† found after proceeding through "a majestic forest like a sanctuary,"‡ (the *"Forest of the Wise"*?) after sailing down the rapids of a river, "she who has been named the Daughter of the Sun," who, against the background, aptly enough, of the rising sun, draped in a red cape, awaits him to consummate the royal marriage, in order to accomplish the incarnation of the Spirit, the Red Work. This, as Yves-Alain Favre, citing Flamand's *Les pierres magiques*, once again emphasizes, "permits the soul to return to its state or original purity and to attain complete whiteness, while one obtains the Philosopher's Stone, the 'quintessence of the spiritual fire enclosed within the universe.'"

This image I am happy to compare, with all the less scruples as

---

*Once again, this quote from Breton's *Second Manifesto* comes to mind: "Recall that the idea of Surrealism tends simply to the total recuperation of our psychic forces by a means which is no other than a *vertiginous descent within ourselves*, the systematic illumination of hidden places, the progressive darkening of all other places." "Blessed vertigo. Spiral descent into the most intimate point of the crystalline silence of the individual," Flamand writes in *Les méandres du sens*!

†Flamand, *Les méandres du sens*. "*Dry water*: a substance extracted from acacia, oak, and fern by a certain manipulation. This body, having the property of being dry and wet at the same time, is therefore called dry-water by the Adepts by virtue of their dual opposing quality." "*Virginal Milk*": Philosophical Salt "but entirely melted." Kamala-Jnana, *Dictionnaire de philosophie alchimique*.

‡Concerning this forest, this is an opportune moment to recall these lines from the famous book by Johann Valentine Andreae, *The Chemical Wedding of Christian Rosenkreutz (Second Day),* that Roger and Camacho quoted and explained in *La cathédrale de Séville*: "'I had barely entered the forest when it seemed to me as if all of heaven and the elements were already adorned in their finery for this wedding,' Christian Rosenkreutz says, telling of the beginning of his journey toward 'the splendid portal on a high mountain' through which he entered the Palace where the wedding of the Royal Fiancés will take place."

we know how much Flamand admired Michael Maier's book,* to this commentary on the twentieth emblem of the book that Canseliet makes in his "Prolegomena" to *Three Ancient Treatises of Alchemy*, where, after recalling that "indeed the Great Stone, in order to become *transmutatory*, and to remove the leprosy of imperfect metals, must be projected onto gold metal of great purity, which then becomes <u>ruby red</u>," he writes, "*Nature, freed from the bonds holding it to its rock, in the company of its liberator, confronts the flames of the Gehanna, which will renew it in its universality in the fourth age of the cycle. This, according to the secret meaning of the initials I.N.R.I. of the crucifixion of the Divine Savior. Acronym that exoterically provide the words: Iesus Nazarenus Rex Judacorum*—Jesus the Nazarene, King of the Jews. *But on the esoteric plane, which is ours, it gives this apothegm of high philosophy:*

> *Igne Natura Renovatur Integra*
> By fire, is all of Nature renewed."[10]

Yves-Alain Favre then concludes his observation, by saying: "In this way, the red work achieves a definitive illumination. Several of Flamand's poems recall this experience through which the White becomes Red and where one ascends to a state in which the opposites are canceled," before quoting some lines from this poet's *Jouvence d'un soleil terminal*:

> *Vigor of the implosive ruby*
> *This Grail always governs my ecstasy.*

Lastly, as a seemingly perfect illustration of André Lagrange's observation that "Flamand borrows from alchemy its language and its

---

*He writes, in *Les méandres du sens*, "This splendid work combines illustrations with texts in verse and prose as well as musical scores," saying about the engravings by Jean-Theodore de Bry, the illustrator of *Atalanta Fugiens*, that they were "works [he had] often admired and studied."

symbols—as the starting point of a spiritual path; the blossoming of the individual, not in search for some kind of philosopher's stone, but a poetic re-creation," *In the Steps of the Daughter of the Sun* ends with this phrase that seems to merge romanticism, symbolism, and surrealism: "I am no more than a tear from the mask of green lightning turning red!"

17

ITHELL COLQUHOUN AND THE
GOOSE OF HERMOGENES

Thence the self-same colors
The alchemists have shown
Lying in the alembic
Thalamus and throne
And have called them the opal
The stone that's not a stone

ITHELL COLQUHOUN, "UNION PACIFIC"

Little known even to specialists and knowledgeable fans, Ithell Colquhoun was born in 1906 in Shillong, Assam, in what was then still called the Raj. The poet, painter, and writer, who died in 1988 in Cornwall, is a kind of meteor within the British surrealist group—and probably one of its most interesting members. Michel Remy, probably the French art historian most familiar with the history of the movement and its players in Great Britain, described her in the *Dictionnaire général du surréalisme* as "surrealism in a perpetual 'fantasmagical' state on the convulsive paths of occultism!"

Having discovered surrealism—in particular the work of Dali—during a trip to Paris in 1931, she visited the London International

Surrealist Exhibition at the New Burlington Galleries organized in that city in 1936, before participating in 1937 and again in 1939 in several group exhibitions, at least one of which was organized by E. L. T. Mesens, as well as a joint exhibition with Roland Penrose, a key figure of the group. After meeting André Breton at rue Fontaine, she went to Chemillieu in the Ain region to a chateau rented by Gordon Onslow Ford, one month before the war started, where Esteban Francis, Matta, and Kay Sage and her husband the Marquis di Faustino—as well as the man who would become the American woman's second husband, Yves Tanguy—were also staying. This is likely when Ithell definitively adopted her methods of pictorial automatism. In 1976, when describing her work of the early forties, she used an expression dear to Matta: "psychological morphology."

After joining the London group led by E. L. T. Mesens and Jacques B. Brunius, she published several texts—including three excerpts from what would become *The Goose of Hermogenes*—in *London Bulletin*, the review they directed, while continuing to take an interest in all forms of esotericism via an approach that openly sought to reconcile the two currents of thought. In April 1940, following a meeting at the Barcelona Restaurant in Soho, she was expelled from the group at the same time as Reuben Mednikoff and Grace Pailthorpe,* but not for the same reasons. Essentially she was thrown out because she refused to break with the esoteric organizations with which she had been spending time since 1927.† For Ithell Colquhoun displayed quite a precocious interest—one she would never belie—in esotericism in

---

*Doctor Grace Pailthorpe (1883–1971), surgeon, and Ruben Mednikoff (1906–1972), artist and designer, came up with a plan together for creating a society that was more livable by combining art, writing, and psychoanalysis. Initially close to surrealism and even considered by Breton as "the best and most authentically surrealist" of all the British artists, the evolution of their creative practice toward what they called "Psychorealism" earned Mesens's displeasure and got them expelled from the group.

†With fine consistency, Mesens would be one of the signers, twenty years later, of the letter excluding Elie-Charles Flamand from the surrealist group for "ruinform esotericism."

all its forms and for the "traditional sciences." In fact, her first text, one she would later call "immature," was published in the magazine *The Quest* in 1930 under the title "The Prose of Alchemy." In about a dozen pages it explores the rich iconography of the Art of Music, into which she had been initiated by a distant cousin, Edward J. Garstin, who was also an author of alchemical treatises. David Gascoyne, one of the first British citizens to join the surrealist movement, wrote in 1946 that this text was "one of the best, most stimulating, short introductions to the subject of alchemy considered as imaginative literature, i.e. a special department of poetry, that exists in English!" We should be careful as well not to underestimate the influence on her of writings—stamped with esotericism, especially alchemy—by William Butler Yeats, whom she admired. Amy Hale even ventures to say that "the images and ideas of alchemy probably reinforced for Colquhoun the 'rightness' of her involvement in surrealism." During the war she again exhibited her interest in the Art of Music by publishing, in 1943, in the Surrealist file compiled by del Renzio, of the review *New Road*, a very short article on the connections between surrealism and alchemy, as well as astrology, "The Water-stone of the Wise." This Richard Shillitoe* considers to be her "most important theoretical text," and it seems to be a response to Breton's *Prolegomena for a Third Manifesto of Surrealism or not* (1942).† Here she clearly advances, and from a female perspective, proposals that match the direction that Breton was starting to present as the plan for the movement after the war. This plan was the elaboration of a new myth, "the collective myth of our time," of which he had already spoken of in the first manifesto. And it is no doubt not insignificant, even if alchemy is far from the only esoteric trail she had set out to blaze,‡ that she

---

*Richard Shillitoe, *Ithell Colquhoun: Magician Born of Nature*. Richard Shillitoe is incontestably one of the authors of reference on the life and work of Ithell Colquhoun.
†An extract of which appears in the said review.
‡She also referred quite a bit to astrology there as well, but the two "traditional sciences" are inseparable.

had chosen for her contribution an excerpt from a treatise by the German alchemist—and heraldist—Johann Ambrosius Siebmacher (1561–1611), a title that reads in full: *The Sophic Hydrolith; or Water Stone of the Wise, that is, a chymical work, in which the way is shewn, the matter named, and the process described; namely, the method of obtaining the universal tincture.*[1]

Before discovering the Lamorna Valley in Cornwall, her "chosen land," where she would eventually settle once and for all, she briefly took part in the activities around a dissident group review, *Arson*, with the person who would become her companion at that time, Toni del Renzio. It is he who writes in the manifesto *Incendiary Innocence* that I mentioned earlier: "To ensure no misunderstanding of what is being said here, let it be repeated that the occultists, Christian Rosenkreutz not the least among them, have supplied surrealism with the form as well as the content of some of its boldest and totally recalcitrant assertions."[2]

Concerning this April 1940 meeting and the reasons stated for excluding her, Ithell Colquhoun, who did not understand this rejection and would consider herself to be a surrealist her whole life, describes again in the biographical supplement of the catalog for her exhibition at Newlyn Orion Galleries in February–March of 1976: "I said I wished to be free to continue my studies in occultism as I saw fit. (It was Mesens's quirk to oppose this aspect of surrealist activity, since Breton, Dominguez, Dr. Mabille, Masson, Seligmann and other continental surrealists pursued such researches without query.)" "But in a late essay, '*Surrealism and Hermetic Poetry*,' she compares," Eric Ratcliffe points out in the book he wrote on her, "the alchemistic search for the elixir with the aspiration of a writer sympathetic to surrealism, and points out that Breton himself stressed the fact that poetry and magic were aspects of the same thing, linking him with magical tradition."[3]

Simultaneously a member of several lodges—at least—of a co-ed Masonic Obedience, the ancestor of Le Droit Humain (The Human

Right), of the scandalous Ordo Templi Orientis,* of the Fraternity of Isis, of the Order of the Keltic Cross, of the Order of the Pyramid and the Sphinx,† headed by Countess Tamara Bourkoun, she was also a druidess. Moreover, Ithell Colquhoun tried unsuccessfully all her life to enter the Hermetic Order of the Golden Dawn. She even wrote a book in 1975, *The Sword of Wisdom*,‡ devoted to the Order and its founder, the Scotsman Samuel Liddell "MacGregor" Mathers (1854–1918). She gave the impression that he could have been an Adept, even suggesting he was "of the race of the Comte de Saint Germain, of those immortals who (as esoteric tradition claims) appear and disappear at will, taking on a temporary humanity for an unknown purpose."

Of the four chapters at the end of the book that discuss his "Legacy," the third one deals specifically with alchemy**—as well as spagyric medicine—and its links with the teachings of the Golden Dawn. The author's approach to the subject from this point of view demonstrates in fifteen pages her deep knowledge of the history and current status of the Art of Music on the continent†† as well as in Great Britain. For the sake of accuracy, she even contrasts alchemy to all esoteric disciplines— and her knowledge of these domains is quite extensive. But from the perspective of this book, it's the definition of the Art that she gives us that I find most valuable. She writes:

---

*This para-Masonic organization founded at the end of the nineteenth century by the masons Karl Kellner and especially Theodor Reuss, the OTO, which states its purpose is helping everyone to discover their true identity and "to instruct individuals in the mysteries of nature through the use of allegories and symbols," was later led astray by the scandalous Aleister Crowley.

†Colquhoun had even apparently received the initiatory deposit of the last Temple of the Alpha Omega in London, Alpha Omega being one of the many splinter groups of the Golden Dawn.

‡Ithell Colquhoun, *The Sword of Wisdom*. A citation from the poem "Du haut de Monserrat" by Georges Bataille and André Masson serves as an epigraph, and is also the source of the book's title.

**The other three are dedicated to magic, Enochian magic inherited from John Dee, and tantra.

††In addition to Roger Caro, she also mentions "Claude d'Ygé de Lablatinière," Armand Barbault, Bernard Husson, Canseliet, and Fulcanelli.

Perhaps I should at once say what I think alchemy is not—difficult though it is to define it positively. It is not a moralistic allegory, but neither is it mere furnace-work, the art of "torturing" metals by extreme heat: authorities unite in decrying the *Souffleurs** [Puffers] whose one idea was to transmute metals into gold in order to get rich quick. It is not chemistry of any kind, not even so-called hyperchemistry; it is rather an aspect of nuclear physics, and its well-attested transmutations result from nuclear reaction brought about by a still-unknown process.

She would conclude this chapter by these words that brook no appeal: "Metallic transmutation, though necessary to the achieved alchemist's end, is no more than a token of the wise's profounder knowledge and wider powers. The toiling Hyperchemist may produce transmutations of a sort in his laboratory, but without the ability to manipulate forces *on 'the confines where matter ends,'* he is no Alchemist."

She focuses particularly on the study of the *Homeri auraea Catena* (*The Golden Chain of Homer*) (1722), by Doctor Anton Joseph Kirschweger, a book partially inspired by the thought of Jacob Böhme that didactically explains the major theories and practices of the Rosicrucians in the seventeenth and eighteenth centuries. This makes it one of the most important alchemical texts but paradoxically one little explored by her surrealist comrades. As with all this literature, she offers a reading with a strong sexual interpretation, comparing, for example, the alembic to the uterus, the bath of Venus to the vagina, "or perhaps the amniotic sac," the aqua vitae to the female fluids "in particular," while the sperm of the philosophers in her opinion would designate nothing but the male fluids. Generally speaking, her notion of the quest for the philosopher's stone is closely tied to sexuality. She finished her work on Kirshweger's book in 1979 when she published "Notes on the Colouring of the *Homer's Golden Chain* Diagram"† in the sixth issue of the *Hermetic Journal*.

---

*In French in the text.
†"The anonymous Unknown Chevalier, like Esprit Gobineau de Montluisant, and Winceslas Lavinius of Moravia," Canseliet writes in the "prolegomena" to his

While some keep only four, "the majority of authors," she suggests in this text "postulate the existence of a greater number of operations; the *Auraea Catena* speaks of ten connections, but it is more often a question of twelve, often compared to the labors of Hercules. Norton* has them symbolized by Twelve Doors while Basil Valentine uses Twelve Keys. I have adopted this latter's nomenclature for the chapters of my esoteric novel, *The Goose of Hermogenes*."[4]

And it is quite true that, among the works Colquhoun published, there is an authentic alchemical novel with the very expressive title, *The Goose of Hermogenes*, which deserves a few words here. Published by Peter Owens in 1961, in London, work on this novel was probably begun much, much earlier, probably 1926, as that is the same year when her novella and one-act play, *The Bird of Hermes*, was published on the same subject. But it is reasonable to assume that, even though some excerpts of the future stories were published before the war in various reviews like the *London Bulletin*, it was not until the mid-fifties that the project really began to take shape, for it was then that she made a series of five drawings—never published—to illustrate the book. One of them even inspired her gouache *The Bed of Empedocles* in 1957. Amy Hale, in her noteworthy essay, *The Supersensual Life of Ithell Colquhoun*,[5] notes that this novel is "saturated with Colquhoun's signature style and themes that define both her written and visual work."

It's the quote of Eirenaeus Philalethes† that the author uses for an epigraph and presents as an extract from *Brevis Manductio ad Rubrem Coelestem*,‡ but which in fact as Shillitoe[6] tells us, comes from another

(cont.d) *Trois anciens traités alchimiques*, "fits into the long lineage of Adepts forming the *Golden Chain of Homer—Homeri auraea Catena*—which remains completely uninterrupted." And he adds, "The last link of the golden, ancestral chain, and no doubt the strongest, is our venerated Master Fulcanelli."

*Thomas Norton (1433–1513), English alchemist and author of a famous alchemical poem dating from 1477, *The Ordinall of Alchemy*.

†In other words, Eirenaeus Philalethes, or George Starkey (1628–1665), who is more famous for another book: *The Open Entrance to the Closed Palace of the King*.

‡In other words, *Brief Guide to the Celestial Ruby: Concerning the Philosopher's Stone and Its Grand Arcanum*. The third book is *The Metamorphosis of Metals*.

book, *The Metamorphosis of Metals*, that provides the full meaning for this book's title. "It's our door-keeper, our balm, our honey, oil, urine, maydew, mother, egg, secret furnace, true fire, venomous dragon, theriac, ardent wine, Green Lion, Bird of Hermes, *Goose of Hermogenes*, two-edged sword in the hand of the cherub that guards the Tree of Life." She strings the names together but it only involves, to use the words of Dom Pernety, "a portion of the names that the Hermetic Philosophers give to their material" although Eric Ratcliffe writes that the "Bird of Hermes is another of the names used by alchemists to designate the Philosopher's Stone (like the Goose of Hermogenes, which she chose as the title for her later novel)."

It is an authentic alchemical novel written in the first person that takes place "on an unnamed island in an eternal present," to quote Shillitoe, although this same observer takes great pains to let us know "that alchemy forms the structure of the novel and informs much of the imagery," even though "the heroine's trials are clearly a metaphor for the quest of the alchemists." "It would be a mistake . . . to attempt an episode by episode of the events into specific alchemical phases," insofar, as Colquhoun herself says in *The Sword of Wisdom*, "one cannot understand an alchemical text by trying to translate it into everyday language. [It] needs some faculty analogous to poetic appreciation." Michel Remy is equally caution when speaking of this little book, describing it as an "initiatory journey through the different alchemical operations seen as so many constituent elements of a landscape that is both geographical and mental," especially since it's not impossible—and it wouldn't be surprising—if Jungian psychology were present in the background, as Eric Ratcliffe assumes. He claims it is possible to glimpse the mark of the *Red Book*'s author and his individuation process in the final lines of the novel. Amy Hale, meanwhile, thinks, "as with the most of [the author's] fiction, *The Goose of Hermogenes* has no characters, only archetypes, seemingly motivated by large external forces."[7] Nonetheless, it's still true that the twelve chapters*

---

*Amy Hale points out that "in the 2018 edition, Richard Shillitoe adds a chapter found only in draft manuscripts, called 'Hexentanz'" (Dance of the Witches). It had been rejected by Colquhoun herself because it was too different from the rest of the book.

are based on the *Twelve Keys* of Basil Valentine, a book she had discovered earlier in A. E. Waite's translation of *The Hermetic Museum*. Each has the name of one of the steps leading to the Great Work: *Calcination, Solution, Separation, Conjunction, Putrefaction, Congelation, Cibation* (which has one of Eugenius Philalethes's* magical aphorisms as an epigraph: "in the wood of wonder her fountain sings"), *Sublimation, Fermentation, Exaltation, Multiplication*, and *Projection*. It should be noted, however, that the twelve-chapter division of her book and their titles seem to be more inspired by the fifteenth-century alchemist George Ripley, and more specifically his *Compound of Alchemy*, a long medieval poem consisting of thirteen chapters of unequal length, ranging from six to fifty-one verses, all of seven, strictly rhyming lines, describing the twelve steps of the Great Work. The thirteenth text, soberly called *The Recapitulation*, brings it all to a close—for a total length of 1561 verses including "recapitulation." Called "gates," these twelve chapters are titled exactly the same as the twelve chapters of Colquhoun's book. And of course in the same order.

However, Richard Shillitoe clearly shows some of the procedures the author uses as well as her use of images from the Art of Music. For example, he explains that "in spiritual alchemy, the phase of *Conjunction* introduces the higher realms of existence, beyond the mundane world," which he says is often symbolized in the texts by the image of a "bird which soars upward free of terrestrial limits." He points out that in the fourth chapter, which bears the name of this operation specifically for its title, "Colquhoun tells the story of two lovers who discover that they have the ability to fly. In their aerial journeying they begin to experience the unity of nature and to sense that the whole cosmos is infused with life," two cousins destined to join together to give birth to the triumphant androgyne, the *rebis*. In the same way, whereas the operation of *congelation* or *coagulation* consists of removing the water from substances, to dry them out, to crystalize

---

*Not to be confused with Eirenaeus!

the metallic salts and to combine sulfur and mercury, Shillitoe stresses that in the chapter with this title, chapter six, the novelist "represents this instability and change of state . . . by contrasting the fluidity of the sea with the solidity of the land" and describes the blossoming of "the relationship between the heroine and the young fisherman" in a sustained process of purification.

Even if, as Amy Hale notes, the alchemical theme is less overt in her artworks after the Forties than in those of Leonora Carrington or Remedios Varo, it nevertheless much inspired Colquhoun the artist and can be seen as a thread running through all her artwork starting in 1938—with the first appearance of *Alchemical Figure*. This figure is recurrent, as shown in the catalog of her artwork compiled by Richard Shillitoe, in which we see another *Alchemical Figure** in 1940, then *Alchemical Figure: Feet in Water*, and finally *Alchemical Mandala*. In 1941 we have *Alchemical Figure: Androgyne*. Sometimes these words appear only as an inscription on the back of the piece, as is the case with *The Homunculus I*† (1940), *The Opal I and II* (1940), *Tidal Wave and Volcano* (1940) as well as with *Communicating Vessels*‡ (1941), in which she "makes the familiar link between alchemical and sexual symbolism."[8] These are works in which the X I have already mentioned often appears, the "Spagyric X of the Crucible," which according to Fulcanelli can be interpreted as a sign of the "fire hidden in matter." Another work from 1942 is called the *Philosopher's Stone,* and we also have a collage from 1960, highlighted with colored inks, *Alchemy up-to-date.* This *Alchemical Figure* still haunted the artist in 1967, this time in the form of a statue,

---

*Shillitoe describes this watercolor as "a standing female figure with arms and legs outstretched in an 'X' position."

†Still according to Shillitoe, at least six watercolors dating from 1940, which closely resemble each other, depict the *Homunculus*, a familiar alchemical concept. They "are to be understood as the alchemical metamorphoses of gendered individuals and the birth of a unified, integrated being."

‡Not to be confused with the 1948 painting called *Les Vases Communicants (André Breton).*

then again in 1978 in an enamel work on paper, *In the Alembic.*

Like Jean-Clarence Lambert said of Elie-Charles Flamand, we could say of Ithell Colquhoun that she "comes close to creating a symbiosis of surrealism and occultism." This gives her work a particularly original style based on her own experiences in the widest variety of esoteric fields, but also on a large number of the surrealist precepts raised at various times by the author of *The Ode to Charles Fourier* (Breton). She seems less close to the operative practices than Breton and her approach to alchemy seems somewhat different. On the one hand, she doesn't reject the Jungian approach, the depth psychology, but considers it a useful tool worthy of consideration, and on the other hand, she doesn't openly reject all forms of transcendence, although she never insists on it, as shown by the fact that she chose to title her 1943 manifesto "The Waterstone of the Wide," a clear allusion to the eponymous treatise by Johan Ambrosius Siebmacher. Now, with its "many references to the Holy Scriptures," this work, which maintains, as Emmanuel d'Hooghvorst points out,* and this should be greatly emphasized, that "wishing to attain the secret of the Philosopher's Stone without divine blessing is a dangerous folly," clearly places the accent on a spiritual dimension of alchemy that I am not sure can be found in André Breton or those close to him like Vincent Bounoure, for example. Bounoure, in his "Preface to a Treatise on Matrices," writes that this "science," that has always seen itself as sacred and whose "language . . . always takes its references from the other traditional sciences: astrology and astronomy, mysteries and metaphysics,

---

*It was the Baron Emmanuel van der Linden d'Hooghvorst (1914–1999), a Belgian alchemist and disciple of the author of the *Message retrouvé*, Louis Cattiaux, "who pulled this wondrous book from oblivion and was the first to partially translate it," in 1955. (Claude Froidebise, in his foreword to the republication of *La pierre aqueuse de sagesse ou l'aquarium des sages* [Paris: La Table d'Emeraude, 1989].) Emmanuel d'Hooghvorst, who worked in the laboratory with his brother Charles (but on gold not stibine), also collaborated on *La tourbe des philosophes.* He also corresponded with Alexander von Bernus.

magic and divination" fits "into the vast current that adopts as its primary goal the regeneration of man," a "regeneration," however, "that appears, in the Christian context of Western alchemy, to respond to the doctrine of original sin, but which is clearly . . . of a fundamentally different nature, as it is not religious in its essence."[9]

TOTAL LIBERATION
OF THE MIND

By losing the purity of the heart, we lose the science.

NICOLAS VALOIS

As we can now see, the matter of the relationship between surrealism and alchemy is complex and vast, all the more vast and complex than what I have been able to share here because, in the words of Jörg Völlnagel, it "tells beautiful, captivating, crazy, fantastic stories, the likes of which we hardly know in the real world." I could also have mentioned Maurice Fourré, whose *La Nuit du Rose-Hôtel** was published by Gallimard in 1950. It appeared in the "Revelation" collection, directed by Breton, but which he had set up in order to republish *The Dwellings of the Philosophers*. In a style, especially in this first novel, and tone that brings to mind those of Irene Hillel-Erlanger and her *Kaleidoscopic Journeys*, Fourré left us works, especially *La marraine du sel, Tête-de-Nègre,* and *Le caméléon mystique,* all published after the Second World

---

*This book appeared in Breton's library with the following dedication: "For André Breton, in central homage of my admiration, my gratitude, and my affection. This first Vowel of my inspiration. Maurice Fourré."

War, which also contain numerous alchemical allusions. These were mentioned by Philippe Audoin, a true expert, in his 1978 book *Maurice Fourré, rêveur définitif,*[1] and again more recently in April 2008 by Jacques Simonelli in his article, "A la recherche de Fol-Yver," published in the nineteenth issue of *Fleur-de-Lune*, the bulletin published by the Friends of Maurice Fourré Association. Cautiously, however, Audoin, who shares Breton's intuition, even wonders whether the author did not "at the end of his life, at the end of his *travels*, have knowledge of an esoteric nature that he secretly taught to those with ears to hear." He even goes so far as to claim that in the novel *Tête-de-Nègre*, for example, "the profound duplicity of the laughing Hilaire and the venomous Basilic, commingled in the same character alchemically marked by the sign of the double nature, is not without inconvenience: chronic transience, volatility," before explaining that "his Clair Harondel," the hero of *La marraine du sel*, "can be seen as a personification of philosophical Mercury, the instable and volatile matter that alchemists had to fix first before undertaking the long coction that completed the Great Work." He develops this as follows: "Clair is volatile by his surname, by his trade, by his fickleness. By his first name, he is a reminder of the purity that Mercury must attain before it is married, in other words combined with the fixed Sulfur."

The author then points out that "Clair is carrying three suitcases, one black, one white, and one red," "the traditional colors through which the philosopher's stone must travel before reaching perfection,"* before making the disturbing observation that "the black suitcase" "black with the preliminary putrefaction" and of "the symbolic death of the material, precondition for its triumphant resurrection" contains "funerary items." The white one, which is the color of "the first stone, the one that allows the transformation of base metals into silver" and whose "appearance testifies that the philosophical mar-

---

*"From Yellow no Red can come, if it has not been a Black made white" (Basil Valentine, *De la nature des métaux*).

riage of Mercury and Sulfur has been canonically consummated in the tomb and is now worthy of being celebrated" contains "wedding articles." Finally, the red one, the color red that "implies the power acquired . . . by the stone to perform the transmutation into gold," is full of "games and toys," which can be presumed to allude to the "*ludus puerorum* dear to the old Adepts." Unless Fourré is thumbing his nose as was his wont and only seeking "to show that for someone who has acquired the power, 'making gold' is a banal distraction" because the "essential acquisition is spiritual in nature and cannot be expressed or transmitted." Jacques Simonelli, who finds "the alchemical context much less clear in *La marraine du sel* (The godmother of salt) than in *Tête-de-Nègre* ("Head of the black one" literally, but refers to the French equivalent of a Mallomar) or *Le caméléon mystique* (The Mystic Chameleon), points out that if the salesmen's suitcases are "really" carrying "the colors of the three phases of the Work," they are "listed in reverse order," which allows us to foresee "the failure of the labor." Among the many other examples he presents in his article, Simonelli, who believes like Audoin that the alchemical quest for Fourré is "the symbol of every spiritual path," explains the transformation in *The Mystic Chameleon* of "The Hotel of the Golden Ball" into the Hotel "of the Silver Ball" by "the alchemical allusions that are so frequent in the work of Maurice Fourré, who shows preference for the Stone's orientation toward silver, symbolized by the white rose." Quoting *The Dwellings of the Philosophers*, he points out that in the "Perfumes" chapter of *The Godmother of Salt*, "on Fol-Yver and his 'green pyramids raised like farmer's huts,'" the author mentions the "gloomy prison of the King," in a symbol-laden phrase in which we find *agriculture* (a metaphor for alchemy), the *fire*, the *green*, and what Fulcanelli calls "our manure that the philosophers designate by the name of black sulfur, *prison of gold, tomb of the King*."[2]

And I can't help thinking that the title of the third book, *Tête-de-Nègre*, has some symbolic connection with the *Caput Mortuum* of the Philosophers by fire.

I'll leave it to Philippe Audoin, who recalls the discussions he had with his friends about Fourré's texts, to conclude with these esoteric and poetic lines: "Fourré appeared to us like one of those wandering alchemists of the seventeenth century who one day, at the home of some *dour scholar*, gave an unexpected demonstration of his art and then disappeared leaving no other trace than a little native gold stuck at the bottom of the crucible. We hold as certain that the *Primal Material* on which Maurice Fourré worked was his life and death, profoundly bound up in a kind of inner illumination!"

I could also have mentioned in greater detail the very curious novel *Aurora** that Michel Leiris wrote at the end of the twenties, but which he didn't publish until after the war, at which time he mocked "the hotchpotch full of apparent symbolism, and the *black* or *frenetic* style of its blustering prose." This book, which combines souvenirs of reading Victor Hugo's *Notre-Dame de Paris* with gothic novel and more directly alchemical texts, ends with these lines seething with mystery: "Further away from me, quite high up on the right, my vitrified stare was riveted to the top of the spire of Notre-Dame. This temple was built by neither Semiramis nor the Queen of Sheba, but they say that on its stones are engraved the principal secrets of Nicolas Flamel, more enigmatic even than those of Paracelsus,"† whose escutcheon was comprised of "a red alembic drawn on a star-studded black background inside which burned a white salamander and from which blond hair rose like wisps of smoke. The whole thing was accompanied by

---

*Whose title cannot help but bring to mind *Aurora consurgens* (1410), the oldest alchemical manuscript, decorated with thirty-seven allegorical engravings and placed under the aegis of Hermes Trismegistus, which we still have. It should be noted that this text was rediscovered by Jung in 1936 and translated by and accompanied by the commentary of his collaborator, Marie-Louise von Franz.

†Michel Leiris, *Aurora*. Aurora, sister of Aurélia and Pandora, a name we are irresistibly tempted—since Pascal Quignard, following the author's suggestions, encourages us to understand her name as "Eau-Rô-Râh, [Water, -Rô, -Râh], OR AUX RATS [Gold For Rats], Horrora, and so forth"—to read "Aurea hora," the hour of gold.

this motto, most appropriate for the greatest man to ever seek the Philosopher's Stone: OR AURA." Paracelsus, moreover, is one of the heroes of this story, whose central theme is the quest of an object created by God, the "Stone" "born of the earth which was bitten to its red core by the first ray of the sun," that restores to man his freedom, that allows him to reach the absolute and transmute all. "This Stone is a funeral urn which controls the process of putrefaction, but which may rot, too, when it changes into a living creature and consequently becomes subject to putrescence," this Stone "the cause of putrefaction and itself putrefied . . . is the very essence of purity, owing to its perpetual undulation which is represented by hair, its dominant symbol." This Stone, "purifying and purified, it is the sign of thought." This "Stone" that never stops transforming itself and the "first syllable of whose name is OR [gold]."

I could have recalled that Jean Biès, who is also the author of a book entitled *The Alchemists* (*Les alchimistes*) in which he develops his firm conviction that their approach is essentially spiritualist, writes of René Daumal, whose quests again are eminently spiritual, that "the Alchemy appeared to him in reality as a sacrificial and sacramental science of earthly substances" and that "if every metal is truly gold that doesn't know itself, every word is virtually a vibrating morsel of spirit," as Elie-Charles Flamand also thinks. "Daumal would never claim to be doing anything different . . . than transmuting the 'black work'—domain of anguish and illusions, the viscous darkness of the *materia* in which the mercurial waters remain congealed—into the white work—kingdom of luminosity—when carrying his poetry *Solve* to *Coagula*, or if you prefer, from Chaos to Order, from Earth to Heaven."[3] "In an article entitled "René Daumal: Alchimie et chamanisme," Biès points out again, "The three stages of the alchemical process are also recognizable in the work of Daumal; especially the first as it is the most well-known. The *Nigredo* is illustrated by the sojourn in the counter-Jerusalem, the *Albedo* by the sun rise and sea voyage, the *Rubedo* by the ascent of Mount Analogue."[4]

But it is time to conclude. Here at the end of this work, it clearly appears that, because of his greater visibility as a painter, and even, as Reinaldo Arenas says, an artist aware "of the imbalance between our thirst for eternity and this ephemeral morsel of reality that we are,"* Jorge Camacho, who through his works, exhibitions, and publications is committed to the transmission of his art, appears, in spite of himself, as a kind of figurehead of the small group of these surrealist "alchemists," these seekers who saw in the Art of Music "a technique intended to make possible the *realization of a dream* stemming from humanity's oldest and most legitimate desire, that of the illumination of their consciousness."[5] Those seekers who, like their Master Canseliet, conformed, as Flamand reminds us, "to the magnificent and harsh precept decreed in the fifteenth century by Nicolas Valois: 'Patience is the ladder of the Philosophers and humility is the gate to their garden.'"[6]

Sharing with them—and Breton—the urge to find with the "philosopher's stone," the means to free the imagination once and for all and to restore its primacy over all the rest in a world that has been disfigured by the misdeeds of positivist reason and the excesses of a science that is more than ever lacking any conscience, the Cuban painter, that rebel for whom alchemy according to Marie-Dominique Massoni, another surrealist close to Alleau and Roger, is the "swing door of freedom," obviously thinks along with all his friends that the goal of the science of Hermes "is precisely to give body to the objects of the fundamental dream of human-ity, in other words to the true *Philosophers* to whom it has restored knowledge of the Word that guarantees, at the same time as victory over death, the awakening of consciousness that the Tradition also promises will characterize the true maturity of the human being."

---

*Invitation card to the February–March 1984 exhibition at the Jacqueline Storme Gallery in Lille.

In a word, for Camacho and his friends, the alchemical approach was never anything other than an absolute search for freedom, specifically to implement, as he did in his painting and in his life, that regenerative enthusiasm that makes it possible to oppose all the forces of death.

Of course, we cannot fail to say that in alchemy, as in other initiatory traditions, discretion is the rule, but it must be noted that Canseliet, Alleau, Roger, Camacho, Gruger, Baskine, and Flamand—as well as to a lesser extent, Audoin and Butor, for their own reasons, which are undoubtedly different, going beyond the "do and keep quiet" motto of *the chemical man*—have opened paths for the uninitiated, and have worked to transmit whatever they may possess of it. And Bernard Roger provides the reason very clearly on the last page of *Paris and Alchemy* when he says:

The legacy is still considerable. We would be fooling ourselves if we did not acknowledge the fact that it is shrinking every day. By pointing out its presence, wherever we find it, we may be helping to save it. In any case it's taking part in the transmission of essential elements of an ancient memory in which is shining an "orient"* without which humanity runs the risk of losing itself.

"To make" ποιειν, "to remove the thick veil from the intellect," as Elie-Charles Flamand says in *Attiser la rose cruciale*, to follow the paths of poetry, but simultaneously to "keep quiet," to observe "the most religious silence"—"because," as Audoin aptly reminds us, "the realization of the Stone would correspond from the spiritual point of view to a

---

*There is a pun here: "Orient" in French has three meanings. It can mean the East in geography. It can also mean the iridescence of a pearl. And finally, it's the part of the Masonic lodge where the Worshipful Master sits.

veritable initiation the arcana of which it would be inappropriate to place at the disposal of the uninitiated."*

However, and this will be the last word, left to those who know a little more than me but are undoubtedly reluctant to "throw the cursed bread to the birds"—even if, as Bernard Roger, Jorge Camacho, and Alain Gruger write in their tract "Nadja Betrayed," "it is undeniable that surrealism and alchemy haunt the same regions of the upper atmosphere," and even if "access to this *supreme point* targeted by surrealism and the acquisition of the Philosopher's Stone by an Adept both correspond to a total liberation of the mind"—"the analogy stops there." Even though "the *Sons of Science* have always given their 'philosopher's stone' the name of Absolute," "the final goal of surrealism is not that of alchemy, and the paths they follow are very different." This includes "psychic automatism, for example," but also that desire of André Breton's to liberate the individual by restoring his lost powers within the context of a new myth in the making, which has "nothing in common with the quest of the name of the 'primal material,'" which remains, as we have seen, "the spiritual adventure of each individual," ending with "the total integration of the Adept into the cosmos, or if you prefer mystical ecstasy,"[7] the "illumination," Flamand says, at the end of "the *internel*† voyage."[8]

---

*Philippe Audoin, *Bourges cité première*. "To my joy, say, do, keep quiet" is also one of Jacques Coeur's mottos, in whom Fucanelli saw a "proven Adept" possessing the "precious gift of the white stone." This should be compared to the last sentence in *The Mystery of the Cathedrals*: "In Science, in Goodness, the Adept must evermore KEEP SILENT" and to Canseliet's mention of "traditional discipline" in chapter six of *L'alchimie expliquée sur ses textes classiques*, which he would violate.

†As the adjective "internel" is rather rare, it is interesting to see that in the article published, at René Nelli's request in the "Lumière du Graal" issue of *Les Cahiers du Sud*, by Christian symbolist and author of the *Bestiaire du Christ*, Louis Charbonneau-Lassay, there is mention of a "little group" that is "absolutely orthodox Catholic [and] strictly secret" whose members were "totally unapproachable" called "L'étoile internelle" (The internal star). We are told by Frédérick Tristan that Charbonneau-Lassay was "one of the last members before the momentary dispersal of this society!" "Internel" (internelle) is a mixture of "inner" and "eternal."

And then the surrealists would have probably had the greatest difficulty sharing an idea like the one Magophon/Dujols, for example, stated in his "peroration," to use Canseliet's word, on the *Mutus Liber*: "Matter is one modality of the spirit at different stages!" But on the other hand, as Van Lennep tells us, Breton "recalling how Éliphas Lévi defined the Great Work as a 'conquest of the central point where the balancing force resides' wrote that 'the idea of Surrealism tends simply to the total recuperation of our psychic forces by a means which is no other than a vertiginous descent within ourselves,'" and thereby seeks "through this katabasis into the well of the universal unconscious . . . like the alchemist, the power to give life."

In this spirit, Breton's famous statement—"Everything tends to make us believe that there exists a certain point in the mind where life and death, the real and the imaginary, the past and the future, the communicable and the incommunicable, the high and the low, cease to be perceived as contradictions. Now, it would be futile to seek in surrealist activity any other motive than the hope of determining this point."—takes on additional meaning when reading these lines from Bernard Roger's text, "Le jour de l'étoile:

> Fountain whose water kills and restores life, we also call it the *mirror* in which, at midnight, in a deep and secret place, are reflected the two natures of the processed material at the same time as the two mental natures of the individual, one of which is in the habit of ceaselessly producing rational concepts that the other will silently plunge anew into the mother waters of the irrational for a new cycle. Thus the two faces of the single *reality*, called "real life" and "dream," are joined, which are only painfully perceived as contradictory because of the faulty position of the observer.

Finally, if Alleau states in his preface to *Aspects de l'alchimie traditionnelle* that "alchemical asceticism . . . testifies to the union of the matter and consciousness, as well as to the sovereign power of the freed mind," in "Hypnos and Thanatos" he is more talkative. "The purpose of alchemy," he says, "is higher than that of the transmutation of metals into gold or the restoration of youth to old men. It's the knowledge of Death and Resurrection, in all the material and spiritual worlds, all the earthly and heavenly worlds." In other words, "what's involved here are the Mysteries *par excellence*." "How not to accept the initiatory discipline of the secret," he goes on to say, that "in all times, in all places, absolutely forbids the casting of these pearls to the profane"!

"*Oculatis abis*"!

APPENDIX

DOCUMENTS OF
THE HERMES CIRCLE

The following pages contain several official documents of the discreet Hermes Circle. These letters and records name some of the key figures of the Hermes Circle, demonstrating that these individuals were active participants in the study of symbolism and Hermeticism. Translations of the text shown in the documents are also included.

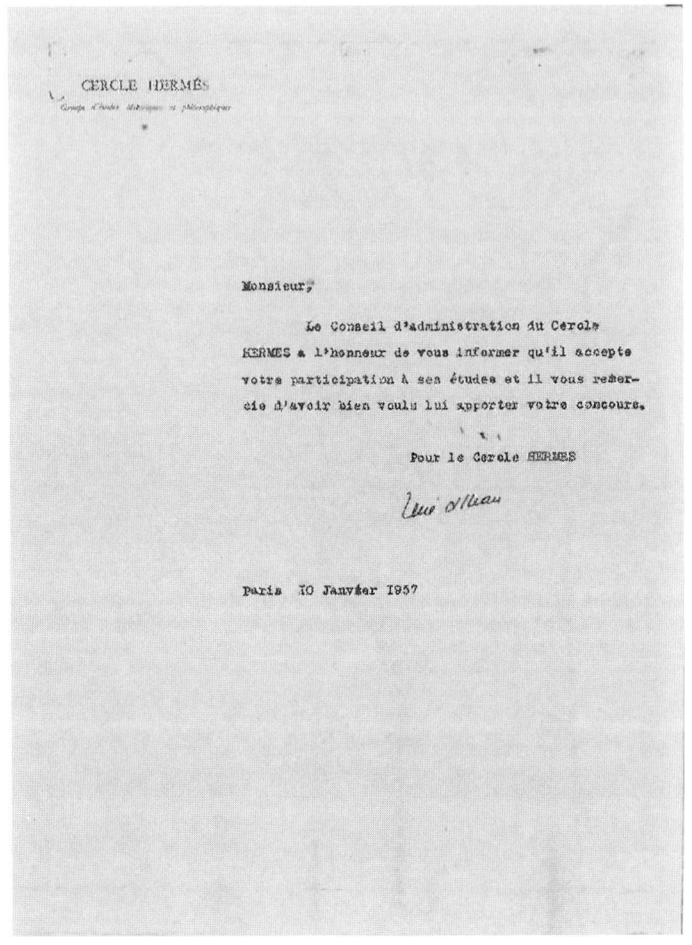

A letter of acceptance to the Hermes Circle.

Sir,

      The administrative board of the Hermes Circle has the honor of informing you that it accepts your participation in its studies and thanks you for having lent us your support.

For the Hermes Circle,

René Alleau

January 10, 1957

CERCLE HERMÉS

Groupe d'études ésotériques et philosophiques

COMPTE-RENDU DU CONSEIL D'ADMINISTRATION

ET DE LA REUNION

DU 20-12-1956

Membres du Conseil d'Administration

Présents :

MM.   ALLEAU

AMADOU

ANDRE

CANSELIET

d'YGE

HAFEZ

HUNWALD

RANQUE

Invités

MM.   BOUILLIER

DOUMAYROU

FLAMAND

MAUHEC

MICHELSON

ROGER

MISRACHI

de la CHESNERAYE

Minutes from the meeting of 12/20/1956 listing members of the Board of Directors and leaders of research groups of the Hermes Circle.
See the translation of the minutes on pages 296–97.

CERCLE HERMÉS
Groupe d'études historiques et philosophiques

Au nom du Cercle HERMÉS, son Président Monsieur
Eugène CANSELIET déclare ouverte la séance du Jeudi 20 Décembre 1956, remercie les personnalités présentes d'avoir
accepté de participer à la réunion; fixe le programme de la
réunion au cours de laquelle seront étudiées les questions
suivantes :

I°) Déclaration légale du Cercle HERMÉS en tant qu'association selon la loi de 1901.

2°) Définition des buts du Cercle HERMÉS, fixation de
son siège social et du lieu de ses réunions mensuelles.

3°) Examen de ses ressources financières et de ses
moyens d'action. Organisation des Cercles HERMÉS en province
et à l'étranger.

4°) Composition de son conseil d'administration et direction des groupes de recherches.

5°) Programme de travail des mois prochains et répartition des tâches à effectuer.

Ces diverses questions sont exposées par Monsieur
ALLEAU assisté du Vice président le Docteur HUNWALD.

Il a été décidé notamment que les groupes de recherches
seraient dirigés par :

Minutes from the meeting of 12/20/1956 listing members of the Board of Directors and leaders of research groups of the Hermes Circle (continued).

CERCLE HERMÉS

Groupe d'études ésotériques et philosophiques

✳

M. ALLEAU	La philosophie de l'hermétisme
M. AMADOU	La symbolique chrétienne
M. ANDRE	La documentation iconographique
M. CANSELIET	La symbolique hermétique
Melle DAVY	La philosophie du Moyen-Age
M. d'Ygé	La littérature Hermétique
M. ELIADE	L'histoire des religions
M. KAFEZ	La symbolique orientale
M. HUSWALD	L'histoire de l'hermétisme

———————

Minutes from the meeting of 12/20/1956 listing members of the Board of Directors and leaders of research groups of the Hermes Circle (continued).

MINUTES OF THE ADMINISTRATIVE BOARD AND MEETING OF DECEMBER 20, 1956

Members of the Administrative Board

Present:

Alleau

Amadou

André

Canseliet

D'Ygé

Hafez

Hunwald

Ranque

Guests

Bouiller

Doumayrou

Flamand

Maubec

Michelson

Roger

Misrachi

De la Chesneraye

In the name of the Hermes Circle, its president Eugène Canseliet, declares that the meeting of Thursday, December 20, 1956, is now open and he thanks the individuals present for having agreed to take part in the meeting; and sets forth the meeting's agenda in which the following matters shall be studied:

1) Legal statement of the Hermes Circle as a non-profit association in accordance with the law of 1901.
2) Definition of the goals of the Hermes Circle, and the establishment of its headquarters and the location of its monthly meetings.

3) Review of its financial resources and the means of action at its disposal. Organization of the Hermes Circle in France outside of Paris and abroad.

4) Composition of its administrative board and the leadership of its research groups.

5) Work program for the coming months and the division of its tasks it requires.

These various matters are presented by Mr. Alleau with the assistance of the vice-president, Dr. Hunwald.

It has been decided that the research groups will be headed by:

Mr. Alleau	The Philosophy of Hermeticism
Mr. Amadou	Christian Symbology
Mr. André	Iconographical Documentation
Mr. Canseliet	Hermetic Symbology
Miss Davy	Medieval Philosophy
Mr. d'Ygé	Hermetic Literature
Mr. Eliade	The History of Religions
Mr. Hafez	Eastern Symbology
Mr. Hunwald	The History of Hermeticism

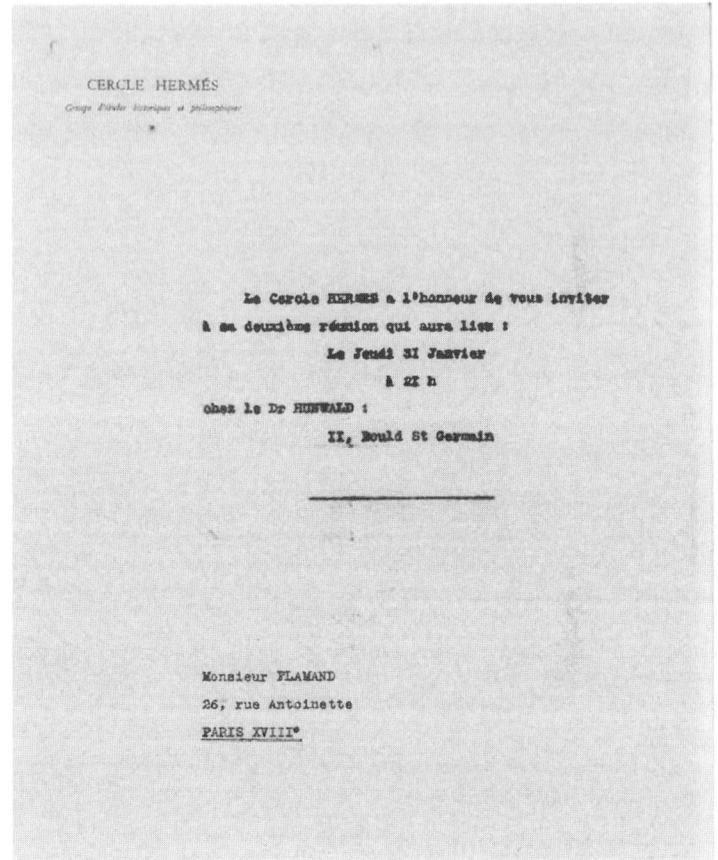

An invitation to the second Hermes Circle meeting.

        It is the honor of the Hermes Circle to invite you to
its second meeting which will take place:

                        Thursday, January 31
                          At 9:00 PM

At the home of Dr. Hunwald,

                11 Boulevard Saint-Germain

Mr. Flamand
26, rue Antoinette
Paris XVIIIe

C O M P T E   R E N D U

de la

Réunion du 31 Janvier 1957

—————

La deuxième réunion du cercle Hermès a eu lieu le 31 Janvier sous la direction du Docteur HUNWALD, vice-Président du cercle.

Au cours de cette séance, des exposés ont été faits par Messieurs ALLEAU, AMADOU, ANDRE, BOUILLIER, FLAMAND, ROGER.

Monsieur ALLEAU s'est attaché à souligner l'importance d'une méthodologie nouvelle, mieux appropriée à l'étude des symboles. Il a insisté sur les différences fondamentales existant entre les "synthèmes" et les symboles et il a montré tout l'intérêt que présenterait la "synthématique" pour l'étude des signes et de la communication en général.

Messieurs AMADOU et BOUILLIER ont exposé l'interprétation de Notre Dame de Paris par la littérature contemporaine et ils ont indiqué les traces décelables de son symbolisme, en particulier dans la "cathédrale" d'Huysmans et dans "Notre Dame de Paris" de Hugo.

Messieurs ANDRE, FLAMAND et ROGER ont présenté la première partie d'une étude iconographique de Notre Dame de Paris.

Après un aperçu d'ensemble au point de vue historique et architectural, ils se sont efforcés de dé-

Minutes of the January 31, 1957, meeting of the Hermes Circle and program for the following meeting. See the translation of the minutes on page 301.

gager l'aspect original de l'Oeuvre d'art avant ses res-
taurations.

Ils ont également établi un parallèle entre
les interprétations des sculptures des portails se réfé-
rant à Viollet-le-Duc, de Guilhermy, Queyron et l'interprétation hermétique notamment celle de Fulcanelli dans
"Le mystère des Cathédrales".

Une série de reproductions photographiques
comportant d'anciennes estampes et documents ayant trait
à la Basilique a été également présentée.

Après ces exposés, une discussion générale a
eu lieu.

*Minutes of the January 31, 1957, meeting of the Hermes Circle and program
for the following meeting (continued).*

MINUTES OF THE MEETING OF JANUARY 31, 1957

The second meeting of the Circle of Hermes took place on January 31, under the supervision of Dr. Hunwald, vice-president of the circle.

During this meetings, presentations were given by Alleau, Amadou, André, Bouillier, Flamand, Roger.

Alleau has devoted himself to emphasizing the importance of a new methodology better suited to the study of symbols. He insisted on the fundamental differences between "systems" and symbols and demonstrated the value of "synthematics" for the study of signs and communication in general.

Amadou and Bouillier presented the interpretation of Notre-Dame de Paris by contemporary literature and they pointed out the detectable traces of its symbolism, particularly in Huysman's *The Cathedral* and in Victor Hugo's *Hunchback of Notre-Dame.*

André, Flamand, and Roger presented the first part of an iconographical study of Notre-Dame de Paris.

After providing an overview from a historical and architectural perspective, they endeavored to reveal the original appearance of the monument prior to its restoration.

They also established a parallel between the interpretations of the sculptures on the portals referring to Viollet-le-Duc, Guilhermy, and Quayron, as well as its hermetic interpretation, mainly that of Fulcanelli in his Mystery of the Cathedrals.

A series of photographic reproductions featuring old prints and documents relating to the Basilica was also presented.

A general discussion followed these presentations.

PROGRAMME
de la
PROCHAINE REUNION

―――――

Au cours de la prochaine réunion qui aura lieu,
sous le Présidence de
Monsieur Eugène CANSELIET,
le Jeudi 21 Mars à 21 Heures chez le

Docteur HUNWALD
11, Boulevard Saint-Germain

les sujets suivants seront étudiés :

1° - Iconographie de Notre Dame (suite)

- rapport de la rose centrale avec les figurines
du portail,
par Messieurs ANDRE, FLAMAND, ROGER.

2° - La Cathédrale. Son importance dans la vie sociale,
sa valeur symbolique.

Discussion générale.

―――――

*Minutes of the January 31, 1957, meeting of the Hermes Circle and program
for the following meeting (continued).*

PROGRAM OF THE NEXT MEETING

During the next meeting, which will take place under the
direction of

Mr. Eugène Canseliet
On Thursday March 21 at 9:00 PM
At the home of Dr. Hunwald,
11 Boulevard Saint-Germain

The following subjects will be studied:
1) Iconography of Notre-Dame (continuation) By André,
   Flamand, Roger
2) The Cathedral. Its importance in social life, its symbolic value.

General Discussion.

CERCLE HERMÈS

Groupe d'études historiques et philosophiques

PROGRAMME DE LA RÉUNION DU 16 MAI 1957

———————————

Au cours de cette réunion qui aura lieu à

21 heures chez le Dr HUNWALD

11 Bd St Germain

les sujets suivants seront étudiés :

I°) Conclusion des recherches iconographiques sur Notre-Dame.

II°) La philosophie hermétique et le symbolique de la Vierge.

III°) Programme des prochaines recherches.

Discussion générale.

———————————

Program of the meeting of May 16, 1957.

PROGRAM OF THE MEETING OF MAY 16, 1957

During the next meeting, which will take place at 9:00 PM
At the home of Dr. Hunwald,
11 Boulevard Saint-Germain

The following subjects will be studied:
1) Conclusion of the iconographical study of Notre-Dame
2) The hermetic philosophy and symbology of the Virgin
3) Upcoming research agenda

General Discussion.

Notes

INTRODUCTION

1. Rolland de Renéville, *Sciences maudites & poètes maudits*.
2. Rolland de Renéville, *Univers de la parole*.
3. Patrick Krémer, preface to *Sciences maudites*, by Andrè Rolland de Renéville.
4. Roger, *A la découverte de l'alchimie*.
5. Biès, *Les alchimistes*.
6. Camacho, *Le mythe d'Isis et d'Osiris et sa relation avec le symbolisme hermétique*.
7. Henri Hunwald, "Origines et destinées de la médecine hermétique, L'héritage de Paracelse," in *L'alchimie*, by E. J. Holmyard.
8. Roger, *Paris et l'alchimie*.
9. Van Lennep, *Art et alchimie*.
10. Roger, *A la découverte de l'alchimie*.
11. Flamand, *Les méandres du sens*.
12. Cited in Remy, *Au treizième coup de minuit*.
13. Flamand, *Les méandres du sens*.
14. Alleau, *Aspects de l'alchimie traditionnelle*, with preface by Eugène Canseliet.
15. Alleau, *Aspects de l'alchimie traditionnelle*, with preface by Eugène Canseliet.
16. Bédouin, *Vingt ans de surréalisme* (italics in original).
17. Flamand, *Les méandres du sens*.
18. Alleau, "Hypnos et thanatos ou le philosophe dans le paysage."
19. Silbermann, *Le saumon, la cerise et le gardien du trait, texte sur l'art*.
20. Crasselame, *La lumière sortant par soi-même des ténèbres*.
21. Canseliet, *Alchimie*.

I. SURREALISM AND ESOTERICISM

1. Caron and Hutin, *Les alchimistes*.
2. Eugène Canseliet, introduction to *Les douze clefs de la philosophie*, by Basil Valentine.
3. Eliade, *Le mythe de l'alchimie*.
4. Fulcanelli, *The Mystery of the Cathedrals*, cited in Roger, "Le jour de l'étoile" (Fulcanelli's italics).
5. Joubert, *Pour le grand surréalisme*.
6. Carrouges, *André Breton et les données fondamentales du surréalisme*.
7. Roger, introduction to *De la nature des métaux*, by Basil Valentine.
8. Alleau, foreword to *Le livre des figures hiéroglyphiques*, by Nicolas Flamel.
9. Van Lennep, "L'art alchimique et le surréel."
10. Flamand, *Les méandres du sens*.
11. Cited in Löwy, *La comète incandescente*.
12. Lepetit, *The Esoteric Secrets of Surrealism*.
13. Kober, "Dans le verger de la salamandre."
14. Roger, *A la découverte de l'alchimie*.
15. Bédouin, *Vingt ans de surréalisme*.
16. Van Lennep, "L'art alchimique et le surréel."
17. Dumas-Pux, "Eros Khalos: Le bel amour."
18. Bachelard, *La formation de l'esprit scientifique*.
19. Backès-Clément and Pingaud, "Le dernier alchimiste."
20. Bachelard, *Le nouvel esprit scientifique*.
21. Mabille, "Contribution à une psychanalyse de la connaissance objective par Gaston Bachelard."

2. SURREALISM AND ALCHEMY

1. Schwaller de Lubicz, *Notes et propos inédits*.
2. Seligmann, *The Mirror of Magic*.
3. Alleau, *Aspects de l'alchimie traditionnelle*.
4. d'Ygé, *Nouvelle assemblée des philosophes chymiques*.
5. Sadoul, *Le trésor des alchimistes* (italics and capitalization in original).
6. Alleau, foreword to *Le livre des figures hiéroglyphiques*, by Nicolas Flamel.
7. Alleau, *Aspects de l'alchimie traditionnelle* (capitalization in original).
8. Bounoure, "Préface à un traité des matrices."

9. Roger, *Paris et l'alchimie.*

10. Audoin, *Bourges cité première* (italics in original).

11. Audoin, *Les capucines aux lèvres d'émail.*

12. Audoin, "La fontaine de fortune."

13. Roger, *Paris et l'alchimie*, citing the words of Fulcanelli in *The Dwellings of the Philosophers.*

14. Roger, *Les demeures de l'invisible.*

15. Artaud, *Le théâtre et son Double.*

16. Chailly, *Héliogabale ou l'alchimiste couronné.*

17. Béroalde de Verville, *Le Voyage des Princes Fortunés.*

18. Flamand, *Érotique de l'alchimie.*

19. Nadeau, "Le surréalisme et la loge maçonnique Thebah."

20. Roger, *Paris et l'alchimie.*

21. Van Lennep, "L'art alchimique et le surréel."

22. Canseliet, "A propos de A un oiseau de houille perché sur la plus haute branche de feu, d'Elie-Charles Flamand."

23. Van Lennep, *Art et alchimie.*

3. EUGÈNE CANSELIET, F.C.H.

1. Van Lennep, *Une pierre en tête.*

2. Bernard Roger, preface to *The Esoteric Secrets of Surrealism*, by Patrick Lepetit.

3. Gérardin, "En souvenir."

4. Preface to Chauvière, *Mémoires d'un alchimiste contemporain.*

5. Rivière, "*Philosophus per ignem*: Philosophe par le feu."

6. Amadou, *Le feu du soleil.*

7. Renaud de la Faverie, "Souvenirs d'Eugène Canseliet."

8. Glasser, "Souvenirs du bon Maître de Savignies."

9. Roger and Camacho, *La cathédrale de Séville.*

10. Canseliet, "Philosophie universelle et spirituelle filiation," in *L'Alchimie*, by E. J. Holmyard.

11. Canseliet, "Hermétiques rudiments d'héraldique."

12. Canseliet, *Trois anciens traités de l'alchimie.*

4. KALEIDOSCOPIC JOURNEYS

1. Khaitzine, *La langue des oiseaux*, vol. 3.

2. Roger, *Paris et l'alchimie*.

3. René Alleau, "Alchimie et cryptographie," in *L'alchimie*, by E. J. Holmyard.

4. Follet, "Préface, les romans de *La défense de l'infini*."

5. Khaitzine, *La langue des oiseaux,* vol. 2.

6. Lorrey, *Stances, sonnets et chansons*.

7. Roger and Camacho, *La cathédrale de Séville*.

8. Canseliet, *Alchimie*.

9. Roger, *Paris et l'alchimie* (italics in original).

10. Roger and Camacho, *La cathédrale de Séville*.

11. Charpentier, *La France des lieux et des demeures alchimiques*.

12. Rivière and Varenne, *La fascinante histoire des maîtres de l'alchimie*.

13. Canseliet, "Mithriaque alchimique," cited by Simonelli, "À la lueur de l'ourse."

14. Canseliet, "Mithriaque alchimique."

15. Fulcanelli, *The Mystery of the Cathedrals* (Fulcanelli's italics and capitalization).

5. ANDRÉ BRETON, ALCHEMIST?

1. Van Lennep, "L'art alchimique et le surréel."

2. Danier, *L'Hermétisme alchimique chez André Breton*.

3. Beaujour, "André Breton ou la transparence," noted by René Alleau.

4. Lamy, *André Breton, Hermétisme et poésie dans Arcane 17*.

5. Breton, "Présentation pour l'ouverture de la galerie *À l'étoile scellée*," in *Œuvres complètes*, vol. 3.

6. Mabin, "La galerie à l'étoile scellée."

7. Flamand, *La tour Saint-Jacques*.

8. Breton, *Position politique du surréalisme*, in *Œuvres complètes*, vol. 2.

9. Rivière, *Soleil noir et main de Feu*.

10. Larguier, *Le faiseur d'or, Nicolas Flamel*.

11. Flamand, *La tour Saint-Jacques*.

12. Fulcanelli, *The Mystery of the Cathedrals*.

13. Rivière, *Soleil noir et main de feu* (italics are Rivière's).

14. Fulcanelli, *The Dwellings of the Philosophers*.

15. Mabille, *Le miroir du merveilleux*.

16. Desnos, "Le mystère d'Abraham juif."

17. Van Lennep, *Art et alchimie*.

18. Etienne-Alain Hubert in Breton, *Œuvres complètes*, vol. 3.

19. Danier, *L'Hermétisme alchimique chez André Breton*.

20. Marie-Claire Dumas in Breton, *Œuvres complètes*, vol. 3.

21. Alleau, *La messe des fous* preceded by *Notes sur la poésie et l'initiation*.

22. Flamand, *Les méandres du sens*.

23. Roger, *Paris et l'alchimie*.

24. Roger and Camacho, *La cathédrale de Séville*.

25. Roger, "Le jour de l'étoile."

26. Cited by Etienne-Alain Hubert in Breton, *Œuvres complètes,* vol. 4.

27. Alleau, *Énigmes et symboles du Mont Saint-Michel*.

28. Roger, "Le jour de l'étoile."

29. Marie-Claire Dumas in Breton, *Œuvres complètes,* vol. 3.

30. Rivière, *Soleil noir et main de feu*.

31. Danier, "André Breton et l'hermétisme alchimique."

32. Danier, "André Breton et l'hermétisme alchimique."

33. Joubert, *Pour le grand surréalisme*.

34. Geyraud, *L'occultisme à Paris*.

35. Alleau, "Au périscope du temps."

36. Nadeau, *L'arche utopique*.

37. Roger, *A la découverte de l'alchimie*.

38. Flahutez, "Quatre questions à René Alleau."

6. RENÉ ALLEAU, FULCANELLI'S *OTHER* DISCIPLE?

1. Béhar, *Dictionnaire André Breton*.

2. Bédouin, *Vingt ans de surréalisme*.

3. Alleau, *De la nature des symboles*.

4. Alleau, "Tradition et invention."

5. Flamand, *Les méandres du sens* (capitalization in original).

6. Alleau, *Aspects de l'alchimie traditionnelle*.

7. Alleau, "Tradition et invention."

8. Alleau, foreword to *Le livre des figures hiéroglyphiques*, by Nicolas Flamel.

9. See Alleau, "Tradition et invention."

10. Cited by Dumas, "Note sur André Breton et la pensée traditionnelle."

11. Bucherie, *René Alleau et l'écriture philosophale*.

12. Genesis 3:24 (footnote in the original).

13. Tristan, *L'obsédante*.

14. Alleau, "Gradiva Rediviva" (italics are Alleau's).

15. Tristan, "René Alleau: Étoile scellée."

7. THE MYSTERIOUS DOCTOR HUNWALD AND THE HERMES CIRCLE

1. Butor, *Portrait de l'artiste en jeune singe*.

2. Canseliet, *Alchimie*.

3. Von Bernus, *Alchimie et médecine*.

4. Vulliaud, *La fin du monde*.

5. Editor's note, Holmyard, *L'alchimie*.

6. Fulcanelli, *The Mystery of the Cathedrals*.

8. ART AND ALCHEMY

1. Roger, *A la découverte de L'Alchimie* (my italics).

2. Van Lennep, *Art et alchimie*.

3. Klossowski de Rola, *Alchimie: Florilège de l'art secret*.

4. Van Lennep, *Art et alchimie*.

5. Bucherie, *René Alleau et l'écriture philosophale*.

6. Bernard Roger, introduction to *La lumière sortant par soi-même des ténèbres*, by Marc-Antonio Crassellame.

7. Van Lennep, *Art et alchimie*.

8. Murphy, "Alchimie des philosophes."

9. Van Lennep, *Une pierre en tête*.

10. Van Lennep, "Jacques Lacomblez."

11. Remy, "L'œuvre de Perahim ou l'athanor du merveilleux."

12. Lebel, *Marcel Duchamp. Von der Erscheinung zur Konzeption*.

13. Choucha, *Surrealism and the Occult*.

14. Tronche, "Une morphologie totémique de l'invisible."

15. Quoted in Moreau, *Joseph Sima*.

16. Völlnagel, *Alchimie, l'art royal*.

17. Simon, "Jorge Camacho, celui qui rencontre."

9. THE PARIS OF BERNARD ROGER

1. Roger, "Esquisse pour une salle de cinéma au fond d'un lac."
2. Also Nadeau, *L'arche utopique.*
3. Lévi, *Dogme et rituel de haute magie.*
4. Solis, *Rituel des grades alchimiques du baron Tschoudy.*
5. Cited earlier by Canseliet, *Deux logis alchimiques.*
6. Roger and Camacho, *La cathédrale de Séville.*
7. Roger, *Paris et l'alchimie.*

10. BERNARD ROGER AND THE LADY OF THE WORK

1. Charpentier, *La France des lieux et des demeures alchimiques.*
2. Eliade, *Le mythe de l'alchimie.*
3. Bernard Roger, introduction to *La lumière sortant par soi-même des ténèbres,* by Marc-Antonio Crasselame.
4. Bernard Roger, introduction to *La lumière sortant par soi-même des ténèbres,* by Marc-Antonio Crasselame.
5. Roger, "De la dame de l'œuvre."
6. Canseliet, *Deux logis alchimiques.*

11. JORGE CAMACHO AND ALAIN GRUGER, SURREALISTS AND OPERATIVES

1. Alleau, "Hypnos et thanatos ou le philosophe dans le paysage."
2. Tronche, *Jorge Camacho: Vue imprenable.*
3. Simon, "Jorge Camacho, celui qui rencontre."
4. Breton, "Brousse au-devant de Camacho."
5. Caradeau, *Le matin des alchimistes.*
6. Flamand, *La tour Saint-Jacques.*
7. Fulcanelli in *The Mystery of the Cathedrals,* quoted by Flamand, *La tour Saint-Jacques.*
8. Albarracin, "Comment Jorge Camacho a écrit un certain *HARR.*"
9. Albarracin, "Comment Jorge Camacho a écrit un certain *HARR.*"
10. Richardson, *International Encyclopedia of Surrealism.*
11. See Davy, *L'homme intérieur et ses métamorphoses.*

12. Camacho, *Le mythe d'Isis et d'Osiris et sa relation avec le symbolisme hermétique*.

13. Durozoi, "Les deux tours."

14. Joubert, "A la découverte de Torgia."

15. Angelini, "L'art cosmique de Jorge Camacho."

16. Waelti-Walters, *Alchimie et Littérature*.

17. Butor, "L'alchimie et son langage."

18. Doumayrou, "Surréalisme, ésotérisme."

19. Roger, *A la découverte de l'alchimie*.

20. Roger, *A la découverte de l'alchimie*.

21. Alleau, "Hypnos et thanatos ou le philosophe dans le paysage."

12. THE OPEN BOOKS OF THE ARTISTS

1. Alleau, "Hypnos et thanatos ou le philosophe dans le paysage."

2. Camacho, Roger, and Parent, *Le hibou philosophe*.

3. Völlnagel, *Alchimie, l'art royal*.

4. Camacho, *Le mythe d'Isis et d'Osiris et sa relation avec le symbolisme hermétique*.

5. Völlnagel, *Alchimie, l'art royal*.

6. Flamand, *La tour Saint-Jacques*.

7. Khaitzine, *Secrets d'alcôves*.

13. THE NEW ALCHEMICAL HERALDRY

1. Roger, introduction to *De la nature des métaux*.

2. Flahutez and Dufrêne, *Art et mythe*.

3. Flamand, *Les méandres du sens*.

4. Canseliet, "Hermétiques rudiments d'héraldique."

5. Canseliet, introduction to preface of *Mutus Liber*, citing *L'œuvre secret de la philosophie hermétique*, Canon XII.

6. Khaitzine, *Secrets d'alcôves*.

7. Roger and Camacho, *La cathédrale de Séville*.

8. Audoin, *Bourges cité première*.

9. Béatrice, "Essai sur les origines alchimiques de blason."

10. Flamand, *La tour Saint-Jacques*.

14. MAURICE BASKINE, FANTASOPHER

1. Ruhaud, "Maurice Baskine (1901–1968)."
2. Alexandrian, *L'érotisme en alchimie.*
3. Aimé Patri, "Apologie" in *Maurice Baskine (1901–1968) Rétrospective.*
4. Monique Escat, in *Maurice Baskine: Peintre, sculpteur, alchimiste.*
5. Alleau, *Aspects de l'alchimie traditionnelle.*
6. Flamand, *La tour Saint-Jacques.*
7. Jonin, "Soeur Âme, ne vois-tu rien venir?"
8. Van Lennep, "L'art alchimique et le surréel."
9. Van Lennep, "L'art alchimique et le surréel."
10. Van Lennep, *Une pierre en tête.*

15. ELIE-CHARLES FLAMAND

1. Biro and Passeron, *Dictionnaire général du surréalisme et de ses environs.*
2. Passelergue, "Elie-Charles Flamand."
3. Kober, "Caresser avec amour les pétales de l'univers."
4. Flamand, *Les méandres du Sens.*
5. Flamand, "Interview by Isabelle Roche," lelitteraire (website, no longer available), June 20, 2006, and reprinted in *Propos mosaïqué.*
6. Khaitzine, *La langue des oiseaux,* vol. 3.
7. Flamand, *Les méandres du sens* (italics in original).
8. Sanda, "Érotisme alchimique, alchimie symbolique."
9. Marc Kober, "Le trésor d'Elie-Charles Flamand," afterword to *Braise de l'unité,* by Elie-Charles Flamand.
10. Starck, "Sur l'œuvre d'Elie-Charles Flamand."
11. Favre, "Alchimie et poésie dans l'œuvre d'Elie-Charles Flamand."
12. Lagrange, "Entrée du médium."
13. Béatrice, "Essai sur les origines alchimiques de blason."
14. Lagrange, "Entrée du médium."
15. Flamand, *Propos mosaïqué* (capitalization is Flamand's).
16. Rabourdin, "Elie-Charles Flamand."
17. Canseliet, review of *La lune feuillée.*
18. Kober, "Caresser avec amour les pétales de l'univers."

16. ELIE-CHARLES FLAMAND IN THE STEPS OF THE DAUGHTER OF THE SUN

1. Flamand, "Interview by Isabelle Roche," lelitteraire (website, no longer available), June 20, 2006, and reprinted in *Propos mosaïqué*.
2. Fulcanelli.
3. Flamand, *Les méandres du sens*.
4. Audoin, *Bourges cité première*.
5. Khaitzine, *Secrets d'alcôves*.
6. Flamand, *Les méandres du sens*.
7. Kamala-Jnana, *Dictionnaire de philosophie alchimique*.
8. Flamand, *Érotique de l'alchimie*.
9. *Le trépied d'Or ou trois traités chymiques très choisis*.
10. Canseliet, *Trois anciens traités d'alchimie* (italics and capitalization are Canseliet's, underlining is mine).

17. ITHELL COLQUHOUN AND THE GOOSE OF HERMOGENES

1. Canseliet, *Trois anciens traités d'alchimie*.
2. Remy, *On the Thirteenth Stroke of Midnight*.
3. Ratcliffe, *Ithell Colquhoun*.
4. Colquhoun, *The Goose of Hermogenes*.
5. Hale, *The Supersensual Life of Ithell Colquhoun*.
6. Shillitoe, *Ithell Colquhoun*.
7. Hale, *The Supersensual Life of Ithell Colquhoun*.
8. Shillitoe, *Ithell Colquhoun*.
9. Bounoure, "Préface à un traité des matrices."

CONCLUSION

1. Audoin, *Maurice Fourré, rêveur définitif*.
2. Simonelli, "A la recherche de Fol-Yver."
3. Biès, *René Daumal*. See also, Biès, *Les alchimistes*.

4. Biès, "René Daumal: Alchimie et chamanisme."

5. Roger, *Paris et l'alchimie.*

6. Flamand, *Les méandres du sens.*

7. Van Lennep, "L'art alchimique et le surréel."

8. Van Lennep, "Art et alchimie," in *L'Alchimie* by E. J. Holmyard.

BIBLIOGRAPHY

Aelberts, Alain-Valery, and Auquier Jean-Jacques. *Poètes singuliers du surréalisme et autres lieux*. Paris: UGE, "10/18," 1971.

Alain Gruger. Exhibition pamphlet. Galerie Sophie Scheidecker, Paris. December 11, 2019, to February 22, 2020.

Albach, Hester. *Léona, héroïne du surréalisme*. Arles: Actes Sud, 2009.

Albarracin, Laurent. "Comment Jorge Camacho a écrit un certain *HARR* (*Hommage à Raymond Roussel*)." *Europe*, no. 1104. April 2021.

Alexandrian, Sarane. *L'érotisme en alchimie*. Cordes-sur-ciel: Editions Rafael de Surtis, 2019.

———. *Histoire de la philosophie occulte*. Paris: Seghers, 1983.

Alleau, René. *Alchimie*. Paris: Editions Allia, 2008. Reprint of article published in *Encyclopaedia universalis*, 1968.

———. *Aspects de l'alchimie traditionnelle*. Paris: Editions de Minuit, 1953.

———. *Enigmes et symboles du Mont Saint-Michel*. Paris: Julliard, 1970.

———. Foreword to *Le livre des figures hiéroglyphiques*, by Nicolas Flamel. Paris: Denoël, Bibliotheca Hermetica, 1972.

———. "Gradiva rediviva." *Le surréalisme même*, no. 1 (1956). Reprint by Gajan: Venus d'ailleurs, n.d.

———. "Hypnos et Thanatos ou le philosophe dans le paysage." In *Jorge Camacho: La danse de la mort*. Exhibition catalog. Galerie de Seine, Paris. November 18–December 18, 1976.

———. "Marx et Guénon." *René Guénon, Les cahiers de l'Herne*, no. 45 (1985). Reprint by Gajan: Venus d'Ailleurs, 2022.

———. *La messe des fous* preceded by *Notes sur la poésie et l'initiation*. Reprint by Gajan: Venus d'Ailleurs, 2022.

———. "Le mystérieux livre d'heures du rêve d'Elisa." In *André Breton, la beauté convulsive*, by Musée national d'art moderne. Paris: Centre Georges Pompidou, 1991. Reprint by Gajan: Venus d'Ailleurs, 2022.

———. *De la nature des symboles*. Paris: Flammarion, 1958.

———. "Au périscope du temps." In *André Breton en perspective cavalière*, by Marie-Claire Dumas. Paris: Gallimard, Les Cahiers de la N.R.F., 1996.

———. "Psychanalyse et alchimie." *Médium*, no. 3. 1954.

———. *La science des symboles*. Paris: Payot, 1982. Translated into English as *The Primal Force in Symbol*, by Ariel Godwin. Rochester, VT: Inner Traditions, 2009.

———. "Tradition et invention." In *Aspects et fonctions du symbolisme dans l'archéologie traditionnelle et dans l'histoire des sciences*. Vincennes: Les Études Atlantéennes, 1973.

Alquié, Ferdinand, ed. *Le surréalisme*. Paris-La Haye: Mouton, 1968.

Amadou, Robert. *Le feu du soleil*. Paris: Jean-Jacques Pauvert, 1978.

Angelini, Surpik. "L'art cosmique de Jorge Camacho." In Jorge Camacho, *Bocetos* [Sketches]. No date, no publisher. Published by Marguerite Camacho.

Artaud, Antonin. *Le théâtre et son double*. Paris: Gallimard, 1938. Translated into English as *The Theater and Its Double*, by Mary Caroline Richards. New York: Grove Press, 1994.

Artero, Julien. *Champagne, apôtre de la science hermétique*. Grenoble: Le Mercure Dauphinois, 2014.

Assouline, Pierre. *Le dernier des Camondo*. Paris: Gallimard, 1997.

Audoin, Philippe. *Bourges cité première*. Paris: Julliard, 1972.

———. *Les capucines aux lèvres d'émail*. Caen: Le Grand Tamanoir, 2019.

———. "La Fontaine de fortune." In *1968, année surréaliste, Cuba, Prague, Paris*, by Jérôme Duwa. Edited by IMEC. Caen: Collection Pièces d'archives, 2008.

———. *Maurice Fourré, rêveur définitif, suivi de Le caméléon mystique*. Paris: Soleil Noir, 1978.

Bachelard, Gaston. *La formation de l'esprit scientifique*. Paris: P.U.F., 1938. Translated into English as *The Formation of the Scientific Mind: A Contribution to a Psychoanalysis of Objective Knowledge*, by Mary McAllester Jones. Manchester, UK: Clinamen, 2006.

——. *Le nouvel esprit scientifique*. Paris: P.U.F, 1941.

Backès-Clément, Catherine, and Bernard Pingaud. "Le dernier alchimiste." *L'Arc* 42 (1970): 1–3.

Béatrice, Guy. "Essai sur les origines alchimiques du blason." *Atlantis*, no. 281. Paris, January–February 1975.

Beaujour, Michel. "André Breton ou la transparence." Postface to *André Breton: Arcane 17*. Paris: Collection 10/18, 1965.

Bédouin, Jean-Louis. *Vingt ans de surréalisme*. Paris: Denoël, 1961.

Béhar, Henri, ed. *Dictionnaire André Breton*. Paris: Classiques Garnier, 2012.

——. "D'un poème-objet." Preface to *André Breton: Arcane 17, le manuscrit original*. Paris: Gallimard, 2008.

Benayoun, Robert, dir. *René Alleau, l'ésotérisme et Breton*. Bibliothèque de Poche, INA/ORTF, April 19, 1970.

Béroalde de Verville, François. *Le voyage des princes fortunés*. Edited and prefaced by Georges Bourgueil. Albi: Les Éditions Passage du Nord/Ouest, 2005.

Biès, Jean. *Les alchimistes*. Paris: Éditions du Félin/Philippe Lebeau, 2000.

——. *René Daumal*. Paris: Seghers, Poètes d'aujourd'hui, 1973.

——. "René Daumal: Alchimie et chamanisme." In *René Daumal*. Lausanne: L'Âge d'Homme, Les Dossiers H, 1993.

Biro, Adam, and René Passeron. *Dictionnaire général du surréalisme et de ses environs*. Paris: P.U.F., 1982.

Bouhier, Marie-Louise. "Bachelard et le surréalisme." In *Le surréalisme*, edited by Ferdinand Alquié. Paris-La Haye: Mouton, 1968.

Bounoure, Vincent. "Préface à un traité des matrices." *Le surréalisme même*, no. 4. Spring 1958. Reprinted in *Moments du surréalisme*. Paris: L'Harmattan, 1999.

Boustani, Claire. "Entretien avec Alain Joubert." In *Art et mythe*, edited by Fabrice Flahutez and Thierry Dufrêne. Nanterre: Presses universitaires de Paris Ouest, 2011.

Breton, André. "Brousse au-devant de Camacho." In *Le surréalisme et la peinture*. Paris: Gallimard, 1965. Reprinted in *Œuvres complètes*, vol. 4. Paris: Gallimard, 2008.

——. *Œuvres complètes*. 4 vols. Paris: Gallimard, 1998–2008.

Bucherie, Gilles. *René Alleau et l'écriture philosophale*. Saint-Gervais: Selena Editions, 2022.

Butor, Michel. "L'alchimie et son langage." In *Répertoire I*. Paris: Éditions de Minuit, 1960.

———. *Portrait de l'artiste en jeune singe*. Paris: Gallimard, 1967. Translated into English as *Portrait of the Artist as a Young Ape*, by Dominic Di Bernardi. Dallas: Dalkey Archive Press, 1995.

Camacho, Jorge [Ohcamac, pseud.]. *L'arbre acide*. Paris: Éditions Surréalistes, 1968.

———. *Hantise de la virginité*. Rouen: L'Instant perpétuel, April 2011.

———. *Le mythe d'Isis et d'Osiris et sa relation avec le symbolisme hermétique*. Paris: La Table d'Émeraude, 1995.

———. "Repères biographiques." In *Jorge Camacho, le miroir aux mirages*. Paris: Somogy/Maison de l'Amérique Latine, 2003.

———. *Semen contra suivi de HARR*. Nérac: Pierre Mainard, 2019.

Camacho, Jorge, and Alain Gruger. *Héraldique alchimique nouvelle*. Paris: Le Soleil Noir, 1978.

Camacho, Jorge, Bernard Roger, and Mimi Parent. *Le hibou philosophe*. Brussels: La Pierre d'Alun, 1991.

Canseliet, Eugène. *L'alchimie expliquée sur ses textes classiques*. France: Pauvert, 1972

———. *Alchimie: Nouvelles études diverses sur les portraits alchimiques*. Paris: Guy Trédaniel, 2014.

———. *Deux logis alchimiques*. Paris: Jean Schemit, 1945.

———. "Hermétiques rudiments d'héraldique." *Atlantis*, no. 281. Paris, January–February 1975.

———. *L'hermétisme dans la vie de Swift et dans ses voyages*. Saint-Clément-de-Rivière: Fata Morgana, 1983.

———. Introduction to *Mutus Liber*, by Isaac Baulot. Paris: Gutenberg reprints, 1996.

———. "Mithriaque alchimique." *Atlantis*, no. 286. Paris, January–February 1976.

———. "A propos de A un oiseau de houille perché sur la plus haute branche de feu, d'Elie-Charles Flamand." In *Les cahiers de la tour Saint-Jacques*. Paris, 1962.

———. Review of *La lune feuillée* by E. C. Flamand (Paris: Belfond, 1969). *Atlantis*, no. 249. Paris, 1969.

———. *Trois anciens traités d'alchimie*. Paris: Jean-Jacques Pauvert, 1975.

Caradeau, Jean-Luc. *Le matin des alchimistes*. Paris: Trajectoire, 2002.

Carletto, Jacques. "Alchimie et Paris." Interview with Bernard Roger. Trédaniel Group website, January 2018.

Caron, Michel, and Hutin Serge. *Les alchimistes*. Paris: Le Seuil, 1959.

Carrouges, Michel. *André Breton et les données fondamentales du surréalisme*. Paris: Gallimard, 1950. Translated into English as *André Breton and the Basic Concepts of Surrealism*, by Maura Prendergast. Tuscaloosa: University of Alabama Press, 1974.

———. *Les machines célibataires*. Paris: Arcanes, 1954. Reprinted, Paris: Editions du Chêne, 1976.

Chailly, Ilios. *Héliogabale ou l'alchimiste couronné*. Paris: Kibil, 2021.

Charpentier, Josane. *La France des lieux et des demeures alchimiques*. Paris: Éditions Retz, 1980.

Chauvière, Bernard. *Mémoires d'un alchimiste contemporain*. Saint-Leu-la-Forêt: Éditions Paginanda, 2022.

Choucha, Nadia. *Surrealism and the Occult*. Oxford: Mandrake, 1991.

Coia-Gatié, André. *La chevalerie errante*. Paris: La Table d'Émeraude, 1992.

———. *Les origines symboliques du blason*. Paris: Berg, 1972.

Colquhoun, Ithell. *The Goose of Hermogenes*. London: Peter Owens. 1961.

———. *The Sword of Wisdom*. New York: G. P. Putnam, 1975.

Crasselame, Marc-Antonio. *La lumière sortant par soi-même des ténèbres*. Paris: Denoël, Bibliotheca Hermetica, 1971.

Danier, Richard. "André Breton et l'hermétisme alchimique." *Question de*, no. 15. Paris: Albin Michel, November-December, 1976.

———. *L'hermétisme alchimique chez André Breton*. Villeselve: Éditions Ramuel, 1997.

Davy, Marie-Madeleine. *L'homme intérieur et ses métamorphoses*. Paris: Albin Michel, 2005.

de Guaïta, Stanislas. *Le serpent de la Genèse*. Paris: Éditions maçonniques de France, 2019.

Desnos, Robert. "Le mystère d'Abraham juif." *Documents*, no. 5. 1929.

Desoubeaux, Henri. "Portrait de l'artiste en jeune singe ou Butor et l'autobiographie: Entre Sartre et Breton." In *Mélusine, no. XXIII: Dedans-dehors*. Lausanne: L'Âge d'homme, 2003.

Desvilles, Jean, dir. *Maurice Baskine*. Résonance, 2004.

De Waal, Edmund. *Lettres à Camondo*. Paris: Les Arts décoratifs, 2021.

Doumayrou, Guy-René. "Surréalisme, ésotérisme." *Docsur*, no. 8. París, April 1989.

Dumas, Marie-Claire. *André Breton en perspective cavalière*. Paris: Gallimard, Les Cahiers de la N.R.F., 1996.

———. "Note sur André Breton et la pensée traditionnelle." In *André Breton: Cahier de l'Herne*, no. 72. Paris, 1998.

Dumas-Pux, Danielle. "Eros Khalos: Le bel amour." *Cahiers jungiens de psychanalyse*, no. 131. Paris, 2010.

Durozoi, Gérard. "Les deux tours." Interview with Jorge Camacho in *Jorge Camacho les détours de soi*. Maubeuge: Editions Idem+Arts, 1998.

d'Ygé, Claude. *Nouvelle assemblée des philosophes chymiques: Aperçus sur le Grand Œuvre des alchimistes*. Paris: Dervy, 1954.

Eliade, Mircea. *Forgerons et alchimistes*. Paris: Flammarion, 1956. Reprinted as *The Forge and the Crucible*. Chicago: University of Chicago Press, 1979.

———. *Le mythe de l'alchimie suivi de L'alchimie asiatique*. Paris: Editions de l'Herne, 1990.

Favre, Yves-Alain. "Alchimie et poésie dans l'œuvre d'Elie-Charles Flamand." Lecture, Second Conference of the Centre de Recherches sur le Merveilleux et l'Irréel en Littérature. University of Caen, September 2, 1989. Reprinted in *À propos de la poésie d'Elie-Charles Flamand*. La Lucarne Ovale, 2011. Also reprinted in *Le merveilleux et la magie dans la littérature*, edited by Gérard Chandès. Rodolfi, 1992.

Feu central: Jorge Camacho dans ses tours. Exhibition pamphlet. Cervantes Institute, Paris. February–March 2013.

Flahutez, Fabrice. "Quatre questions à René Alleau." *La sœur de l'ange, pensées iniques*, no. 8. Paris: Hermann, September 2010.

Flahutez, Fabrice, and Thierry Dufrêne, eds. *Art et mythe*. Nanterre: Presses universitaires de Paris Ouest, 2011.

Flamand, Elie-Charles. *Braise de l'unité*. Paris: Recours au poème, 2014.

———. *Érotique de l'alchimie*. Paris: Le Courrier du livre, 1989.

———. *Les méandres du sens*. Paris: Dervy, 2004.

———. *Les pierres magiques*. Paris: Le Courrier du livre, 1981.

———. *Propos mosaïqué*. Saint-Ouen-en-Brie: La Lucarne Ovale, 2021.

———. *La tour Saint-Jacques*. Paris: La Table d'Emeraude, 1991.

———. *À un oiseau de houille perché sur la plus haute branche du feu*. Lyon: Armand Henneuse, 1957.

Follet, Lionel. "Préface, les Romans de *La défense de l'infini*." In *La défense de l'infini*, by Louis Aragon. Paris: Gallimard, 1997.

Fulcanelli. *Les demeures philosophales*. 2 vols. Paris: Jean-Jacques Pauvert, 1976. Translated into English as *The Dwellings of the Philosophers*. Boulder, CO: Archive Pr & Communications, 1999.

———. *Le mystère des cathédrales*. Paris: Jean-Jacques Pauvert, 1964. Translated into English as *The Mystery of the Cathedrals*, by Daniel Bernardo. Sojourner Books, 2019. Also translated as *Fulcanelli: Master Alchemist: Le Mystère des Cathédrales, Esoteric Interpretation of the Hermetic Symbols of The Great Work*, by Mary Sworder. Las Vegas: Brotherhood of Life, 1984.

Gérardin, Lucien. "En souvenir." In *Hommage au maître alchimiste Eugène Canseliet*. Special issue. *Atlantis*, no. 322. Paris, January 1982.

Geyraud, Pierre [Raoul Guyader, pseud.]. *L'occultisme à Paris*. Paris: Emile-Paul Frères, 1953.

Gissey, Olivier. *Frédérick Tristan: L'appel de l'Orient intérieur*. Paris: Entrelacs, 2015.

Glasser, Jean. "Souvenirs du bon Maître de Savignies." *Atlantis,* no. 322. September-October 1992.

Grasset-d'Orcet, Claude-Sosthène. *Archéologie mystérieuse*. Vol. 1. Paris: Éditions E-dite, 2000.

———. *L'histoire secrète de l'Europe*. Vol. 1. Paris: Éditions E-dite, 2000.

Hale, Amy. *The Supersensual Life of Ithell Colquhoun: Genius of the Fern-Loved Gully*. London: Strange Attractor Press, 2020.

Hillel-Erlanger, Irène. *Voyages en kaléidoscope*. Paris: Éditions Allia, 1996.

Holmyard, E. J. *L'alchimie*. Paris: Arthaud, 1979.

Un jardin universel, une anthologie de regards sur Jacques Lacomblez. Exhibition catalog. Caen: Éditions du Grand Tamanoir, 2019.

Jody, Bernard. *La rationalité de l'alchimie au XVIIᵉ siècle*. Paris: Vrin, 1922.

Jonin, Jean-Gabriel. "Soeur Âme, ne vois-tu rien venir? ou *Celui qui révèle de tout Cœur*." In *Maurice Baskine (1901–1968) Rétrospective*. Exhibition catalog. 2003

Joubert, Alain. "A la découverte de Torgia." Preface to the exhibition pamphlet accompanying the Torgia exhibit, at the Sophie Scheidecker Gallery, Paris. June 3, 2021.

———. *Pour le grand surréalisme: La clé est sur la porte*. Paris: Maurice Nadeau, 2016.

Jung, Carl Gustav. *Psychologie et alchimie*. Paris: Buchet-Castel, 2004. English translation is *Psychology and Alchemy*, translated by Gerhard Adler. Princeton, NJ: Princeton University Press, 1980.

Kamala-Jnana. *Dictionnaire de philosophie alchimique*. Argentières: Éditions G. Charlet, 1961.

Khaitzine, Richard. *Le cabaret du chat noir*. Grenoble: Le Mercure Dauphinois, 2018.

———. *La langue des oiseaux*. Vol. 1. Paris: Dervy, 1996.

———. *La langue des oiseaux*. Vol. 2. Paris: Dervy, 2012.

———. *La langue des oiseaux*. Vol. 3. Paris: Dervy, 2019.

———. *Secrets d'alcôves: Fulcanelli et la cosmosphère*. Bosguérard-de-Marcouville, Eure: Éditions Philomène Alchimie, 2020.

Klossowski de Rola, Stanislas. *Alchimie: Florilège de l'art secret*. Paris: Dervy, 2013.

Kober, Marc. "Caresser avec amour les pétales de l'univers." *La sœur de l'ange*, no. 13. Paris: Éditions Hermann, Spring 2014.

———. "Dans le verger de la salamandre." *La sœur de l'ange*, no. 3. Cluny: Éditions A Contraria, Spring 2005.

Kyrou, Ado. *Le surréalisme au cinéma*. Paris: Le Terrain vague, 1963.

Lagrange, André. "Entrée du médium." *Jointure*, no. 38. Summer 1993. Reprinted in *A propos de la poésie d'Elie-Charles Flamand*. La Lucarne Ovale, 2011.

Lamy, Suzanne. *André Breton, Hermétisme et poésie dans Arcane 17*. Montreal: Presses universitaires de Montréal, 1977.

Larguier, Léo. *Le faiseur d'or, Nicolas Flamel*. Paris: Les Éditions Nationales, 1936. Reprinted, Paris: Arléa, 2010.

Lassalle, Jean-Pierre. "Témoignage d'un ami de longue date." *La sœur de l'ange*, no. 1. Paris: Éditions Hermann, Spring 2014.

Lebel, Robert. *Marcel Duchamp. Von der Erscheinung zur Konzeption*. Ostfildern, Germany: DuMont Reiseverlag, 1962.

Leiris, Michel. *Aurora*. Paris: Gallimard, 1946. Translated into English as *Aurora*, by Anna Warby and Michel Leiris. London: Atlas Press, 1990.

Lepetit, Patrick. *Le surréalisme: Parcours souterrain*. Paris: Dervy, 2012. Translated into English as *The Esoteric Secrets of Surrealism*, by Jon Graham. Rochester, VT: Inner Traditions, 2014.

Lévi, Éliphas. *Dogme et rituel de haute magie*. 1854. Translated into English as *Transcendental Magic*, by A. E. Waite. London: George Redway, 1896.

Lorrey, Claude. *Stances, sonnets et chansons*. Paris: Grasset, 1910.

Löwy, Michael. *La comète incandescente: Romantisme, surréalisme, subversion*. Orange: Éditions Le Retrait, 2020.

Mabille, Pierre. "Conférence sur la poésie I." In *Traversées de nuit*. Paris: Plasma, 1981.

———. "Contribution à une psychanalyse de la connaissance objective par Gaston Bachelard." In *Traversées de nuit*. Paris: Plasma, 1981.

———. *Le miroir du merveilleux*. Paris: Les Éditions de Minuit, 1962. Translated into English as *The Mirror of the Marvelous*, by Jody Gladding. Rochester, VT: Inner Traditions, 1998.

Mabin, Renée. "La galerie à l'étoile scellée." *Mélusine*, no. 28. Lausanne: L'Âge d'Homme, February 2008.

Maurice Baskine (1901–1968) Rétrospective. Exhibition catalog. Maison du Grand Fauconnier, Museum of Modern and Contemporary Art of Cordes-sur-Ciel, curated by Jean-Gabroel Jonin and Paul Sanda. June 27–September 2, 2003.

Maurice Baskine: Peintre, sculpteur, alchimiste. Exhibition catalog. Grenier du Chapitre in Cahors, curated by Monique Escat. July 1–September 15, 1990.

Moreau, Patrice. *Joseph Sima: Visions du monde perdu, aquarelles inédites et peintures*. Editions Gourcuff-Gradenigo and Musée Saint Roch d'Issoudun, 2016.

Mourier-Casile, Pascaline. *André Breton, explorateur de la Mère-Moire*. Paris: P.U.F., 1986.

Murat, Michel. *André Breton: Cahier de l'Herne*, no. 72. Paris, 1998.

Murphy, Juliette. "Alchimie des philosophes." Exhibition catalog. Château Gala-Dali of Pubol, Editions Distribucions d'Art Surrealista. March 14–December 31, 2009.

Nadeau, David. *L'arche utopique: Le surréalisme et la loge maçonnique Thebah*. Quebec: La Vertèbre et le Rossignol, 2021.

———. "Le surréalisme et la loge maçonnique Thebah: I. Jean Palou." *Chroniques d'histoire maçonnique*, no. 77. Paris, 2016.

Passelergue, Michel. "Elie-Charles Flamand: Une quête du verbe dans les méandres du sens." Lecture, given at "Arts et Jalons." Saint-Mandé, October 27, 2018.

Perahim 1914–2008. De l'avant garde à l'épanouissement, de Bucarest à Paris. Exhibition catalog. Edited by Claude Miglietti and Gaëlle Rageot-Deshayes. MASC, the Museum of Modern and Contemporary Art, Sables d'Olonne.

June 13–September 26, 2021. Cantini Museum, Marseilles. November 26, 2021–April 24, 2022.

Plussihem, Antoine. "Le tombeau de François II à Saint-Pierre de Nantes." In *Bretagne mystique*. Special issue. *Atlantis*, no. 401. Vincennes, May 2000.

Rabourdin, Dominique. "Elie-Charles Flamand." *Infosurr*, no. 130. March–April 2017.

Ratcliffe, Eric. *Ithell Colquhoun: Pioneer Surrealist Artist, Occultist, Writer, and Poet*. Oxford: Mandrake, 2007.

Remy, Michel. "L'œuvre de Perahim ou l'athanor du merveilleux." In *Perahim 1914–2008. De l'avant-garde à l'épanouissement de Bucarest à Paris*. Exhibition catalog. Edited by Claude Miglietti and Gaëlle Rageot-Deshayes. MASC, Museum of Modern and Contemporary Art, Sables d'Olonne. June 13–September 26, 2021. Musée Cantini, Marseilles. November 26, 2021–April 24, 2022.

———. *Au treizième coup de minuit. Anthologie du surréalisme en Angleterre*. Paris: Dilecta, 2008. Translated into English as *On the Thirteenth Stroke of Midnight*. Manchester: Carcanet, 2013.

Renaud de la Faverie, Bernard. "Souvenirs d'Eugène Canseliet." In *Ces hommes qui ont fait l'alchimie de XXᵉ siècle*. Grenoble: Geneviève Dubois Éditions, 1999.

Richardson, Michael, ed. *International Encyclopedia of Surrealism*. London: Bloomsbury Visual Arts, 2020.

Rivière, Patrick. "André Breton: *Soleil noir et main de feu*." In *L'Hermétisme alchimique chez André Breton*, by Richard Danier. Villeselve: Editions Ramuel, 1997.

———. "*Philosophus per ignem*: Philosophe par le feu." *Hommage au maître alchimiste Eugène Canseliet*. Special issue. *Atlantis*, no. 322. Paris, January 1982.

———. *Soleil noir et main de feu—Surréalisme et alchimie*. Gajan: Venus d'Ailleurs, n.d.

Rivière, Patrick, and Jean-Michel Varenne. *La fascinante histoire des maîtres de l'alchimie*. Paris: Éditions de Vecchi, 2012.

Roger, Bernard. "De la dame de l'oeuvre." In *Bulletin de liaison surréaliste*, complete edition. Paris: Savelli, March 1977.

———. *À la découverte de l'alchimie*. Saint-Jean de Braye: Dangles, 1988.

———. *Les demeures de l'invisible*. Gajan: Venus d'Ailleurs, 2022.

———. "Les emblèmes de la rue Monbel." *L'archibras*, no. 2. Paris, October 1967.

———. "Esquisse pour une salle de cinéma au fond d'un lac." *Surréalisme*. Special issue. *L'âge du cinéma*, no. 4–5. Paris, August–November, 1951.

———. Introduction to *De la nature des métaux*, by Basil Valentine. Brussels: La Pierre d'Alun, collection Haute Pierre, 1997.

———. "Le jour de l'étoile." *L'archibras*, no. 7. March 1969.

———. *Paris et l'alchimie*. Paris: Editions Williams–ALTA (Umbra solis), 1981.

Roger, Bernard, and Jorge Camacho. *La cathédrale de Séville et le bestiaire alchimique du portail de Saint Christophe et de l'Immaculée Conception*. Huelva, Spain: Fondation Pol Lambert, 2001.

Roland de Renéville, André. *L'expérience poétique ou le feu secret du langage*. Paris: Gallimard, 1938.

———. *Sciences maudites & poètes maudits*. L'isle sur la Sorgue: Le Bois d'Orion, 1997.

———. *Univers de la parole*. Paris: Gallimard, 1944.

Ruhaud, Etienne. "Maurice Baskine (1901–1968), Cimetière du Père-Lachaise. Mémoire des poètes." *Diérèse* 82. Autumn 2021.

Sadoul, Jacques. *Le trésor des alchimistes*. Paris: Publications Premières, 1970.

Sanda, Paul. "Érotisme alchimique, alchimie symbolique." In *L'érotisme en alchimie*, by Sarane Alexandrian. Cordes-sur-Ciel: Rafael de Surtis, 2019.

———. *Le labyrinthe hermétique*. Sainte-Colombe-sur-Gand: La rumeur libre, 2021.

Schwaller de Lubicz, René. *Notes et propos inédits*. Vol. 2. Apremont, Vendée: MCOR/La Table d'Emeraude, 2006.

Seligmann, Kurt. *The Mirror of Magic*. Rochester, VT: Inner Traditions, 2018.

Shillitoe, Richard. *Ithell Colquhoun: Magician Born of Nature*. N.p.: Lulu, 2010.

Silbermann, Jean-Claude. *Le saumon, la cerise et le gardien du trait, texte sur l'art*. Mulhouse, Médiathèque, 1994. Paris: HC and D'Arts, 1999.

Simon, François-René. "Jorge Camacho, celui qui rencontre." In *Jorge Camacho 1934–2011*. Exhibition catalog. Sophie Scheidecker Gallery. April 22–June 2, 2017.

Simonelli, Jacques. "À la lueur de l'ourse." Afterword to *Voyages en kaléidoscope*, by Irene Hillel-Erlanger. Paris: Éditions Allia, 1996.

———. "A la recherche de Fol-Yver." *Fleur-de-Lune*, no. 19. Paris, April 2008.

Solis, Jean. *Rituel des grades alchimiques du baron Tschoudy*. Maisongoutte: Éditions Aureus, 2018.

Starck, Julien. "Sur l'œuvre d'Elie-Charles Flamand." *Poezibao.* May 2015.

Tristan, Frédérick. *L'obsédante.* Paris: Le Cherche Midi, 1992.

———. "René Alleau: Étoile scellée." *Les chroniques de Mars*, no. 14. Rennes-le-Château: Éditions Arqa, Christmas 2013–March 2014.

Tronche, Anne. *Jorge Camacho: Vue imprenable.* Plomelin, France: Éditions Palantines, 2004.

———. "Une morphologie totémique de l'invisible." In *Wifredo Lam: Voyages entre Caraïbes et avant-gardes.* Exhibition catalog. Museum of Fine Arts, Nantes. April 29–August 29, 2010.

Valentine, Basil. *Les douze clefs de la philosophie.* Paris: Minuit, 1956.

Van Lennep, Jacques. *Art et alchimie.* Brussels: Meddens, 1966.

———. "L'art alchimique et le surréel." In *L'alchimie*, by E. J. Holmyard. Paris: Arthaud, 1979.

———. "Jacques Lacomblez." In *Un jardin universel, une anthologie de regards sur Jacques Lacomblez.* Caen: Editions du Grand Tamanoir, 2019. Exhibition catalog.

———. *Une pierre en tête: Travaux d'alchimie.* Cisnée, Belgium: Éditions Yellow Now, 2007.

Völlnagel, Jörg. *Alchimie, l'art royal.* Paris: Imprimerie nationale, 2012.

Von Bernus, Alexander. *Alchimie et médecine.* Paris: Editions Dangles, 1960.

Vulliaud, Paul. *La fin du monde.* Paris: Payot, 1952.

Waelti-Walters, Jennifer. *Alchimie et littérature: À propos de "Portrait de l'artiste en jeune singe" de Michel Butor.* Paris: Denoël, Les Lettres Nouvelles, 1967.

INDEX

Page numbers in *italics* refer to illustrations.

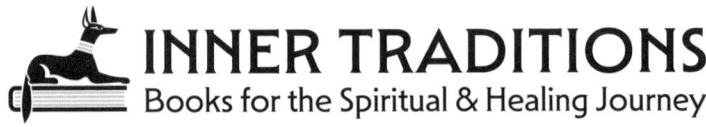

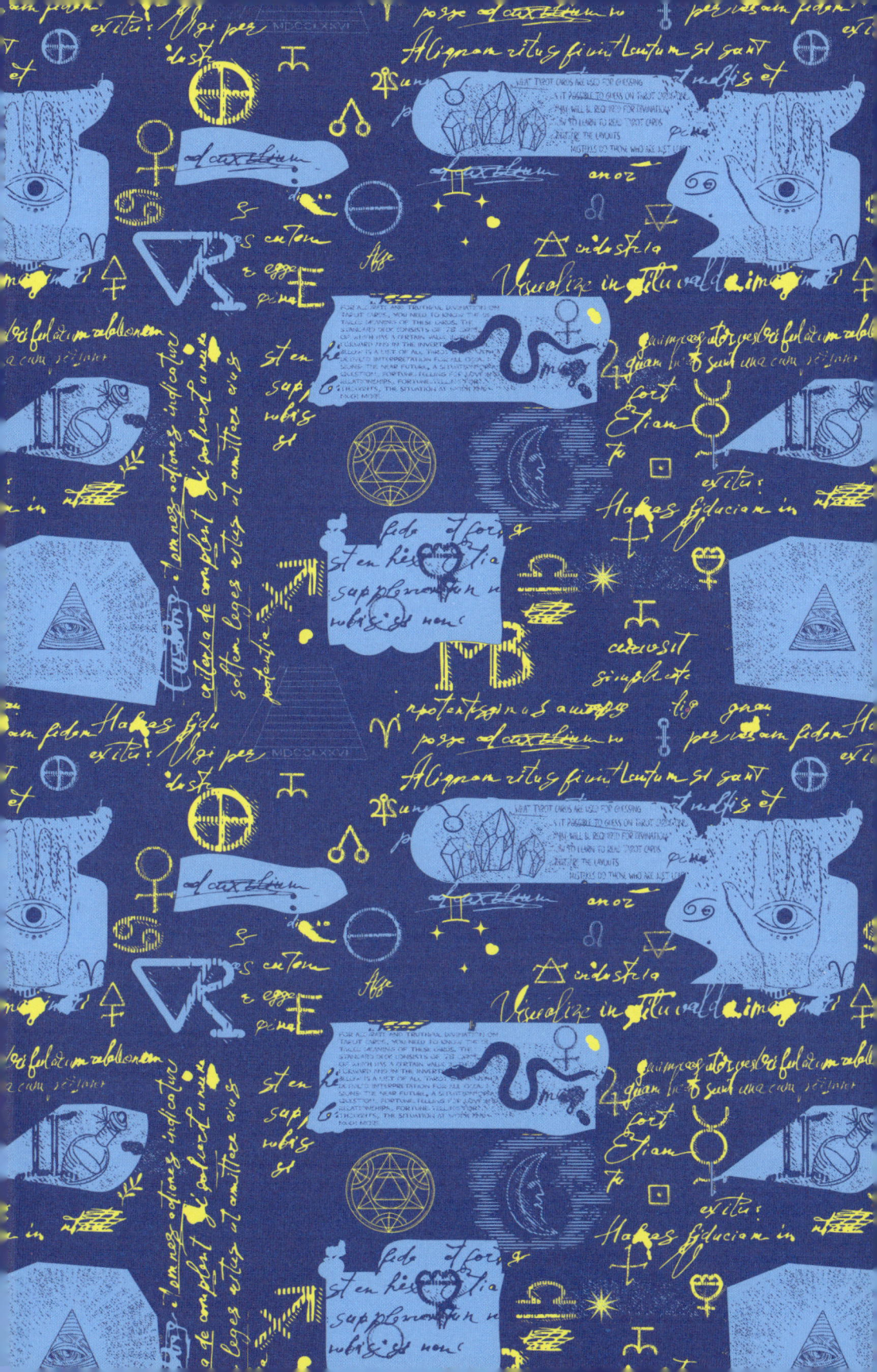

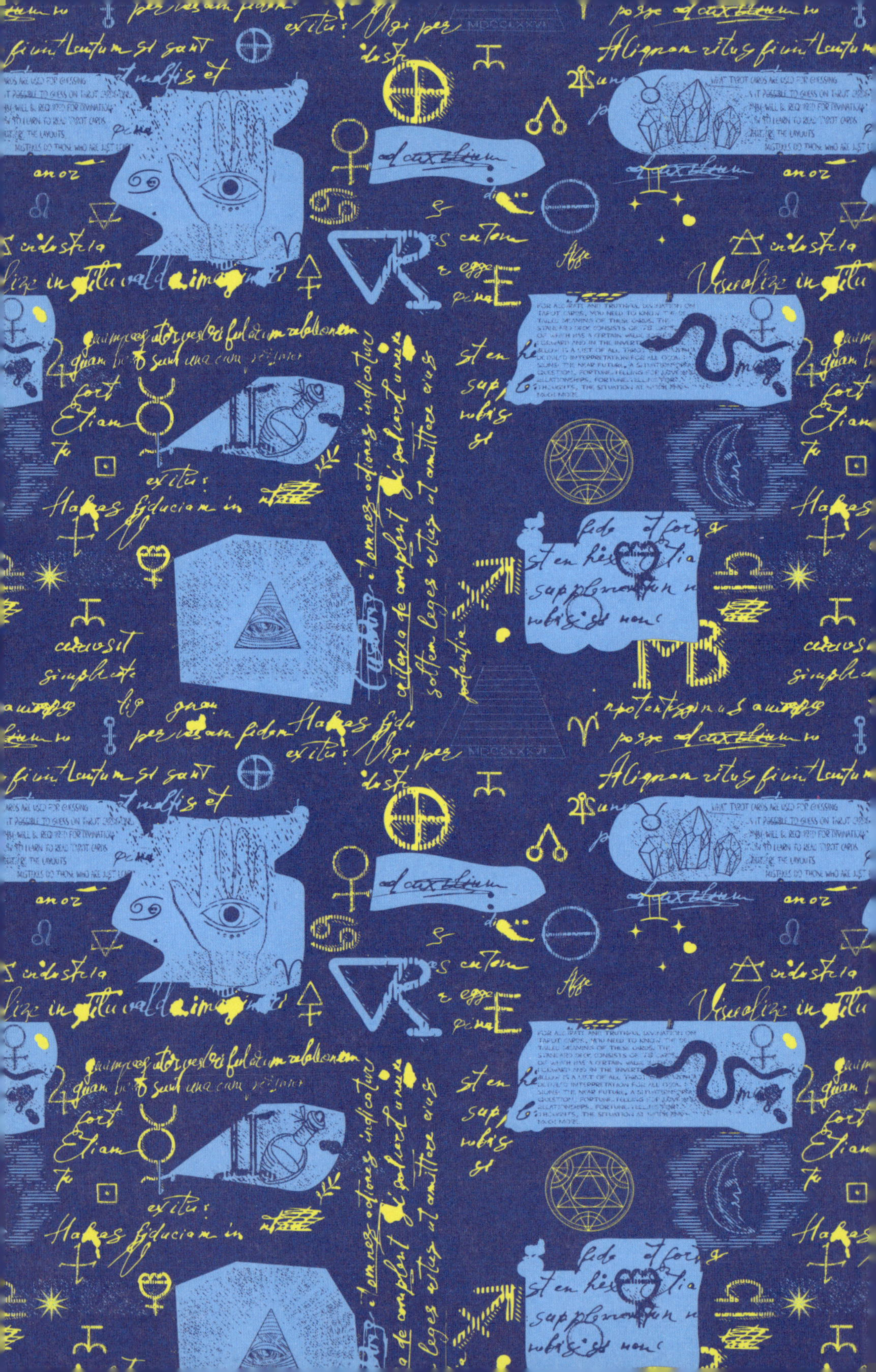